William *Charles*
WENTWORTH

William *Charles*
WENTWORTH
Australia's greatest native son

ANDREW TINK

ALLEN&UNWIN

This project has been assisted by the Commonwealth Government
through the Australia Council, its arts funding and advisory board.

Allen & Unwin
83 Alexander Street
Crows Nest NSW 2065
Australia
Phone: (61 2) 8425 0100
Fax: (61 2) 9906 2218
Email: info@allenandunwin.com
Web: www.allenandunwin.com

The Cataloguing-in-Publication entry is available from
the National Library of Australia
www.librariesaustralia.nla.gov.au

ISBN 978 1 74175 192 5

Typeset in 12/16 pt Bembo by Post Pre-press Group, Brisbane, Queensland
Printed by McPherson's Printing Group, Maryborough

10 9 8 7 6 5 4 3 2 1

For my parents, Margaret and Arnold, who introduced me to books.

CONTENTS

NOTE ON THE JACKET

The original of Wentworth's portrait on the front cover has been on display in the New South Wales Legislative Assembly since 1859. On 11 October that year, Henry Parkes moved a motion to hang the massive painting in the Chamber, noting that it was 'by an Italian master' whose commission had been paid by public subscription. 'The money had been forwarded to Mr Wentworth,' Parkes said, 'and that gentleman himself undertook the selection of an artist.' Most likely, Wentworth sat for the portrait during his visit to London in 1854 when he lobbied the British Government to grant self-government to the Australian colonies.[1]

Although there is no signature or date visible on the painting, an official publication of the New South Wales Parliament attributes it to the English portrait artist Richard Buckner (1812–83). After spending many years in Rome studying under the Italian master, Giovanni Battista Canevari, Buckner returned to London in the mid 1840s and counted Queen Victoria among his patrons.[2]

Following bitter opposition from the Reverend John Dunmore Lang and many other Assemblymen, Parkes's motion was only passed on the casting vote of the Speaker. No one doubted that the painting was an accurate likeness of Wentworth. Rather, the concern among his former colleagues was that he might return to the Colony and resume active politics. If that happened, they argued, the portrait's location in the Chamber would give him an unfair advantage.

Early photographs show the painting, which measures nine feet three inches by six feet six inches in its ornate gilt frame, hanging from the top of the Chamber's eastern wall above the press gallery and the Speaker's chair. In more recent times, it has been displayed above the door leading to the old Legislative Council Chamber— the room in which Governor Gipps forced Wentworth to relinquish his claim over the South Island of New Zealand.

The hand writing on the back cover is an extract of a letter Wentworth wrote to Lord Fitzwilliam on 15 January 1817. In it he announced his intention to study for the Bar to acquaint himself 'with all the excellence of the British Constitution . . . to advocate successfully the right of my country to a participation in its advantages'.[3]

ACKNOWLEDGEMENTS

As someone whose formal study of history finished at undergraduate level, I am very grateful to Emeritus Professors Alan Atkinson, Brian Fletcher, Bruce Kercher and Associate Professor Carol Liston for their generous advice and encouragement, including their comments on an early draft of this book. Each of them has given me the confidence to persevere with Wentworth's story. However any mistakes are mine.

Some lawyers struggle to write plain English. My natural 'on the one hand/on the other hand' style has been further complicated by my time in Parliament attempting to write punchy press releases. Despite this, Rebecca Kaiser, the Editorial Director at Allen & Unwin has championed my proposal from the start. But for her support and that of my agent, Lyn Tranter, both of whom have expended great energy weaning me away from my lawyerly phrases, this book would not have been published. And copy editor Liz Keenan has given me a new understanding of the word 'relevance'. I cannot thank them enough.

For me, writing a life is about addressing what happened, not what did not happen, what might have happened or what I would like to have happened. Evidence is the key and I have many people to thank for helping me come to grips with the trail Wentworth left (and sometimes hid) during his long and complex life.

The Dixson Librarian, Mark Hildebrand, and the staff of the State Library of New South Wales provided invaluable assistance, enabling me to navigate the library's vast holdings, especially its priceless collection of Wentworth family correspondence. With Mark's assistance, in particular, coming to an understanding of what is not there as well as what is, has helped me to better understand Wentworth himself.

The New South Wales Parliamentary Librarian, Greig Tillotson, and the Director of Research, David Clune, gave me access to books and papers Wentworth would have borrowed when he was a Member of Parliament. As long-time students of parliamentary history and procedure, their insights were invaluable. For this and much else besides, I am grateful to both them and their staff.

Whatever Wentworth may have been reading or talking about in Parliament, it all happened in a physical environment which affected his moods. For information relating to Parliament House itself, including nineteenth century correspondence about coal fires, gas lamps, security, Vice Regal visits and the layout of the Chamber, I am indebted to the Parliamentary Archivist Robert Lawrie and his staff.

The same can be said of Wentworth's legal career. Without the work of Bruce Kercher, who has placed all the important early colonial court cases on line, I would simply not have been able to research this book in a time frame acceptable to any commercial publisher. Bruce's colleagues on the executive of the Francis Forbes Society, including Geoff Lindsay SC and Philip Selth, have helped too. The society's 2006 legal history lecture presented by Rosemary Annable gave me a better understanding of the physical layouts and limitations of the court rooms Wentworth appeared in. And at State Records, the staff gave me generous access to the Chief Justices' Letter Books.

For an understanding of Wentworth's domestic life, the role of the Historic Houses Trust was vital. Through its superintendence of Vaucluse House and its publication of many books which shed light on Wentworth's domestic arrangements, The Trust brings Wentworth the family man alive. My particular thanks go to Mark Lillis and to Scott Carlin, the curator of Vaucluse House.

During a trip to New Zealand to better understand Wentworth's purchase of that country's south island, I was grateful for advice from Graham Langton and the staff of Archives New Zealand, Amy Watling and the staff of the Alexander Turnbull Library in Wellington and John Martin, the New Zealand Parliamentary Historian. The courtesy extended to me by the then Australian High Commissioner to New Zealand John Dauth and the Deputy High Commissioner Frank Ingruber is also greatly appreciated.

I am indebted to the Speaker of the New South Wales Legislative Assembly, Richard Torbay, the Clerk Russell Grove, and the Deputy Sergeant-at-Arms Greg Kelly, for permission to photograph the painting of Wentworth which hangs in the Assembly chamber and for their assistance in doing so.

To Vice Chancellor Steven Schwartz, Emeritus Professor Bruce Kercher and Professors Andrew Buck and Rosalind Croucher, my thanks are due for the courtesies they have extended to me as a Visiting Fellow at Macquarie University's Law School.

And to Derek McDonell of Horden House Rare Books whose cataloguing of a certain mezzotint in 2001 rekindled my interest in Australian history, a special thank you for your generous support ever since.

For general discussion and encouragement, as well as for advice and information on topics as diverse as premature birth and Latin translation, I want to thank many people including Carol Baxter, John Bennett, Gregory Blaxell, Stuart Braga, Jerelynn Brown, Paul Brunton, Peter Cochrane, Russell Cope, Elizabeth Ellis, Angus FitzSimons, Peter FitzSimons, Luis Garcia, Ian Hancock, Trevor McCaskill, Beverly McClymont, John McDonald, Mari Metzke,

Milton Osborne, Joan Ritchie, Brent Salter, Rachel Spratt and Alan Tasker.

Last, but by no means least, I thank Kerry, Michael and Peter for putting up with me living in Wentworth's world for three years.

Andrew Tink
July 2009

INTRODUCTION

When the hearse carrying the body of William Charles Wentworth passed along Sydney's streets in 1873, more than 70,000 people stood silently to pay their last respects. Half the city's population turned out to honour the man who was primarily responsible for bringing them trial by jury, a free press and the first Parliament in Australia. Most of all, they came to salute Australia's first patriot. For despite his reputation as a divisive political rogue, Wentworth was the first native-born Australian of European parents to articulate a distinctly Australian identity to the world.

The man who claimed to be his father, D'Arcy Wentworth, was related to one of England's most distinguished families, whose head, Charles Watson-Wentworth, had twice been British Prime Minister. But D'Arcy was the black sheep of the family. And after being tried and acquitted of four highway robberies, he sailed to Sydney as a private passenger on board a convict transport. During the voyage, D'Arcy began an affair with a female convict, who gave birth to Wentworth some time after the ship arrived in Sydney. Many years later, one of Wentworth's political opponents accused him of being 'the son of a . . . highwayman by a convict whore'. The *People's Advocate* called him a 'convict brat'.[1]

Strong, active and awkward in his movements, with a harsh, booming voice and a quick but not often vindictive temper,

Wentworth was distinctly Australian in his manner, despite his largely English education. Developed in company with the children of other convicts, Wentworth's 'decided drawl' was similar to today's broad Australian accent. These attributes, combined with his high intelligence and sharp wit, later helped him rally public meetings behind his catchcry of 'taxation by representation', a demand for self-government in all but defence and foreign affairs.[2]

After joining the first expedition to cross the Blue Mountains Wentworth became a barrister, turning Sydney's courts into a forum to push his political agenda. A fearless and inventive advocate, he ran rings around the government lawyers. However, his professional conduct sometimes bordered on criminal. At times drunk and disorderly, and responsible for fathering at least one illegitimate child during his marriage, he nevertheless remained close to his long-suffering wife Sarah until the day he died.

Author of the first book written by a native Australian to be published, founder of Australia's first university, co-editor and joint proprietor of Australia's first independent newspaper and, for a few weeks, owner of the whole of New Zealand's South Island, Wentworth called himself an 'Australasian'. He was also a man of the land, a squatter who ran livestock by the tens of thousands. Although he pushed for the creation of a local Parliament, Wentworth was always concerned to protect the squatters' interests. At one stage he called for a Legislative Council of 'bunyip' aristocrats to keep the popularly elected Legislative Assembly in check. Despite being the son of a convict, Wentworth opposed the abolition of transportation because that system had supplied him and his fellow squatters with 'convict shepherds'. However, even some of Wentworth's squatter friends baulked at his offensive comments about Aborigines.

In 1843, Wentworth was one of the first members elected to the Legislative Council. His colleagues included a future British Chancellor of the Exchequer and a man who was to be five times Prime Minister of New South Wales. But they all acknowledged

Wentworth, a man who stood head and shoulders above them physically and intellectually, as their leader. Wentworth could be hard,
bullying and duplicitous when it served his purpose, and many of
his colleagues later fell out with him, especially over his attempts
to limit the right to vote. But they all agreed with one of Britain's
top public servants that Wentworth's New South Wales Constitution Bill of 1853 was an unprecedented 'legislative declaration
of independence' which served as a model of self-government for
all the Australian colonies. In London to lobby for this Bill, and
faced with a British Government preoccupied by the Crimean War,
Wentworth advised Sydneysiders not to rely on Britain to defend
them against possible Russian naval attack. 'Perfect self-reliance,'
he said, 'is the only safe principle the Australian Colonies [*sic*] can
now adopt.'[3]

No one has ever been widely identified as Australia's founding father in the sense that Americans use the term, and to elevate
politicians to that status is probably not the Australian way. But
if it were, Wentworth would have a claim to the title at least as
strong if not stronger than Governor Arthur Phillip, Henry Parkes,
and Australia's first Prime Minister, Edmund Barton. Indeed, it
was Parkes himself, so often Wentworth's bitter political opponent,
who said that Wentworth's constitution had been drafted 'with the
painstaking care of a man having a fatherly regard for his country
to make the broad foundations for it'. And Parkes, whom Barton
described as the 'Father of Federation', said his inspiration had come
from Wentworth, who had advocated a confederation of the Australian colonies almost half a century before the Commonwealth of
Australia came into being. Most tellingly, while the English-born
Parkes had called his paper *The Empire*, the native-born Wentworth
had called his *The Australian*.[4]

It is therefore surprising that while comprehensive biographies
have been written about Phillip, Parkes and Barton, no such biography has been written about Wentworth, a man described by

historian Manning Clark as 'Australia's Greatest Native Son'. Perhaps this is because much of the material relating to Wentworth's life has only recently become readily accessible. For example, Emeritus Professor Bruce Kercher of Macquarie University has put the important early colonial court cases online, and the Sesquicentenary Committee of the New South Wales Parliament has done the same with the early Parliamentary debates.[5]

With ready access to these important records, and with the benefit of scholarly work done on key aspects of Wentworth's long life by historians including C.M.H. Clark, Peter Cochrane, Carol Liston, A.C.V. Melbourne, Michael Persse and John Ritchie, I have attempted a life of the man whose larger-than-life portrait loomed over my workplace for the nineteen years during which I was a member of the New South Wales Legislative Assembly.[6]

Andrew Tink, Sydney 2009

DRAMATIS PERSONAE

SECRETARIES OF STATE FOR THE COLONIES	TERM OF OFFICE
Baron Glenelg, 1778–1866	1835–1839
Duke of Newcastle, 1811–1864	1852–1854
Earl Bathurst, 1762–1834	1812–1827
Earl of Liverpool, 1770–1828	1809–1812
George Grey, 1799–1882	1854–1855
George Murray, 1772–1846	1828–1830
Henry Dundas, 1742–1811	1791–1794
Henry, Earl Grey, 1802–1894	1846–1852
Henry Labouchere, 1798–1869	1855–1858
John Pakington, 1799–1880	1852
Lord John Russell, 1792–1878	1839–1841, 1855
Lord Stanley, 1799–1869	1833–1834, 1841–1845
Marquess of Normanby, 1797–1863	1839
Viscount Castlereagh, 1769–1822	1805–1806, 1807–1809
Viscount Goderich, 1782–1859	1827, 1830–1833
William Gladstone, 1809–1898	1845–1846
William Huskisson, 1770–1830	1827–1828

COLONIAL SECRETARIES	TERM OF OFFICE
Alexander McLeay, 1767–1848	1825–1837
Edward Thompson, 1800–1879	1837–1856
Frederick Goulburn, 1788–1837	1821–1825

NSW GOVERNORS	TERM OF OFFICE
Arthur Phillip, 1738–1814	1788–1792
Charles FitzRoy, 1796–1858	1846–1855
George Gipps, 1791–1847	1838–1846
John Hunter, 1737–1821	1795–1800
John Young, 1807–1876	1861–1867
Lachlan Macquarie, 1762–1824	1810–1821
Philip King, 1758–1808	1800–1806
Ralph Darling, 1772–1858	1825–1831
Richard Bourke, 1777–1855	1831–1837
Thomas Brisbane, 1773–1860	1821–1825
William Bligh, 1754–1817	1806–1808
William Denison, 1804–1871	1855–1861

NSW PRIME MINISTERS	TERM OF OFFICE
Charles Cowper, 1807–1875	1856, 1857–1859, 1861–1863, 1865–1866, 1870
Henry Parker, 1808–1881	1856–1857
Henry Parkes, 1815–1896	1872–1875, 1877, 1878–1883, 1887–1889, 1889–1891
James Martin, 1820–1886	1863–1865, 1866–1868, 1870–1872
John Robertson, 1816–1891	1860–1861, 1868–1870, 1875–1877, 1877, 1885–1886
Stuart Donaldson, 1812–1867	1856

MEMBERS OF THE WENTWORTH FAMILY

Alice Fisher, 1844–1898 — Eldest granddaughter of W.C. Wentworth

Catherine Crowley, 1772?–1800 — Mother of W.C. Wentworth

Charles Watson-Wentworth, 1730–1782 — Marquis of Rockingham, twice Britain's Prime Minister and head of the Wentworth family in England

D'Arcy Wentworth, 1762?–1827 — Father of W.C. Wentworth

D'Arcy Wentworth, 1793–1861 — Brother of W.C. Wentworth

D'Arcy Wentworth, 1848–1922 — Youngest son of W.C. Wentworth

Edith Dunbar, 1845–1891 — Youngest daughter of W.C. Wentworth

Eliza Wentworth, 1838–1898 — Fourth daughter of W.C. Wentworth

Fanny Reeve, 1829–1893 — Second daughter of W.C. Wentworth

Fitzwilliam Wentworth, 1833–1915 — Second son of W.C. Wentworth

Henry Eagar, 1830–? — Illegitimate son of W.C. Wentworth

Isabella Wentworth, 1840–1856 — Fifth daughter of W.C. Wentworth

John Reeve, 1804?–1875 — Husband of Fanny

John Wentworth, 1795–1820 — Brother of W.C. Wentworth

Laura Keays-Young, 1842–1887 — Sixth daughter of W.C. Wentworth

Maria Hunt, 1809–1885 — Sister of Sarah Wentworth and tenant at Vaucluse

Mary Ann Lawes, 17??–1849 — Mother of W.C. Wentworth's half brothers and sisters

Robert Hunt, 1805?–1892 — Husband of Maria and tenant at Vaucluse

Robert of Wentworth Woodhouse, 1240?–1275? — The Wentworth family's thirteenth century ancestor

Sarah Wentworth, 1805–1880 — Wife of W.C. Wentworth and daughter of Francis Cox

Sarah Wentworth, 1835–1857 — Third daughter of W.C. Wentworth

Thomas Fisher, 1813?–1875 — Husband of Thomasine

William *Charles* **WENTWORTH**

Thomasine Fisher, 1825–1913 — Eldest daughter of W.C. Wentworth

William Charles Wentworth, 1790–1872 — Australia's greatest native son

William Charles Wentworth, 1827–1859 — Eldest son of W.C. Wentworth

William Fisher, 1846–1868 — Eldest grandson of W.C. Wentworth

William Wentworth Fitzwilliam, 1748–1833 — Lord Fitzwilliam, head of the Wentworth family in England from 1782

OTHERS

Alexander Riley, 1778?–1833 — D'Arcy and W.C. Wentworth's business partner

Alfred Stephen, 1802–1894 — NSW Chief Justice 1844–1873 and fourth son of Justice Stephen

Atwell Hayes — Editor of *The Australian*

Charles Buller, 1806–1848 — Succeeded Bulwer as Commons Advocate for NSW

Charles Cookney — D'Arcy Wentworth's London agent

Charles, Earl Grey, 1764–1845 — Prime Minister 1830–1834

Charles Mitchell — Captain of HMS *Slaney*

Daniel Deniehy, 1828–1865 — Lawyer, orator and NSW Legislative Assemblyman

Duke of Wellington, 1769–1852 — Field Marshal and Prime Minister 1828–1830, 1834

Edward Hall, 1786–1860 — Editor of *The Monitor*

Edward Hargreaves, 1816–1891 — Gold prospector

Edward Wakefield, 1796–1862 — Member of the Commons and instigator of the early settlement of South Australia and New Zealand

Elizabeth Macarthur, 1766–1850 — Wife of John Macarthur

Elizabeth Macarthur, 1792–1842 — Second daughter of John Macarthur

Francis Forbes, 1784–1841 — NSW Chief Justice 1824–1837

Francis Grose, 1758?–1814 — Commandant of the NSW Rum Corps 1792–1794

DRAMATIS PERSONAE

Francis Stephen, 1804–1837 — Agitator for constitutional reform and fifth son of Justice Stephen

Frederic Rogers, 1811–1889 — Permanent Head of the Colonial Office in London 1860–1871

George Cookney — Architect and son of Charles Cookney

George Johnston, 1764–1823 — Arrests Governor Bligh and succeeds him in 1808

George Molle, 1773–1823 — Lieutenant-Governor of NSW 1814–1817

Gregory Blaxland, 1778–1853 — Leader of the Blue Mountains expedition

Henry Bennet, 1777–1836 — Law reforming member of the House of Commons

Henry Bulwer, 1801–1872 — House of Commons Advocate for NSW

Henry Douglass, 1790–1865 — Doctor and Magistrate

Henry Hayes, 1762–1832 — First owner of Vaucluse House

James Busby, 1801–1871 — Official British Resident in New Zealand 1832–1840

James Dowling, 1787–1844 — NSW Justice 1828–1837 and Chief Justice 1837–1844

James Macarthur, 1798–1867 — Grazier, Legislative Councillor and fourth son of John Macarthur

James Stephen, 1789–1859 — Permanent head of the Colonial Office in London 1836–1847 and nephew of Justice Stephen

Jane New, 1805?–? — Escaped convict harboured at Vaucluse

Jeffrey Bent, 1781–1852 — Judge of NSW Supreme Court 1814–1816

John Bigge, 1780–1843 — Royal Commissioner into NSW 1819–1823

John Darvall, 1809–1883 — Barrister, Legislative Councillor and later Assemblyman

John Dickinson, 1806–1882	Judge of NSW Supreme Court 1844–1861
John Jamison, 1776–1844	Doctor, landowner and NSW Legislative Councillor
John Lamb, 1790–1862	Merchant and NSW Legislative Councillor
John Lang, 1799–1878	Clergyman and NSW Legislative Councillor
John Macarthur, 1767–1834	Founder of the Australian wool industry
John Macarthur Jnr, 1794–1831	Barrister and second son of John Macarthur
John Mackaness, 1770?–1838	Sheriff of NSW 1824–1827
John Oxley, 1784?–1828	NSW Surveyor-General and explorer
John Stephen, 1771?–1833	Solicitor-General and NSW Supreme Court Judge 1826–1832
John Stephen Jnr, 1798?–1854	Court Registrar and second son of Justice Stephen
Joseph Foveaux, 1767–1846	Commandant of the NSW Rum Corps 1796–1799
Joseph Sudds, 1800?–1826	Private soldier who died chained in an iron collar
Maurice O'Connell, 1812–1879	Army officer, political opponent of W.C. Wentworth and grandson of Governor Bligh
Ralph Mansfield, 1799–1880	Editor of the *Sydney Gazette*
Richard Jones, 1786–1852	Merchant, pastoralist and NSW Legislative Councillor
Richard Windeyer, 1806–1847	Barrister and NSW Legislative Councillor
Robert Howe, 1795–1829	Editor of *The Sydney Gazette*

DRAMATIS PERSONAE

Robert Lowe, 1811–1892	Barrister, NSW Legislative Councillor, Member of the House of Commons, British Cabinet Minister
Robert Wardell, 1793–1834	Newspaper editor and barrister
Samuel Marsden, 1765–1838	Chaplain, Magistrate and farmer
Te Maiharanui	Maori Chief of the Ngai Tahu
Te Rauparaha	Maori Chief of the Ngai Toa who murdered his enemy Te Maiharanui
Thomas Scott, 1783–1860	Bigge's secretary and later Anglican Archdeacon
Tuhawaiki	Te Maiharanui's successor as Maori Chief of the Ngai Tahu
Saxe Bannister, 1790–1877	NSW Attorney-General 1824–1826
William Bland, 1789–1868	Doctor and NSW Legislative Councillor
William Hobson, 1793–1842	Lieutenant-Governor and then Governor of New Zealand 1840–1842
William Lawson, 1774–1850	Blue Mountains explorer and NSW Legislative Councillor
William Macarthur, 1800–1882	Sheep breeder, wine maker and fifth son of John Macarthur
William Molesworth, 1810–1855	Chairman of the Commons Committee into Transportation
William Redfern, 1774–1833	Doctor and friend of D'Arcy Wentworth
William Wakefield, 1801–1848	Leader of the first colonising expedition to New Zealand and younger brother of Edward Wakefield

Chapter 1

PLUCKED FROM
THE PUTRESCENT PILE

In the spring of 1846, the grand old man of Australasian politics, William Charles Wentworth, compared the rotting ships that housed British convicts to decaying dumps of dead animals. 'There can be no aggregations of humans . . . in hulks,' he told the New South Wales Legislative Council, 'without calling this putrescence into existence.' Although Wentworth himself had been conceived in just such conditions, on board the *Neptune*, the worst convict transport ever to set sail, he now recommended that transportation to New South Wales, abolished in 1840, be renewed.[1]

William Charles Wentworth's long life was to be littered with such paradoxes, beginning with his ancestry and the mysterious circumstances of his birth.

The man who claimed to be his father, D'Arcy Wentworth, was descended from one Robert of Wentworth Woodhouse, who lived in Yorkshire in the thirteenth century. Members of the Wentworth family had subsequently migrated to Ireland, where D'Arcy was born in 1762. Three years later, a member of the family's English branch, Charles Watson-Wentworth, Marquis of Rockingham, became British Prime Minister. But even though he had inherited great wealth and titles through the female line of his family, Rockingham always acknowledged D'Arcy's poor commoner family as the senior male line of Wentworths.[2]

During his brief tenure as Prime Minister in 1765–66 Rockingham repealed the infamous American Stamp Act, which had introduced a direct tax on a range of documents, and angered many of King George III's American subjects. This action, in turn, angered the King, and Rockingham was soon dismissed from office. Over the next fifteen years, when he was not breeding his horses or betting on them at the Newmarket races, Rockingham led the Whig Party (which believed that the power of the Crown had to be balanced by the power of Parliament) in opposition to the King's war against the Americans. After General George Washington's victory over the British Army at Yorktown in 1781, Rockingham again became Prime Minister and forced George III to recognise American independence.[3]

Exhausted by this struggle Rockingham died in July 1782, whereupon his enormous estate passed to his nephew, William Wentworth Fitzwilliam. At the age of thirty-four, Lord Fitzwilliam now had a total annual income of £60,000 pounds, the equivalent today of $8 million. But D'Arcy Wentworth, the son of a Portadown innkeeper, shared in none of it. Instead, at fifteen, he became apprenticed to a local surgeon, before going to London to continue his medical studies. After qualifying as an assistant surgeon in 1780, D'Arcy tried to copy Fitzwilliam's expensive London lifestyle. Living way beyond his modest surgeon's income, he was soon in trouble with the law.[4]

In January 1787, D'Arcy was arrested for a number of highway robberies on the Blackheath and Kentish roads. A surprised editor of *The Times* noted that although the accused was from a good family and trained as a surgeon, he now faced the death penalty owing to 'a destructive connection' with 'bad characters at the Dog and Duck'. At his trial three months later, D'Arcy was acquitted thanks to the ingenuity of his barrister. Some of D'Arcy's London contacts, including an MP named James Villiers, then tried to get him a job overseas. One rumour had it that D'Arcy was to be a surgeon on the First Fleet convict transport *Charlotte* but that he ran away before the ship sailed in May 1787. Whatever the case, D'Arcy had another narrow escape on 11 July as he sat in the public gallery at the Old Bailey to watch the trial of young Thomas Alger who, as *The Times* put it, 'used to attend upon Wentworth [at the Oxford Coffee House] and carry messages to his ladies who were pretty numerous'. Moments after Alger had been sentenced to death for highway robbery, a barrister who had been the victim of another robbery pointed to D'Arcy in the public gallery, identifying him as his assailant. Seized immediately, D'Arcy was brought to the front of the court. However, six months had passed since the robbery and upon closer inspection of D'Arcy, the barrister became uncertain about his identification. So D'Arcy was released. But no sooner had he left the court than the person who had taken his place in the public gallery dropped his handkerchief on the floor. While stooping to pick it up he discovered a gold watch, which had been advertised as stolen on Hounslow Heath by a person fitting D'Arcy's description.[5]

Although a warrant was immediately issued for D'Arcy's arrest, he managed to avoid apprehension for five months until he faced trial for yet two more highway robberies. In the first of these trials, the victim and his companion struggled to identify the highwayman, who had worn a black silk mask. 'He appeared to be a man of rather large size, a lusty man,' one said, 'but I . . . could not distinguish him.' So the prosecution called D'Arcy's landlord to try to trace the stolen property, which D'Arcy's live-in lover was accused of receiving. Cross-examining the landlord himself, D'Arcy got him to concede that he had never seen any suspicious people visit the accused, 'who behaved . . . and paid his way like a gentleman'. Duly impressed, the jury returned a verdict of not guilty. The second trial was much tougher because D'Arcy had been caught near the scene of the crime in possession of a pistol, a black silk mask and a purse. This time, D'Arcy wisely retained a barrister, who managed to get the victim to agree that the highwayman was 'a different person' from the prisoner in the dock. Again, the verdict was not guilty.[6]

Apparently returning to a quieter life, D'Arcy managed to avoid the courts for almost two years. When he next appeared before a magistrate, charged with yet another hold-up, *The Times* described him as 'the famous D'Arcy Wentworth' and no less than King George III's brother came to watch. Immediately after the hold-up the victim, John Heywood, a barrister who had met D'Arcy, told his travelling companion, 'if D'Arcy Wentworth were in the kingdom, I would say that he was'. D'Arcy tried to explain that he had been nabbed when he was 'just about to set sail [as a surgeon] for Botany Bay, where a birth [*sic*] had been provided for him by his friends'. After being duly committed for trial, D'Arcy stood in the dock of the Old Bailey as Heywood said under oath, 'I do verily believe the prisoner to be the man that committed the robbery,' recalling the highwayman's strong Irish brogue, 'as you will hear if you hear him [D'Arcy] speak'. This time, the wind had blown at the highwayman's mask. '[It] flew up and I saw the lower part of his face very distinctly, about as far as his nose.' But D'Arcy's counsel got Heywood to admit that he had not seen enough of the highwayman's face. And of his earlier meeting with D'Arcy, Heywood conceded that he was 'a very agreeable young gentleman . . . of an excessive good family in Ireland'. Sensing the prosecution's difficulty the judge, who had heard D'Arcy's brogue at a previous trial, asked him if he would like to say something. 'No, my Lord,' his counsel answered, 'I would not advise him to.' The jury returned a verdict of not guilty, whereupon D'Arcy's lawyer said, 'My Lord, Mr Wentworth . . . has taken a passage . . . in the fleet to

Botany Bay . . . as Assistant Surgeon, and desires to be discharged immediately'. In committing himself, D'Arcy would have been aware of Watkin Tench's best selling and generally positive account of his voyage with the First Fleet. But he was probably unaware that, in order to cut costs, the government had appointed a slavery firm to organise the fleet he would be travelling with.[7]

While D'Arcy had been in court, the transport ship *Neptune* had been loading convicts at its berth on the Thames. Among them was seventeen-year-old Catherine Crowley, who had been sentenced to seven years' transportation for stealing sheets and clothes, valued at £1.11.0, from the house of her employer.

After weighing anchor, the *Neptune* made for Plymouth to load 300 male convicts before sailing to Portsmouth to join the Second Fleet to the colony. During this short trip Lieutenant John Macarthur, of the New South Wales Corps, complained about the swearing of the convict women and the stench of their toilet buckets, which upset his wife Elizabeth. With a reputation for being 'proud and haughty', Macarthur became so angry that he fought a duel with the *Neptune*'s captain, Thomas Gilbert. This resolved nothing, and before long the escalating fights and death threats among the female convicts led to Gilbert's replacement. But Macarthur was soon complaining about the new captain for ignoring his concerns that Elizabeth had to share a passageway with convicts. For Catherine Crowley, the long voyage ahead could only get worse.[8]

According to one account D'Arcy Wentworth boarded the *Neptune* on 12 December 1789, although as late as 30 December *The Times*, which had developed a keen interest in his fate, reported that he was still ashore. If he did remain ashore a little longer, it was no doubt to enjoy for one last time the delights of London. After all, he was leaving a vibrant city of almost a million people at the centre of the civilised world for a settlement of about 1000 souls, three-quarters of them convicts, perched on the edge of a continent whose coast had not yet been fully mapped. Whenever D'Arcy did finally board the *Neptune* for what was then the longest voyage in the world, to be sailed at the pace of a person walking, his status as a private passenger guaranteed him the sort of accommodation that Catherine Crowley could only have dreamed about.

Unlike the male convicts, the females aboard the *Neptune* were not chained and were given access to the poop and quarter deck. It was probably here, early in the voyage, that something about Catherine caught D'Arcy's roving eye. As no picture or description of Catherine exists, just what the attraction was remains a mystery. But knowing D'Arcy, she was no doubt pretty or voluptuous or both. For her part, Catherine wanted to escape her violent convict companions, who were 'abandoned creatures' covered in filth and vermin. So D'Arcy plucked her from this putrescent pile into his quarters. After a few weeks the Macarthurs, exasperated with the conditions on board, undertook a hazardous transfer to the *Scarborough* by rowboat at sea.

For those who remained on the *Neptune*, especially the convicts, the voyage degenerated into a living hell as illness swept the ship. The miasma below decks nauseated the prisoners and turned the officers' shiny metal buttons black. Despite his medical qualifications, D'Arcy did not help. Like everyone else on board he was cowed by the captain, a violent man who was later tried for the murder of the *Neptune*'s cook. But this did not stop the Navy's Commissioners from later trying to exculpate themselves by saying that in addition to a surgeon and surgeon's mate, there was 'a passenger of the [medical] faculty on board'.

When the *Neptune* finally arrived at Sydney on 29 June 1790, its bilge sloshing with disease-laden sewage and its holds crawling with rats, one observer said of her convicts that 'they were almost half dead, very few could stand . . . and they died ten or twelve a day when they first landed'. The *Neptune* had lost 147 men and eleven women, or 31 per cent of those aboard, the worst record of any convict transport ever to sail to Sydney. One anonymous female convict later claimed she overheard Governor Arthur Phillip say that the convicts' deaths amounted to murder. But in the middle of all this misery some small miracles occurred, including, apparently, Catherine Crowley's pregnancy.[9]

As D'Arcy and Catherine soon found out, the tiny Sydney settlement, established just over two years earlier, was in a desperate state. It was so short of food that many of the colony's residents were now eking out an existence ten miles to the west, at Rose Hill, or 1000 miles to the northeast, on Norfolk Island. As a result, Sydney's population had shrunk from 1000 to fewer than 600 starving inhabitants, who dressed in rags and sheltered in shacks. Although Governor Phillip was responsible for the whole of eastern Australia, from roughly today's Western Australian border to the east coast, as well as for Van Diemen's Land, those who dined with him at his modest little abode overlooking the mud flats of Sydney Cove had to bring their own bread rolls.[10]

The Second Fleet swelled Sydney's already hard-pressed population to over 1700. Many of the emaciated new arrivals now lay dying in tents pitched along a grassy slope on the western side of Sydney Cove. To relieve this pressure, Governor Phillip sent the healthiest new arrivals, including D'Arcy and Catherine, to Norfolk Island. Despite their past brushes with the law, New South Wales gave the couple the opportunity for a fresh start. Apart from Elizabeth Macarthur, just about every woman in the colony had a convict background. And of D'Arcy, the Colony's Deputy Judge Advocate, David Collins, noted in a book published eight years later that:

> There came out in the *Neptune* a person by the name of Wentworth, who being desirous of some employment . . . was now sent to Norfolk Island to act as an assistant to the surgeon there, being reputed to have the necessary requisites.

Many in the colony would have been aware of D'Arcy's past thanks to a combination of gossip and newspapers like *The Times*. Therefore Collins probably thought that D'Arcy's trials were so notorious that they required no mention, or that in a colony full of convicts no one cared anyway.[11]

As D'Arcy set out with the heavily pregnant Catherine for Norfolk Island on board the *Surprize* on 1 August 1790, he turned his back on his family in Ireland. His brother and sister later complained about his failure to respond to their letters. For Lord Fitzwilliam and his London agent Charles Cookney, it was a different story. D'Arcy began with them a remarkable correspondence which helped to sustain him and his sons well into the next century. Prior to Darcy's departure from England, Fitzwilliam had arranged for Cookney to act as D'Arcy's agent as well as his own to look after their respective business affairs in London. Both men wanted D'Arcy to succeed and were delighted when he later did so.[12]

Early victualling records clearly show that when D'Arcy and Catherine arrived on Norfolk Island in mid-August, they were accompanied by the infant William Crowley. But when that infant, later known as William Charles Wentworth, died in England in 1872 in his eighty-second year, his obituary in the *Illustrated London News* said he was born in 1794. By then, his date of birth had become a source of confusion and embarrassment. If he was born on the *Surprize*, then either his birth was premature or he was conceived before Catherine and D'Arcy met. Perhaps someone else in the *Neptune*'s putrescent pile was his father. The first alternative is more likely, since the only known image of D'Arcy indicates a strong physical resemblance to William and they shared a number of buccaneering character traits. Whatever the case, D'Arcy acknowledged William as his son and doted on him for the rest of his life.[13]

William was thus Australian born. He was one of the first 'currency lads', a term used by a regimental paymaster to distinguish native-born Australians of European descent from their British-born counterparts, and so named because at the time the pound currency was inferior to the pound sterling. William's parents had survived extraordinary perils to arrive off Norfolk Island; now he joined them in facing new hazards as they disembarked from the *Surprize* for a dangerous small boat ride through the island's surf.[14]

Chapter 2

CURRENCY LAD

As their vessel approached Norfolk Island, the wreck of the First Fleet flagship *Sirius* was a stark warning to D'Arcy and Catherine of the hazardous landing ahead. Only five miles long by three wide, this lush subtropical paradise was buffeted by the full force of the South Pacific Ocean, which had recently claimed the *Sirius* and now threatened the *Surprize*. Indeed, one of the *Surprize*'s boats was soon capsized by a rogue wave, drowning seven, including three female convicts and a small child. D'Arcy, Catherine and the infant William were not among the dead, but when they finally landed ten days later they joined a community crowded by shipwreck survivors—one where food was in such short supply that people lived under martial law and survived by eating native birds.[1]

Despite the food shortage John Hunter, who had commanded the *Sirius*, shared Governor Phillip's hopes that the island might support 2000 people if it were cleared and cultivated. This claim sparked an intensive search for fertile land, and 100 acres of treeless ground were soon under cultivation. As an unpaid assistant to the island's surgeon Dennis Considen, D'Arcy attended to the medical needs of those who worked this ground, soon known as Queenborough. By 1791, it comprised a small hamlet of eight houses and a jail, but D'Arcy still had to walk two miles from the main settlement at Kingston to see his patients. It was not until late summer that a timber-framed house, finished with logs and thatch, was ready for him and his family. Although he was sometimes troubled by his convict patients, D'Arcy was not a stern disciplinarian. When one Sarah Lyons was ordered to receive fifty lashes for abusive language, he stopped the flogging after she had endured sixteen. Such flexibility impressed the island's Lieutenant-Governor, Philip Gidley King. Noting that D'Arcy carried out his duties 'with the greatest propriety', King appointed him Superintendent of Convicts at Queenborough, a job he added to his medical duties.[2]

It was at Queenborough, too, that D'Arcy became an entrepreneur, laying the groundwork for what would later become the Wentworth family fortune. Buying up other people's land grants to farm with convict labour, D'Arcy sold his produce to the government store. Lord Fitzwilliam's London agent, Charles Cookney, set up a London account into which he deposited D'Arcy's superintendent's salary together with loans from Fitzwilliam. These were repaid as and when D'Arcy had enough money. Out of this London account, for an annual fee to himself of two guineas, Cookney also purchased linen, china and groceries, which D'Arcy began to trade. Always a risk taker, D'Arcy now redirected the charm and quick wit that had repeatedly saved his neck in the English courts towards business associates and colonial officials in his quest for wealth and promotion.[3]

Lord Fitzwilliam took a keen interest in D'Arcy's progress, writing in June 1793 to say how pleased he was with the Lieutenant-Governor's praise of him as assistant surgeon. But this job carried no salary until D'Arcy's appointment was confirmed in London. And although Fitzwilliam was an active member of the

House of Lords, he was then in opposition so could not directly lobby the Secretary of State, Henry Dundas. He therefore lobbied the Under Secretary, whose response was mixed. D'Arcy would be paid as an assistant surgeon rather than as a superintendent, so there was still only one salary for two jobs. But the new Governor, John Hunter, would be asked to appoint D'Arcy to any future medical vacancy.[4]

At least one English newspaper, *The Advertiser*, also took an interest in D'Arcy's progress, noting that 'Wentworth the highwayman' was assisting the surgeon on Norfolk Island and 'behaves himself remarkably well'.[5]

In the formal hierarchy of Norfolk Island's Victualling Book, D'Arcy ranked No. 6 in the Civil Department, behind the Lieutenant-Governor. The Military Department was listed next, followed by the categories of 'Settlers and Free People', 'Male Convicts', 'Female Convicts', 'Children of Civil, Military and Free' and finally 'Convicts Children'. As Catherine Crowley's child, young William—who was known by his mother's surname even though D'Arcy claimed to be his father—came right at the bottom of the pile. But the real hierarchy of the island was not so formal. During his first term there Lieutenant-Governor King had lived with a convict, fathering two sons by her. So D'Arcy's de facto relationship with Catherine, which later produced William's brothers Dorset and Matthew Crowley, born in 1793 and 1795 respectively, raised few eyebrows. After King returned to the island with a Cornish wife for his second term he continued with his liberal approach, building a school house and appointing 'a Careful Woman' to teach William Crowley and the island's other children.[6]

During 1795, word reached D'Arcy that one of Sydney's assistant surgeons was ill and wanted to return to England. Keen to fill this vacancy, D'Arcy returned to Sydney with his family on 5 March 1796. Governor Hunter did not disappoint them, formally appointing D'Arcy as an assistant surgeon two months later. Meanwhile, in England, Fitzwilliam pursued D'Arcy's claim for back-pay as an assistant surgeon on Norfolk Island, finally reaching a satisfactory compromise with the government.

Walking Sydney's dusty streets, the tall, dark and handsome D'Arcy was often accompanied by William Crowley, a clumsy little red-head with a turned-in eye. In this primitive village of mean shacks and draughty lean-tos clustered around the Tank Stream, D'Arcy must have pined for the delights of London. But for young William, this village and its often rum-sodden, brawling inhabitants were all he knew. These surroundings only increased his natural feistiness, contributing to the violent side of his personality as an adult. But the brilliant sunlight and the natural beauty of the harbour infused his sharp intelligence with optimism and energy. Such were the beginnings of William Charles Wentworth's formidable and distinctly Australian personality.[7]

D'Arcy's trading gathered momentum in Sydney as he took advantage of a new market created by Governor Phillip's successor, Major Francis Grose, who allowed his officers and men to pay the convicts who worked for them in rum. Although these payments by the so-called Rum Corps debauched many, rum became a substitute for money. By 1800 D'Arcy had 3000 gallons (13,600 litres) on hand, conservatively worth £1500. Despite his growing wealth, D'Arcy continued to practise medicine. The previous year, he had been appointed as an assistant surgeon at Parramatta and obtained a twenty-year lease on six acres of land there. As a result, he and Catherine were again neighbours of the Macarthurs. When the Parramatta lease was added to a grant of 140 acres D'Arcy had been given at a place he later called 'Home Bush', it was clear that he and Catherine had come a long way from the convict sewage buckets on the *Neptune* that had so nauseated Elizabeth Macarthur. Still, when D'Arcy went to dine with Governor Hunter on Christmas Day 1799, he went alone. His domestic arrangements with Catherine were intensely private.[8]

A fortnight later, on 6 January, Catherine died. Although it is known that she was buried at St John's Church in Parramatta after a service conducted by the well-known Reverend Samuel Marsden, there is no record of what killed her at the age of twenty-seven. It may have been a complicated pregnancy, then a common cause of death among women her age. But whatever the cause, D'Arcy was sufficiently recovered by 28 January to have visiting Irish surgeon John Price spend 'a pleasant afternoon' with him and stay over-night. For the three boys, the loss of their mother would have been much more traumatic. And there were more shocks in store, as D'Arcy changed their surname from Crowley to Wentworth, and renamed Dorset and Matthew D'Arcy and John. Years later William wrote of:

Scenes, where my playful childhood's thoughtless years
Flew swift away, despite of childhood's tears.[9]

Shocks were in store for D'Arcy Sr, too, when the new Governor, Philip Gidley King, cracked down on the rum trade, placing his lucrative business in jeopardy. When Francis Grose, by now a Brigadier-General in England, wrote to the Rum Corps' Commander, Joseph Foveaux, that the Commander-in-Chief would 'turn . . . out of the service' anyone who associated with D'Arcy Wentworth, it was clear that D'Arcy had by no means shed his past. But there is no evidence that young William, who was now old enough to understand such things, knew of his father's run-ins with the law. Although John Price noted during his stay with the Wentworths that he had met George Barrington, a well-known former pickpocket who had appeared at London's Old Bailey on the same day as D'Arcy in 1789, he made no reference to D'Arcy's past.[10]

D'Arcy decided to continue his elder sons' education in England, and twelve-year-old William and his nine-year-old brother D'Arcy Jr departed on 8 October 1802. Leaving Sydney, which did not extend further south than modern-day Martin Place before meeting open countryside, they sailed for the capital of the British Empire. Travelling without their father, they were placed in the care of the captain, Richard Brooks, for the long voyage, via China and India, which would take them across the Equator three times. These unaccompanied children from a primitive colony were now exposed to sights, smells and sounds that their father and most other Englishmen would never experience. Chinese junks and Indian dhows jostled their ship, while the smell of cats, rats and dogs which had been split open for sale as food assailed their nostrils and their ears filled with the unintelligible talk of strange-looking people.

Travelling in the opposite direction was a letter from Lord Fitzwilliam to D'Arcy, again praising him for his good conduct and hoping that he would 'leave the name of Wentworth one of the most considerable and . . . respectable in New South Wales'. This comment may have prompted the increasingly wealthy D'Arcy to name his new Parramatta country house 'Wentworth Woodhouse', in honour of his ancestors. It certainly suggested that D'Arcy's sons would be well looked after in England. [11]

In London Charles Cookney took them under his wing, paying their expenses out of D'Arcy's account, which was frequently topped up by Lord Fitzwilliam. In October 1803, having been 'innoculated [sic] with the cow pox' in the then-novel practice of vaccination, the boys began attending the Reverend Richard Midgley's school in Bletchley with Cookney's sons, returning to stay with the Cookney family during the summer holidays. While all reports of their behaviour were excellent, William was keen to move to a school that taught French as well as Latin and in 1805 he began attending Dr Alexander Crombie's 'superior school' at Greenwich. The boys wrote to their father about seeing St Paul's Cathedral, visiting the Exeter show, where a kangaroo from Botany Bay was on display, and meeting Fitzwilliam. In a joint letter they said, 'we waited one day on Lord Fitzwilliam at his request. He seemed glad to see us and presented each of us with a guinea'. The boys' letters, in which affection was tempered by the formal politeness of the era, made their father miss them all the more. Fitzwilliam began lobbying the Secretary of State, Viscount Castlereagh, to grant D'Arcy leave of absence to visit them. Then in his mid-fifties, Fitzwilliam bore on his distinguished, owl-like face the expression of a man who was comfortable with life. Active though he was as a Whig politician, he lacked the drive and rat cunning needed to get to the top.[12]

During William's early days at Greenwich, Charles Cookney wrote to D'Arcy that although Dr Crombie was an excellent master he was also a 'very sharp disciplinarian', and William did not like his new school 'quite as well' as his old one. With a hint of concern, Cookney inquired 'what business or profession' D'Arcy intended for his eldest son, who would struggle to follow in his father's footsteps as a surgeon because of a cast in his eye, which 'leads him differently to the object he intends'. It was hard to determine William's future from the other side of the world, and despite Lord Fitzwilliam's best efforts D'Arcy's leave application remained up in the air for two years. The good news from Cookney in the dying days of 1807 was that William was doing better at Greenwich. 'William tends to be a very clever fellow,' he said, 'and Dr Crombie has made him a monitor.' Crombie, a renowned advocate of liberal principles, including civil and religious liberty, was also an admirer of the British Constitution, and his teaching influenced William's career. But this was all in the future, and Cookney continued to wait for a decision from D'Arcy. William, who 'had grown quite a man', Cookney noted, now spent money on lotteries and bottles of port, a sign that his appetites for risk taking and drinking were emerging along with his intellect.[13]

At the end of 1807, the Secretary of State finally granted D'Arcy leave. But less than a month later, D'Arcy and John Macarthur signed a petition asking the Rum Corps' commander to arrest

Governor William Bligh because, they claimed, he was endangering 'every man's property, liberty and life'. As a result, the Governor was deposed by Lieutenant-Colonel George Johnston, who took his place in what amounted to a rebellion during Britain's war with Napoleon. D'Arcy therefore decided it might not be wise to return to England after all. A tentative plan for William to join the army had been ruled out as too expensive, and Lord Fitzwilliam, whose brief time in the British Cabinet had ended, advised that he 'could not ask any favour' of the new government. In November 1809, Cookney told D'Arcy that he was sending William back to Sydney with Captain Brooks.

The indecision about William's future attracted the attention of John Macarthur, who had been summonsed to London for his leading role in the rebellion against Governor Bligh. 'I am very sorry Mr Wentworth has omitted to send positive instructions for the disposal of his son,' Macarthur wrote to his wife, 'he is a very pleasing lad.' Having satisfied himself that Fitzwilliam could not help, Macarthur agreed with Charles Cookney that there was 'nothing else to be done but to send [William] out by the first good opportunity'. On his voyage home, William could only guess at the ramifications of the rebellion that had forced Macarthur's return to England.[14]

Chapter 3

A VERY VALUABLE INVESTMENT

On 24 March 1810, *The Sydney Gazette* reported with unintended irony that 'on Monday arrived . . . Captain Brooks who imports a very general and valuable Investment, as per advertisement will appear.—Passenger, Mr Wentworth, jun'.[1]

Uppermost in William's mind as the *Simon Cock* anchored would have been concerns about his father's fate at the hands of the new governor, Colonel Lachlan Macquarie. In 1801, the future Duke of Wellington had described Macquarie as an 'excellent man' with significant limitations. 'He wants that decision in difficult cases which is the life of everything,' the future Duke said, 'although he has the habits of business.' Such was the man the Crown had assigned to deal with the rebels against Governor Bligh. William knew that Bligh had tried D'Arcy in 1807 and suspended him as an assistant surgeon for admitting convicts to hospital and then using them for private labour, charges D'Arcy strongly denied. William also knew that Bligh's subsequent arrest and trial of John Macarthur had triggered the boil-over that led to Bligh's overthrow on 26 January 1808. But it is unlikely that he knew that D'Arcy was deeply implicated in the rebellion, having been one of those who had asked Lieutenant-Colonel Johnston to arrest Bligh in the first place. William was probably unaware, too, of D'Arcy's concern that he might be hanged for his part in this insurrection.[2]

Macquarie's first acts were indeed ominous for D'Arcy who, under Johnston's rebel administration, had been acquitted by a kangaroo court and reappointed as an assistant surgeon. In a series of page one proclamations in The Sydney Gazette of 7 January 1810, Macquarie had reinstated Bligh for a day and cancelled all rebel court orders and appointments, leaving D'Arcy dangerously exposed. But on the same page, Macquarie had also expressed the hope that 'harmony and union' would be restored. And the following week, The Sydney Gazette carried a proclamation protecting certain office holders who had not actually been involved in any 'gross acts of rebel oppression'. This still left D'Arcy in an ambiguous position, but thanks to Lord Fitzwilliam's aggressive lobbying of the Secretary of State, Lord Liverpool, Macquarie had come out to the colony with an order reinstating him as an assistant surgeon. This the Governor duly announced in The Sydney Gazette, alongside a tirade against unmarried couples living in sin.[3]

Some years after Catherine Crowley's death, D'Arcy had had an affair with his housekeeper, Maria Ainslie. He then began a live-in relationship with Mary Ann Lawes, who was three years younger than William. But despite D'Arcy's private life and his involvement in the rebellion, Macquarie now nominated him as Principal Surgeon of New South Wales on account of his 'considerable professional abilities'. And the Governor was in a position to know. D'Arcy had treated him for venereal disease, suggesting that Macquarie was more broad-minded than his tirade against de facto relationships indicated.[4]

In many ways, D'Arcy and William now looked alike. But whereas D'Arcy in his prime was 'a handsome, tall man with blue eyes, who was invariably popular with all classes and both sexes', William at twenty was variously described as rugged, untidy, heavy shouldered, sloppily dressed, solidly built, clumsy and coarse featured, with a shock of auburn hair and that cast in his eye. His formidable intelligence and knowledge of the classics coexisted with speech and manners as coarse as his looks. William's aggressive, risk-taking nature soon made its public debut at the Hyde Park races, held over three days in October 1810. D'Arcy's horse Gig, a black gelding, raced on each of those days. In the first heat on the last day, Gig fell when a dog crossed the racecourse. The rider was too badly hurt to go on, but Gig was 'not much injured'. So William saddled up to ride in his place and, as the *Gazette* reported, 'beat Mr Broughton's bl[ack]. g[elding]. Jerry, rode by the owner; 3 miles, 20 [guineas]. play or pay. Gig won in a canter.'

Sydney had had its first taste of William's capacity for headstrong and ruthlessly effective improvisation. Clearly, the vigour of the currency lad had not been entirely tamed by an English education. Ten years later, a visiting British official would remark that native-born Australian men were 'active in their habits . . . remarkably awkward in their movements . . . [with] tempers that are quick and irascible but not vindictive'. He might have been describing young William Wentworth.[5]

Principal Surgeon was just the first of the senior appointments showered on D'Arcy during 1810. He was also made treasurer of the Police Fund, commissioner of the turnpike road to the Hawkesbury River, Magistrate for Sydney and Superintendent of Police. The Wentworth family fortune surged as Macquarie allowed D'Arcy to resume co-mingling his public duties and his business affairs. The Governor had a passion for building. His efforts soon began to transform Sydney, whose most prominent buildings in 1810 were a couple of old windmills and the fortress-like tower of St Phillip's Church. Macquarie's top priority was to replace the hospital, which he said was 'in a most ruinous state'. At the same time, he recommended to the Secretary of State that restrictions on rum imports be eased. Within a year, the Governor astonished even the roughest rum traders by granting D'Arcy and his fellow merchants Garnham Blaxcell and Alexander Riley the exclusive right to import up to 45,000 gallons (204,300 litres) of spirits for three years in return for building a 200-bed hospital. Lord Liverpool was astonished, too, but when he expressed concern about D'Arcy's conflict of interest, Macquarie reassured him that the Principal Surgeon brought much-needed experience and capital to the 'Rum Hospital' project.[6]

William also benefited directly from Macquarie's largesse when, in late 1811, he was appointed Acting Provost Marshal, the first native-born Australian to be appointed to a senior post. For a salary of just under £100 a year, William was now the executive officer for the courts, responsible among other things for arranging hangings, transmitting requests for public meetings to the Governor, and convening those approved. In January 1812, he called a meeting at the request of Sydney residents to congratulate Macquarie on his safe return from Van Diemen's Land. After this resolution had been put and passed, the meeting gently but firmly noted that New South Wales enjoyed only some of the benefits of the British Constitution and encouraged Macquarie 'to model the laws that rule us after their revered original'. At meetings in Liverpool and the Hawkesbury, perfunctory congratulations were answered by equally perfunctory vice-regal thanks. But in Sydney, Macquarie said he had anticipated residents' requests and recommended 'such alterations to . . . our Courts . . . as the inhabitants . . . so justly demand'. As a student in England, William had witnessed the drama of the British Parliament, and the Sydney meeting must have seemed tepid by comparison. Yet it did show that an all-powerful Governor could be responsive to public sentiment. The insights into the courts and public meetings that William gained as Acting Provost Marshal would prove useful when he later set out to drive constitutional reform.[7]

D'Arcy, Blaxcell and Riley's income from the Rum Hospital contract began to slow, and they protested that their exclusive right to import rum was being undercut by smugglers. But when Macquarie allowed the trio to increase their rum imports to compensate, they complained that there were not enough people in Sydney to drink that much liquor. Macquarie countered that there were not enough pillars to support the main hospital building. When he refused to negotiate further, D'Arcy, Blaxcell and Riley threatened to petition the Secretary of State. Although this resulted in a compromise further disputes plagued the project, and it was not until 1816 that the hospital's three wings, which were to dominate Sydney's skyline from the top of Macquarie Street for decades, were sufficiently completed to admit the first convict patients.[8]

Despite their ongoing dispute with Macquarie over the Rum Hospital, D'Arcy, Blaxcell and Riley soon entered a new agreement. In early January 1814, reading through a ship's log that had been submitted to him in one of his official capacities, D'Arcy noticed an entry about a South Sea island covered in sandalwood trees. Within days, he signed a contract with Blaxcell and Riley to import this wood. A group of islanders was then visiting Sydney, and at a public meeting of the Philanthropic Society the three partners expressed their support for their welfare. William was also a party to D'Arcy's sandalwood agreement, along with Captain William Campbell. The hurriedly prepared document committed them all to charter the schooner *Cumberland* to sail to Rarotonga, where the wood could be obtained by bartering with the locals. William was to sail on the *Cumberland* and manage the deal-making. He was to take any cargoes of sandalwood to Palmerstone Island for storage and repeat the process. Campbell would 'purchase or hire' another 'fit for purpose vessel' and 'act in conjunction' with William. The wood itself would be jointly owned by all of them and sent to 'the best markets for sale'.[9]

Arriving in Rarotonga, the schooner's landing party was attacked by natives who 'with surprising dexterity' used slings to hurl large stones at them. But after being placated with gifts of tomahawks, they helped load the *Cumberland* with sandalwood. All went well until mid-August when, in William's presence, one of the crew was attacked by a club-wielding islander. *The Sydney Gazette* reported that as soon as William saw the crewman go down, he aimed his pistol at the culprit but the weapon mis-fired. He then rushed forward to help, but the crewman was already dead. 'Mr W. having now only to provide for his own safety', the paper said, 'took a pistol from the dead man's belt and menacing and menaced made his way to his boat'. Three other crew members were massacred by the locals and the captain's mistress, who had earlier been shown kindness by female islanders, was slaughtered when she went to call upon her new friends. *The Sydney Gazette* reported that 'the murdered persons' were later eaten at 'a cannibal festival'.[10]

If William thought his fight had ended on the beach at Rarotonga, he was wrong. Back in Sydney, the Philanthropic Society's secretary, Samuel Marsden, urged the Society to investigate the killings, but D'Arcy, Blaxcell and Riley used their numbers to block him. William's next challenge came from his partners. After the Wentworths' side of the contract had been trashed on the beach at Rarotonga, Campbell did arrive in another ship, the *Governor Macquarie*, so he and Blaxcell argued, to help William 'as a matter of necessity not choice' after which they collected sandalwood worth £4000. But when it was sold, Campbell and his friend Blaxcell refused to give Riley and the Wentworths any of the money, equivalent to $325,000 today. Writing to his lawyer on 4 June 1815, William regretted that the agreement had been so loosely worded. His assumption had been that the parties were all honourable men. 'Legal forms were . . . disregarded and the framing of the agreement was left entirely to Mr Blaxcell,' Wentworth said, '. . . almost justifying the conclusion that the ambiguity was intentional.'[11]

As the twenty-five-year-old William saw it he had put his life on the line to keep his side of the contract, only to be cheated by 'men of honour'. It was another lesson he would not forget, and in later life he developed a reputation for ruthlessly exploiting legal loopholes. But not all his partnerships ended in rancour. One of the most successful partnerships in Australian history—between Wentworth, Gregory Blaxland and William Lawson—was built on a handshake.

Chapter 4

BLAXLAND, LAWSON AND WENTWORTH

At the beginning of 1813, the European population of continental Australia was living in Sydney, on the surrounding Cumberland Plain and in small settlements to the north and south. While this population of 12,000 would not fill a small Sydney suburb today, local agriculture then could not comfortably sustain it during difficult times. As far as is known, all European attempts to cross the Blue Mountains in search of fertile country to the west had failed. Yet in *The Sydney Gazette* of 22 May the lead item concerned the discovery of a man's body floating in Sydney Harbour after he had fallen in drunk. Only after came a story that 'Lieutenant Lawson . . . Mr G. Blaxland and Mr. W.C. Wentworth' had set out west from Emu Island (near Penrith) on 18 May (in fact it was a week earlier) with stores for a six-week 'excursion of discovery' on a track which 'had not before been attempted'.[1]

A friend of the influential botanist Sir Joseph Banks, Gregory Blaxland, aged thirty-four, had arrived in New South Wales as a wealthy free settler in 1806, while William Lawson, a thirty-eight-year-old surveyor, had been an officer in the Rum Corps. Both men had joined D'Arcy Wentworth in the revolt against Governor Bligh, and Lawson had also been one of D'Arcy's patients. In 1812, Governor Macquarie had issued William Wentworth, aged twenty-two, with cattle worth £168 and granted him 1750 acres of land near the Nepean River. Blaxland and Lawson had cattle properties nearby. They all shared the problem of overgrazing on the Cumberland Plain.[2]

Blaxland, in particular, had been keen to find new pastures. He made enquiries about 'discovering a passage over the Blue Mountains', noting that every person who had tried 'described it as impossible'. In the company of the Governor and Mrs Macquarie, Blaxland had travelled west up the Warragamba River, which cut through the lower mountains, until the further navigation of their vessel was prevented by 'immense blocks of stones . . . confined on each side by perpendicular cliffs'. On a separate trip Blaxland had followed the river's south bank, but as he again tried to travel west he had found himself 'turned eastwards towards the coast'.[3]

Blaxland's next idea was to climb and then follow the ridge running west between the Warragamba and Grose Rivers, which would give him 'a fair chance of passing the mountains'. Macquarie supported this plan and asked Blaxland to attempt it. He invited Lawson and Wentworth to join him in an expedition, and they agreed. On 11 May 1813 they left Blaxland's farm at South Creek, accompanied by four servants, five dogs and four horses and crossed the Nepean not far from today's Penrith railway station. Each of the principal explorers kept a journal. Blaxland's was written as a daily narrative in the third person, while Lawson's was dominated by the carefully logged compass bearings of a surveyor. Wentworth's gave every appearance of having been written later: it began with a description of the country they found on the other side of the mountains. [4]

Thanks to Lawson's precise calculations, it is possible to say that the modern Great Western Highway follows the explorers' route quite closely. On their first full day in the mountains they hiked along a very crooked ridge with deep rocky gullies on each side, and that night camped midway between the modern railway stations of Warrimoo and Valley Heights. The next day there was some excitement when the explorers came across a track marked by a European, but their spirits fell when shortly afterwards they encountered very thick brushwood blocking the main ridge. Attempting to sidestep it, they tried other ridges, but each one ended in a deep rocky precipice. Again they set up camp, this time near modern Springwood Station, and stayed there for the next four nights while they hacked a path through the brushwood. Exhausted by this heavy work, they rested on Sunday, doing their best to ignore the howling of nearby dingoes. Resuming their journey on the 17th, they ducked and weaved from north-north-west to south-south-west and spent the next two nights on a narrow ridge near modern Linden Station. They ran short of water: Blaxland noted that they had to 'fetch [it] up the side of a precipice about 600 feet high' and the horses went without. The next day, they found that the ridge they were travelling on, which was now less than twenty yards wide with deep precipices on each side, was blocked 'by a perpendicular mass of rock, nearly 30 feet high'. But they discovered a small, rugged track in its centre up which they were able to scramble, after removing some large stones.[5]

The explorers began climbing the second ridge of the Blue Mountains on Wednesday, 19 May. But they had not gone far when they found 'a pyramidal heap of stones'. They thought this pyramid had been built by George Bass in 1797 to mark the end of a journey in which he exhausted himself trying to climb the cliffs with ropes. Others later suggested that it could have been built by Aborigines or by earlier explorers. William Dawes may have reached as far as Mount Twiss, three miles north of Linden station, in 1789, and Henry Hacking was believed to have been in the same vicinity and possibly further west five years later. The pyramid had almost certainly not been built by George Caley, who had blazed a path to Mount Banks in 1804 from the other side of the Grose River Valley, not far from the modern Bell's Line of road. Even so, Macquarie later referred to this pyramid as 'Caley's Repulse'. Whatever its origin and whatever the most westerly point of their predecessors' journeys, Blaxland, Lawson and Wentworth, rightly or wrongly, assumed that in passing the pyramid they had penetrated further than any other Europeans. Over the next day or so they pushed on in a generally westerly direction, making camp on the 21st near modern Bullaburra station. That night their dogs barked violently, scaring off some Aborigines who, so the explorers thought, had been following their track intending to spear them by the light of their fire.[6]

Next morning, Blaxland noted that at a point eighteen miles due west of the Nepean River and just south of what is now known as Wentworth Falls they had 'reached the summit of the third and highest ridge of the mountains southward of Mount Banks'. This meant they had matched the furthest point of Caley's 1804 expedition, albeit on the other side of the Grose River, and were nearing the most westerly point of the high ground they had been traversing for almost two weeks. They therefore began to look for a way down to the valley below. But they were also in the vicinity of the King's Tableland and soon faced 'an impassable barrier of rock which appeared to divide the interior from the coast, as with a stone wall, rising perpendicularly out of the side of the mountain'. Wherever they tried to climb down, by following either a stream or fallen rocks, they were frustrated by perpendicular cliffs 400 feet high. So they continued west along the high ground, then began turning north as they followed the edge of the west-facing escarpment, 'expecting to find a passage down the mountain further northward'. They camped near the Explorers' Tree at Katoomba, and looked down on the fires of Aborigines in the apparently sandy Megalong Valley. Not far from Mount Victoria, they failed to notice a natural pass down into the valley (which now carries the Great Western Highway) and continued on until they reached what Macquarie later named Mount York, where they camped on 28 May.[7]

Stationing themselves on the edge of the precipice at Mount York, the explorers went in search of water and found some in the valley below, after clambering down through a thirty-foot wide pass in the rock. As Blaxland later put it to Macquarie, 'this pass was discovered by the suggestion of Mr Wentworth'. So steep was the gradient here that the horses had to be unloaded so they could keep their footing, and the explorers were obliged to carry their packs themselves. At the bottom they found that the country was quite lush, although the climate was much colder than on the Sydney side. They continued west through the Hartley Valley, and on Monday, 31 May made their furthest camp just beyond the junction of the River Lett with the Cox's River, before proceeding to a high hill shaped like a sugar loaf, later called Mount Blaxland. From its summit they saw country capable, in their opinion, of supporting the colony's stock for the next thirty years. At this, 'the extreme point of their journey', they had travelled fifty miles through the mountains and eight miles beyond them. 'They had sufficiently accomplished . . . their undertaking,' Blaxland said, 'having surmounted all the difficulties which had . . . prevented the interior . . . being explored and the Colony . . . being extended.'[8]

On the return trip, which coincided with the first days of winter, the explorers made most of the distance in just four days by taking full advantage of their marked trail. After briefly getting lost on the one section of the track they had not marked, they crossed the Nepean River and reached their homes, according to Blaxland, 'all in good health'—although Wentworth later claimed he had contracted a lung inflammation that almost 'terminated in consumption'. *The Sydney Gazette* carried a short report on their return, but it was buried by the momentous news that New South Wales had been at war with the United States since October 1812 and that the frigates USS *President* and *Constitution* were menacing the shipping route to Australia.[9]

In his own journal, Wentworth was surprisingly circumspect about what he and his companions had achieved. Although the tract of land they discovered beyond Mount York looked large and green, Wentworth admitted that it was impossible to know just how large it was without further exploration. It was quite likely, he said, that 'perpendicular walls of stone from 500 to 1000 feet in height [might] entirely surround it'. Elsewhere, he admitted that the explorers had 'not traversed the mountains' but said they had 'proved that they are traversable and that too, by cattle'. Wentworth correctly concluded that they had discovered the only track through the mountains between the Warragamba and Grose Rivers, and noted that it was so narrow in parts that it could 'be easily defended by a few against the efforts of thousands'.[10]

Blaxland said that when he told Macquarie they had succeeded, the Governor 'did not doubt my statement but appeared dissatisfied'. Just why, Blaxland did not know. But when Macquarie failed to publicly acknowledge the explorers' efforts, Blaxland concluded that 'he neither expected nor wished us to succeed'. Perhaps the Governor feared it might be impossible to control settlement west of the mountains. Five months passed before Macquarie dispatched the Deputy Surveyor of Lands, George Evans, to follow up the explorers' discoveries. Taking advantage of Blaxland, Lawson and Wentworth's marked trail, Evans reached and named Mount Blaxland on 26 November, covering his journey out in about the same time the explorers had taken to get home. Still fresh, Evans continued and four days later became the first European to officially record his crossing of the Great Dividing Range. (John Wilson may have achieved the same thing in 1798 by using the so called 'Marulan ramp' to get to the outskirts of the future town of Goulburn.) Whatever the case, Evans was the first European to see westward-flowing rivers and the first to discover the Bathurst Plains.[11]

After Evans' return, Macquarie wasted no time in getting a General Order published on the front page of *The Sydney Gazette*. Its centrepiece was praise for Evans' efforts, along with a 1000-acre grant and a 'pecuniary reward'. Buried further down the page was Macquarie's acknowledgment that Blaxland, Lawson and Wentworth had been 'the first Europeans . . . over the Blue Mountains' and that their 'enterprising and arduous exertions' had assisted Evans. Right at the bottom was the news that the explorers had each been granted 1000 acres as well. Macquarie now commissioned William Cox to build a road to the Bathurst Plains. With the aid of twenty-eight convicts and six soldiers, he completed it just over six months after the first sod had been turned.[12]

On 25 April 1815, the Governor began a tour of the newly discovered country and fixed the site of a town to be called Bathurst. In a General Order published on the front page of the *Gazette* after his return, he expressed his 'surprise and admiration' at Blaxland, Lawson and Wentworth's 'patient endurance'. But Macquarie suggested that they had only made 'the first passage over the most rugged and difficult part of the Blue Mountains', implying that they had not made a complete crossing. Even worse for the explorers, Macquarie named the pass down Mount York Cox's Pass and the river where Blaxland, Lawson and Wentworth had made their furthest camp Cox's River. This prompted Blaxland to fire off an angry letter:

> I claim . . . a victory where and on the same ground on which all others had been defeated . . . even Mr Cox . . . Your Excellency having so named the Pass and River will be the means . . . of attaching the honour of a first discoverer to Mr Cox . . . [when] the pass was actually discovered by the suggestion of Mr Wentworth and the River was actually discovered by Mr Lawson.[13]

An even more irritable explorer than Blaxland was George Caley, who in 1804 had almost crossed the mountains before retreating at Mount Banks. Caley had previously denounced Francis Barrallier's claims to have succeeded near the upper Kowmung River, saying Barrallier 'could not compute distances'. And he was at it again in February 1816, writing that the mountains 'are not yet crossed'. Caley's friendship with Sir Joseph Banks may have prompted Blaxland to tell Banks that 'the business of our having passed the mountains has . . . been misrepresented'. But Blaxland's anger was mainly focused on Macquarie, who had 'endeavoured to give others as much of the merit due to us as possible'. In official correspondence, Macquarie described Blaxland as a 'lazy discontented drone'. Four years were to pass before Blaxland had his revenge at an inquiry into Macquarie's administration.[14]

Although Blaxland implied that he was speaking on behalf of Lawson and Wentworth in his letters of complaint, this was not so. Generally content, Lawson took up his 1000–acre grant west of the Blue Mountains and soon became a wealthy grazier. As for Wentworth, he remained a staunch Macquarie fan. In *Australasia*, a poem he dedicated to the former Governor in 1823, Wentworth melodramatically described the explorers' moment of triumph:

> And, as a meteor shoots athwart the night,
> The boundless champaign burst upon our sight,
> Till nearer seen the beauteous landscape grew,
> Op'ning like Canaan on rapt Israel's view.[15]

Macquarie initially took advantage of the explorers' observation that their mountain trail was narrow enough for a few to hold back thousands. But although the Governor placed guards at pinch points to do just that, nothing could stop the relentless westward movement of agriculture or the discovery of gold.

These changes, which drove the European settlement of the Australian continent, also shaped Wentworth's career in the Legislative Council where, for one term, an elderly William Lawson sat beside him.[16]

Chapter 5

A SHOWDOWN LOOMS

No one who had a copy of the malicious poem, or 'pipe', thrown over their front fence in early March 1816—least of all Lieutenant-Governor George Molle—was in any doubt about its target.

> Of all the mongrels, that to wit lay claim,
> The basest breed, that e'er prophan'd the name!
> And now farewell thou dirty grov'ling M–ll–
> Go with thy namesake burrow in thy hole.

Nor was there any doubt that the pipe's author saw Molle and his 46th Regiment as a direct threat to Governor Macquarie and the ex-convicts he championed. The only mystery was the author's identity. A free pardon was therefore offered for information leading to the poet's arrest, and the officers of the 46th put up their own £100 reward.[1]

At the same time, William Wentworth prepared to return to England—'on account of his health', Lord Fitzwilliam was told. He seemed preoccupied—and not just by the question of whether to be a lawyer or a soldier. While packing his bags, he showed his brother John and a friend a bundle of poems he had written and admitted with some concern that he was the author of the pipe defaming Molle. So they suggested that he work up one of the other poems, 'An Imitation of the Ode to Horace', into a pipe defaming someone else. This would be distributed after Wentworth had departed, 'as a cloak to cover me', he said, from any suspicions that he had been the author of the pipe defaming the Lieutenant-Governor. The target this time was William's business partner Alexander Riley, who had stood by him during the *Cumberland* affair. A pipe that defamed a friendly partner was an ideal cloak, especially given that Riley and Molle were also friends. It was an early sign of Wentworth the political activist's talent—and readiness—to deceive.[2]

On 25 March 1816 Wentworth sailed for England, via Hobart and Capetown, aboard the *Emu*. Also on board were three officers of the 46th Regiment, little dreaming that their commanding officer's defamer was in their midst. D'Arcy, now fifty-four, was well settled with Mary Ann Lawes and their two young children, with another on the way, but his eldest son remained much in his thoughts. Realising that a military career was unlikely to meet William's expectations, D'Arcy wrote that he would pay for him to study law.[3]

By the time D'Arcy's letter reached Hobart, the *Emu* had already crossed the Great Australian Bight and was taking on wood and water at King George's Sound (near Albany). Wentworth noted that the Aborigines there were 'most pacific and obliging'. But as the *Emu*'s shore party prepared to leave, the Aborigines nearby suddenly withdrew and moments later there was a 'general discharge of spears', one of which 'just grazed Mrs Napper's bonnet'. While Wentworth relied on Dr Napper's account of this incident, he drew the harshest conclusions.

Based in a state of ferocious and solitary independence, what ideas can . . . [Aborigines have] of society or its obligations? . . . If they commit an outrage on the . . . relatives of their own tribe . . . [those] relatives are constantly on the spot to avenge . . . This however is not the case with strangers. If they can commit an outrage on them with impunity, they have no after-reckoning to pay [and] no future retaliation to fear.

The weather was also working against the *Emu*'s passengers. Hit by a gale and massive breakers as it tried to tack into the Southern Ocean, the ship lost half its topmasts and was delayed by some days. Wentworth was highly critical of the captain, who was paid by the day and thus, he believed, encouraged to delay further. The slowdown meant the *Emu*, which was full of dry rot, had to face midwinter gales. These tossed up howling mountains of green water and stinging spray, rolling the ship on her beam-ends—almost capsizing—while she struggled west. When the *Emu* again approached land, the captain admitted that he was unfamiliar with this part of the South African coast. Soon afterwards the vessel was in the breakers, hard aground and badly holed. Making his way overland to Cape Town, Wentworth likened himself to Don Quixote, the mythical traveller bedevilled by mishaps.

In 1816, Cape Town was the transport hub between London and Sydney, awash with news and rumours. Wentworth was alarmed to hear that someone called Maxwell was tipped to replace Macquarie but pleased that the 46th Regiment was to be transferred to India, thereby removing Molle as a threat to the ex-convicts. Forced to rent a room in a Cape Town boarding-house, Wentworth was now seriously short of money. Any hope he had of obtaining a government job in England was dashed by news of cutbacks by the Liverpool ministry following the Duke of Wellington's emphatic victory at Waterloo. Wentworth could only pray that the Whig party would soon be in government and that Fitzwilliam would be able to get him a job.[4]

After obtaining a loan Wentworth secured a berth to England on the frigate *Revolutionaire* [*sic*], which docked at Plymouth on 27 November 1816. John Macarthur, who had been sent to England to testify over the Bligh business, noted that William had arrived on the same frigate as Lieutenant Smith of Molle's 46th Regiment. 'Tell his father he is well,' Macarthur wrote to his wife Elizabeth, 'and very highly spoken of by . . . Lieutenant Smith.' It was a tribute to Wentworth's ability to keep a poker face that Smith had no idea his commanding officer's defamer shared the same mess, where the Regiment's reward of £100 must have been discussed in his presence.[5]

Detained eight days in Plymouth by a severe cold that worsened his lung ailment, Wentworth was grateful to be able to stay with Charles Cookney and his family when he finally arrived in London. Still unaware that his father was now prepared to pay for him to study law, Wentworth contacted Lord Fitzwilliam to seek his advice but Fitzwilliam would not be drawn. After mulling things over at the Cookneys' Castle Street home, Wentworth advised his lordship, with a display of precociousness unlikely to be bettered in Australian public life:

> My deliberations have entirely confirmed the bias I have always felt towards the Bar . . . and I calculate upon acquainting myself with all the excellence of the British Constitution and hope at some future period to advocate successfully the right of my country to a participation in its advantages.

Fitzwilliam strongly approved and D'Arcy's account was duly debited £35 to enrol his eldest son as a law student. Lacking a degree, William had to be enrolled at Middle Temple for five years, but he had to be present for only twelve quarter-long terms, leaving him two years to fill in. So he talked about going to Oxford but decided that his health ruled it out. He talked about a return voyage to Sydney, during which he could study law books while improving his health in the sea air. But that too came to nothing. He wrote to the Secretary of State, Lord Bathurst, to apply for the job of Vendue Master (government auctioneer) at Sydney but received no answer. So he wrote again, flamboyantly offering to traverse Australia 'from its eastern extremity to its western . . . a space of two thousand miles and upwards'. That idea too came to nothing, and he remained at a loose end.[6]

Wentworth rented rooms at No. 22, The Terrace, Pimlico and tried to keep up the appearances of a young gentleman as he again toyed with the idea of going to Oxford. But he would have to study the classics to get a degree there. Adopting a supercilious air, he claimed that he was 'already a far better classical scholar than nine-tenths of the persons who have taken degrees.' At the same time, he hinted that his plan to make 'powerful connections' at Oxford could not succeed because he did not have the money to socialise with the student sons of the aristocracy. Still unsettled, he wrote to his father of going to France for a year and also said he would need extra income to keep a proper London house for his health's sake.

Not surprisingly Charles Cookney, who provided his allowance, was now keeping his distance. As for D'Arcy's family in Britain, cousin Maria had married a bankrupt and cousin William 'failed some time ago', while another cousin 'made some disgraceful match [with] a common soldier'. The truth was that although Wentworth had settled on his life's goal, he was financially fragile and emotionally erratic. And as he saw it, he had little help from his father's patrons or family.[7]

It was during these difficult days that Wentworth turned to John Macarthur. The older man supported his decision to become a barrister and said he should prepare himself for a change in the colony's Constitution, which would allow him to obtain a judicial appointment or practise in the courts there. 'Macarthur has indeed transferred that friendship . . . he entertains for you to your son,' Wentworth told his father, 'and I really do not know what I should have done . . . without him.' Filled with frustration at his inability to make his own influential connections in London and concerned that his father's patrons were keeping him at arm's length, he now hatched a plan to marry Macarthur's daughter Elizabeth and establish a dynasty in the Antipodes. Although Wentworth claimed that he had cherished Elizabeth for a long time, the nature and timing of his proposal suggested he had other motives. As he explained to his father, the union would be for 'the future respectability and grandeur of our family'. Just a few years before, Wentworth had ridiculed Macarthur's pretensions, which he thought were 'meant to cast a shadow on . . . [their] owner's low extraction'. So although Elizabeth Macarthur was in colonial terms a great catch, Wentworth's about-face on the Macarthur family's social standing was yet more evidence of his instability.[8]

Macarthur soon returned to Sydney, and Wentworth finally went to Paris to study French and improve his health. But he went without Fitzwilliam's blessing, and his gift of a parrot to Lady Fitzwilliam just before his departure could not come close to covering the huge debt he now owed her husband: almost £250 ($22,000 today). While that was no more than small change for Fitzwilliam, he was far from pleased that Wentworth was compounding his own debt with his trip to Paris.[9]

In Sydney, the 46th Regiment's reward offer for the author of the pipe mocking Molle had drawn a blank. Macquarie ordered an inquiry, during which D'Arcy admitted that William was the likely culprit. So Molle arrested D'Arcy in September 1817 for 'aiding and abetting' his son's criminal libel. He also recycled the old note from Grose to Foveaux that had undermined D'Arcy's reputation. Because D'Arcy was a civilian officer he could not be court-martialled, so

Macquarie referred the case to the Secretary of State in London.[10]

While the author of the pipe tried to enjoy himself in Paris on a rapidly shrinking budget, an agitated D'Arcy wrote to Lord Fitzwilliam to seek help. Fitzwilliam had some success interceding with Secretary of State Bathurst on D'Arcy's behalf, but William remained unrepentant. His first reaction when cornered was usually to talk tough: he was even prepared, he said, to challenge Molle to a duel. But the duel never materialised.

The Molle affair added to a growing pile of complaints about Governor Macquarie's administration, including one from Gregory Blaxland. This pile was being noticed in the House of Commons. A few months before, William had read in *The Times* that Henry Grey Bennet MP, a crusader for law reform, was about to present a petition complaining about Governor Macquarie's 'oppressive' conduct. Open-faced and earnest, Bennet looked like a man who would listen to reason. But, although William wrote immediately offering to demonstrate the 'absolute falsehood' of the petition's claims, Bennet tabled it anyway. Wentworth, who was in the Commons gallery at the time, later said that if Bennet had simply argued that it was wrong for any individual to possess unlimited power, he would have agreed with him. But Bennet's attack on Macquarie went too far, and Wentworth was pleased to see the Secretary of State come to the Governor's defence. Nevertheless, Bathurst, who was once described as 'generally averse to changes but acquiescing in many', now decided to hold a Commission of Inquiry into Macquarie's administration.[11]

The petition that had triggered the inquiry covered many issues, but the complaint that the 'most inexperienced persons' were magistrates bore the mark of Jeffrey Hart Bent, the colony's first Supreme Court judge. Bent, whose face was so shrunken that it resembled a death's head skull, had been appointed as an indirect result of the public meeting Wentworth had called as Acting Provost Marshal back in 1812. But Macquarie and Bent later clashed over the independence of the judiciary and Bent's refusal to open his court to convict attorneys. Bent had taken his claim of independence to absurd lengths when, in 1815, he was confronted by the operator of a toll-bar at the entrance to the Parramatta Road, near modern-day Railway Square. 'I'll pay no toll [while] I am a judge of this Colony,' Bent yelled, 'and if you don't let me pass, I'll send you to jail.' Bent then dismounted from his horse and attacked the toll gate with such force that the chain flew off. The gate swung open and the judge leaped into the saddle and rode straight through. Refusing to answer for this before magistrate D'Arcy Wentworth, he was fined £2 in absentia. There was more Bent rage to come. Not only was the judge recalled to London for refusing to open his court, but before he left his successor Justice Field was joined on the Supreme Court Bench for a ceremonial sitting by D'Arcy Wentworth and his fellow magistrate, the ex-convict Simeon Lord. Bent fired off a furious letter to Lord Bathurst denouncing Macquarie for having 'associated with the judge one person who had been a transported felon, and another a notorious highwayman'. As far as the hardheads in London were concerned, this generous treatment of ex-convicts undermined the deterrent effect of transportation.[12]

Bent's letter echoed ex-Governor Bligh's (inaccurate) evidence to a Parliamentary Committee in 1812 that 'D'Arcy Wentworth, a man transported for highway robbery, acted as an assistant surgeon of the colony'. When the irascible judge arrived in London in May 1818, Henry Bennet had a ready source of misinformation about Macquarie and his associates close at hand. Bennet also happened to be related to John Thomas Bigge, who was chosen to conduct Bathurst's promised Commission of Inquiry into New South Wales. Wentworth later claimed that Bigge—who began proceedings by reading the evidence given to the 1812 Parliamentary Committee—had been appointed through Bennet's influence. The scene was set for a monumental showdown.[13]

Chapter 6

HUMILIATION

'I arrived late last night from Paris and went to your lodgings early this morning in the hope of seeing you . . . to refer me to any banker who would be willing to advance me money . . . I await your reply with the greatest impatience.' Fitzwilliam had cut off Wentworth's funds in mid-August and suggested he return to London, which he did two weeks later. In his desperate note to John Macarthur's second son, John Jr, Wentworth said he had also been refused a loan by Alexander Riley, by this time also in London, who now knew that Wentworth had defamed him while attempting to cloak his authorship of the Molle pipe. John Jr, who was just starting out as a barrister at Lincoln's Inn, appeared to be Wentworth's last hope of obtaining money from anyone, including D'Arcy. Described by Macarthur Sr as being as 'soft and winning as could be wished', John was nevertheless fiercely independent and obstinate in pursuing his goals.[1]

In June, Wentworth had written to D'Arcy for the first time in seven months, blaming a gout attack for his long silence. In fact he had been too embarrassed to write because he had not told D'Arcy that he was the author of the Molle pipe and because Fitzwilliam was furious with him for wanting to extend his trip and go to Italy. So he had only himself to blame for the long delay with his father's mail and money.[2]

No doubt Wentworth hoped young John would help him the way both Macarthurs had helped him in the past. After all, he counted the younger John as a friend. William had stayed at his Paris apartment while he was in France and, at his host's suggestion, had begun writing a book on the 'political state of the colony'. But he also had reason to be wary because an earlier letter of his from Paris, begging John Jr for a loan of £250, had gone unanswered. There was no satisfaction this time, either. Both men referred their correspondence to their respective fathers. John Jr in any case lacked his father's authority to lend Wentworth large sums or act as a banking middleman. He had told him as much at the beginning of 1818, when William suggested a 'union' between the two families—and a loan of £200. It was the proposed union that brought matters to a head. Shortly after William's return from Paris, Macarthur Sr informed him that he could not marry his daughter Elizabeth. Precisely why is a mystery. Perhaps it was Wentworth's support for ex-convicts that rankled with the older man. Perhaps it was D'Arcy's criminal past—or Wentworth's demands for money. Perhaps Macarthur had found out about Wentworth's ridicule of his social pretensions. Or perhaps Elizabeth simply said no. Whatever the reason, Wentworth was furious. He vowed to 'pay . . . [Macarthur] off in his own coin', and described John Jr as a 'complete chip off the old block'. So powerful was this enmity that it decisively determined the relationship between the two families until both Macarthur men were dead. While they had well-deserved reputations for unforgiving pigheadedness, Wentworth outdid them both on this occasion.[3]

In the months that followed, Wentworth somehow arranged a loan of £100 from a Mr Birnie, whose brother in Sydney had given William a letter of introduction. Nevertheless, his finances remained precarious. He even visited the dead letter office in search of his father's mail and money. But he was soon over any feelings he might have had for Elizabeth Macarthur. In November 1818 he wrote to D'Arcy about a lady who had shown a 'partiality' for him and who he hoped would become his wife. This liaison too evaporated. A frustrated Wentworth settled down to serious study of the law, using some of Birnie's loan to pay for chambers 'in the Temple'. Despite an advance by Cookney in November of £100 Wentworth was still in great need of money, but his pride was greater. He wrote to Alexander Riley, one of the few people who might have been persuaded to help financially, that 'my decision never to make any concession to Colonel Molle is unalterably confirmed . . . however much your friendship with . . . [him] may lend you to deplore this inflexibility'. Wentworth's pigheaded pride came ahead of a pound.[4]

Although Henry Bennet MP had publicly welcomed Commissioner Bigge's appointment in late 1818, he continued his own criticism of how New South Wales was being run. To keep up the momentum, Bennet began 1819 by publishing a long pamphlet in which he launched a general assault on Governor Macquarie's administration. Using information provided by Judge Jeffrey Bent, Bennet attacked Macquarie's appointment of ex-convicts to the Bench and also referred to the employment of Magistrate D'Arcy Wentworth—who, he joined Bent in alleging, had been transported for highway robbery.[5]

The wide publication of this devastating slur on his father's reputation electrified Wentworth. He immediately sought out the 'preying slanderer' Bennet and demanded that he make D'Arcy a full public apology for 'so infamous a calumny'. Should Bennet refuse, Wentworth threatened to shed his 'last drop . . . of blood in the effort'. But things were not quite as clear-cut as the hotheaded Wentworth imagined. When the two men met on the morning of 12 February, Bennet told William that his source was not Bent but Lord Erskine, who claimed he had defended D'Arcy on a highway robbery charge. Appalled, Wentworth rushed to see Charles Cookney, who confirmed that D'Arcy had been tried for highway robbery but said he had been acquitted. After making further inquiries around the Bar, it was no comfort to Wentworth to discover that it was in fact not Erskine but William Garrow, until recently Attorney-General and now an Exchequer Judge, who had represented D'Arcy. After composing himself Wentworth wrote to Bennet that same night, conceding that D'Arcy had indeed been tried but saying Bennet must accept from the verdict that D'Arcy was 'innocent'. Warming to his father's defence, Wentworth explained that D'Arcy had 'sought by voluntary exile . . . to efface . . . an unjust accusation' and had now spent many years of 'unimpeachable rectitude' in New South Wales. 'By his single merit,' Wentworth said, D'Arcy had risen to the 'highest point of distinction.' He therefore deserved 'all the public reparation in your power'.[6]

Two days later, Wentworth wrote to his father that a Member of Parliament had asserted 'you went out to the colony [sic] as a convict' and that unless this slur was withdrawn, he would challenge the MP to a duel. Still, he wrote, he had been 'cut . . . to the quick at the discovery that you were once arraigned on a criminal charge'. Improbable as it may seem Wentworth, now twenty-eight, had clearly had no inkling about his father's past.[7]

On 18 February, Bennet followed through on his pamphlet and moved in the Commons for a Committee to review transportation to New South Wales. But he also followed through on his promise to withdraw the slur against D'Arcy, telling the House he had been 'misinformed' and that D'Arcy was never a convict. Bennet said he understood that in the colony D'Arcy had conducted himself 'with the utmost propriety'. Wentworth, who was in the public gallery to hear this speech, later told his father that 'it was impossible that anyone could have made a handsomer apology'.[8]

But questions remained in Wentworth's mind about the precise circumstances in which D'Arcy had gone out to New South Wales. By now he knew William Garrow had told the judge that 'Mr Wentworth the prisoner at the bar . . . has taken a passage to . . . Botany Bay; and has obtained an appointment . . . as Assistant Surgeon'. But when he questioned how someone in custody could organise such an appointment without some kind of official intervention, Lord Fitzwilliam testily denied any involvement. 'I never made application to Government for permission for [D'Arcy] . . . to go out to New South Wales,' he said, 'and it is undoubtedly a gross misconception if he is supposed to have gone out [other than] as a free settler.'[9] Wentworth's most senior legal colleagues might have told him that during the late 1780s prosecutors, who often appeared without Counsel, were notorious for failing to 'take the necessary steps to bring forward evidence'.

When Wentworth next wrote to D'Arcy, it was clear that he was still mulling over his father's past. Lord Erskine may have been mistaken about representing D'Arcy and mistaken too about the outcome. But D'Arcy had made so many court appearances that Erskine could have represented him at some stage. Wentworth remained troubled by Erskine's claim that it was only 'by some ingenious contrivance of his' that D'Arcy had been acquitted. And he now conceded that Bennet, who had accepted Erskine as a reliable source, was 'a really good man'. This was a complete backdown for Wentworth. Fortunately, he soon had something to offset his humiliation.[10]

Chapter 7

THE FIRST BOOK

On 4 May 1819, a triumphant Wentworth wrote 'my work is this day published' as he rushed three copies of his book about New South Wales to a ship then leaving for the colony. One was for his father, one was for D'Arcy's colleague Dr William Redfern, and one was for Governor Macquarie. In targeting the colony's administration, William hoped that his friend Macquarie would accept that he had been dealt with by an 'impartial writer' who had not been 'tamed' by the administration's enemies.[1]

Wentworth called his book *A Statistical, Historical, and Political Description of the Colony of New South Wales and its Dependent Settlements in Van Diemen's Land: with a Particular Enumeration of the Advantages which these Colonies offer for Emigration, and their Superiority in many Respects over those Possessed by the United States of America.* This tortuously long title also served as a kind of table of contents, as was the publishing convention of the day. The title page described the author as 'a native of the colony', and the book was the first by an Australian-born author ever to be published. The goal implied in its title was ambitious indeed: to set up New South Wales in direct competition with the United States as the preferred destination of British migrants, even though they had to sail four times as far to get to Sydney as they did to reach New York. No one in the newly United States cared a fig about New South Wales, so the competition was more a sign of Wentworth's soaring ambition than anything else. At times almost childishly grandiose, the 466-page book was full of moving references to the author's 'country', which were calculated to seize the attention of anyone in Sydney or London who was able to read.[2]

But the title did not convey Wentworth's real agenda. He had always intended to tell the world that the colony's 'impoverished' situation arose from the nature of its administration. As a remedy, he planned to argue that a 'free constitution' should be granted to his country—and naturally to be offered a seat in any new Legislative Council that might result. Little wonder, then, that he was worried about Macquarie's reaction.[3]

In his preface, Wentworth connected this issue to the title thesis by arguing that free settlers were discouraged from going to New South Wales rather than the United States by the former's 'arbitrary government'. But if such people could be encouraged to migrate in the right direction, he foresaw that they would not tolerate arbitrary rule for long. After harshly dismissing the Aborigines in what was becoming for him a regular pattern of abuse, saying they occupied 'the lowest place in the gradatory scale of the human species', Wentworth turned to the promise of the lands west of the Blue Mountains. Going by reports of John Oxley's recent exploration, Wentworth wrote that there must surely be 'a navigable river communicating with the western coast'. This, he believed, would open up Australia to free settlers just as the Mississippi had opened up the United States.[4]

Though forced to admit that Australia's geography was harsh and that the country bordering the sea was 'one of the most barren spots on the globe', Wentworth argued that 'the prosperity of nations' depended more on 'the wisdom of their institutions' than on the fertility of their soil. He gave the rise and fall of ancient Rome as an example. He likened former Governor William Bligh's conduct to that of 'the most atrocious monster of antiquity' (he gave no name, but Caligula or Nero might be imagined), adding that Bligh had demonstrated the 'impropriety of confiding unlimited power to any individual'. About Macquarie's use of power, however, Wentworth had no complaint.[5]

Arguing that Britain should remove certain commercial constraints on the colony, Wentworth gave wool as an example: 'No country . . . is so well adapted to the growth of fine wool' he said, noting that its price per pound had doubled to 5s. 6d. in just three years. Despite his falling-out with John Macarthur Sr, Wentworth acknowledged Macarthur's role in developing wool as an 'exportable article of immense consequence'. Indeed, the book provided important publicity for this fledgling industry, which Macarthur had complained 'still creeps on almost unheeded'.

Wentworth then turned to his core political philosophy:

Every community which has not a free government is devoid of that security of person and property which has been found to be the chief stimulus to individual exertion and the only basis on which social edifice can repose in a solid and durable tranquillity.[6]

Wentworth knew his readers would take some convincing that a society of convicts was ready for this 'free government'. He argued that the 18,443 free people in the colony made it a potential electorate much bigger than some West Indian colonies. Wentworth admitted that many of this free population (whose numbers he exaggerated) 'had been subject to the lash of the law', but he praised Macquarie for supporting their return to full citizenship. At the same time, he bitterly criticised the faction in the colony that wanted to deny ex-convicts the rights to vote and sit on juries. The aim of these 'exclusives', Wentworth said, was 'to convert the ignominy of the great body of the people into a hereditary deformity . . . and raise an eternal barrier of separation between their offspring and the off-spring of the unfortunate convict'. John Macarthur Sr had made this very distinction, or so Wentworth imagined, when he turned down Wentworth's request for his daughter's hand.[7]

But even in Wentworth's model of a free society there were still limits, generous for their time, on who among the free people could vote. Although ex-convicts would be included, any who reoffended would be disenfranchised for life. Otherwise, voters had to own at least twenty acres of land or have a leasehold of £5 a year. In the towns, a rental of £10 a year would suffice. Generally speaking Wentworth said, the Canadian Constitution was the best one to follow. But as in Canada and everywhere else at that time, women would not be allowed to vote.[8]

The prime business of Wentworth's popular assembly would be to approve all purely colonial taxes, many of which had been imposed illegally by governors. But having staked his assembly on 'the fundamental maxim of the British constitution that no taxes shall be levied on the subject without his consent expressed by his representatives' Wentworth then appeared to backtrack, endorsing, on a transitional basis at least, the creation of a council whose members would be named by the British Government. He noted that it was already moving to establish such a council, which had been supported in the Commons by Henry Bennet.[9]

Wentworth also argued for reform of the justice system. He proposed a Supreme Court with a chief justice and three associate justices to replace the existing single judge and two magistrates. Most fundamentally Wentworth advocated trial by jury, saying that 'it was disgusting to an Englishman to see a culprit, however heinous may be his offence, arraigned before a court clad in full

military costume'. Ironically, Wentworth's 'most atrocious monster' William Bligh had called for just such a reform in 1812.[10]

Wentworth wound up his book by returning to his title theme,
the competition with the United States for free settlers. He identified the profit from farming in Illinois as 'the principal magnet of
attraction possessed by the United States', then boldly claimed that
capital invested 'in the growth of fine wool in this colony' would
do much better. But he concluded that it was the United States'
free government that was the 'decisive ground of preference' for
free settlers.[11]

After allowing for 100 extra copies Wentworth sent to his father,
the book—priced at 12s.—sold well, netting him about £150.
According to Wentworth the reviews were generally positive,
although he was concerned about *The Quarterly*. Being a government 'ministerial publication', he thought it might be 'sore' about
his reform proposals, and he had heard that its editors joked about a
'Botany Bay Parliament'. On the other hand, the opposition journal
The Edinburgh Review wrote that the colony 'appears to have suffered
a good deal from the tyranny . . . and ignorance of its Governors'. Even so, Governor Macquarie found the book 'informative'
and, after reading it in Portadown, D'Arcy's sister inquired about
emigrating. By far the most explosive reaction came from John
Macarthur Sr, who interpreted Wentworth's compliments about
him as 'payment for the free use' of his own plans to reform the
colony. In Macarthur's eyes, Wentworth had 'fancifully rearranged'
these plans in a form of twisted plagiarism which was 'highly mischievous'. He told his son John:

> You must remember my decided disapprobation of Trial
> by Jury and anything in the shape of a Legislative Assem-
> bly . . . The establishment of either one or the other at this
> time would seal the destruction of every respectable person
> here.

Macarthur added that he hoped John Jr had already informed the Colonial Office of his opposition to these dangerous proposals. And he trusted that his son 'had no hand in' calculating Wentworth's alleged wool profits or his 'delusive statements' about the profit to be made breeding fine-wooled sheep.[12]

In August 1819, Wentworth began planning a second edition. It appeared the following year with '*and a Word of Advice to Emigrants*' tacked on to the title. It also contained a large folding map detailing the land discovered by Blaxland, Lawson and the author. Travel tips to emigrants included 'laying in their own sea-stock' of preserved meat to offset the 100 guineas fare and converting their pounds into dollars. Wentworth had grudgingly bowed to John Macarthur Sr over wool prices: he now said 5s. 6d. per pound applied only to 'the best samples'. But he noted that he had agreed to substitute this reduced price only to avoid the charge that he intended to mislead 'those who are desirous of emigrating'.

On a more positive note, Wentworth wrote that many of the 'oppressive and impolitic regulations' he had raised in the first edition were already being addressed. Reforms in the works included a limitation on the Governor's power to tax, the imminent creation of a Legislative Council and a revised Court system. As he summarised it:

> It is probable that all the privileges, which the author has contended for will be conceded excepting perhaps Trial by Jury and the establishment of a House of Assembly; and if these privileges should be withheld a little longer . . . it will only be from a conviction . . . that the colony has not yet arrived at a sufficient degree of maturity for the reception and exercise of them.

In fact, those privileges would be withheld for a lot longer. Indeed, they became a major focus of Wentworth's public life.

First, however, came Commissioner Bigge's inquiry into the colony, which now had a total population of 24,000. Of these, almost 10,000 were convicts—9000 men and 1000 women. And most of the remainder were ex-convicts or children. The extent to which they would be allowed to join in the colony's decision-making, as voters and as jurors, was the pivot point on which its future teetered.[13]

Chapter 8

A BOOBY COMMISSIONER

Commissioner Bigge left for Sydney to hear from Governor Macquarie in person. Realising that he would now be thousands of miles from the Commissioner's key hearings, William begged his father to lobby Bigge to support judicial and electoral reforms. But he privately doubted D'Arcy would lift a finger to do so.[1]

It was all very well for Wentworth to rail in print against 'arbitrary government', but D'Arcy was one of its greatest beneficiaries. John Macarthur Sr would soon inform Commissioner Bigge that the elder Wentworth owned 40,000 acres. An increasingly bitter opponent of the ex-convicts and their allies since his return to New South Wales, Macarthur asked, 'Is not every clever active scoundrel in the Colony becoming the proprietor of large estates?' This question summed up the resentment of many so-called 'exclusives' who were determined to block increasingly wealthy ex-convicts from the business and society of Government House. Unpalatable as it might have been for Wentworth to accept, it was D'Arcy's money, obtained from the colony's 'arbitrary government', that was helping to sustain him in London's rarefied legal and political circles. Even so, it was a struggle to survive.[2]

Although Wentworth was 'at last' able to tell his father that he had 'got into chambers in the Temple', his financial needs, quite apart from the rent and fees of £130 per year, were huge, including more than 200 guineas for furniture and £500 to purchase 'anything like a tolerable library'. (£10 was the equivalent of about $1200.) Admitting that he was almost £200 in debt, Wentworth itemised yearly expenses of £50 for clothes, £20 for washing and £10 for candles. It was impossible even 'with the utmost care' to keep within his budget. So he demanded that it be increased to £250 per year, made retrospective for two years. D'Arcy was by now one of the wealthiest men in New South Wales. Still, Wentworth feared his father would baulk, and demand to know just how long he would be obliged to support his thirty-year-old son in this style. Wentworth therefore re-emphasised his ambition. 'I will not suffer myself to be outstripped by any competitor,' he said, 'and I will finally create for myself a reputation which shall reflect a splendour on all who are related to me.' Wentworth probably had in mind John Macarthur Jr, his antipodean competitor at the Bar. The reference to reputation was to remind D'Arcy that the former criminal defendant had been less than forthright with his son about his own. Wentworth was working up to yet another plea: 100 guineas to enter a special pleader's office, which was the only way to acquire 'the practical part' of his profession. With this shopping list, it was hardly surprising that Wentworth had not seen Lord Fitzwilliam lately. Yet despite his plaints of penury, Wentworth revealed that he was about to leave for Normandy for six weeks to visit friends.[3]

On his return Wentworth resumed the pressure, declaring that his income was 'utterly inadequate to maintain the character and appearance of a gentleman'. He reassured his father that he was absorbing Britain's political tradition as well as studying its laws. Each morning he walked to the 700-year-old Westminster Hall, site of a number of courts and the venue of some of England's most famous trials including that of King Charles I, who had been found guilty of treason there in 1649. At the nearby Parliament buildings, Wentworth saw firsthand the political fallout of the economic depression that followed the Napoleonic wars. On 16 August 1819, the cavalry charged a crowd of 80,000 that had assembled to hear a reformer talk about giving everyone the right to vote. Nine were killed and over 400 were wounded. Quickly dubbed the Peterloo Massacre, it was a clear sign, Wentworth told his father, 'that the most vigorous measures will be proposed for repressing . . . the lower orders'. Lord Fitzwilliam, true to his Whig beliefs, chaired a protest meeting against the massacre and was dismissed from his government posts for his trouble. Wentworth fretted that if the unrest continued it might lead to a civil war. But he was also hopeful that recent favourable accounts of New South Wales would encourage dissenters to migrate there.[4]

Commissioner Bigge, who would never have been mistaken for a dissenter, arrived in New South Wales on 26 September 1819 bearing a commission to replace Macquarie in the event that he should resign. There were rumours that the governor was about to be sacked, although William thought that he was unlikely to be disturbed just yet for fear of what he might then say. But Macquarie's views were the least of Bigge's concerns as he went about the colony asking, 'Have you any complaint to make against Governor Macquarie?' Bigge's priority was to ensure that the system was still suited for the punishment of criminals. 'The settlements of New Holland,' Secretary of State Lord Bathurst had said, 'must chiefly be considered as receptacles for offenders . . . Their growth as colonies must be a secondary consideration.' This was the antithesis of everything Macquarie had worked for and William had hoped for. Indeed, Bigge and Wentworth were polar opposites. While the Commissioner was detached and controlled, carrying out his instructions with a neat integrity, Wentworth was scruffy, passionate, biased and far less than honest when it suited him. About all the two men had in common was a cast in the eye. William was deluding himself if he thought Bigge might support trial by jury or an elected house of assembly, let alone be impressed by any endorsement of them from D'Arcy.[5]

Part of the Commissioner's brief was to investigate the conduct of prominent office-holders, including Wentworth's father. Bigge's interviews with D'Arcy ranged over his conduct as Superintendent of Police, Treasurer of the Police Fund, Magistrate and Principal Surgeon. At one point, when D'Arcy dissembled over Bigge's request for drug records that implicated his colleague Dr Redfern in illegal distribution, Bigge became testy and formally demanded 'the production of the General Hospital's Books'. Bigge's interviews with John Macarthur Sr took a different course. Having lent Bigge a 'high bred stallion of Arab blood', Macarthur sketched out his plan for a wool industry that would enable the colony to become self-sufficient. Bigge was not interested in the colony's growth, but he was interested in reducing its cost to the British government. So he listened closely to Macarthur, who managed to get in some jibes about D'Arcy's enormous landholdings and his eldest son's stupid overstatements of wool profits. Bigge's secretary, Thomas Hobbes Scott, who also happened to be the Commissioner's brother-in-law, said that Macarthur's evidence was 'the touchstone' of all they had heard.[6]

After almost eighteen months of inquiries, Bigge's reports covering 'The Colony', 'Judicial Establishments' and the 'State of Agriculture and Trade' were published in June 1822 and February and March 1823 respectively. Overall, D'Arcy was criticised for mixing his public duties with his private interests, for his handling of the Rum Hospital contract and for failing to prosecute spirit merchants. While Bigge found that D'Arcy had carried out his Treasurer's duties with 'punctuality and credit', he faulted him for storing medicines in the loft above his own kitchen and for allowing

Dr Redfern inappropriate access to drugs. Although D'Arcy was miffed by this criticism, the great survivor had survived yet again.[7]

For the former governor, Macquarie, the stakes were much higher. He bitterly criticised Bigge's attempts to tar him with 'neglect and mismanagement as governor'. In 1820, Lord Bathurst had been unimpressed by Macquarie's observation that 'above nine-tenths of the population . . . are or have been convicts or the children of convicts' and that they had made 'wonderful efforts' to obey the law and build a community. Bathurst was equally unimpressed when Macquarie told him, after resigning and leaving the colony in 1822, that he had been proud of 'admitting no distinction' between ex-convicts and others where their 'merits were equal'. But Macquarie had not forced his troops to accept this change in social situations and he was especially angry at Bigge's suggestion that he had pressured military officers to dine with former felons at Government House. However, his fury was nothing compared to William Wentworth's when he read Bigge's assertion that an anonymous poem defaming Lieutenant-Governor Molle had 'afterwards [been] acknowledged by Mr D'Arcy Wentworth to be the composition of his son'.[8]

Having decided to deny authorship of this poem, in public at least, Wentworth's reaction was explosive. He challenged the Commissioner to a duel and became so dangerously agitated that the Under Secretary of State had to place him under police restraint. Although Bigge had relied on one of Macquarie's dispatches to make his claim, Wentworth responded that D'Arcy had only ever said that 'he had reason to believe' he was the author. In a later report Bigge attempted a correction, writing that:

> whether [Wentworth] was the author of the poem or not, (and it is distinctly understood that on this point he makes neither avowal nor denial) I . . . was not justified in [naming him because] . . . it was not competent to me to investigate

any part of his conduct . . . and because his name was cou-
pled with an admission to his prejudice that was made by
another person in his absence and without his authority.[9]

This whole episode reflected poorly on Wentworth's character. He had long ago privately admitted that he was the author
of the poem, and Bigge's apology, if it could be called that, had
resulted from a combination of bullying and legalistic nitpicking.
But Wentworth was also angry because Bigge's attitude towards ex-
convicts meant that, in a colony where they comprised the bulk of
potential voters, a house of assembly was out of the question. The
Commissioner's general attitude was summed up by his conclusion
that it would be 'dangerous to submit the property or life of a free
person . . . to a jury of remitted convicts'.[10]

As Wentworth had feared, the government, heeding Bigge's
advice, refused to legislate for Wentworth's parliamentary and jury
reforms. So in the third edition of his book, published in 1824, he
unleashed volleys of abuse against Bigge. Trial by jury had been
supported by the overwhelming majority of colonists, all governors
for the last twenty years and nearly all the judges, Wentworth said.
Yet the British Government refused to budge.

And upon what grounds was this mischievous and contemptible obstinacy sought to be justified? Why, forsooth, on the
recommendation of a booby commissioner—himself either
the unconscious dupe, or the corrupt coadjutor of as turbulent and tyrannical a faction, as ever any community was yet
cursed with.[11]

Turning to Bigge's attacks on Macquarie, Wentworth blamed
Henry Bennet: 'Bigge went to the colony,' Wentworth said,
'predetermined to support all the charges which his patron had
made against the Governor, both in his speech in Parliament and

in a pamphlet.' And in relation to Bigge's treatment of D'Arcy and himself, Wentworth wrote the most vicious description of a Commissioner of the Crown ever published in Australia:

> Instead of confining his report to public objects . . . he has polluted almost every page of it with private scandal and vituperation, as if these had been the exclusive ends of his appointment. This nauseous trash . . . he has not scrupled to promulgate to the world on the faith of mere *ex-parte* evidence collected with mischievous industry from . . . the whores, and rogues, and vagabonds of Sydney . . . with a good share of . . . embellishment besides.

At the Colonial Office, successive Secretaries of State saw Bigge's report rather differently, treating it as a virtual textbook on New South Wales until 1838. But though the exclusives had won the day in London, the ex-convicts had found their champion in Wentworth.[12]

Chapter 9

TRANSITION

Wentworth was called to the Bar on 8 February 1822, and this report on his progress, made six months later by Charles Cookney, would not have pleased his father:

> 'Tho' fortune has not yet favoured him in his legal pursuits . . . some happy event will arrive when his abilities can be made to appear as they deserve.'

Cookney regularly described Wentworth as a very clever and promising young man. But the promise was taking its time to mature. Wentworth was now thirty-two yet still unable to fully support himself. Meanwhile D'Arcy, now over sixty, an advanced age for that time, was in poor health and cutting back on his official work. He still had to support Mary Ann Lawes and their six children. John, his youngest son by Catherine Crowley, had died at sea in 1820, but he was also under pressure from D'Arcy Jr in relation to his Army expenses. As a result, D'Arcy was again in debt to Lord

Fitzwilliam, this time for £300. The long-suffering Fitzwilliam was still prepared to lend William money, but he drew the line at its being used for European travel.[1]

After a year at the Bar and without warning his father, Wentworth wrote that he had become a fellow at Peterhouse, at the University of Cambridge, for a few terms 'as I am at present doing scarcely anything in my profession'. The London-based judges were travelling the country on circuit, and although Wentworth understood that he could not succeed at the Bar without doing circuit work, the travel involved would cost him more than he was earning. Indeed he was reaching a professional crisis. He had already cast around for alternatives, including an appointment as New South Wales Attorney-General. But his application had been rejected by the Colonial Office, perhaps because of his lack of professional success or more likely because of the company he was keeping. One of his closest associates in London was his father's friend, the ex-convict Dr William Redfern. They both supported Macquarie while the former Governor fought for his reputation, and Redfern helped his ally with the odd loan.[2]

Wentworth's falling-out with the Macarthur family had become a major problem for him. In some ways the ambitions and experiences of Wentworth and John Macarthur Jr had run in parallel. John too had studied law to make himself 'most useful to his country' and after being admitted to the Bar had also struggled to make ends meet. But whereas Wentworth tended to tell the Colonial Office what was on his mind via attacks in his books and poems, John Jr had taken his father's advice to form 'a friendly connection in Downing Street'. He claimed to have been responsible for the appointment of Saxe Bannister as New South Wales Attorney-General, the job Wentworth had wanted. He had met Governor Macquarie's replacement Sir Thomas Brisbane in London. And he had swapped notes with Commissioner Bigge, who blamed Wentworth for an anonymous attack on him in *The*

Times. It did not surprise John Jr 'that suspicion should rest upon one who has been the author of so many anonymous attacks'. In addition, someone had gone to a lot of trouble to provide the Macarthur family with full reports of D'Arcy's trials in 1787 and 1789.[3]

Whatever reason the Colonial Office had for rejecting Wentworth as Attorney-General it would come to regret its appointment of Bannister, a barrister who 'had never held a brief in his life'. Wentworth wrote to his father in March 1823:

> If I ever do return to the Colony . . . I wish only to return as an individual. I have fully made up my mind to hold no situation under Government. As a mere private person, I feel that I might lead the Colony but as a servant of the Governor I could only conform to his wishes which would neither suit my tastes nor principles.

Meanwhile Wentworth had something to prove at Cambridge, Macarthur Jr's alma mater. After only a month at Peterhouse, he composed a poem which he felt confident would win him the Chancellor's Gold Medal. The topic set that year was 'Australasia', and Wentworth boasted to D'Arcy that he had written 'rather more than four hundred lines . . . the longest prize poem that ever was written in this University'. As it turned out, the prize was won by one Winthrop Mackworth Praed, who had not been to the colony and who imagined seeing it for the first time:

> On thee, on thee I gaze, as Moslems look
> To the blest Islands of their Prophet's book

Wentworth by contrast, described what he had seen, including the Blue Mountains:

Hail mighty ridge! That from thy azure brow
Survey'st these fertile plains, that stretch below

And he gushed about his ambitions for his homeland, imagining a time when Britain might 'to some proud victor bend'st the vanquish'd knee'. Then, he said:

May this, thy last-born infant then arise,
To glad thy heart, and greet thy parent eyes;
And Australasia float, with flag unfurl'd,
A new Britannia in another world.

Although Wentworth's effort came second he prevailed on his book publishers, G. and W.B. Whittaker, to publish his poem without seeking 'to impugn the decision of the learned . . . judges'. He described himself on the title page as simply 'An Australasian' and dedicated his 'crude effort' to Lachlan Macquarie, who had 'watched over and promoted [Australasia's] growth rather with the warm solicitude of a parent than the frigid superintendence of a governor'. He felt it important to express his gratitude to Macquarie at a time when 'a few dastardly and privileged calumniators have dared, not openly but by insidious implication to impugn . . . your administration'.[4]

Wentworth's poesy, as he called it, was also directed towards his love interests, including Miss Bella Taylor:

And shall my tongue alone be mute?
Shall I be wanting here?
Ah no, dear girl, my author's lute,
Shall speak while I am near.

And also towards 'Jane', whom he had evidently wanted to marry:

Why Jane, oh why, thou glory of thy kind,
Supreme in loveliness, and grace and mind . . .
Relentless charmer, I must love thee still.

These relationships, like his earlier ones, came to nothing. Wentworth, ever the optimist, wrote to Alexander Riley asking for a
character reference to impress the family 'of a lady whom I hope at
no very remote period to lead to the altar'. Riley, still fuming over
the decoy pipe that had covered Wentworth's tracks in the Molle
case, refused.[5]

Struggling through personal, professional and financial difficulties, Wentworth thought increasingly often of home. He encouraged
others to migrate, including a large group of Quakers. Although
they told him that 'there is no part of the world which affords equal
encouragements', they found the nature of the colony's government
'a decisive obstacle'. Charles Cookney's brother-in-law, a Mr James,
proved to be a more willing emigrant. Wentworth and Cookney
agreed that, having been 'bred to farming', James would be 'a most
useful man' for D'Arcy. Just over six months later, Cookney's second son George, a trained architect who was teetering on the edge
of insolvency, also decided to resettle in Sydney.[6]

During 1823 Wentworth worked on the third edition of his
book, which now ran to two volumes. The additions he made
re-emphasised the advantages New South Wales offered to emigrants, noting that 'the fevers of the backwoods of America have
become proverbial'. Bridling at explorer John Oxley's conclusion
that western New South Wales 'is useless for all the purposes of
civilised man' Wentworth spent seventy-five pages trying to argue
otherwise, though like Winthrop Mackworth Praed he was now
describing land he had never seen.[7]

While Wentworth worked on his book, the government worked
on a Bill that would turn Commissioner Bigge's recommendations
into reality, with a Legislative Council appointed by the Crown and

a new Supreme Court. There was still no provision for comprehensive trial by jury and no hint of a house of assembly. After a short debate, which Wentworth witnessed from the public gallery, the new legislation, soon known in the colony as 'the Act of 1823', passed the House of Commons on 7 July. Writing over 130 years later, the noted legal historian Sir Victor Windeyer said that this Act 'made New South Wales a colony with a civil as distinct from military government'. But Wentworth had been less impressed at the time.[8]

Although he had grudgingly accepted that a legislative council might be a necessary step on the way to an assembly, he now wrote defiantly in his book 'what a wretched mongrel substitute it is'. Wentworth had been almost alone in his call for an assembly, which arose from his view that such bodies had made the United States more attractive to emigrants. Now furious at the rejection of his original idea, Wentworth drew attention to weaknesses in the new system—flaws that he would one day exploit. In particular, he noted that no proposal could become law until the Chief Justice had certified it was consistent with the laws of England. 'It is evidently a power', he wrote, 'which cannot fail to set the Governor and Chief Justice by the ears.' Although Wentworth was also angry that juries would be empanelled only in civil actions where all parties agreed to it, he took some comfort from a provision that allowed for the future extension of jury trials.[9]

The exclusives came in for more savaging, as Wentworth defended Macquarie's enlightened work on behalf of the ex-convicts. 'Like the Indian juggler's bag of serpents', he wrote of Bigge and Bennet's cronies, 'their nature is not altered, but they have happily lost their poisonous fangs.' In the dedication of his poem *Australasia*, Wentworth had predicted that 'his Majesty's ministers [would] soon form a more correct estimate of [Macquarie's] zeal, ability and integrity'. He was right. Macquarie wrote to Wentworth on 22 June 1824 that after a series of meetings the Home Secretary had agreed to restore emancipists' rights under the Transportation Continuance

Act. Within days, the former Governor was dead. But Wentworth did not find out for months because he had sailed for Sydney aboard the *Alfred*, back in February.[10]

Although the Act of 1823 had disappointed Wentworth it had led to the creation of a new Supreme Court, based on the courts at Westminster, with the power to admit British barristers to practise in the colony. For Wentworth, who had struggled to make a living at Westminster, the opportunity to be admitted as one of the first barristers in this new colonial court was irresistible. And so he used some of a £250 loan Fitzwilliam had advanced him in December 1823 to relocate to Sydney. One of his fellow passengers on the voyage was Robert Wardell. Although he was three years younger than Wentworth, Wardell had become a barrister a year earlier. Like Wentworth, he had applied to be New South Wales Attorney-General and was also fascinated by newspapers. Wardell had been the proprietor of an evening newspaper called *The Statesman* which he had recently sold; Wentworth had reproduced almost every word of *The Sydney Gazette* of 20 February 1823 in his book to show how dull the government publication was. Wentworth noted:

> Anything in the shape of political discussion is a novelty . . . An independent paper, therefore, which may serve to point out the rising interests of the colonists, and become the organ of their grievances and rights, their wishes and wants—is highly necessary.

When they boarded the *Alfred* Wentworth and Wardell took with them a printing press, remnants of lead type and the steel letter punches, copper blanks, moulds and frames necessary for publishing a paper in Sydney.[11]

Other passengers on the *Alfred* included the Sheriff of New South Wales, John Mackaness, and Dr William Redfern. They all expected that the captain would treat them as gentlemen and keep a good table with fresh food, but the menu consisted of little but salted meat. At Madeira the passengers bought their own meat, but the captain would not wait for their purchase of fifty dozen bottles of dark brown beer to clear customs. To add to the gentlemen's misery, some of their cabins were ankle deep in water. So when the *Alfred* arrived in Sydney on 15 July 1824, Wentworth and Wardell had not just their printing equipment but a bad case of traveller's rage.[12]

Chapter 10

PLEADERS AND PAPERS

It took over a year for Wentworth to sue the owner of the *Alfred*. But with Wardell as his barrister and the Sheriff of New South Wales as his witness he won £80 in damages, exactly what he had paid for the voyage. Wardell's separate claim was then settled even before Wentworth began to present it.[1]

Wentworth had returned to Sydney something of a celebrity. On 18 March 1824, *The Sydney Gazette* announced the imminent arrival of the Australian-born barrister whose poem dedicated to Macquarie it would soon publish in full. Two weeks later the paper lamented that Wentworth's verse had not won the Chancellor's Medal, since 'we see and feel . . . the generous mind breathing patriotically in every line'.[2]

Although the *Sydney Gazette* was wrong about the date of Wentworth's arrival, the build-up raised his public profile. When he did finally land four months later, the paper reported, 'The Australian Bar assumes increasing importance.' During Wentworth's absence, Governor Macquarie's building program had transformed

Sydney. Even before sailing through the Heads, Wentworth would have been struck by the sight of Macquarie's Light House. Inside the harbour stood Fort Macquarie, on the site of today's Opera House. Prominent on the ridge running south behind the Fort were Macquarie's stables and, along Macquarie Street, the three Rum Hospital buildings and the Convict Barracks. Nearby rose the St James Church spire, now more prominent than the familiar old St Phillip's Church tower. Down towards The Rocks were new wharves and warehouses bustling with the trade generated by settlements as far afield as Port Macquarie, the outskirts of Goulburn and Wellington in the central west. The colony's European population was now over 30,000. It was a lively and volatile brew of convicts, ex-convicts, native-born children, free settlers and soldiers, who answered to Macquarie's replacement as Governor, Sir Thomas Brisbane. A general who had seen action during the Napoleonic wars, Brisbane was a keen amateur astronomer who, in the Duke of Wellington's words, 'kept the time of the Army'.

At first, Wentworth found it hard to settle down. Perhaps it was because he was almost thirty-four and still unmarried, perhaps it was because his ageing father was still a magistrate and still making babies with a woman younger than Wentworth himself. Or perhaps it was because he had been months on the *Alfred* without a dark brown beer. Whatever the reason, Wentworth was soon behaving badly. Rumours spread about drunken carousing at a house in Castlereagh Street. Before long, he had been placed under restraint three times for being drunk and disorderly.[3]

Despite his misconduct, Wentworth was admitted to practise as a barrister in September 1824 before the colony's first Chief Justice, Francis Forbes, who had commenced sittings of the new Supreme Court four months earlier. Unusually for his time, Forbes did not wear a wig in court, and his bald head gave him 'a round head republican look'. His court was convened in the Georgian Public School, an 'elegant and spacious' two-storey brick building with a steeply pitched grey roof built on the block between Castlereagh and Elizabeth Streets, facing the northern end of Hyde Park. This was to be the Supreme Court's home until a purpose-built courthouse was opened next to St James Church in 1827. Because of his seniority in England, Wardell was admitted before Wentworth; after the Attorney-General, Saxe Bannister, and the Solicitor-General, John Stephen, they were the most senior barristers in the colony. Immediately upon their admission, Wentworth and Wardell asked the Chief Justice to ban solicitors from acting as barristers. Whether they had removed their British barristers' wigs out of deference to the bare-headed Forbes or kept them on to highlight their pre-eminence over solicitors is unknown. Whatever the case, their application naturally prompted strong opposition from the solicitors. According to the *Gazette*, Wentworth spent almost two hours arguing with 'considerable ardour and abundant talent'. But it was all to no avail. Forbes ruled in the solicitors' favour.[4]

If solicitors could still act as barristers, then Wentworth the barrister took it that he could still act as a solicitor. So he set up an office overlooking Macquarie Place, next door to rooms in which he lived, and entered into a profit-sharing arrangement with Charles Chambers, one of the solicitors he had tried to ban. Although Macquarie Place was some distance from the courthouse, the Chief Justice also lived there. Previously described by its namesake as 'about two acres . . . planted with shrubbery', the square contained a stone obelisk engraved with distances to other settlements, a constant reminder to Wentworth of the rapid expansion that had followed his journey over the Blue Mountains. Having maintained his right to appear in court, Chambers generally contented himself with supporting Wentworth the advocate, who would sometimes appear alongside Wardell for the same client. But although they also shared adjoining chambers, Wentworth and Wardell were never in partnership and just as often appeared against each other for different clients.[5]

★   ★   ★

Business was another matter. On 14 October 1824 the first edition of their weekly newspaper *The Australian*, priced at 1s. ($5 today), appeared on the streets of Sydney. Page one was covered in Government Orders and private ads for West India rum and the first Sydney Grammar School. In their editorial, Wentworth and Wardell wrote that 'a free press is the most legitimate and . . . powerful weapon that can be employed to . . . frustrate the designs of tyranny'. For the first time, the colony had a voice independent of officialdom. And, as the paper's name implied, its tone was nationalistic.[6]

Wentworth and Wardell had not sought Governor Brisbane's permission to publish their paper in a colony where the only other paper, the government's *Gazette*, had always been subject to rigorous censorship. As it turned out, Brisbane did not attempt to block *The Australian*. Instead, the Governor decided 'to try the experiment of the full latitude of freedom of the press'. He also lifted his censorship of the *Gazette*, which noted defensively that 'this last week we have lost ONE subscriber while . . . [gaining] TWENTY-FOUR'. The first edition of *The Australian* sold out its entire print run of 625 copies and was unable to meet demand. Despite fretting about the cost, Brisbane decided that official advertising would be placed in both papers. This gave Wentworth and Wardell vital income.[7]

A major part of the first edition of *The Australian* reported on the criminal prosecution of a magistrate. It was Wentworth's first major case, the first prosecution initiated on the information of a private citizen, and the first major civil-liberties action heard by Chief Justice Forbes. A man named Vickers Jacob complained that when police executed a warrant to search his Newcastle house for stolen fence palings, Magistrate Gillman, who was nearby, called out, 'See that there is nothing else concealed.' After the search turned up nothing Jacob sent a strong letter to Gillman, who aggressively replied that he was 'always to be seen at Newcastle'. Speaking for Jacob, Wentworth argued that Gillman's remark was a thinly veiled challenge to a duel and that the magistrate had thereby committed 'an act of the most unjustifiable oppression'. Although Forbes dismissed the action he ordered Gillman to pay all costs, saying that magistrates must exercise their power with 'gentleness'. It amounted to a win for Wentworth, although *The Sydney Gazette* predictably took a pro-government line, arguing that 'it was only the strong arm of the law which held [Newcastle] together'. Wentworth, under pressure from the law and order lobby, had opened his address to the court with a passionate defence of the barristers' role, reported in full by *The Australian*:

> It is the habit of this . . . [colony] to confound the man with the advocate and to consider him privately and individually responsible for whatever he may say or do in his public and forensic capacity . . . I consider it my duty . . . which I owe to myself and the profession at large . . . to enter my solemn protest.[8]

Under the banner headline 'Important Decision', the second edition of *The Australian* carried a full report of a case that bore on one of Wentworth's pet causes, the introduction of civil jury trials. While the Act of 1823 banned such trials in the Supreme Court unless both parties agreed otherwise, Governor Brisbane had received conflicting advice from the government lawyers, Bannister and Stephen, about whether juries should be used in the new Magistrates' Court of Quarter Sessions. Bannister said yes and Stephen said no. So they placed the issue before the Chief Justice, who ruled for juries. *The Australian* called this ruling 'a partial experiment' with jury trials and blamed the exclusives, with their insistence on keeping ex-convicts at arm's length, for having delayed their introduction. Two weeks later that former great beneficiary of jury trials, D'Arcy Wentworth, who was by now Chief Magistrate, empanelled the colony's first Grand Jury, saying he hoped they would have 'the same beneficial effects' in New South Wales as in England.[9]

But the exclusives were far from defeated. On the very day *The Australian* reported that their nemesis Macquarie was 'no more', disturbing news emerged that the names of ex-convicts had been 'carefully weeded' from the new jury lists nailed to church doors. Wentworth and Wardell blamed Attorney-General Bannister for siding with the exclusives and claimed that instead of bonding 'two discordant . . . classes', trial by jury would now 'cleave society to its centre'. As they saw it, Bannister had said yes to juries only because he planned to keep ex-convicts off the lists. Wentworth thought the exclusives were growing far too influential. The newly created Australian Agricultural Company, a brainchild of John Macarthur Jr, was in his view a front for key exclusives and their London backers who, thanks to the British government, would receive a million acres of prime land for initial paid-up capital of just £10,000. But the exclusives were just as wary of Wentworth—especially when on 1 December he was elected as a director of the Bank of New South Wales.[10]

Early in the New Year, Wentworth and Wardell launched a fresh assault on the jury problem, this time targeting the Sheriff with a writ to force him to add ex-convicts' names to the jury lists. When the court ruled against them, Wentworth and Wardell transferred their campaign to the editorial pages. If the existing jury lists were not augmented with the names of 'respectable' ex-convicts, *The Australian* said, then the constables responsible for compiling them would be prosecuted. Wentworth kept up the agitation at a dinner for eighty to celebrate the colony's 37th birthday. Toasts were drunk to 'Trial by Jury', 'a House of Assembly' and 'Freedom of the Press'. So impassioned were the diners that it took Wentworth an interjection-studded three-quarters of an hour just to propose the jury toast. It was just one of at least fifteen drunk on a night steeped in alcohol.[11]

Wentworth's love of drink and rough, aggressive ways continued to get him into trouble. Less than a month later, after dining at Macquarie Place, Wentworth and two guests took a summer evening stroll towards the government Domain. But a sentinel refused to let the drunken trio into the park. 'Upon my questioning him as to the nature and extent of his order,' Wentworth said later, 'he brought his flintlock to the charge and ordered me into the sentry box.' The sergeant was then called and Wentworth was marched off to the guardhouse, where he was detained for ten minutes until one of his guests prevailed on the commandant to release him. Back at his chambers next morning, Wentworth fired off a furious letter to the governor complaining he had been arrested without cause and demanding the names of those involved so he could 'punish this violation of my personal liberty'. However, a military inquiry heard only the evidence of the soldiers involved and was, in Wentworth's words, 'exculpatory of the accused . . . incriminatory of the accuser . . . a solemn mockery of justice . . . and a premeditated attempt to add a military insult to the military outrage'. Part of the reason for Wentworth's bad behaviour may have been that he lacked a female companion. Like many colonists, he was a victim of what *The Australian* described as one of the colony's 'worst features . . . the comparative amount of males and females'. There was only one woman to every four men, and the competition did not seem to be favouring Wentworth.[12]

In May 1825 Wentworth took the case of one Francis Cox, who was suing over a breach of promise of marriage. An ex-convict blacksmith who specialised in making ships' anchors, Cox lived and worked on the waterfront at Sydney Cove. The aggrieved party was not Cox but his twenty-year-old daughter, Sarah, whose thin lips and receding chin were offset by big, determined yet sensuous eyes and raven hair parted severely across a high forehead. Wardell appeared for the defendant, John Payne, a wealthy sea captain and businessman, and at the request of both parties the case was tried by a jury. Instead of formally asking for Sarah's hand, Wentworth told the court, Payne 'one morning handed the plaintiff a slip of paper asking her whether she had any objection to change her name to Sarah Payne'. Shortly afterwards the two became lovers. At the time, Sarah was living at the home of Mrs Foster, a milliner to whom she was apprenticed. In *The Sydney Gazette*'s summary, Mrs Foster 'has heard the defendant make love to the young lady; cannot exactly prove a promise having been made; has heard of no rumours to the disadvantage of the plaintiff'. Sarah's sister Elizabeth said Payne had told her he would marry Sarah 'when he left off the sea' and that this arrangement was accepted by Sarah's family. But in 1824 Payne began seeing a Miss Redmond. Confronted by Sarah, he backed off—only to 'go off at right angles' with the recently widowed Mrs Leverton, who had inherited a lot of money. Payne had compounded the insult by keeping up his liaison with Sarah while making love to the widow. 'A case of greater treachery,' Wentworth said, 'never came before a court.'

To Wardell's explanation that 'when a good catch presents itself there is always an anxiety to get hold of something like a promise', Wentworth retorted, 'The ladies in this country are like horses very scarce, and my learned friend would make them still dearer.' Citing a letter Sarah had written to Payne, Wardell argued that she had released Payne from any promise. Moreover, since she was still capable of getting a husband, 'Where was the injury?' He summed up wittily: 'Captain Payne was the only pain that could give her pleasure; yet he was not the only suitor that would suit her.'

Unmoved by Wardell's puns, the jury awarded Sarah's father £100 damages with costs. Whether the jurors would have seen things differently had they been aware that Sarah and Wentworth were lovers will never be known. But most of them might later have learned that in mid-December 1825, Sarah Cox gave birth to a daughter, Thomasine, who was accepted by Wentworth as his own daughter. Those involved in Cox v Payne never forgot the case, and its sensational reporting by *The Sydney Gazette* meant that few of the many exclusives who read the paper forgot it either.[13]

Wentworth did not marry Sarah, but in the middle of 1825 after he began leasing the Petersham Estate, a 295-acre farm with a house, orchard and grazing paddocks on the road to Parramatta, Sarah lived there as his de facto wife. *The Australian* had vigorously defended such relationships, editorialising that they prevented 'dissoluteness and crime'. It was another major point of difference with *The Sydney Gazette*. Its editor, Robert Howe, a God-fearing Methodist, wrote that the colony had to be rescued from 'the depths of awful depravity to Righteousness in the Son of God'. But *The Australian* said, 'There are persons . . . who while the genuine precepts of Christianity are foreign to their hearts, make a show of austerity and humiliation for temporal purpose and laugh at the credulity of their dupes.'

As a founding member of the Sydney Turf Club, Wentworth was also angry with the colony's 'devout pastors' for railing against horse-racing. *The Australian* noted that Protestantism, which most of the exclusives practised, was 'well taken care of because it is the religion of the land by law established'. Wentworth had more sympathy for Catholics, though he noted rather cynically that 'having a Catholic place of Worship may prevent many evils to which unoccupied . . . thoughts give rise'. Wentworth himself did not believe in organised religion. He was far more interested in the goings-on around him.[14]

Chapter 11

SHOOT THE ATTORNEY-GENERAL

'The dull monotony of Sydney . . . has been a little broken by a comical incident,' so said *The Australian* on 24 February 1825. It all began when the Superintendent of Police, D'Arcy Wentworth, warned that the shortage of grain posed a threat to law and order. Governor Brisbane therefore sent a ship to Batavia (today's Jakarta) for fresh supplies. But when the *Almorah* returned its hold contained, along with the rice it had been chartered to fetch, 350 chests of tea. The East India Company held a monopoly on products such as tea, so these chests were contraband. Accordingly, an officer of Sydney's naval guard padlocked the ship's hatches and his commander, Captain Charles Mitchell, declared the ship to be a lawful prize. *The Sydney Gazette* wrote up this incident as a clash of authority between the Governor and a Navy Captain.[1]

After days of unsuccessful negotiations between Attorney-General Bannister on behalf of the governor, and Wentworth and Wardell on behalf of the captain, Brisbane told Bannister to seize the rice. Arming himself with a warrant, Bannister set out in a rowing boat to board the *Almorah*, which was anchored in the harbour. Naval Lieutenant Matthews, who was preparing to sail this East India Company prize to Calcutta, told Bannister to back off. When the Attorney-General kept coming, warning shots were fired wide of his boat. Through the musket smoke he was then seen to jump up, vigorously waving the warrant in one hand and a white pocket handkerchief in the other. With his little boat now rocking from side to side, he ordered his men to keep rowing. The muskets fired again, closer this time. Still Bannister kept coming, attracting a third volley, which now fell so close to him that he was forced to retreat. That afternoon he tried again, and again was forced to retreat. A furious Bannister gave his side of the story to *The Sydney Gazette*, which reported Lieutenant Matthews 'daringly and wantonly fired on' the Attorney-General by signalling his men to shoot, whereupon musket balls 'came whistling about' the first law officer's rowing boat. As for the afternoon confrontation, 'this [Bannister and his men] might have expected as Captain Mitchell . . . very considerably advised them not to think of going on board—so HE was well aware of the instructions he had given to his Lieutenant to shoot the Attorney-General'.

The Australian claimed that the sound of gunfire was caused by 'a few blank cartridges' and that Bannister had simply imagined musket balls had landed near his boat. Governor Brisbane attributed this tame version of events to the fact that the paper's editors happened to be Captain Mitchell's lawyers. An explosion of litigation followed, driven by an angry Attorney-General, two naval officers who wanted to clear their names and a *Gazette* editor who thought he had been told the truth. Because Lieutenant Matthews had left for Calcutta, or 'cut and run' as the *Gazette* put it, Wentworth and Wardell on his behalf sued the editor, Robert Howe, for libel. At the same time, Bannister prosecuted Mitchell for aiding and abetting Matthews' perceived attack on him.[2]

Matthews' claim against Howe failed because the case could not be heard without the lieutenant being present. So Bannister's case against Mitchell went before Chief Justice Forbes the following day. On Mitchell's behalf, Wentworth and Wardell argued that the order to fire, which was in any case 'an order to fire wide', had come from Matthews, not his captain. It took the jury only twenty minutes to agree and return a verdict of not guilty. But neither side was finished. Bannister now sued Mitchell for trespassing upon the government's rice, while Mitchell sued *Gazette* editor Howe for defamation for claiming he had told Matthews to 'shoot the Attorney-General'. Mitchell and his lawyers would not consent to a jury trial in the libel case, and when Mitchell won Howe attacked Wentworth and Wardell for denying him what 'they in similar circumstances would have been the first to claim'. Meanwhile the trespass action became mired in technicalities although an Admiralty Court in Calcutta ultimately ruled that the *Almorah*'s seizure had been illegal.[3]

At the beginning of 1825, Wentworth and Wardell had been proud to address Gregory Blaxland and his fellow jurors on the first jury ever to be assembled for a civil action in the Supreme Court. In saying no to a jury now in Mitchell's claim against Howe, Wentworth and Wardell had put their client's interests ahead of their own views. Howe's anger was not surprising, since the pair had used other cases to push jury reform. They had even sued Wentworth's father D'Arcy, trying to force him to issue a fresh warrant requiring colonial constables to compile 'true lists of jurors'. Such lists, they argued, should include ex-convicts like their client Simeon Lord, who had been fit to be a magistrate under Macquarie but was apparently not good enough to be a juror now. Lord was exactly the sort of person the exclusives wanted to keep off juries, and their man Bannister fought hard to block him. But although the Chief Justice turned down Wentworth and Wardell's suit, he thought Bannister had gone 'much too far' and severely criticised the constables for failing to include Lord in their jury lists. This judicial dressing-down proved to be enough, and by September 1825 the constables were including the names of 'respectable' ex-convicts on their jury lists.[4]

The Australian's first anniversary coincided with the magistrates' formal assessment of jury trials in Quarter Sessions. It gave the paper's editors 'infinite satisfaction that the experience of the Magistracy accords with our own—trials by jury work well'. Abandoning all modesty in their fifty-second issue, Wentworth and Wardell told their readers 'the first Authors of *The Australian* will be referred to as the founders of liberal politics in the Colony'.

At the *Gazette*, Robert Howe saw it all rather differently. Describing his competitors' boast as 'an elaborate nothing', Howe took exception to *The Australian*'s claim that it had twice the *Gazette*'s sales. 'We would not give 400 of our subscribers for their 650,' Howe said, haughtily noting that the 'mercantile world' preferred to advertise in his paper. Howe also questioned *The Australian*'s financial viability. Still smarting over the *Almorah* affair, he declared that 'the combined duties of the barrister and the editor [were] destructive to the liberty of the press'. No doubt he hoped that Wentworth, at least, would quit the paper.[5]

Wentworth's approach to the cases involving the *Almorah* showed his characteristic ingenuity and aggressiveness, particularly in the increasingly important area of defamation. Dr Peter Cunningham, who visited Sydney in 1826, noted that 'the affairs of the mother country [are] soon comparatively of no interest . . . while colonial news . . . politics and conversational discussions about the private affairs and personal good qualities or failings of individuals and families engross . . . the whole of public attention'. In short, the colony was a defamation lawyer's paradise. And Wentworth's attacking style in court soon became legendary, leading one of his opponents to claim that 'counsel for the defendant had . . . indulged in a strain of virulent invective towards the plaintiff . . . such as was never before heard or tolerated in a Court of Justice'.[6]

Although *The Australian*'s main reforming focus had been on trial by jury, its owners had not forgotten the state of the Legislative Council. This Council was originally convened on 25 August 1824. After it had considered its first, purely procedural item, Governor Brisbane 'was pleased to say that he had nothing further'. Limited at this time to the colony's five senior office-bearers, the Council continued to meet in desultory fashion for several months. *The Australian* attacked it as 'a confined contracted conclave of five—the penumbra of a legislative body'. An elective council was needed, the paper said, so that 'the people alone' could make decisions about taxes. In the first edition of his book, Wentworth had written of his ambition to be one of the Council's first non-official appointees, but when Lord Bathurst announced his decision in July 1825 Wentworth did not rate a mention. Instead John Macarthur Sr got one of the three new positions, with no little thanks, Wentworth thought, to his son's influence on the spot in London.[7]

The same went for the choice of Governor Brisbane's replacement. On 28 April 1825, *The Australian* reported, 'We can state with certainty that General Darling has been appointed to the Government of New South Wales.' John Macarthur Jr had already known this for months and had impressed the exclusives' views on the new Governor in London long before Wentworth and his fellow colonials set eyes on him in Sydney.[8]

But if the Macarthurs had the ear of the Colonial Office in London, Wentworth made sure he had the ear of the people in Sydney. On 21 October 1825 a public meeting was held at the courthouse to pay tribute to Sir Thomas Brisbane for his term as Governor. After a short and polite address to Brisbane had been moved and seconded, 'Mr Wentworth presented himself' and loudly condemned the address as a 'mere milk and water production'. His huge frame, barrel chest and majestic head combined to produce an unforgettable voice that commanded attention. Interrupted by constant cheering, Wentworth thanked Brisbane for his firmness and impartiality and then set about haranguing the crowd in earnest. After calling the exclusives 'the yellow snakes of the Colony' and saying he hoped 'to deprive them of their venom and their fangs', he proposed that Brisbane be requested to lobby the British Government 'for the immediate establishment . . . of Trial by Jury and Taxation by Representation'. Wentworth's amendment to establish a house of assembly pointedly noted 'that there are colonists of . . . very great influence at home who are inimical to the establishment in New South Wales of the British Constitution'.

Just as the Chairman was about to decide the motion on a show of hands, opposition emerged from an unexpected quarter. Stepping forward, Wardell, of all people, said he wanted to delete the demand for an assembly because it reflected on the 'fitness of the Council'. In another surprise, Gregory Blaxland seconded him. But Wentworth would have none of their squeamishness, and he was strongly supported by Edward Smith Hall. Once described by Governor Macquarie as 'a useless and discontented free gentleman settler', Hall said that Wardell spoke of form, not substance. So Wardell withdrew, whereupon Wentworth's original amendment was carried 'most triumphantly'. Five days later Brisbane responded to the address. He promised that when he got back to England he would support the colonists' claims for 'an extension of their civil rights'. (Less than two months later, Wentworth and Sarah named their newborn daughter, Thomasine, in his honour.) To Wentworth and Wardell, the meeting had been something of a revelation. As they wrote in *The Australian*:

Public meetings open the eyes of the people—shew them their own strength—moral as well as physical and convey to their reasoning faculties truths, to which, but for them, they might remain strangers. Public meetings expose the irresistibility of the people, if they firmly and legally claim their political due.

John Macarthur Sr, however, was appalled, saying the meeting had inflamed the worst passions of the lower orders and contempt for all legitimate authority.[9]

Chapter 12

THE CALM BEFORE THE STORM

Wentworth organised a similarly political public meeting to welcome Brisbane's replacement, Lieutenant-General Ralph Darling, who had ruled Mauritius, his last posting, with military simplicity. The new Governor of New South Wales—recently extended to the present-day Western Australian border—wasted no time reconstituting the Legislative Council, adding John Macarthur Sr and two other exclusives as non-official members. This was a backward step, Wentworth told the welcoming meeting on 12 January 1826. What they all wanted, he thundered, was 'an elective assembly and unlimited trial by jury'. And he repeated these now mantra-like themes at the Colony's Anniversary Dinner just over two weeks later. Of Darling himself, Wentworth simply said 'he is yet unknown to us'. Darling too was feeling his way. He was by no means enamoured of Macarthur, whose talents, he said, 'are rendered nugatory . . . by his intemperance and violence'. In fact it was an official member of the Legislative Council, the arbitrary and autocratic Anglican Archdeacon Thomas Hobbes Scott, who first opened Darling's eyes to what was in store for him with Wentworth the barrister.[1]

The Archdeacon was both the brother-in-law of and secretary to 'booby Commissioner' John Bigge when Wentworth first met him. Scott was now in charge of the colony's established Church, so when a case came up that gave Wentworth the chance to challenge his credentials in the Supreme Court, Wentworth must have pounced on it avidly. His client was William Walker, master of the Female Orphan School. Located on the northern bank of the Parramatta River in what is now Rydalmere, the school centred around a handsome three-storey brick building connected by corridors to side buildings, each two storeys high. It accommodated over 100 girls from as young as two, who were given a basic education before being apprenticed as domestic servants. Walker was accused of being absent from the school without permission and Archdeacon Scott, who was the school's Official Visitor (or inspector), proposed hearing the complaint in his Spiritual Court. But on Walker's behalf, Wentworth demanded that Scott formally prove his appointment as Official Visitor. If he could not do so, Wentworth argued, Scott had no jurisdiction over his client. Chief Justice Forbes asked Attorney-General Bannister, who appeared for Scott, to produce evidence of his appointment. But Bannister could not do so because the paperwork had not yet arrived from London. The Chief Justice therefore barred Scott from hearing the complaint against Walker even though, as an official member of the Legislative Council, he knew Scott's appointment was genuine. As a fellow Legislative Councillor, Bannister complained to Darling that Forbes the Judge had ignored a fact that Forbes the Councillor knew would soon be formally confirmed. But Forbes' decision could not be interfered with. This case showed Wentworth the barrister at his best: technically inventive and fearless of officialdom.[2]

Six months later this heavyweight bout went into a second round. Archdeacon Scott had finally visited the Orphan School in his official capacity. Based on information he provided, a bench of seven Parramatta magistrates had convicted a Mr and Mrs Broadbear of leaving their jobs at the school without giving proper notice. At the time, this was a criminal offence carrying a maximum penalty of three months' jail. Wentworth, who appeared for the Broadbears on their appeal, succeeded in getting the convictions overturned. But what really galled the Archdeacon was Wentworth's argument that the Broadbears' employer was not in fact Scott but William Walker, whose evidence had supported the defendants.[3]

In March 1827 came yet another round. The Broadbears, still retaining Wentworth as their barrister, sued three of the seven magistrates who had originally convicted them. Wentworth alleged that the magistrates, Lachlan Macallister, James Bowman and his brother-in-law James Macarthur, were stooges who rarely heard cases at Parramatta and were only there to help their friend Archdeacon Scott. One of the magistrates who had heard the case with them was Wentworth's old exploring partner William Lawson. Under cross-examination, he admitted that the defendant magistrates were 'the intimate friends of the Archdeacon and it certainly struck him as extraordinary that they should be there'. The clerk of the Parramatta Court went further, saying that the defendants had been on the bench that day by Scott's 'solicitation'. Although Scott denied all this under oath, the court awarded the Broadbears £290 damages. The Archdeacon was left seething. He was all the more enraged because the court had allowed Wentworth to ask him whether he had 'indelicately examined' female orphans' bed-clothes and entered a washroom where young girls 'were in a state of nudity' before ruling that those questions were irrelevant.[4]

Wentworth did well at the Bar. Between August 1825 and June 1826 he grossed £3108. After expenses, he was left with a net income of £2153 ($225,000). By comparison, his clients the Broadbears jointly received £30 per year as servants at the Female Orphan School, and the Attorney-General's annual salary was

£1200. Increasingly wealthy ex-convicts—described by Dr Cunningham as 'the most enterprising portion of the community who owned all the distilleries, nearly all the breweries and the greater portion of the mills and manufactories'—provided plenty of litigation. But Wentworth was not content to wait for business to come to him. Once he happened to meet a John Coghill, who complained that Magistrate D'Arcy Wentworth had fined him for smuggling spirits without hearing his witnesses. 'I hope you do not intend to pay . . . as [your conviction] is unjust and illegal,' replied Wentworth the barrister. 'Give me twenty-five pounds and I will indemnify you,' he said. As good as his words, he then had his father's conviction of Coghill overturned by the Supreme Court.[5]

In March 1826, *The Sydney Gazette* declared that Wentworth was no longer associated with *The Australian*, a fact the barrister confirmed. Wardell still used 'we' in his editorials, but it was clear from *The Australian*'s more turgid style that he had been on his own at least since the beginning of the year. Just why Wentworth left is not clear. The two men might have fallen out over Wentworth's farewell address to Governor Brisbane. Wentworth may have thought the £4000 he had contributed to the paper was too big a drain on his finances. He might have wanted to concentrate on being a lawyer. Or perhaps his enthusiasm had waned. The *Gazette* later claimed that Wentworth had been 'sickened with the fatigue and responsibility of editorial duties'. Whatever its cause, the change freed Wentworth the barrister, allowing him to represent other newspapers in court. And although Wentworth and Wardell still sometimes acted together for the same client, as often as not Wentworth now took the lead.[6]

Speculation soon mounted that a new paper would shortly be published by Edward Smith Hall, the man who had defended Wentworth's farewell address to Brisbane. But even before the first edition of *The Monitor* appeared on 19 May 1826, Wentworth had been preparing to defend the feisty Hall in a defamation case. Hall had written letters to the *Gazette* in late 1825 implying that the principles advocated by Dr Laurence Halloran, headmaster of the Sydney Free Grammar School, were immoral. Much evidence was given about a play Halloran had produced, a 'horrible production' called *Count O'Candle*. One witness described it as 'a wedding and a bedding' though full details, which included a description of sexual intercourse 'in the grossest of terms', were suppressed by the judge, who 'thought it unnecessary to shock the ears of the Court'. Wentworth argued in Hall's defence that since Halloran held 'a public situation of trust', his conduct could be subjected to 'public scrutiny'. It did not help Halloran's case that he had written letters of his own to the *Gazette*, some of which editor Robert Howe regarded as 'too foul for insertion'. After listening to the evidence until 9 p.m., the jury took fifteen minutes to award Halloran 1s. damages.[7]

Wentworth's status as the newspaper editors' advocate of choice was confirmed five months later, when he appeared for Howe to defend a libel action brought by former Attorney-General Saxe Bannister. Among other things, Howe had written that 'an Attorney-General should never allow any party or faction to . . . give bias to his views'. Bannister, though he no longer occupied that post, still practised as a barrister. He now made the mistake of appearing for himself, claiming that Howe's remark implied he had been corrupted by the exclusives. Wentworth responded that Howe's criticisms were made about Bannister's conduct as a public official and had not 'exceeded those limits . . . allowed by the law to be exercised towards all public men'. *The Australian* was scathing about Bannister's performance, reporting: 'For six hours did this poor man rant and roar . . . resembling an over-driven ox . . . then whining pitifully like a lamb.' The jury agreed, taking only five minutes to find in Howe's favour. Chief Justice Forbes privately questioned Bannister's sanity. Supporting his man Bannister to the end, John Macarthur Sr claimed that Forbes had probably helped to write the offending article.[8]

Macarthur and other key exclusives petitioned Lord Bathurst to oppose the demands for trial by jury and taxation by representation that had been agreed to by the meeting to farewell Governor Brisbane. They demanded instead an enlarged Legislative Council, whose membership should be limited to respectable colonists chosen by the King. They also wanted severe restrictions on the selection of jurors. However, much of the political heat went out of these issues during 1826. This was due, Robert Howe thought, to the nature of Australian society. One moment, he wrote, 'a spark will quickly rise into a flame'; the next moment, 'the utmost labour will . . . [not] originate so much as a desire'. Of the jury question, the *Gazette* noted that it had lost its 'high importance'. Indeed, many jurors now found their duties irksome. *The Australian* was unsympathetic. 'They must endure inconveniences,' it said, 'with a cheerful disposition.'[9]

Wentworth had, as it turned out, placed too much faith in Sir Thomas Brisbane's ability to lobby the British government. Brisbane and his official secretary, Frederick Goulburn, had been at loggerheads before both were recalled to London. And Goulburn's brother Henry happened to be a senior government minister. This, added to the Macarthurs' constant sniping against Brisbane at the Colonial Office, meant that the former Governor had little standing to deliver on Wentworth's demands. But it would be almost a year before this reality filtered back to Sydney.[10]

Apart from his busy practice, Wentworth had other things to divert his attention. On 15 January 1826 Thomasine, 'the daughter of Sarah Cox and W.C. Wentworth of Petersham', was baptised at St James Church. And in September Wentworth purchased Petersham farm, which he had been leasing for over a year, for £1500. Located off Parramatta Road near today's Petersham Oval, the farm was isolated, especially at night. The only stagecoach service passed by on its way to Parramatta at about 7.30 a.m. and back again at about 6 p.m. Wentworth stayed at Petersham with his family on weekends, but spent weeknights at his chambers. Sarah had several farm servants to protect her during the week, but when Wentworth returned from Macquarie Place on Friday nights he rode alone. On 27 September, the *Gazette* reported:

> After dining with the Chief Justice on Friday evening, [Wentworth] was returning to Petersham about eleven; and when near home, in the act of going at a pretty quick pace, his attention was arrested by a fellow . . . by the roadside who . . . instantly snapped up a loaded piece . . . Providentially the dreadful instrument missed fire and the favourite Barrister of Australia escaped being laid, by the hands of a base assassin.

Unarmed and unharmed, Wentworth managed to gallop off, doubtless displaying the same turn of speed that had led him to victory on Gig sixteen years earlier.

Wentworth was an active member of the Turf Club, which held its first race meeting in mid-June 1826 with Governor Darling as guest of honour. On the first day, Wentworth's horse Currency Lad came up against Captain Piper's Currency Lass. 'In the second heat,' *The Australian* reported, 'the filly followed the example of Currency Lad by bolting. Her rider made a complaint about jostling but there did not appear to have been any cause for it.' Wentworth did better with Don Giovanni, which beat Colonel Dumaresq's horse Abdullah. On the second day, Currency Lad came good in one heat but Currency Lass did better overall, before a crowd estimated at 'no fewer than 2000'.[11]

Wentworth was also diverted by the affairs of the Bank of New South Wales, which his father had helped to found in 1817 to provide a safe place of deposit and to lend money to traders, settlers and agriculturalists. Wentworth had been elected to the board of directors on 16 November 1824 by a landslide 152 votes to seven.

Within a year the bank was embroiled in the ongoing political struggle between the Wentworths and the Macarthurs as it faced a credit squeeze. At a stormy meeting of the bank's proprietors to elect new directors, Wentworth proposed Dr Henry Grattan Douglass and 'censured' his opponent, a Mr Brown, for aligning himself with Macarthur. Brown's supporters, including James Norton and John Oxley, then criticised Wentworth for allowing politics to taint the directors' election. But Douglass won convincingly in what was seen by the Macarthurs as a takeover of the bank by the 'convict party'.[12]

Douglass and Wentworth soon fell out, however. Wentworth wanted the bank's discount rates lowered further to help poorer borrowers, but Douglass maintained that the bank had already discounted 'to the full extent of its means'. Wentworth won the argument, but Douglass was right about the economics. Within a fortnight all the bank's notes were in circulation, forcing its cashiers to honour cheques with 'solid dollars'. The formation of the Australian Agricultural Company had meant that barristers, doctors and even clergymen borrowed to outbid each other for every scabby sheep and scarecrow horse available. As a result, by May 1826 the bank's loans stood at £95,408, more than twice the level of a year earlier. To make matters worse, Macarthur and his fellow exclusives Norton, Oxley and Brown set up the rival Bank of Australia, which drained off deposits. On 13 May, *The Australian* declared that nothing short of an earthquake could shake the Bank of New South Wales' credit. Four days later, it admitted its mistake. In just five weeks, the bank's dollar holdings had plunged from £122,933 to £4739. Now the paper said of the directors: 'Their paper flew—kites flew—and last of all the few dollars flew, and then—and then—they came to their senses.'[13]

What stopped the rot was Governor Darling's agreement to lend the bank £20,000. The mere promise of this loan was sufficient to restore a shaky level of confidence. The bank survived, but the crisis had taken a toll on Wentworth. As the bank's solicitor he had held grave doubts about the validity of its charter which, as he knew, the British government regarded as 'null and void'. In March, as the crisis was gathering momentum, Wentworth had fronted a general meeting of the proprietors and 'strongly reprobated those that entertained such silly notions regarding the Charter'. He had lied to save the bank. And, not incidentally, to save himself.[14]

The bank would face many more crises during the 1820s, including a motion by Wentworth in December 1828 that it should cease operations altogether. But these dramas were eclipsed by the complete breakdown in relations between Wentworth and Darling. What triggered it was the theft of some calico cloth by two soldiers. Privates Sudds and Thompson had committed the crime in hopes of being discharged from the Army, even though Darling had warned that any troops who tried this exit ploy 'would be held up as examples of just abhorrence to their comrades'. After being sentenced to seven years' transportation, they were paraded before their regiment on 22 November 1826 in special chains designed by the Governor. Each set weighed about fourteen pounds, and comprised an iron collar with two protruding spikes linked by chains to ankle irons. After listening to the Governor's Order that Sudds and Thompson were to work in chains for the whole of their sentence and then be put back into the Army, the regiment watched while the soldiers were stripped naked, dressed in convict clothes and made to stand as their irons were riveted around their necks and ankles.[15]

At first *The Australian*, which had been running a strong law-and-order campaign against bushrangers, had a bet each way. On 25 November it backed the 'unusual severity' of the soldiers' sentences, but noted that the chains prevented the soldiers from 'laying their heads down to rest' and made it difficult for them to breathe.[16]

Then, on 27 November, Private Sudds died.

Chapter 13

THE STORM BREAKS

'We were appalled!' *The Australian* screamed two days later. 'How much does a single event prove the superiority of . . . a Civil Court over the impassioned emanations of one man [Darling]?' Wardell demanded to know as he steered his paper onto a new tack.[1]

Governor Darling also scrambled—to justify himself. He had been happy for Wardell to examine the chains, he insisted, and unaware that Sudds was ill when they were fitted. But the more Darling said the more questions Wardell asked, keeping the story running into the New Year. The Chief Justice's opinion that the Governor had been wrong to increase the court's sentence only added to the pressure. So Darling turned to Wentworth, beseeching him 'for God's sake' to persuade Wardell to stop his attacks. Wentworth refused because he agreed with them. 'Up to that period . . . I had always been treated by His Excellency with marked hospitality and respect,' Wentworth said, 'but all private communication . . . immediately ceased . . . and I have since been exposed to an incessant system of persecution.'[2]

Only a month earlier, *The Australian* had lamented 'the inertness' of the people and the difficulty of calling a public meeting in Sydney. In this political climate the Act of 1823, which had put off a popular assembly and most jury trials thereby underscoring the power of the exclusives, was likely to be renewed unchanged for another five years. What frustrated *The Australian* delighted Darling, who blamed the public's apathy on ill-feeling between free settlers and ex-convicts. But the alleged torture of Sudds and Thompson fired up just about everyone, save the exclusives, to support reform. So while Wardell whipped up public feeling in his paper, Wentworth concentrated on London's parliamentarians. His goal was to build 'Sudds' case' into a cause that would unite the majority behind constitutional change.[3]

Wentworth's plan was to formally complain about Darling's conduct to the Secretary of State, Lord Bathurst, who was facing a Parliamentary debate over a continuation of the Act of 1823. He would circulate copies of his complaint among his friends in the Commons and send over drawings of the soldiers in chains to be published in London. To rub dirt into the wound, he would transmit his complaint to Bathurst through the Governor himself. Darling wrote bitterly about this 'young demagogue':

> From the first he has evinced a feeling of hostility without my being able to discover any cause. I have endeavoured to conciliate him by courtesy and attention; but he is a vulgar, ill bred fellow, utterly unconscious of the common civilities due from one gentleman to another. Besides he aims at leading the emancipists and . . . his return to England is now spoken of in order to his conducting their cause in person.[4]

Wentworth did not go to England. Instead he decided to remain in Sydney to capitalise on the public's renewed interest in politics. At first, Wentworth had planned to delay a meeting until he received word from Sir Thomas Brisbane in London about the British government's response to the last one. But Wardell's inflammatory articles had stirred up even the likes of Gregory Blaxland and William Lawson. They demanded a meeting, which was duly convened at the courthouse on 26 January 1827. Wentworth, 'in his usual energetic, lucid and unsophisticated style', moved motions for trial by jury and taxation by representation. He did not refer to Sudds' case, but compared local taxation levels to those that had helped spark the American War of Independence fifty years earlier. He demanded that in the Supreme Court civil juries replace assessors in civil actions and military juries in criminal actions. And he moved that copies of the meeting's resolutions, signed by the Sheriff on behalf of all those in attendance, be presented to the King and Parliament. Gregory Blaxland was duly deputised to take these to London.[5]

Embittered by what he called *The Australian*'s 'perverted and distorted' coverage of the Sudds case, Darling advised the Colonial Office that the 'evil' of New South Wales was its determination to be 'the counterpart of England'. Darling also rubbished Brisbane's support for reform, saying that the former Governor had 'shut himself up at Parramatta' and embraced Wentworth's demands only when he was leaving. As for the people generally, 'they were not ill disposed if left to themselves . . . but are susceptible to Wardell and Wentworth . . . who are ever ready to inflame their minds'. And there the matter rested while the Governor's dispatch made its long voyage to London.[6]

Conflict between *The Australian* and *The Sydney Gazette* was just as fierce, though in the beginning it was driven less by disagreement over constitutional change than by a circulation war. This intensified in early 1827, when the *Gazette* became the colony's first daily in an attempt to beat its weekly competitor. It was not long before the newspaper editors' preferred advocate was forced to decide which of them to defend. In an early attack on *The Australian*'s viability, Robert Howe had published an article in the *Gazette* saying that his rival Wardell had come to Sydney because his London paper had failed and that *The Australian* 'was likely to suffer a similar fate'. On behalf of Wardell, Wentworth sued. He won the action, but only 1s. in damages—and the ridicule of the *Gazette*.[7]

Darling continued to fume about the colony's free press, in which the convict 'is taught to believe he is ill treated'. Secretary of State Bathurst agreed. He was appalled by the clippings from *The Australian* that Brisbane had proudly sent him. These articles were written at a time when Wentworth was still a co-editor, and Lord Bathurst found them 'highly dangerous to a society of so peculiar a description'. Indeed, Bathurst had suggested before Darling left for Sydney that the colonial press should be registered and required to pay stamp duty. At first, however, Darling was reluctant to interfere. Then in March 1827 Attorney-General Saxe Bannister brought an action against Wardell as 'Editor and Proprietor' of *The Australian*. This time, Wentworth appeared as a witness. He did not know whether Wardell was the editor, he said, but he had no doubt he was a proprietor. Deciding that Wardell's responsibility had only been 'partly proved', the jury found in his favour. Following this technical win, Darling obtained Legislative Council support for a law to register the press. This would make it easy to identify the 'editors and proprietors' of defamatory papers. No doubt with Bannister's case in mind, *The Sydney Gazette* helpfully published contact details for *The Australian*'s editor. But it noted that 'Doctor Wardell intends leaving the country rather than submit' to registration.[8]

Wardell did neither. Instead he set about circumventing Darling's other law, which charged a 4d. stamp duty on every 'newspaper'. *The Australian* exploded. Darling, it thundered, 'had gone further than the most tyrannous and despotic of British Governors'. After consultation with Wentworth, Wardell set about avoiding the duty by turning *The Australian* into a magazine. But Chief Justice Forbes soon made this unnecessary, ruling that 4d. per paper was an attempt 'to tax the papers to death'. The *Gazette* tried to apologise for the law, saying it was needed to control the 'unremitting licentiousness of the press', while *The Australian* continued to accuse the Governor of trampling on the 'liberty of the subject'.[9]

Fond as Wentworth and Wardell were of liberty, it was not a notion they extended to Aborigines in court. In May 1827 they defended Lieutenant William Lowe, who was charged with murdering an Aboriginal by the name of Jackey Jackey. Arguing that New South Wales had been settled rather than conquered by the British, they submitted that the court had no jurisdiction to try a British subject for an offence committed against an Aboriginal. As Wentworth put it:

It is because [the Aborigines] possess the free demesne . . . without any Sovereign laws among themselves besides . . . native customs . . . that . . . by the law of nature [they] are not subject to the jurisdiction of this Court . . . From the inability of this Court to punish [them] . . . it has no jurisdiction to punish any British subject who may have committed an offence against them.

The Chief Justice instructed the jury that Aboriginals were 'entitled to the protection of our laws', but they took only five minutes to return a verdict of not guilty. Lowe's many supporters, who had crowded into the public gallery, immediately broke into a round of 'loud applause'. Was Wentworth simply putting forward an argument for his client, or did he really believe what he was saying? His reaction to the Aboriginals he encountered during his voyage on the *Emu* in 1816 suggests that he was speaking from personal conviction. In his poem *Australasia*, Wentworth had romanticised the Aboriginal in nature:

Ye primal tribes, lords of this old domain,
Swift-footed hunters of the pathless plain,
Unshackled wanderers, enthusiasts free,
Pure native sons of liberty,
Who hold all things in common, earth, sea, air,
Or only occupy the nightly lair.

But in Wentworth's world the Aboriginal had no place in court, either as a victim or as a witness. Their only place there was as a defendant. And in January 1828, when another Aboriginal called Jackey Jackey was arrested for murder, there was no debate about whether he was subject to British law: the judge sentenced him to death.[10]

Wentworth's appearance in Lowe's murder trial was unusual because the bulk of his practice was devoted to far more lucrative commercial and defamation cases. Freed from his financial obligations to *The Australian*, he amassed enough money to buy Vaucluse House in June 1827 for £1500. The owner had fallen into debt and his creditors sold the property, which was situated on the route to the southern headland guarding Sydney Harbour. In the first edition of his book, Wentworth had written about the 'romantic' views that open up 'from the hills on the south head road'. He enjoyed similar views from his new estate, a 105-acre property with a secluded cove, stables, dairy, gardens and orchards. The residence, however, took five months to make habitable. Only then did Wentworth and his family move from their Petersham farm, which Wardell bought not long afterwards.[11]

On 7 July, Wentworth's father died of pneumonia at his Homebush estate. D'Arcy was sixty-five and had been ill for some time. Nevertheless, he had maintained his zest for life: seven months later, Mary Ann Laws gave birth to their eighth child. The *Gazette* suspended hostilities with Wentworth to note that he had been 'indefatigable in his attention to his sire' and was at his side when he died. The funeral of the 'oldest Colonial Public Servant' was attended by 150 people of the 'highest respectability', along with hundreds of the colony's more humble folk. Afterwards, many of them adjourned to Walker's Inn for some 'handsome entertainment' provided by the executors of his will, who included Wentworth and William Lawson. All the obituaries were generous, and none mentioned D'Arcy's Old Bailey appearances. Wentworth had his father's tombstone inscribed: 'An honest man the noblest work of God.' He also arranged for his mother's remains to be reburied under an inscription that began, 'Here lie the Mortal Remains of D'Arcy Wentworth . . . Also of Catherine his wife'. In fact they had never married, but whether Wentworth knew this is unknown. One way or another D'Arcy had amassed a fortune, including 34,145 acres of land and an income of more than £23,000 a year from land rentals and livestock sales. Even after his surviving brother and all his half-brothers and -sisters had been provided for, Wentworth's share of his father's estate allowed him to increase his holdings to over 7000 acres of the best land in New South Wales.[12]

Wentworth was soon back in court challenging the Governor's attempts to regulate newspapers. From August 1827 these battles took place in a new Supreme Court building on the corner of King and Elizabeth streets, which is still in use today. Despite an imposing façade, which included an entry porch supported by Greek columns, the courthouse was draughty, with smoking chimneys and unsafe floors. Some of the building remained under construction, and for a while tables and chairs substituted for a judge's bench. Those in court could hear discussions in the jury room, and a lack of waiting rooms forced opposing parties and witnesses to sit side by side.

When the editor of *The Monitor* was charged under Darling's new press laws with failing to forward copies of his newspapers to the Colonial Secretary Alexander McLeay, Wentworth successfully argued that *The Monitor* was 'no more a newspaper than the Encyclopaedia Britannica' because it consisted of several sheets of paper sewn together in the form of a book. Besides, McLeay had failed to formally appoint someone to receive the papers. An embarrassed McLeay admitted that he 'had no idea that any written appointment was necessary'. He later denounced Wentworth as 'an infamous blackguard . . . worthy of his birth being the son of an Irish Highwayman by a convict whore'. Wentworth responded with yet more cases to embarrass the Governor.[13]

In December, Darling launched his third libel suit in a year against Wardell. What upset him this time was an allegation that the Governor had 'acted tyrannically and . . . illegally punished Sudds and Thompson', the soldiers who had been chained up for theft. Wentworth argued in Wardell's defence that the military jurors at their trial had been hopelessly compromised because if they disobeyed the Governor, they were 'liable to be . . . cashiered'. In the end, the jury could not agree on a verdict. As the Governor saw it, Wardell had got off yet again. These three cases had created immense community interest and the public gallery of the new courtroom was 'crowded to an extent never before witnessed' as the Governor and his critics slugged it out.[14]

Back on 16 May, John Macarthur Sr had written to his son John that 'our vile press may publish as many libels as they please with impunity. Wardell and Wentworth will defend and [Chief Justice] Forbes will if possible shelter the libellous.' Darling evidently agreed. He told the new Secretary of State, Viscount Goderich, that Sydney's courts had become 'a theatre for vilifying the Governor and Government . . . holding up both to the contempt and hatred of the public'. Because the Governor lacked competent legal assistance, he suggested Wentworth and Wardell had been able to turn the courts into a de facto Parliament.[15]

At a dinner at the Turf Club in November this long-simmering conflict reached boiling point. The purpose of the dinner was to accept a trophy cup donated by the club's former patron, ex-Governor Sir Thomas Brisbane. The cup arrived from London at the same time as news that Brisbane, now a champion of Wentworth's reform agenda, would be in the Commons gallery when the Bill to renew the anti-reform Act of 1823 was debated. Darling, the Turf Club's new patron, declined to attend the dinner, pleading illness.[16]

What happened that night was to be hotly contested, even by people who were not at the dinner. The only thing everyone agreed on was that Wentworth had presided. He proposed a toast to Brisbane and then one to Darling. Some claimed that he made a 'grossly indecent speech . . . provoking an odious parallel between the two', a claim Wentworth angrily denied. But there was no doubt the toast to Brisbane had been followed by the singing of 'Auld Lang Syne', while after the toast to Darling the 'factious' members of the Club, including Wardell, had suggested the songs 'Over the Hills and Far Away' and then 'There Is No Luck About the House'. Choosing to believe the worst rumours, Darling resigned as the club's patron. A specially convened meeting of the club then declared that no offence to the Governor had been intended. Darling responded that he did not hold the bulk of club members responsible, but he believed Wentworth was intent upon 'the most determined and unprovoked hostility to the Government' and said he could not associate with a club that counted Wentworth as a member. However, the club met again and resolved to approve the speech Wentworth had given.[17]

At the height of this Turf Club war, the appointment of Sheriff John Mackaness—who also happened to be the club chairman—came up for renewal. Citing Mackaness' involvement in public attacks on him and as a 'common associate' of Wentworth, the Governor refused to reappoint him. And he now moved ruthlessly against the other public servants involved in the club's dinner. Dr Douglass was dismissed as commissioner of the Court of Requests for proposing a toast to Wentworth the horse breeder, C.D. Moore was dismissed as assistant clerk of the Supreme Court for being the club secretary, and W.H. Moore was suspended as Solicitor General for agreeing to the final club resolution approving Wentworth's speech. Darling was especially incensed at the continuing association of these men with Wentworth, who was now threatening to impeach him over the Sudds case. To explain this bureaucratic bloodbath, Darling instructed Colonial Secretary Alexander McLeay to publish a notice blaming the victims for associating with 'five or six factious individuals'.[18]

Wentworth and Wardell immediately sued McLeay for defamation, claiming that in calling them 'factious individuals' he and the government were attempting to 'hunt them out of society'. The court dismissed their suit, saying it had been 'calculated to . . . revive feelings which it were better should be suffered to subside'. But no one was satisfied. Darling was furious with Chief Justice Forbes, who had expressed the view that McLeay's words were probably libellous. Wentworth and Wardell were equally unhappy, because Forbes now seemed bent on preventing them from using the court as a de facto Parliament. So both sides attacked the Chief Justice. While the Governor accused him of republican tendencies, Wentworth and Wardell criticised him for refusing to wear a wig in court. If pressured to wear a wig, Forbes replied, 'it will be a great consolation when I find my brains boiling under it in the summer to know that I am performing my duty and silencing a great scandal'. The need to fix the 'abominable' stench of the outside toilets, which regularly overpowered the courtroom, was about the only thing they all agreed on.[19]

Wentworth wrote to Secretary of State Goderich that 'a variety of unforeseen causes' had prevented him from framing Darling's impeachment 'until the session of Parliament was too far gone'. But he promised he would do so by the time Parliament next sat in January 1828. John Macarthur Jr, meanwhile, had quietly continued his successful lobbying of the Colonial Office on the spot in London. The Act of 1823 was up for review.[20]

Chapter 14

A LITTLE CRACKED IN THE UPPER STOREY

Just after 9.30 p.m. on 17 December 1827, a man approached Chief Justice Forbes' house in Macquarie Place. 'Who goes there?' the military sentry called. Receiving no reply, he asked again. 'Friend,' came the reply. But when the sentry told him to pass, the stranger questioned his authority. After an exchange of words, the man said he would report the sentry to 'the judge' and the sentry arrested him. Soon a sergeant arrived and began an interrogation.

'Who are you?' the Sergeant asked.

'Mr Wentworth,' the prisoner replied.

'Mr Wentworth the Attorney?' the Sergeant asked a Mr Gilchrist, who had emerged from Forbes' house.

'I am no Attorney. I am Mr Wentworth the Barrister,' the prisoner replied.

When the sergeant said that he would take the prisoner to the watch house overnight, Gilchrist warned him that although Wentworth was 'overheated by wine . . . this might appear an act of military oppression towards a man known to be at variance with the

Government'. So the sergeant let him go. And Wentworth disappeared into the night, vowing to 'find the sentry in the morning'.[1]

No appeal to his civil liberties could hide the fact that Wentworth was—as so often these days—drunk and disorderly. Since his father's death, he had slipped badly. A few months earlier the *Gazette* speculated that he was 'either a little cracked in the upper story [*sic*] . . . [or] downright mad'. More recently, it had observed that Wentworth's popularity was 'gradually declining', even among ex-convicts. This was soon confirmed when Wentworth and Turf Club chairman John Mackaness advertised a public meeting to protest the former Sheriff's dismissal. But the Governor had no need to worry. The owner of the hotel where the meeting was to be held refused to host it, so it had to be moved to Wentworth's office. And a total of just eight people showed up, including Mackaness, Wardell, Wentworth and Edward Smith Hall.[2]

Worse was to come in the New Year, when the colony first learned that the Act of 1823 was likely to be renewed unchanged. The Wentworth-inspired reform petition sent to London a year before had merely been noted, not acted on. And *The Australian* reported that 'every backdoor tale . . . against the establishment of liberal institutions had been attended to at the Colonial Office'. Clearly, the exclusives' London agent John Macarthur Jr had trumped the ex-convicts' champion, Sir Thomas Brisbane. On 18 January came Gregory Blaxland's report that sympathetic MPs had told him the petition he had delivered, signed by the Sheriff alone, 'was only a petition of the Sheriff's . . . the Colonists ought to forward another . . . signed by the inhabitants of the Colony generally'. In short, Wentworth's tactics had been wrong.

At a dinner of ex-convicts and their supporters to celebrate the colony's fortieth anniversary, the usual toasts to 'trial by jury' and 'taxation by representation' were drunk. But Wentworth was not there, because he had been warned off indulging in his 'red-hot politics'. Darling now gleefully told London that his nemesis had been humiliated nonetheless: 'A . . . clerk in Mr Wentworth's office conceiving that due honour had not been paid to his patron, at length proposed his health which the company *repeatedly* rejected . . . The proposer . . . [then] drank it alone and immediately retired.'[3]

Although Wentworth's parliamentary sympathisers in London suggested that he draft a Bill incorporating his reform agenda, he was in no mood to act. His drinking aside, Wentworth seemed preoccupied by family matters. His first priority was to mend fences with Sarah. When their second child, William Charles, had been born on Boxing Day Sarah had not named the father, registering young Willie under the name of Cox. It may not have been sheer coincidence that Wentworth now turned his attention to improving what he still called a 'very uncomfortable residence' at Vaucluse.[4]

It was a house with quite a history. If there was anyone in Sydney's early days who had a past as interesting as D'Arcy Wentworth's it was Sir Henry Browne Hayes, the first owner of Vaucluse. Hayes, an Irish baronet and a widower with small children, had abducted a young heiress and forced her into a bogus marriage. As a result, he was sentenced to death for kidnapping, later commuted to transportation. Hayes resolved never to cut the hair on his upper lip until he was free to return to Ireland. A constant thorn in the side of authority, who called Governor Philip Gidley King 'a tyrant gaoler', he nevertheless managed to build a stone house at Vaucluse, where he lived when he was not in jail for insubordination. According to rumour he surrounded his house with a ring of Irish turf to keep the snakes out, but it was not until late 1812 that Hayes was finally able to shave his upper lip.[5]

Wentworth was determined to transform the house into an elegant *château* fit for the senior member in Sydney of the ancient and noble Wentworth-Fitzwilliam family. He engaged as his architect his old English school friend George Cookney, the son of Lord Fitzwilliam's London agent. After heavy lobbying by Wentworth, Governor Brisbane had appointed Cookney as Government

Architect in April 1825. One year on, Cookney was dismissed. As Darling explained it to Secretary of State Goderich:

> Cookney was removed . . . because his services were not required and he was not considered eligible from his general habits for a public situation. Even his friend . . . Wentworth admitted when urging his being continued in his situation that he should not himself be disposed to employ him.[6]

Luckily for Cookney Wentworth changed his mind, and the two men were soon discussing new stables and a coach-house. Sarah would no doubt have been more interested in the discussions about the new dining room, bedrooms, sitting room and drawing room with French windows which opened on to a verandah, all with fine furniture and fittings to match. Together with the new wing, which included a large kitchen, domestic quarters for the servants and a nursery on the first floor, the renovations may have convinced her to forgive Wentworth at least some of his drunken escapades.[7]

Preoccupied as he was with his house and his practice, Wentworth never failed to keep up with political events. However, ships brought only an erratic stream of news bulletins from England, and they were inevitably months old and often distorted. Nonetheless, it was clear that Lord Bathurst, who had been Secretary of State for most of Wentworth's adult life, had left the Colonial Office at a time of great political upheaval. He was followed by no fewer than three Secretaries of State for War and the Colonies in less than a year: Goderich, William Huskisson and Sir George Murray. In early January 1828, Huskisson (who would go down in history as the first person to be killed by a train) introduced a Bill to 'gradually assimilate the administration of justice in New South Wales to that of England'. But three months later, when the petition delivered by Blaxland demanding jury trials and popular representation was tabled in Parliament, he responded that juries would operate to the colony's 'disadvantage' and said he would end the experiment of jury trials before magistrates in Quarter Sessions. When petition-influenced amendments to his Bill were then proposed by Wentworth's Parliamentary supporters, the Secretary of State replied that juries were 'altogether inapplicable' to Sydney's 'peculiar society' and adjourned debate until June.[8]

At the end of May Huskisson was replaced by Sir George Murray, a general who had developed a close professional friendship with the new Prime Minister, the Duke of Wellington, during the Napoleonic wars. Sir Thomas Brisbane, who had fought alongside both men, melodramatically lobbied his old comrade Murray, pledging 'his life that the Colony was quite fit for trial by jury'. But when debate resumed on Huskisson's Bill, Murray had little to say. So Sir James Mackintosh, the Whig MP, put up two amendments:

> For the immediate establishment of trial by jury . . . [with] the governor and council to frame regulations . . . respecting the number and qualifications of jurors . . . [And for] . . . the election of one third of the Legislative Council (till an Assembly shall be called) to be chosen for five years by all persons enjoying a clear yearly income of £100 who shall have been free inhabitants for three years.

While this was hardly Wentworth's idea of taxation by representation, it was a start. But that was all it was. Wellington's government opposed the amendments, taking the view that New South Wales had too much liberty rather than too little. The Bill became law unchanged.[9]

The new Act did abolish the requirement for both parties to agree to a jury trial in Supreme Court civil cases, allowing the judges to make this decision, but juries in criminal cases were still to be made up of military officers. And while the number of non-official members of the Legislative Council was increased, so far those selected had almost all been exclusives. John Macarthur Jr was exultant, seeing the new law as a renewal of the Act of 1823 and 'the death blow' to the ex-convict party. Naturally, Wentworth was furious and resumed his ferocious vendetta against Darling, who had advised the government that the infant colony was 'not prepared' for a Legislative Assembly.[10]

Page 98
Sudds & Thompson
sentenced to
transportation

P 106
DITTO

Chapter 15

DARLING EMBARRASSED AND EMBARRASSING

In a 25,000-word submission to Secretary of State Murray, Wentworth now accused Governor Darling of murder in the case of Private Sudds. He demanded Darling's removal—and pointedly noted that the Governor of Senegal, Joseph Wall, had been executed for murder in 1802 for sanctioning an excessive punishment that had led to a soldier's death.[1]

Determined to blame Sudds' demise on the Governor's iron collar, Wentworth said a post-mortem had shown that his existing illness could not have been the cause. He then quoted Sudds who, as he lay dying, had complained of 'them irons'. The collar was so tight that it could not be turned around and nothing more than a cotton handkerchief would fit between it and the prisoner's neck. Such a device, Wentworth said, was 'unknown to the law'. It was all about 'The Irons!! The Irons!!' he wrote. 'They were the alpha and omega of this catastrophe.' There had been no formal inquest into Sudds' death and Wentworth alleged that his body had been moved from jail to hospital to avoid one. Wentworth further claimed that in organising an inevitably biased inquiry by his Executive Council, Darling had sought to answer the press with 'a counter recorded opinion by those of his creatures who compose the majority of [the] Council'.[2]

Accused of not just a murder but a cover-up, Darling now reconvened his Council, which heard evidence all over again. But it did not give Wentworth a chance to put his side and ignored his 'extreme indignation about . . . such a farce'. Sending the collected facts and opinions to London, Darling echoed the Chief Justice's view that the Sudds case had been exploited 'to answer Party purposes'.[3]

Wentworth alerted British MPs to what was going on and a pamphlet highly critical of Darling began circulating in England and, before long, in Sydney. So harsh was it that it inspired counter-petitions. One of these described Wentworth's impeachment charge as 'a gross and absurd compound of base and incredible calumnies'. When this counter-petition was published in *The Sydney Gazette* in mid-1829 Wentworth sued the paper's new editor, Ralph Mansfield, for criminal libel.[4]

Addressing the military jury, Mansfield's advocate said of Wentworth: 'The liberty of the press is with . . . [him] a good thing just so long as it leaves [him] uncriticised and uncensored. Liberty of the press with . . . [him] consisted in unbounded licence to attack the Governor.'

But the Chief Justice agreed with Wentworth's counsel, Wardell, that it was publication of the attack on Wentworth that was illegal; the content of the original pamphlet was irrelevant. So Mansfield, the Governor's editor of choice, was found guilty and fined £10. Wentworth thus chalked up a win against Darling in the Sudds affair, but it was a win based on the same carelessness with the truth and tricky tactics that had allowed him to evade responsibility for his verse attack on Lieutenant-Governor Molle.[5]

Secretary of State Murray had by now received Wentworth's letter of impeachment, yet refused to act on it until Darling could respond from Sydney. But supporters of Wentworth kept up the pressure. 'The conduct of Darling appears indefensible,' MP Daniel O'Connell said, 'because he had imposed an additional punishment on a man already convicted of a felony.' Joseph Hume, another MP, noted that Wentworth enjoyed 'much more of the confidence of the inhabitants of the colony than the Governor'. So Murray backed down and agreed to table all papers relating to Darling, who was becoming an embarrassing liability.

Meanwhile, the Governor proceeded to erode his own support in London with his belligerent use of the libel laws. The new court building itself now symbolised the burden created by this storm of libel cases. The weight of the clerks and their files on the second floor threatened to collapse into the courtroom below, forcing its ceiling to be held up by 'unsightly poles'.[6]

A year before, Atwell Edwin Hayes, the new editor of *The Australian*—and a nephew of Vaucluse's original owner—had written of the Sudds case: 'The House of Commons will decide whether will is to be substituted for law—and whether or no an iron collar could be a fitting decoration for the neck of an Englishman . . . we can never believe . . . that the author of Sudds' punishment . . . is a fit person to rule over a British Colony.'

Darling immediately sued him for libel. Wentworth, who appeared for Hayes, argued that having a military jury, which was answerable to the Governor as Commander-in-Chief, effectively meant Darling was judging his own case. Although they had to rule against Wentworth because military juries were established by law, the judges noted that the 'general force of Wentworth's reasoning . . . is impossible to deny'. These comments were not lost on Wentworth's allies in the British Parliament, who moved that criminal cases in New South Wales should be decided by juries of civilians. The Secretary of State agreed to such trials where 'the conduct or character' of the Governor was in question, and Darling was duly authorised to make such a law. To widespread outrage, he refused.[7]

This impasse in the reform of military juries was a direct result of the worst in the Governor colliding with the worst in the press. Darling was unwilling to give up any of his prosecutorial advantages against the press so long as it continued its attacks, while the press was determined to continue those attacks until he gave up his advantages. In July 1829, Darling reported with great satisfaction to London that 'the editors of *The Monitor* and *The Australian* are both in jail, the former having been sentenced fifteen months and the latter six months' imprisonment for libellous publications.' But the press had become so vicious that even some of Wentworth's supporters in the Commons were leaning towards Darling's side. MP Charles Jephson warned the colony's newspapers to 'abstain from that coarseness of vituperation . . . towards all who are placed in authority'.[8]

The worst offender was Edward Smith Hall, editor of *The Monitor*. Much of the work at *The Monitor* was done by its foreman printer, a convict servant named Peter Tyler. So the Governor revoked Tyler's assignment to the paper and redeployed him to a road gang, hoping to cripple *The Monitor* by giving Hall 'less means of disseminating his poison'. But Tyler ran away and returned to Hall, who was then convicted of harbouring an escaped prisoner.

However, Wentworth had Hall's conviction overturned by citing the recent case of Jane New. As it turned out, this female convict did more than (unwittingly) save Hall's hide. She ended up hurting Darling's.[9]

Transported for larceny, Jane had been assigned to work for one James New. He fell in love with her, and she was permitted to marry him. In January 1829 Jane was convicted for another theft, but her conviction was overturned on a technicality. Governor Darling then revoked Jane's assignment to her husband and held her in custody. Her angry husband engaged Wentworth, who argued that the Governor had no power to cancel Jane's assignment unless it was to her benefit. To this the Attorney-General replied that the Governor had 'the absolute right at his pleasure' to do so. Relying on a series of technicalities, the judge ruled that Jane was indeed a prisoner at large and should remain in custody. This allowed him to avoid any decision about the Governor's power to revoke assignments.[10]

Darling thought his power to cancel convict assignments at will was inarguable. Having withdrawn *The Monitor*'s printer Peter Tyler only days earlier, he now demanded a firm ruling on the question. So confident was Darling of his power that he had also withdrawn two convicts from the editor of *The Australian*: Edward Ledsham, a reporter, and Joseph Monks, a compositor. But the Court declined to oblige the Governor, ruling that, as Wentworth had argued, Darling could withdraw assigned servants only if that would be to their benefit. This meant that Tyler, Ledsham and Monks had all been withdrawn illegally, so Darling referred the matter to London. There, the Attorney-General advised that Darling was right and the court was wrong.[11]

But as Secretary of State Murray looked into the circumstances in which Darling had used his power, his sense of embarrassment and anger grew. On 3 May 1830 he wrote to the Governor:

> in each case, the parties directly affected . . . were the editors . . . who are habitually opposed to your administration . . . Nothing can be more opposite to the intentions of Parliament in conferring this power upon you . . . than that the right of revoking assignments should be made subservient to any political purpose.

Soon afterwards, Parliament changed the law to incorporate Wentworth's argument in the Jane New case and require the Governor to consult his Executive Council before he revoked convict assignments in future. It was an embarrassing slap in the face for Darling, whose days in office were now numbered.

Meanwhile, Jane New had escaped.[12]

Chapter 16

VAUCLUSE INTRIGUE AND CELEBRATION

After slipping out of the Parramatta Female Factory in June 1829 Jane New fled to a house at Minto, leaving just in time to avoid a police raid. Among her hurriedly abandoned possessions was a letter signed by Supreme Court registrar John Stephen certifying that 'Jane New became free on 27 April'. Governor Darling thought differently. 'Mr Stephen has been guilty of a flagrant dereliction of duty . . . in granting [Jane New] certificates of freedom,' he fumed, 'which he knew to be contrary to the fact [and] . . . were not within his province . . . to grant.' Stephen had apparently become infatuated with New, a renowned beauty, and after her narrow escape from Minto he helped her to make her way to Vaucluse. As Darling later reported to London: New 'went to the residence of Mr William Wentworth, near the entrance to Port Jackson, for the purpose of embarking from thence with Mr John Stephen', and had been seen at Vaucluse by a Mr Cole. Dressed as a boy, New tried to board a ship but a heavy security presence kept her away. However, on 6 July she boarded another vessel bound for New Zealand and made good her escape.[1]

If Cole had seen New in Wentworth's home, it is inconceivable that Wentworth did not know he was harbouring an escapee. Reporting what may have been a deliberately planted cover story, *The Australian* announced 'the recovery from his recent severe fit of illness of W.C. Wentworth of Vaucluse'. If he was involved in New's flight Wentworth was endangering his own liberty, not to mention his professional reputation and livelihood. Perhaps he helped her because he genuinely believed she deserved to be free or because John Stephen was a drinking partner of his. Perhaps he too was infatuated with the convict's beauty. Whatever Wentworth's motivation may have been, Vaucluse was ideal for New's purpose. Unable to be seen from the town of Sydney, yet close to shipping lanes, its private beach was the perfect place from which to smuggle an escapee.[2]

Overall, Darling became obsessed with pursuing John Stephen rather than Wentworth over the Jane New affair, perhaps because Stephen had become obsessed with clearing his own name. In this, Stephen was unsuccessful. While trying to convince Darling's successor, Governor Bourke, of his innocence at a hearing before the Executive Council in 1833, Stephen offered to call Wentworth to give evidence. But when the Council demanded that Wentworth take an oath, he declined to appear—strong evidence that he had willingly harboured Jane New at Vaucluse.[3]

Altogether, New was at Vaucluse for approximately three weeks. This was at a time when Wentworth's de facto wife Sarah Cox was about four months pregnant with their third child, at the same time caring for Thomasine, not yet four, and young William, just one and a half. Perhaps Wentworth felt some remorse about the risks he had taken in hosting New, because on 23 September a love poem he dedicated to Sarah appeared in *The Australian*:

For I must love thee, love thee on,
Till life's remotest latest minute;

And when the light of life is gone,—
Thou'll find its lamp—had thee within it.

Three days later, Wentworth and Sarah were married at St
Phillip's Church. With its fortress-like clock tower the church was
visible from anywhere in Sydney, but the Wentworths' marriage
there did not rate a mention in the press. Nor did the birth, on
20 November, of Fanny Catherine Wentworth.

Whether or not Jane New had somehow triggered Wentworth's
apparent surge of devotion to Sarah is unknown. What is known is
that Wentworth's good friend Edward Eagar, who had helped him
with his book, had married Jemima McDuel at the same church some
years before. And on 4 November 1830, Jemima had given birth
to a son. Eleven years later, when this boy was baptised Henry, the
paperwork stated that his father was 'William Charles Wentworth,
Gentleman of Vaucluse'. At the time of Henry's birth, Edward Eagar
had long since abandoned Jemima, and Wentworth had helped her
with money and a house in Macquarie Street. However, Henry's con-
ception, which must have happened within months of Wentworth's
marriage to Sarah, casts a very different light on their relationship. And
it raises questions about the nature of his friendship with Jane New.[4]

Wentworth's probably duplicitous conduct at home matched his
erratic approach to politics. By early 1830 his zeal for constitutional
reform seemed to have stalled. Although three years had passed
since the last pro-reform public meeting it was Sir John Jamison, a
wealthy doctor and grazier, and some of Wentworth's other friends,
including Francis Stephen, one of John's brothers, and C.D. Moore
who organised the next one. Wentworth attended the 9 February meeting, but it was Jamison who took the lead, delivering a
workmanlike speech in support of the petition for trial by jury and
taxation by representation. Not until a vote was called did Wentworth step forward.[5]

After paying lip service to the petition's goals, Wentworth launched into a criticism of its wording. It implied, he said, that the colonists were happy with everything save the jury and taxation issues. But the petition failed to mention other rights they ought to be demanding. As he was about to spell them out, the Sheriff called him to order. Replying that he was not 'an inch out of line', Wentworth plunged into an encomium on freedom of the press. But after further calls to order for what the Sheriff called a 'wholly irregular' speech, Wentworth 'cordially' seconded the motion to approve the petition. Having been repeatedly cheered by the 350 people present, it seems strange that Wentworth did not propose an amendment to include freedom of the press. This is all the more surprising given that the Legislative Council, at Darling's urging, had just passed a law under which any editor convicted twice of seditious libel would be banished from the colony. But as Chief Justice Forbes had actively supported the new law, Wentworth may have felt it would be better to oppose it in the courts, where he continued to appear for newspaper editors. His client, Edward Smith Hall of *The Monitor*, was seen as the main target of the 'two strikes and you're out' law. Implacably hostile to Darling, he had continued to write defamatory articles from his jail cell while serving time for criminal libel and had published a drawing of a large black coffin, accusing the Governor of strangling the press.[6]

The banishment laws did choke off the worst press criticism of Darling, but Hall found other ways to get under the Governor's skin—and Wentworth was right behind him. In March 1830 Hall and Hayes, the editor of *The Australian*, separately sued the Principal Superintendent of Convicts for illegally depriving them of their assigned convicts, Tyler, Ledsham and Monks. Wentworth acted for both editors and won. The two men received £25 damages for each servant lost.[7]

The indefatigable Hall—again with Wentworth as his artillery—now sued Ralph Mansfield, the editor of the *Gazette*, three times in succession for defamatory attacks on him. After winning two of the three cases Hall had two days off, then loaded the Wentworth cannon again to fire at Archdeacon Scott for unlawfully depriving Hall of his rented pew at St James Church. As he hurried to court across a windswept stone patio thronging with litigants and witnesses, Wentworth must have relished the prospect of cross-examining the hapless Archdeacon yet again. When Scott repossessed the pew and reserved it 'for certain civil officers', Hall climbed over the panels Scott had put up around it and sat in his pew regardless. Hall and Wentworth won this case too when Justice Dowling ruled that Scott 'had no power to determine the temporal contract between the church's Pew Committee and Hall, whatever authority he might possess . . . in spiritual matters'. But as the full import of the anti-press laws sank in, even Hall lost his taste for vituperation. Governor Darling, however, lost none of his distaste for Wentworth. He wrote to the Secretary of State:

> It has been . . . the object of the Opposition papers supported by Wentworth . . . to convey a belief that a formidable party exists against the Government; while the truth is that Mr Wentworth is entirely excluded from society . . . [His] . . . character is too well known ever to permit . . . [him] . . . having any influence except amongst individuals of the lowest orders.[8]

With press litigation almost wiped out by Darling's banishment laws, the focus of Wentworth's practice shifted to commercial and criminal cases. In 1828, a gang had managed to tunnel into the coffers of the Bank of Australia and steal the then huge sum of £12,000. The culprits got clean away—until, two years later, one William Blackstone, sentenced to death for another crime, confessed to the robbery and named his accomplices. But under English law, Blackstone's evidence could not be used against them because he was a convict still under sentence. Even though the courtroom had been built to accommodate a large public gallery, there was a queue waiting to witness Wentworth and Wardell prosecute this case. They persuaded the court it was in the interests of the colony to allow 'any testimony which may . . . give vigour to the arm of justice'. Blackstone's accomplices were convicted, and from then on the evidence of convicts was accepted in New South Wales courts.[9]

In October 1831, Wentworth took on the government when it tried to recover forty acres near the South Head Road from one Thomas West. Twenty years before, West had undertaken to build a water mill on a stream that ran through this land into Double Bay. Governor Macquarie had scribbled a note promising that the land would be formally granted to West when the mill was finished. West duly built the mill, but no formal grant was ever made. The dispute now hung on measurements made by Surveyor-General Thomas Mitchell. Strong-willed, efficient and imperious, Mitchell had in just two years surveyed new roads to Goulburn and Bathurst. But, in a brutal cross-examination, Wentworth tied him in knots:

> The black stump pointed out to me by the defendant as his boundary was some distance beyond the old fence; the south-eastern fence, I think runs very near the stump; there was a line of fence on the east side but it did not extend to the tree . . . I asked the defendant where his boundary was; he said it ran upon a stump and that the fence was not a boundary; the stump he pointed out was a stump which he said was on his eastern boundary . . . I think what is called Double Bay in the memorial is in fact Rushcutting Bay.

Wentworth pointed out to the jury that if his client lost, 'three parts of the landholders in the Colony might in the same way be ousted from their property'. Not surprisingly, they decided in West's favour.[10]

While Governor Darling congratulated himself on the relative quiet that his banishment law had achieved, news of the law was met with near-apoplexy in London. At the Colonial Office James Stephen, then a senior legal officer, described it as 'indefensible . . . and repugnant to the law of England'. Accusing Darling of 'needlessly embittering the exercise of his authority by a severe temper and ungracious manners', Stephen said that, so long as he remained Governor, 'it would be idle to hope for any moderation in . . . the newspapers'. Added to the steady drip of complaints from Wentworth's supporters in the Commons, this sealed the Governor's fate. Just after Secretary of State Murray decided to replace Darling with Major-General Richard Bourke, the Duke of Wellington's government fell. But the new government, led by the Parliamentary reformer Charles, Earl Grey, now best remembered for the tea named after him, confirmed the decision. Indeed, it went further, disallowing Darling's banishment law altogether. When he finally found out about these developments in late 1831, Darling knew at once whom to blame. 'It must be unnecessary to say anything of Mr Wentworth,' he told the new Colonial Secretary, Viscount Goderich, 'to prove the malignity of his mind.'[11]

On 19 October, the day of Darling's departure, a prominent advertisement appeared in *The Monitor* under the headline 'Mr Wentworth's Fete and Illuminations'. It said that an ox and half a dozen sheep would be roasted at Vaucluse and that an abundance of Cooper's beer would also be available to celebrate the Governor's departure; his farewell song would be 'Over the Hills and Far Away'. According to *The Australian*, almost 4000 people turned up. Carriages thronged the South Head Road all day, about fifty boats stood offshore, and those who could afford neither carriage nor boat came on foot. While Wentworth was carried around by the crowd in a chair, his party got out of control. The *Gazette* reported:

The offer of a full swig at the bung-hole of a gin-cask without charge was not to be resisted by that very thirsty and
long winded . . . rabble . . . [with its] . . . roaring, bawling,
screeching, blaspheming, thumping, kicking, licking, trick-
ling, cheating, beating, stealing, reeling, breaking of heads,
bleeding of noses, blackening of eyes, picking of pockets, and
what not.

Looking around at this drunken crowd from the elevation of his
shoulder-borne chair, Wentworth must have found it hard to see in
them a future base of political support.[12]

Chapter 17

ECHOES FROM THE PAST

About the only thing Ralph Darling and his successor Richard Bourke had in common was high rank in the British Army. But where Darling was rigid and narrow-minded, Bourke was genial and given to flights of philosophy. Bourke was a kinsman of Edmund Burke, the Irish-born Whig philosopher and statesman, for whom he maintained a lifelong affection. Burke had been a close political ally of Wentworth's kinsman the Marquis of Rockingham, whose nephew Lord Fitzwilliam had been one of Burke's executors. (In the 1840s, as old men, Fitzwilliam's son and Bourke would edit and publish Burke's correspondence.) Bourke's formal education had also been much broader than Darling's. Before deciding on an Army career, he had attended Oxford and studied law. As Governor of Mauritius, Darling had demanded strict adherence to regulations and the unquestioning loyalty of his subordinates. As Governor at the Cape of Good Hope, on the other hand, Bourke had upheld press freedom, helped to introduce a jury system and extended the Cape's Legislative Council. From the beginning,

Wentworth had a great deal more in common with Bourke than he did with Darling.[1]

Bourke's commission as Governor of New South Wales did not extend to Western Australia, which had had its own Governor since it was claimed by Britain in 1829. Nevertheless his domain was still immense, and on 22 December 1831 a public meeting was held at the courthouse in Sydney to welcome him. Speakers at the gathering rejoiced that Darling's 'reign of terror' had passed and hoped a 'wise and fostering government' would restore 'good fellowship among us'. Britain was again called on to establish 'those institutions which are the birth-right of Englishmen'. The locals lost no time informing the new Governor of the need to change press laws and promote immigration. Wentworth attended, but ignored 'the most deafening shouts' to speak to the crowd. In doing so he passed up an opportunity to address the burning issue of the day, new land regulations that threatened to bankrupt him.[2]

The British government had abolished free grants of the colony's waste or Crown lands. From now on these lands would be auctioned, with a minimum price set at 5s. an acre. Forcing colonists to buy, it was thought, would slow unchecked settlement, provide a fund to finance immigration and ensure that migrants stayed in the labour market until they could afford their own land. Wentworth was unhappy with a minimum price but his greatest objection was to a government demand for immediate payment of all outstanding quit rents—nominal rents that were attached to land grants but rarely collected. So great was his alarm over this move that Wentworth temporarily joined forces with John Macarthur Sr's fourth son, James. Wentworth and James, who was eight years his junior, had been acquainted in London years before, but the falling-out between Wentworth and James' brother and father had soured things. John Jr, however, had died, and rapidly advancing insanity had ended his father's involvement in public affairs.[3]

James and Wentworth had crossed paths in a Sydney street and got talking about their common interest in protesting the new land law. At a public meeting on 28 November, Macarthur proposed a petition objecting to the land price of 5s. per acre. Instead, he suggested 1s. 6d. The meeting had to be adjourned to another day, but when it convened at the Red Crow Inn in mid-January Wentworth moved for a further, indefinite adjournment. His land problem had been resolved, he explained: 'Instead of being called upon to pay a ruinous sum of £60,000 at once, the term of credit . . . had been extended to three years.' No longer needed, his alliance with James Macarthur now came to an end.[4]

Meanwhile, in Wentworth's eyes, Governor Bourke had got off to a good start, promising to enlarge the role of emancipist jurors, repeal the anti-press banishment law and use proceeds of land sales to promote immigration. He achieved all this despite entrenched opposition in the Legislative Council, where those appointed by Darling still had the numbers. In London, however, things were not going so well. In June 1832 the colonists' 1830 petition demanding trial by jury and taxation by representation was tabled in Parliament. The government declared that civilian juries would soon be introduced in criminal trials but said giving ex-convicts the vote 'was a startling proposition'; the colonists' demand for 'legislative representation' was also voted down, by 66 to 26.

News of this precipitated yet another public meeting in Sydney on 26 January 1833. Wentworth had developed the theatrical habit of waiting in the wings until the crowd demanded that he speak and even then sometimes refusing. But when James Macarthur asked if the colony was yet 'ripe' for a full representative Assembly, Wentworth bristled. Soon he took the stage and, to the crowd's delight, started savaging his way through a list of senior officials. Of the Government Resident in New Zealand, he said:

This gentleman may be sent to New Zealand to strut about in his uniform and be stared at by the savages—they may make a roast of him for all I care—but why should £500 a year of our money be voted into his pocket without our consent?

Of the Archdeacon, an official member of the Legislative Council whose stipend was £2000 a year, Wentworth asked, 'Gentlemen, do any of you know the *meaning* or *use* of an Archdeacon?' If the British Government now believed ex-convicts were capable of voting as jurors in criminal trials, then surely ex-convicts were also capable of voting for representatives to replace men like the Archdeacon. Wentworth wanted the Commons to clearly understand that 'nothing short of a Representative Assembly . . . will satisfy our wishes'. To general acclamation, he proposed that Governor Bourke provide £1000 for a Parliamentary Agent to be chosen by 'householders of £10 a year and upwards' to better argue their case in the Commons. As *The Australian* put it, 'thus ended a meeting the most remarkable yet extant in the annals of New South Wales'.[5]

Because Bourke freed up the press and pursued a liberal agenda, Wentworth's work at the Bar moved away from highly charged political cases and refocused on conventional matters. One of these no doubt reminded all Sydney's gossips of the highly unusual circumstances in which Wentworth had originally seduced his own wife, Sarah. Wentworth's client, a Mr Nowlan, was being sued by a Mr Earle for seducing his step-daughter Mary Ann Home. Nowlan had promised to marry Mary Ann, so Earle said, but had then abandoned her. Earle further alleged that Mary Ann had been persuaded to visit Nowlan's house by a promise that she would soon be mistress of it. But when her sisters duly attended with her to inspect the property, Earle told the Court that they were called into another room, whereupon Nowlan 'locked the door and . . . [Mary Ann] became pregnant'. At this point Earle's barrister, who caught Wentworth smiling, said he did not think it was funny. 'With all allowances for flesh and blood and the opportunities afforded to this young man,' Wentworth replied, 'he only did what very many in similar situations would have done.' Even so this exchange had stung Wentworth. And when Mary Ann entered the witness box with a child in her arms, he conducted a savage cross-examination to show that she had been 'seduced by the Plaintiff [her step-father] before her acquaintance with the Defendant'. By this time in the proceedings the immaculately bewigged trial judge, Dowling, would have presented a stark contrast to Wentworth, whose naturally unkempt appearance, with wig askew and gown falling off his shoulders, became even more untidy under pressure. Whatever his motivation in smearing Mary-Ann's stepfather, Wentworth's tactics did not work as Dowling ordered the assessors to ignore 'every inflammatory topic tending . . . to pervert their judgment'. Earle was duly awarded £100 damages. It was exactly the same amount Wentworth had obtained for Sarah's father in 1825.[6]

To many of the so-called exclusives, Sarah's reputation was not worth £100 and their refusal to consider ex-convicts as their equals affected not just the colony's political life but Wentworth's personal life. Though Wentworth and his wife were free-born Australians, Sarah's parents were convicts, and prior to her marriage she had lived in sin with Wentworth for years. Although Wentworth was the other party to this arrangement, and his mother had been a convict too, his father's illustrious family and his own standing as a barrister made him harder to pigeonhole. Still, the exclusives relished any tidbit of gossip that confirmed their prejudices about low-born Sarah, and in May 1832 they got a good one.

One day the Wentworths went sailing on the harbour, leaving the servants in charge of Vaucluse House. Taking advantage of their master and mistress' absence, the servants raided the liquor cabinets and got roaring drunk. Wentworth had them charged with theft, and told the court:

On going round to the back door near the kitchen, I found the prisoner Lewis lying near the kitchen door speechless drunk . . . Elizabeth Smith was also drunk . . . I called Lockhart who answered that he was in bed and . . . I found that he was also drunk and had been fighting [with another servant Ward] . . . his face was disfigured with blood . . . I found the door of the store open and missed eleven bottles of claret, some shrub, a quantity of brandy, gin and other articles.

In Sydney's rough society such a scene was not unusual, but because of Wentworth's prominence the case was written up in all the papers. Wentworth would not have given a damn about the publicity so long as the servants were punished. But it gave ample ammunition to those who wanted to think the worst of Sarah, the lady of the unruly house.[7]

Some of those people were even in London. Their role model was Eliza Darling, the wife of the former Governor and one of the leading lady exclusives. She had helped to establish Sydney's Female School of Industry, where girls aged between five and eighteen were trained as sober, chaste and God-fearing domestic servants. When Eliza was mistress of Government House, she had never had to decide whether Sarah should be invited there because relations between their husbands were so poisonous that the issue never arose. But when Bourke became Governor, Sarah was invited to a ball. It had to be cancelled due to Elizabeth Bourke's illness, but Eliza Darling let fly when the gossip reached London:

People ought to be born and educated as gentle-folks before they should be admitted to Government House—Mr Wentworth himself as a Barrister . . . might certainly have been asked but his wife, having lived with him for years, has only recently become his wife . . . and used to sit at a stall selling beef, in consequence of the very low price of cattle and

Mr Wentworth having so many thousands he had set up a butcher's shop.[8]

Eliza Darling was right about the shop. Wentworth's interest in cattle, which had begun in 1812 when Macquarie granted him some land and livestock, grew throughout the 1820s as he added to the land he inherited from his father. He owned much of his land outright through grant or purchase but the remainder he claimed as a 'squatter', through mere possession. During the 1830s Wentworth claimed land as far away as Port Phillip, but his livestock interests were centred mainly in the upper Hunter Valley. These properties provided Wentworth and his wife with a welcome escape from the pretensions of Sydney's exclusive society, as did their growing family. In 1835 they added Sarah to their brood of four: Thomasine, aged nine, Willy seven, Fanny six and Fitzwilliam nearly two. Wentworth also took responsibility for his much younger half-brothers and sisters, so Vaucluse House was always full of extended family members who made up for the absence of visits by the children of 'respectable' colonists.

Wentworth continued adding to the house as he and Sarah added to their family. As the children grew, they became increasingly strong-willed and Sarah relied on persuasion rather than force to get them to do things. Her husband, such a fierce public figure, was an indulgent father.

Over the years, their home came increasingly to resemble a Gothic Revival mansion—not unlike the new Government House later built in the Domain. But inside its walls, Wentworth found a kind of peace. Sarah, an intensely practical woman, apparently put up with her husband's carousing and was a loyal and patient domestic companion. And at the Bar, Wardell was his ideal professional colleague.[9]

Chapter 18

EXIT WARDELL

Aggression was a characteristic Wentworth and Wardell shared both inside and outside the courtroom. Ever ready to defend his family honour, Wentworth had threatened to fight more than one duel. In 1827 he acted as Wardell's second when Governor Darling's brother-in-law, Colonel Henry Dumaresq, challenged the then editor over an article in *The Australian* entitled 'How-e to live by plunder'. The parties and their seconds duly met in a quiet Homebush field. After being placed thirty feet apart, Wardell and Dumaresq exchanged shots, both of which flew wide. While the pistols were being reloaded, Wentworth tried to talk Wardell into an apology, but before he could get anywhere Dumaresq demanded a rematch. Again the shots flew wide. As Wentworth went to intercede, Dumaresq's second approached him with a written apology for Wardell to sign. Waving the paper aside, Wardell now demanded another rematch. Again the duellists fired, and again the shots went wide. Finally Wentworth suggested that Wardell make a verbal apology. This was accepted by Dumaresq, so ending the contest.

But the exchange of three volleys underscored just how hot-headed and impulsive Wardell could be, even in the face of mortal danger. His only known likeness, a marble relief in St James' Church, has the haughty air of a Roman consul. These qualities soon got Wardell killed.[1]

Travel in the colony was a dangerous business. Bushrangers preyed on anyone who ventured too far from Sydney town by day or night. Wentworth's narrow escape in 1826 near his home at Petersham, when only the misfiring of a bushranger's pistol had saved him, was just one of many incidents. In 1830 Darling finally took action, and the so-called Bushranging Act was passed. If anyone reasonably suspected that another man was a transported felon illegally at large, he could now arrest him without a warrant. And unless the suspect could prove that he was lawfully at large, he could be detained indefinitely. As a leading liberal Governor Bourke was unimpressed with this law, and when it came up for renewal in 1834 he suggested that it be scrapped. But in the face of protests from prominent colonists, including Gregory Blaxland, William Lawson and James Macarthur, Bourke backed down and the Act was renewed for another two years.[2]

In early June 1834 a man called Elder, worried about bushrangers on the road from Sydney to Parramatta, hid £131 in his stockings. He had been given the money by a man named Farringdon to buy eleven tons of flour. But when Elder reached Parramatta, he found to his horror that all the money had fallen out of a six-inch hole in his stocking. Farringdon believed him at first, but a bush lawyer advised him to sue because there was 'something rotten in the state of Denmark'. He engaged Wardell, and the hapless (or thieving) Elder hired Wentworth. Wardell won the case and the court ordered Elder to repay the £131.[3]

The two friends appeared together to prosecute two law-and-order cases in August 1834. The first was against a number of men who had a stolen ox. One of them, Bartholomew Cullen, was also rumoured to have robbed a policeman of £80 'on the road'. Despite their best efforts, Wentworth and Wardell could not crack his alibi that he had been cleaning his master's windows when the ox was stolen, although they did obtain a conviction against one of the other men. Because the Supreme Court's watch house was located some distance from the main court building, prisoners await-ing trial were confined in an iron cage fixed in the middle of the courtroom itself. 'The construction of the court is such,' the judges complained, 'that the prisoners [watch] . . . cases tried before their own and [benefit from] the various tricks they see employed.' Apart from distracting witnesses with their chatter, the prisoners rattled their chains as they were led to and from the toilet during court proceedings. Such conditions may have helped Cullen to avoid a conviction but they did not help Thomas Brigdens two weeks later. Relying on circumstantial evidence, Wentworth and Wardell suc-cessfully prosecuted Brigdens for receiving three stolen oxen, three steers, one cow and three calves. It was their last court appearance together.[4]

On the morning of 7 September, a Sunday, Wardell dressed him-self in a fustian coat and rode out on a white horse to look over his Petersham estate. At this time, Sydney did not extend far into what is now the inner-city suburb of Chippendale, so Wardell's estate was still very much in the country. After a while, Wardell came across three runaway convicts, John Jenkins, Thomas Tattersdale and Emanuel Brace, camped in a rough hut. When he demanded to know who they were, Jenkins reportedly answered, 'We are men.' Wardell then stooped in his saddle to pick up a stick and began waving it as if to summon assistance, saying, 'You are only three poor runaways who had better come with me.' Still mounted, he began prancing about the hut, but Jenkins jumped out of the way and began menacing him with a large stone. No doubt both men were thinking of the Bushranging Act. When Wardell was unfazed by the stone, Jenkins drew his pistol. Wardell said, 'Oh, for God's sake don't do that,' to which Jenkins replied, 'By God I will.'

When Wardell's horse pranced back, Jenkins aimed his weapon and fired. Wardell groaned, 'Oh dear, I'm killed.' The horse then turned and bolted away with Wardell still in the saddle. Next morning, the blood-spattered animal was found wandering in a paddock, and Wardell's body was located half a mile away under an oak tree. He had evidently fallen from the horse, tried to get up and run, and fallen again. Wentworth watched as Surgeon Neilson cut open his old friend's body. Pushing a probe into the gunshot wound on the left breast, the Surgeon concluded that it must have burst an artery, killing Wardell within minutes.[5]

At Wardell's funeral four days later, Wentworth was the chief mourner in a cavalcade of chaises and horsemen that stretched for half a mile along the road from the Petersham estate towards the cemetery. Meanwhile, after a short time on the run, Jenkins, Tattersdale and Brace were captured. Brace turned witness for the prosecution, and his evidence saw his two accomplices sentenced to death. On 10 November, Jenkins ran up the ladder to the scaffold and pulled on the ropes, addressing his fellow prisoners:

Good morning, my lads. As I have not much time to spare I shall only just tell you that I shot the Doctor for your benefit; he was a tyrant and if any of you should ever take to the bush, I hope you will kill every bloody tyrant you come across.

At first Jenkins refused a request to shake hands with his accomplice, but when he finally did so Tattersdale became very emotional. Jenkins then said, 'Don't cry, in ten minutes you will be happy enough.'[6]

Wentworth continued to mourn privately, but his practice could not be put on hold. In mid-November, news arrived from London that barristers and solicitors would be separated. This was confirmation of a court ruling Wentworth and Wardell had finally obtained in mid–1829, but which had been suspended pending London's approval. At a celebratory Bar dinner, the table was laid for ten but only nine diners, dressed in their wigs and gowns, were present. The tenth chair was occupied by a tub full of uncorked wine bottles; a wig made of black sheep's wool hung from its back. The function was also an informal wake for Wardell but Wentworth, as the most senior barrister, presided with considerable cheer. Numerous toasts were drunk; among them, 'good Fees and plenty of them', 'take no Briefs without the cash' and 'the deluded Attorneys'. So noisy did the gathering become that Wentworth had to ring a massive auctioneer's bell with both hands for five minutes before he could address his eight drunken colleagues. Then he said:

> Look at me, the father of the Australian Bar, yet here I stand with six bottles under my belt and none the worse. I feel for your degeneracy, my sons, but trust that practice will soon make you perfect, and that by punctual attendance at bar dinners under my tuition you will emulate the British Barrister in all his habits. Next to wine, my brethren, devotion to the fair sex is the characteristic and pride of the English Barrister—but in this respect you are not wanting—so I have good hopes for you. For myself, I had thought to pass the rest of my days in growing cabbages and pruning my vines, but the glorious era which has at length dawned upon the profession, calls me like a second Cincinnatus [a reference to the retired Roman general who returned to war] from my retirement to assume the station which my seniority gives. Whether I shall hold briefs or not is not a question on which I have yet decided, but I shall always be ready to preside at your convivial meetings.[7]

The following year, 1835, turned out to be Wentworth's busiest at the Bar as he shrugged off the challenge, shared with his colleagues, of handling drunken witnesses who had wandered off to nearby taverns because there was no waiting room for them at the courthouse. Despite this irritation, he appeared in no fewer than thirty-five major cases. And his professional pre-eminence was formally recognised when he was presented 'with a silk gown and something equivalent to a "Patent of Precedence" at the Australian Bar'.[8]

In June he had a courtroom clash with the fiery John Dunmore Lang, a Scottish Presbyterian minister. Like Wentworth Lang had written about migration but, unlike him, Lang had also organised a successful migrant voyage, setting a precedent that would soon change the face of the colony. A highly intelligent and energetic wowser, Lang was determined to erase Sydney's convict immorality with a wave of God-fearing migrant tradesmen. He despised ex-convicts, including the editor of *The Sydney Gazette*, E.W. O'Shaughnessy. In his court affidavit, Lang broadened his criticism of O'Shaughnessy by asserting 'the moral unfitness' of any ex-convict to manage a paper. Representing himself in O'Shaughnessy's libel suit, Lang kept the packed courtroom including his opponents, Wentworth, entranced with his oratory. With onlookers clearly impressed by his address, the prosecution was 'forthwith withdrawn'. A new and formidable political opponent had arrived on the scene.[9]

At the end of 1835, forty-five-year-old Wentworth had a shock that changed the course of his life. His twenty-ton schooner, *Alice*, was moored as usual in Vaucluse Bay when two crew members abducted her master and waved several more of Wentworth's servants aboard, including Wentworth's butler, who was the apparent ringleader. Their plan was evidently to sail to New Zealand, but they only got as far as Port Stephens. During their short voyage, the butler said to the master, 'Tell Mr Wentworth that if I had not got away . . . [I] would have settled him in another way,' an apparent reference to revenge for punishment Wentworth had inflicted for drunkenness and insolence. In their hurry to depart, the nine prisoners had left a packet of poison. With Wardell's murder fresh in his mind, Wentworth—who might once have scoffed at the threat—took this very seriously. He left the Bar for good, and turned his attention to his family and his growing pastoral interests. Even in court, Wentworth had been reminded of squatting by the flocks of sheep which grazed in Hyde Park. Whenever a southerly breeze blew the sounds and smells of these animals wafted straight into the courtrooms, offending many of his colleagues but not Wentworth the grazier.

The Bar he left was a changed Bar from the one he had joined eleven years before. Under Governor Bourke the courts had ceased to be a quasi-parliament. And thanks largely to Wentworth's advocacy and the bravery of editorial clients like Edward Smith Hall, freedom of the press was now a reality. This moved the political debate away from the courts just as Wentworth was leaving them himself.[10]

Chapter 19

THE AUSTRALIAN PATRIOTIC ASSOCIATION

After Bourke became Governor, Wentworth's hot-headed harangues were replaced by humour and logic as he set about pleading the case for self-government. The precedent of American Revolution meant the end result was never in doubt. But it still took another twenty years as the colonial factions fought each other and the British government over transportation, immigration, land ownership and taxation. In this environment Wentworth's 1816 decision to become a lawyer rather than a soldier matched his talents to the challenges of his time.

Wentworth's changing attitude first showed itself in July 1833 during a public meeting at the courthouse to protest the misuse of local tax revenue, especially on the salaries and pet projects of certain colonial officials. Only six months before, Wentworth had said that he would not mind if one of these officials, the British Resident in New Zealand, was roasted by the natives. And just a month earlier, he had been accused of addressing 'an assemblage . . . met together for the purposes of charity, with the gesticulation of a maniac . . . and [the] language of political warfare'. But in place of such 'violent' performances, *The Australian* now noted that Wentworth's speech was 'temperate and replete with facts'. And a little jest. Protesting at £700 being spent on the Colonial Botanist, he said that 'to call a mass of walks and trees covering 10 acres a botanical garden was a misnomer. They grow excellent cabbages and pines—articles very pleasant when no money was paid for them.' Wentworth pushed forward Sir John Jamison to chair the meeting. A wealthy landowner who was sympathetic to ex-convicts, Jamison had earned his knighthood as a doctor in the Royal Navy before migrating to Sydney in 1814. Although he had taken a prominent part in previous public meetings, Jamison was at first reluctant to take the chair. But Wentworth prevailed. Jamison, 'a pleasant man of a vain, ostentatious . . . character' who rode to hounds and was famous for his fancy dress balls at Regentville, had been promised the next Legislative Council vacancy. This made him Wentworth's perfect front man not just for the meeting but for its petition to the Governor and Council.[1]

For a short while there appeared to be a welcome shift in the Government's tax policy, but it soon became clear that the Secretary of State had been involved in a sleight of hand. He was now paying the British Resident in New Zealand from 'droits of the Crown', a fancy name for a local land tax. Another beneficiary of these droits was Alexander McLeay, whose salary as Colonial Secretary was topped up with a pension of £750 from his old job at the Transport Board in London. This British pension, Wentworth said, should not be paid by the people of New South Wales. So on 28 August 1834—and in defiance of the Sheriff, who refused to call a meeting at all—Wentworth organised a protest at the courthouse.

It did not go according to plan. Jamison, who had agreed to chair it, was unavoidably detained and attendance was poor. Wentworth expressed his frustration: 'A subject of this importance ought to have attracted a multitude instead of a half-filled Court-house.'

The Boston Tea Party it was not. But Wentworth resisted the temptation to boost the numbers by rabble-rousing and, as the *Sydney Gazette* noted, he denounced 'measures not men'. Again showing his lighter approach, in questioning the effectiveness of immigration spending he referred to three shiploads of women recruited from English workhouses. Noting that they had arrived in the *Red Rover, Bussorah Merchant* and *Layton*, Wentworth said, 'the very names of these vessels excite laughter'. The meeting unanimously passed his motion that local taxes 'should be applied to the benefit of the Colony', which most of those present agreed meant constructive spending on immigration. A petition incorporating the motion was then forwarded to London.[2]

One parliamentarian who had demonstrated a consistent interest in New South Wales was Henry Lytton Bulwer. His reply to this petition triggered demands for another meeting. When the Sheriff refused to call it, just as he had refused to call the previous one, a furious Wentworth dismissed him as 'a mere Bailiff' and the meeting went ahead anyway. Those who assembled at the courthouse on 29 May 1835 established the important principle that they could meet when and where they chose to discuss what they chose, which on this occasion turned out to be Bulwer's job application. After explaining that there had been great apathy in Britain about New South Wales for many years, Bulwer suggested that the colonists form a permanent, broad-based committee to act through a parliamentarian, thereby 'blending with England's daily affairs'. And he had suggested himself for this job. A man of charm and self-possession who had won £700 in one night at Paris' gaming tables, Bulwer had dabbled in diplomacy and literature. He was duly proposed as the colony's Parliamentary Advocate. His appointment was urgent, because the Governor had just been ordered to use local funds to pay for the police who superintended convicts. They were Britain's convicts, Wentworth said, and the order was thus a misuse of local taxes. Those assembled resolved to raise £2000 to fund Bulwer's position by forming the Australian Patriotic Association. Ordinary Members were to subscribe £1 and 'directing members' £5, prompting one speaker to complain that the £5 qualification was giving influence to property ahead of ability. 'Ignorance and poverty went together,' Wentworth was reported as replying, 'and the sum . . . would ensure . . . men of talent, education and experience and would exclude only the ignorant pretender.' He then personally pledged £50.

Wentworth's transformation from rabble-rousing man of the people to 'respectable' man on the land was by now well underway. In December the Governor added Wentworth's name to a special list of twenty-five, which already included Sir John Jamison and James Macarthur. The people on this list, Bourke thought, would form a suitable pool of talent from which the Secretary of State could make appointments to the Legislative Council. Meanwhile, hoping to add to the fund it was raising to pay the Parliamentary Advocate, the Australian Patriotic Association applied to the Governor for an annual grant of £2000.[3]

Although the Macarthurs were never members of the Australian Patriotic Association, the property qualification for membership initially attracted a number of pastoralists who were otherwise opponents of the ex-convict cause. These men included Richard Jones, who had been appointed to the Legislative Council by Darling and who, although he opposed restoring ex-convicts' civil rights, accepted the principle that all British colonies should have a representative legislature. Moderates such as Gregory Blaxland and William Lawson joined too, and the Association thus began life with the broad base Bulwer had suggested. But it did not last. With Jamison as president, Wentworth and the former Sheriff John Mackaness as vice-presidents and Edward Smith Hall as secretary, this was not surprising. In November 1835, the *Gazette* reported that 'party spirit has found its way into the newly formed

Association' and a public meeting scheduled for 4 December had to be postponed because the directing members could not agree on an agenda. Jones, it seems, was concerned about Governor Bourke's ongoing efforts to abolish military juries in criminal trials, which would expand the civil rights of ex-convicts. Convinced that Bourke was biased against so-called 'Tory' exclusives like himself, Jones decided he could no longer work with Wentworth and the association's other ex-convict sympathisers. Adding to the pressure were two Bills drafted for the association by Wentworth, which repealed all restrictions on trial by jury. In addition, Bill 'A' provided for a Legislative Council of fifteen nominated members and an Assembly of forty elected members, while Bill 'B' provided for a combined 'House of Legislative Council and Assembly' with a mixture of ten nominated and forty elected members.[4]

Recognising that some form of representative government was desirable, Richard Jones now called his own meetings, which attracted a number of like-minded exclusives. The petitions they drew up conceded that the Governor and his executive were too powerful and the Legislative Council too weak, but suggested that any changes should be put off until there were enough free migrants to swamp the political influence of the ex-convicts. To that end, they urged the British government to end transportation and boost free settlement. The exclusives also attacked the reformed jury system and called for any constitutional changes to be drafted in Britain. Their petition gained 398 signatures.[5]

All pretence of a broad-church Patriotic Association was now dead. To counter the exclusives' move Wentworth scrambled to organise a public meeting on 12 April 1836 at the old Royal Hotel, the venue of choice for 'settlers and squatters on business or pleasure bent'. Taking the meeting's main pulpit, Wentworth agreed with the exclusives that immigration should be encouraged, but he strongly objected to their attacks on ex-convict jurors and accused them of wanting to postpone a representative legislature for as long as possible. Something more was bothering him—the news that a Commons committee had exonerated Darling over Sudd's death without hearing Private Thompson's evidence. Even worse, the very next day the hated ex-Governor had been knighted by the King. An infuriated Wentworth slipped back into his bad old ways, ranting that Darling's acquittal 'was analogous to the acquittal of a murderer . . . in a case where the witnesses had been kept back'. But the meeting ended constructively with a petition calling for a blended legislature of fifty, three-quarters of whom were to be elected—a variant on Wentworth's Bill 'B'. The petition ultimately attracted 5000 signatures. However, the new *Sydney Herald*, which sympathised with the exclusives, dismissed the gathering as 'a meeting of the great unwashed'.[6]

Unwilling to be pushed around by the unwashed, the exclusives met again in May to hear James Macarthur denounce the idea of ex-convicts playing any role in electing a law-making body. 'Once a convict, always a convict,' Macarthur claimed. 'By what test could it be ascertained that [a convict] had reformed?' Macarthur offered to go to London and present the exclusives' petitions himself.

This animated speech aside, Macarthur was not much of a dema-gogue. His forte was negotiating behind the scenes, massaging his contacts in London the way his late brother John had done. A grave and pensive man with a dreamy, imaginative side, Macarthur was the antithesis of Wentworth in both character and belief. He believed that immigrants should be industrious and orderly, that any changes should be introduced gradually, and that to prevent social chaos the vote should be reserved for the rich and respectable. Unlike the coarse, scruffy Wentworth, Macarthur took a gentleman's care with his appearance. Although a currency lad like Wentworth (who increasingly shared his views about limiting the vote to the colony's wealthier inhabitants), Macarthur favoured delaying a representative legislature, while Wentworth wanted one as soon as possible.

Meanwhile, the Secretary of State, Lord Glenelg, had turned

down the Patriotic Association's request for the government to fund Henry Lytton Bulwer's salary. Paying a member of the Commons for what amounted to parliamentary services 'would be alien to . . . the British Constitution', he said. So, while James Macarthur was on the spot in London doing what Macarthurs had always done best, Wentworth was stuck in Sydney with the status of his hoped-for agent under a cloud.[7]

If ever there was a time when the ex-convict camp needed a powerful advocate in London, it was now. Unlike Macarthur, Secretary of State Glenelg believed it was against the spirit of English law to bar respectable ex-convicts from voting and sitting on juries. And the Colonial Office Under-Secretary James Stephen, suspicious of partisan claims from either the exclusives or ex-convicts, was looking for a compromise. But in the absence of a strong voice for the ex-convicts on the spot, Stephen was soon encouraging Macarthur and the former Chief Justice, Francis Forbes, to negotiate a compromise.

Why did Wentworth remain in Sydney? Unlike Macarthur, who was still a bachelor, Wentworth had a wife and five children under the age of eleven. He had been made a Justice of the Peace, and his name had been put forward for the Legislative Council. In addition, Governor Bourke had been seen to visit Vaucluse House, and there were rumours that Wentworth might be appointed to the Supreme Court. The old rabble-rouser was now extremely comfortable in New South Wales.[8]

In 1835, when he was still Chief Justice, Forbes had drafted a Bill at Governor Bourke's request that provided for a blended legislature of twelve hand-picked members and twenty-four elected ones. But Forbes shared the exclusives' view that ex-convicts should not be allowed to join it. Under Macarthur's influence, Forbes' attitude hardened still further. As a general rule, he now thought ex-convicts should also be kept out of jury service. Far from being capable of negotiating a compromise with Macarthur, Forbes had been captured by the leading exclusive himself. Macarthur, for his part, had lost none of his disdain for the ex-convict party. In an 1837 book entitled '*New South Wales: Its Present State and Future Prospects*', he said the Australian Patriotic Association's petition of April 1836 had been signed 'by the very offscourings of the convict system . . . at gatherings in tap-rooms' and was 'intended to perpetuate the debasement of the Colony'. Describing Wentworth's jury proposals as 'perverted', he then quoted Alexis de Tocqueville, the author of *Democracy in America*. 'To yield to the clamour of those who seek to obtain a House of Assembly for New South Wales under the present circumstances of that colony,' Macarthur wrote, 'would be to establish [what Tocqueville called] "the liberty of corrupt nature".' [9]

If Macarthur had given the dithering British government an excuse for postponing a representative legislature in New South Wales, the Molesworth Committee on Transportation, established on 7 April 1837, provided another. Sir William Molesworth's agenda was to end transportation altogether, but he and his supporters had mixed motives. Some saw the practice as evil and thought any society based upon it must inevitably be evil, too. Others believed transportation and its pool of cheap convict labour would undermine the current effort to settle South Australia (founded as a separate colony in 1836) with fare-paying free migrants. Macarthur told the committee that transportation should be gradually phased out. And John Dunmore Lang, the prohibitionist Presbyterian minister Wentworth had tangled with in court, testified that New South Wales' corruption had to be purified through free immigration; transportation must end. [10]

While Macarthur, Lang and Forbes appeared before the Molesworth Committee in person, the Patriotic Association had to rely on its parliamentary advocate. Bulwer sat on the committee, but joined it a month late. His only question of any consequence was to Lang. 'When you speak of the reputable classes of society there, do you exclude such persons as Sir John Jamison?' he asked. To this query about the wealthy doctor, grazier and ex-convict sympathiser Lang replied, 'By no means.' Not exactly earth-shattering stuff to the ear of a cross-examiner like Wentworth. Soon afterwards, while the Committee was still sitting, Bulwer went off to Constantinople as a diplomat. Before leaving, and without consulting the Patriotic Association in Sydney, Bulwer transferred his responsibilities as advocate to Charles Buller, who had taken acting lessons to improve his performance in the Commons. A more active member of the Molesworth Committee than Bulwer, Buller was a disciple of Edward Gibbon Wakefield, the man behind the free settlement of South Australia. He and the rest of the committee recommended the immediate end of transportation which had, they said, 'created a moral cesspool in the antipodes'. But that finding, with its implied condemnation of ex-convicts, gave the British government an excuse to further delay introducing a representative legislature.[11]

When news of the Molesworth Committee's recommendations reached Sydney in January 1839, Wentworth and his fellow ex-convict sympathisers held a protest meeting. In a new petition, they argued that the colony relied on the almost cost-free labour of assigned convicts for its prosperity. No one supported convict gangs, which only entrenched criminal behaviour. But the solitary and contemplative life of the assigned convict shepherd, Wentworth said, 'tends to humanise and raise . . . [his] mind to a fitter state'.

While Wentworth may have briefly thought here of his mother, who had been a convict but given a second chance, his financial interests as a squatter were uppermost in his mind. Many of the free migrants who arrived in Sydney were tradesmen, unwilling to work in the bush. One such was Henry Parkes, a bone and ivory turner. Arriving in Sydney from London on 25 July 1839 with his wife Clarinda and an infant child, Parkes complained bitterly about being 'compelled to seek the means of existence in a foreign wilderness'. Parkes even preferred working alongside a convict road gang on Jamison's Regentville estate to finding work in the bush. Faced with an acute shortage of labour, Wentworth was furious that the Molesworth Committee had been dominated by members with a financial stake in South Australia's success as a free colony. They wanted to end the supply of cheap convict labour to New South Wales, he knew, because it undercut their investments.[12]

Wentworth might as well have named Buller outright. As a supporter of Wakefield and his free colony, the Patriotic Association's advocate had been working against the association all along. For a time he had kept his real loyalties hidden. But in August 1839, when the new Secretary of State, the Marquess of Normanby, moved to renew unchanged the law on the colony's local government, Buller revealed himself. Transportation should long since have been discontinued, he said, claiming that five years of emigration would be needed before New South Wales was in a fit state to 'enjoy free institutions'. Behind the scenes Buller had been working with Macarthur to lobby London's power brokers, and it was said that 'when Macarthur led . . . Buller followed'. But it was not until the following May, when Buller got around to writing to the association, that the extent of his double-dealing sank in. 'All parties are agreed in withholding free institutions . . . while New South Wales continues to be a Penal Colony', he wrote, evidently unperturbed. At that time there were still 38,300 convicts in New South Wales, representing almost one-third of the colony's population. The association pointedly replied that all parties were not 'agreed' and complained that, even though Buller had been its advocate since 1837, 'nothing but a few garbled extracts [of the Molesworth Committee's work] reached us till the early part of the year 1839'.[13]

James Macarthur no doubt thought he had triumphed. But he soon found that he had been too clever by half when the committee recommended raising the fixed price of Crown land from 5s.

to £1 an acre. No longer would Wakefield's free migration program to South Australia be undermined by the release of cheap land in New South Wales. It was Wakefield who had triumphed. This recommendation, which dramatically increased the cost of buying new grazing land, boded disaster for pastoralists like Macarthur. It would soon form the basis for his reconciliation with the ex-convict camp, who also had to pay more. On the other hand, Macarthur was not to be reconciled with Wentworth for some time.[14]

Chapter 20

WENTWORTH BUYS UP
NEW ZEALAND

*This is not in the
English language — purely Yank*

On 1 December 1837 'The Friends of Sir Richard Bourke' met
to farewell the Governor, who had resigned after squabbling with
the exclusives over the selection of a chairman of Quarter Sessions.
To Wentworth and the ex-convicts Bourke was a hero who had
reformed the jury system, proposed a partly elected legislature and
pushed for a secular, government-funded education system. In his
speech to the crowd, Wentworth indirectly snubbed Bourke's predecessor, Darling:

> When Governor Bourke arrived, the Colony was one vast
> scene of rapine, crime, violence and disorder . . . it was posi-
> tively a work of danger to travel by land from Sydney to
> Parramatta. What is the scene now? Look where you will,
> there is one wide scene of peace, quiet and order.

The new Governor, Sir George Gipps, was expected to arrive
early in the New Year. 'He was one of the Commissioners who

148

went out to Canada . . . in 1835,' *The Australian* said, 'and for the information of our Tory [exclusive] friends . . . he is a staunch Whig.' Major Gipps had developed a reputation as a civil administrator. With an army rank well below that of the colony's military commander, he was in that sense the first civilian Governor of New South Wales, from which the colony of South Australia had now been excised. Wentworth assumed that he would be able to work as well with Gipps as he had with Bourke. And, initially, Gipps did not disappoint him.[1]

The new Governor quickly recommended that military juries be abolished, and London promptly complied. Gipps also agreed with his predecessor that the Legislative Council was in need of reform. In the short term, he wanted to create a council that was partly nominated and partly elected. But his medium-term plans were more ambitious. 'No form of representative government will be acceptable to the people,' Gipps said, 'which is not in its fundamental principles analogous to the mother country.' Wentworth himself could not have put it better.

These days, Wentworth mostly kept a low profile. He spent much of his time on his properties outside Sydney, especially Windermere, near Maitland, which he had bought in 1836 for £25,000. Windermere became the family's Hunter Valley base after Wentworth lavished another £4000 on a thirty-room home on the property. The first leg of the trip to Windermere, from Sydney as far as Morpeth, took twelve hours by paddle steamer. One of these boats, the eighty-foot-long *William IV,* or 'Puffing Billy', weighed 100 tons and had separate ladies' and gentlemen's cabins. The second leg, from Morpeth to Windermere, was by carriage. Sometimes Wentworth went there alone and sometimes with his family, which soon included Eliza, born in 1838. While his focus at Windermere was mainly on farming, he would occasionally sally forth with a letter to the editor. In March 1837 he wrote to the *Gazette,* 'let my name be erased from the list of subscribers to your pestilent publication . . . if you publish a lie I will indict you for it', a threat that cost him £225 when he lost the ensuing court case.[2]

As promised by the Secretary of State some years previously, Sir John Jamison, Wentworth's chairman of choice at protest meetings, was appointed to the next Legislative Council vacancy, which came up in 1837. Of the twenty-five names that remained on Bourke's 1835 list of potential appointees, Wentworth's stood high. In April 1839, Gipps informed Whitehall that he favoured Wentworth over James Macarthur. The latter's exclusive faction was already over-represented, and Wentworth would be 'very obnoxious' to that faction. But he had positive qualities, too:

> He is a man of vast influence . . . vast possessions . . . great knowledge . . . and experience; and though in former days he was extremely violent in his opposition to Government, he has now for a long time past, and especially since his retirement from the Bar, become moderate in his politics . . . It would be . . . sound policy to attach such a man to the Government by placing him in the Council, instead of leaving him to find his own way into it, as he undoubtedly will in the event of a Representative form of Government being . . . introduced.[3]

But the final choice belonged to the Secretary of State, and in late 1839 he chose Macarthur to fill the next vacancy. No doubt Macarthur had impressed the government with his display of moderation during his most recent stay in London. Wentworth, despite Gipps' praise, had still not shed his old reputation for rabble-rousing. His focus had also strayed abroad—to New Zealand. Although claimed by Britain, New Zealand had not been formally annexed and Maori tribes, armed by British investors who purchased their land for a pittance, were at war with each other. In November 1830 the chief, Te Rauparaha of the Ngati Toa, asked a sea captain named John Stewart of the brig *Elizabeth* to invite his rival Te Maiharanui to the ship to discuss the flax trade. But after going on board, Te Maiharanui and some of his Ngai Tahu relatives were taken below deck as prisoners. Stewart and Te Rauparaha then raided the Ngai Tahu tribe, killing many. After returning to the *Elizabeth* Stewart handed the captive Te Maiharanui over to Te Rauparaha, who tortured the other chief to death and ate him. The *Elizabeth* sailed for Sydney, and when it docked Stewart was charged with murder. One of the imprisoned Maori was still alive, but as a heathen he could not take the oath and give evidence against Stewart. The prosecution was abandoned 'for the time being', whereupon Stewart left Sydney 'as advised by Mr Wentworth' and was never brought to justice. This outcome so enraged the Secretary of State that he dispatched James Busby to New Zealand as the British Resident. Busby, a collector of internal revenue in New South Wales, had written a paper about New Zealand which had led to his appointment. His duties included preventing the several hundred European settlers from attacking the Maori, protecting British subjects and seizing escaped convicts. To Wentworth's annoyance, the cost of all this was borne by New South Wales taxpayers.[4]

Although Lieutenant James Cook had 'taken possession' of New Zealand for the British Crown, James Stephen, now permanent head of the Colonial Office, was concerned that by 1839 this was meaningless. Abel Tasman had been the first European to discover New Zealand, and Britain had done nothing to keep Cook's claim alive. On the contrary, James Busby's instructions as Resident referred to New Zealand as a foreign country and Busby was duly accredited to the Maori chiefs. At Busby's suggestion, ships built in New Zealand were to have their own register under the chiefs who, 'in their collective capacity', also selected a flag. In 1834, this flag was declared to be 'the National Flag of New Zealand' and given a twenty-one-gun salute by HMS *Alligator*. The Admiralty instructed its officers to give effect to the register and respect the flag. But Busby went further, and on 28 October 1835 he formally acknowledged a declaration by the hereditary chiefs of the 'Northern parts of New Zealand' that they were 'to be an Independent State under the designation of The United Tribes of New Zealand'. They would 'meet in Congress at Waitangi' once a year to make laws. What now vexed James Stephen was the prospect that France might seek to 'obtain sovereign jurisdiction in New Zealand', where British speculators had already purchased huge tracts of land from the Maori.[5]

Having become involved in the Captain Stewart case, Wentworth now took an increasing interest in New Zealand. He joined the land grabbers and in late 1838, when he learned that a company was being formed in London to purchase New Zealand land for colonisation, he went into a frenzy of buying. Within two years his holdings totalled 100,000 acres. The company that had spurred his speculation was called simply 'The New Zealand Company'. Its shareholders included Sir William Molesworth and five other MPs. The government did not entirely approve. In late April 1839, after the Secretary of State learned that the company's ship *Tory* was about to sail for New Zealand to purchase land from the Maori and establish an independent administration, rumours flew that it would be prevented from leaving English waters. This prompted a 'stout, fresh-complexioned, middle-aged gentleman' to leave London in a post-chaise and drive furiously to Plymouth, where the *Tory* was soon expected on its last port of call in England. He was none other than Edward Gibbon Wakefield, the promoter of South Australia, the man behind Molesworth's recommendation to abolish transportation and now the man behind the New Zealand Company. Wentworth's nemesis got to the *Tory* first and convinced its captain to sail immediately. After saying goodbye to his brother William, an army colonel, who was the company's representative on board, Wakefield watched as the ship departed unmolested. Having spent three years in Newgate Jail for abducting an heiress, Wakefield had fought his way back to respectability by studying the causes of crime and advocating organised free emigration to prevent it. The Wakefield brothers were not to be underestimated.[6]

Unable to stop the *Tory* reaching New Zealand, the Secretary of State now dramatically upped the ante, deciding that 'certain parts of the Islands of New Zealand should be added to the Colony of New South Wales as a dependency'. Captain William Hobson, RN, was now dispatched as Lieutenant-Governor of the colonial annexe reporting to Governor Gipps in Sydney. At the same time, the Secretary of State warned the New Zealand Company in London that the government would seek 'to obtain [New Zealand's] cession in sovereignty' and that the company's title to lands purchased from the Maori could not be guaranteed.

When Hobson arrived in Sydney on Christmas Eve 1839, Gipps learned for the first time that his jurisdiction as Governor was to be extended to New Zealand. It was not long before Sydney's land speculators, including Wentworth, learned for the first time too that their New Zealand title deeds might be worthless. On 6 January 1840, a sale of New Zealand land in a Sydney auction house was about to commence when a clerk of the Legislative Council burst in and announced to the large assembly of land sharks that the Governor would shortly be issuing a proclamation calling into question any land titles derived from the Maori. Captain Hobson tried to allay the speculators' fears about their existing titles but two weeks later, after he left for New Zealand, the dreaded proclamation appeared:

> All purchases of land in any part of New Zealand which may be made by any of Her Majesty's subjects from any of the Native Chiefs or the tribes of these Islands upon the date hereof will be considered absolutely null and void.[7]

The *Tory*, meanwhile, had long since arrived in New Zealand. In late 1839 Colonel Wakefield, nicknamed Wide-awake by the

Maori, purchased millions of acres, including the northern third of the South Island, from the Ngati Toa tribe. The purchase price Te Rauparaha demanded from Wakefield included over 250 guns, sixty-two kegs of gunpowder and eight kegs of ball cartridges. These were to be used against his old enemy, the Ngai Tahu tribe, who claimed to own the whole of the South Island, including the part that the chief had just sold to Wakefield. The mere threat of the weapons was enough to persuade the Ngai Tahu's new chief, Tuhawaiki, to abandon a planned attack on the Ngati Toa in late November. Six weeks later Tuhawaiki sailed for Sydney with four other chiefs and the vessel's owner, one Johnny Jones. The chiefs wanted to see Governor Gipps to obtain 'the protection of the Queen of England' and get the Ngai Tahu's ownership of the South Island recognised by the British. *The Sydney Herald* soon reported that 'the Chiefs . . . are continually to be seen near a certain Attorney's office, where a large quantity of deeds are . . . [being prepared] for their signatures'. The attorney was Wentworth, who still gave legal advice to his friends and business associates, among them Johnny Jones. His old client Captain Stewart had been an enemy of the Ngai Tahu, but Wentworth could not resist advising its chief, whose goal of having the tribe recognised as the true owners of the South Island neatly dovetailed with his own interests—and would foil the Wide-awake Wakefields. If the Governor recognised the Ngai Tahu ownership, Wentworth might be able to purchase from them the very land Colonel Wakefield thought he had bought from the Ngati Toa.[8]

As it turned out, Governor Gipps was as keen to meet the chiefs as they were to meet him. Having just seen off Captain Hobson to the North Island to sign up as many chiefs as possible to what became known as the Treaty of Waitangi, Gipps now had an opportunity to sign up chiefs from the South Island. On 14 February, with Jones in tow, the chiefs duly arrived at Government House, where they were ushered into the presence of the Governor and the Colonial Secretary. After Gipps explained that only land purchases 'approved by Her Majesty' would be confirmed, each chief was presented with ten sovereigns and each invited to return two days later to sign a treaty that would be drawn up in the meantime. The Governor also gave Tuhawaiki a British flag.

Despite these overtures, the chiefs did not return to Government House. Instead, Gipps received a note from Jones saying he had 'been advised not to . . . [get] the . . . Chiefs . . . to sign away their rights . . . until my purchases are confirmed . . . by the Crown'. A furious Governor soon discovered that this advice had been provided by Wentworth. On the day after the chiefs had visited Government House, Wentworth and Jones had signed a deed with them to purchase almost all of the South Island for a pittance. To confirm Jones' purchases as the note demanded would have meant that Gipps recognised Wentworth's purchase of the South Island. The Governor was worried, too, that in merely offering to treat with the chiefs he had somehow acknowledged their ownership in a way that Wentworth could exploit. Gipps later wrote to Secretary of State Russell that the chiefs 'had been advised [by Mr Wentworth] to sign no treaty which did not contain full security for the . . . purchasers of all lands acquired from the natives'.[9]

By their deed, Wentworth and Jones agreed to pay Tuhawaiki a lump sum of £100 together with £50 a year for life, while the other chiefs were each to receive a lump sum of £20 and an annuity for life of £10. In return the chiefs 'granted, alienated, enfeoffed, released, ratified and confirmed' to Wentworth and Jones virtually all of New Zealand 'situate between the degrees of forty and forty nine degrees south latitude'; that is, the whole of the South Island including the third already purchased by Wakefield from the chiefs' enemy Te Raupahara. The deed was 1000 words long and written in a dense legalese that would be unintelligible to some English lawyers, let alone Maori chiefs. But it conveyed well over

20 million acres. The chiefs 'signed' by having their distinguishing tattoos, known as *mokos*, drawn onto the deed. Wentworth and Jones signed and sealed their purchase of New Zealand's South Island in the traditional British way, with red wax.[10]

Within days of this debacle, Governor Gipps received news from Lieutenant-Governor Hobson across the Tasman that on 6 February no fewer than forty-six head chiefs and 500 chiefs 'of inferior degree' had signed the Treaty at Waitangi. Among other things it provided that, in return for British protection, the chiefs would yield to Queen Victoria 'the exclusive right of pre-emption' over their lands at prices to be agreed. Although the British claimed sovereignty over New Zealand from that day, the reality was that Hobson and his emissaries now had to travel all over the country to obtain other signatures. In these circumstances, any deal between Gipps, Wentworth and Jones over the South Island was out of the question. And so the battle lines were drawn. While the Governor prepared a Bill to legislate the Wentworth–Jones deed out of existence, Wentworth set up the New Zealand Association to keep a close eye on the Bill's progress. Meanwhile, Tuhawaiki and his fellow chiefs had left for New Zealand with Johnny Jones. Tuhawaiki carried the Governor's British flag as well as the full dress uniform of a British aide-de-camp, and now looked on himself as the Maori King.[11]

At the end of May 1840 the Governor introduced his New Zealand Land Claims Bill, the purpose of which was to invalidate the Wentworth–Jones deed by turning his proclamation of 19 January into law. Just over a month later, Wentworth appeared before the Legislative Council to attack Gipps and his Bill head-on. This confrontation occurred in what is today a photocopying room next to the Legislative Assembly Chamber. Wentworth began by noting that a proclamation could not itself make law. Therefore, he argued, although his deed was signed after the proclamation was issued, his purchase remained valid. The proclamation could not change the fact that he had bought the South Island from chiefs who were independent of Britain and could rightly sell land to a British subject. Wentworth referred to the Magna Carta and to Abiel Holmes' *Annals of America*, which detailed the 1639 purchase of all the lands between Connecticut and Boston from the American Indians for 'twelve coats and twelve blankets'. Sensing that Wentworth might be making headway with his argument that he could purchase from people who were then independent of Britain without the British government's consent, the Governor began clutching at straws. He even alleged that the chiefs had been taken drunk to the Sydney watch house after spending the sovereigns he had given them, implying that they were under the influence when Wentworth signed them up.

In the hand-picked Legislative Council, passage of the Governor's Bill was never really in doubt. All the same, Gipps was livid with Wentworth. Always sensitive about what London thought of him and embarrassed at Wentworth's brazen attempt to undermine the government's land policy, Gipps let fly:

He [Wentworth] will never get one acre, one foot, one shilling for the land which he bought under the proclamation; and . . . he is not yet safe from prosecution for conspiracy . . . All the jobs that have taken place since the expulsion of the Stuarts . . . would not equal this job effected by Mr Wentworth . . . who purchased a whole island at the rate of four hundred acres for a penny.[12]

Listening to this tirade, Wentworth was probably unaware that on 10 June one of Hobson's emissaries had tracked down Tuhawaiki at the southern tip of New Zealand. The chief, dressed in his aide-de-camp's uniform with its gold lace trousers, cocked hat and plume and clutching his British flag, signed the Treaty of Waitangi 'without hesitation'. A year later Gipps' Bill was adopted by the newly formed New Zealand Legislative Council, and Wentworth was shut out of his 'ownership' of the South Island. The New Zealand land commissioners also dismissed his claims for compensation after noting that 'he had not appeared . . . or brought forward evidence'. The Wide-awake Wakefields, with their clout in the Commons, did better. Although they waived their claim to a third of the South Island, they accepted Whitehall's offer of an acre of land for every 5s. they had spent on colonisation.

In August the Governor withdrew his 'recommendation of Mr Wentworth for a seat in the Legislative Council', citing his land sharking in New Zealand as the reason. From that day on, Gipps and Wentworth were bitter enemies.[13]

Chapter 21

WENTWORTH ECLIPSES MACARTHUR

'His day is gone by. His opinion is worth nothing', so observed *The Australian* in January 1842. It had a point. Three years had passed with hardly a peep from Wentworth on the issues that had once stirred him to tub-thumping oratory. The torch seemed to have passed to his opponents. James Macarthur was now one of the Legislative Council's leading lights. Naturally, he approved of the Governor's move to freeze Wentworth out of his ill-gotten New Zealand acres. Wentworth's personal humiliation in that affair was compounded by political humiliation. His public meeting in January 1839 endorsing the convict assignment system had been ignored, thanks to the Australian Patriotic Association's double-dealing agent Charles Buller. And in May 1840, the government announced it would end transportation to New South Wales.[1]

A chastened Wentworth disengaged from public life and focused on his family. To accommodate his brood of seven—Eliza and Isabella were born in 1838 and 1840—a new three-storey Gothic-style bedroom wing, complete with a castellated tower, was built at the rear of Vaucluse House. This wing also provided accommodation for guests, including Wentworth's surviving brother D'Arcy. After long military service in India, D'Arcy was now the police magistrate in Launceston, Van Diemen's Land, but he and his wife, Elizabeth, were regular visitors to Vaucluse. William and his family, for their part, continued to make regular visits to Windermere. As a result Willie boarded for a time at Sydney College, a non-denominational school opened in 1835. The school, which now forms part of Sydney Grammar, focused on teaching the classics to prepare its students for English universities. Like his father, Willie was an outstanding classics student. He came first in his class in Latin verse composition, and made a speech in Greek titled 'Pagondas to the Boeotians'. Only Consett Stephen, son of the Chief Justice, could equal him and it was said that the two lads were 'so much in advance of the other pupils that they formed a class by themselves'. In 1842 Willie won the school's medal for classics, while Stephen won the medal for mathematics. Wentworth had been a shareholder in the college from its inception and the headmaster, William Cape, was a regular visitor to Vaucluse along with the school's treasurer, Dr William Bland. Fitzwilliam, Wentworth's second son, was sent to the Normal Institution, which prepared its students for a teaching career in secular schools. Facing Hyde Park not far from Sydney College, it employed a sergeant-major to instruct the pupils in gymnastics and military drill. However, Fitzwilliam preferred academic subjects and in December 1842 won a prize in history.[2]

Wentworth's daughters also went to school though, as was the fashion of the day, their education was less academically rigorous than the boys'. Nevertheless, they received a strong grounding in written English. And dealing with the large staff of domestic servants at Vaucluse House gave them practice in managing a household, important for young women who hoped to marry well. Sarah took the lead in her daughters' education, which extended to religious instruction. They regularly attended St James Church of England—in search of respectability, some gossips said. Wentworth, however, struggled to share their faith. He had difficulty reconciling the Church of England's spiritual message with the distinctly temporal political activities of leaders like Archdeacon Scott.[3]

Wentworth and his women might not have seen eye to eye on religion, but they shared a passion for gardening—and were very good at it. In the first edition of his book Wentworth had written about 'The Colonial Garden', offering advice on the cultivation of fruit and vegetables. 'Peaches and plums are best budded upon their own stocks', he wrote, '[while] apricots may be budded on peach stocks.' In January 1830, *The Australian* reported that a peach nine inches around had been picked from the Vaucluse orchard. A decade later, as Wentworth nursed his wounds at Vaucluse, he and his ladies won prize after prize at floral and horticultural shows, for African marigolds, 'pine-apples' and sugar cane.[4]

But the financial pickings were meagre. By the end of 1840 it was clear that New South Wales had entered a prolonged depression, due in part to the fall in the value of wool. Many colonists pointed the finger at the British government's decisions to abolish transportation and rein in the squatters' relentless expansion. As concerns about the price of labour and land increased, the speculative bubble around the wool industry burst. Land sales plummeted and the Land Fund, which the colonial government relied on to pay for immigration, contracted so dramatically that it was unable to cover debts already incurred. When Governor Gipps withdrew government deposits from the banks to cover this shortfall, he only worsened the overall credit squeeze. During the height of the economic depression, in 1842–43, over 1000 colonists went bankrupt. Wentworth stayed solvent, but he was forced to rein in his spending. The work of turning Vaucluse House into a Gothic-revival mansion was abandoned. The proposed grand façade was never built. Work on the *porte-cochère* was halted. And the entrance hall was left without its main external door. To this day, there is no formal entrance to Vaucluse House: visitors enter via the verandah or the courtyard near the kitchen. At the time this strange arrangement was evidence of Wentworth's tight financial straits, but in later years, after he had recovered his fortune many times over, Vaucluse remained much the same: 'a fragmentary muddled house with a character particularly evocative of its owner'.[5]

After surviving the depression's initial shocks, Wentworth used much of the money he saved on Vaucluse to buy up more Hunter Valley sheep stations at reduced prices. These properties included Belltrees, near Scone, which by the mid-1840s was being used to muster, wash and shear up to 180,000 sheep. Having used his inheritance and income from the Bar to invest wisely, Wentworth was able to ride out the depression better than most, taking advantage of other people's financial problems. A squatter by the name of Hobler, who later lost his run to Wentworth, called him a 'dirty dog' for ruining him. A new 'boiling down' factory at Windermere, which turned sheep fat into tallow for candles and soap, creating an overpowering stench in the process, also helped him to make the most of low sheep prices.

While Wentworth focused on his properties, James Macarthur emerged as a prominent colonial politician, and a popular one. One of his most acclaimed moves was to block the introduction of local councils by opposing ex-convicts as aldermen. Since councils were seen by many as a device for imposing new taxes, this gained Macarthur considerable support. He also backed the use of income from land sales to finance free migration. This made him appear forward-looking compared to Wentworth, who had supported a tax on convict labour to pay for police and jails. And Wentworth's stance seemed even more old-fashioned when the news arrived that transportation to New South Wales had been stopped.[6]

Another piece of news, however, set Macarthur's success on its ear. The government had decided to implement Edward Gibbon

Wakefield's suggestion and fix uniform land prices throughout Australia to fund migration and promote more concentrated settlement. It would now be harder for wealthy squatters and landowners like the Macarthurs to dominate the market in new land. The government would continue to allow new land in the so-called 'nineteen counties' (which stretched from the Manning River in the north to Bateman's Bay in the south and Wellington in the west) to be sold by auction at the existing minimum upset price (lowest price) of 5s. an acre. But new land further afield would have to be sold at a uniform £1 an acre. For landowners like Macarthur, whose family held huge squatting runs south of the nineteen counties, it would now be impossibly expensive to build up large freehold estates. Worse, the government also planned to divide New South Wales into three colonies, a move certain to reduce the influence of Legislative Councillors like himself. Driving this plan to partition the colony, which still covered almost half the continent, was a separatist movement in the Port Phillip District, where the population had exploded from just over 200 in 1836 to more than 20,000 in 1841. Adding weight to the argument for a three-way split was significant population growth around the Brisbane River, which had first been settled in 1824.[7]

A public meeting was called for 7 January 1841 at the School of Arts in Pitt Street. Addressing a large crowd, Macarthur dismissed Wakefield's system of concentrated settlement as 'merely theoretical' in a land where squatters relied on huge open spaces to generate the colony's wealth. He also strongly endorsed a petition to the Queen protesting the 'dismemberment' of the colony. Notable by his absence was one of the colony's largest squatters, Wentworth.

When *The Australian* expressed concern that the petition might 'never actually come under Her Majesty's notice', a second meeting was called to petition Parliament as well. This time, Macarthur told the crowd it should show it was 'ripe for representative institutions' and stressed the importance of a united front with the ex-convicts. 'The more advisable course,' Macarthur said, 'would be to allow . . . [the ex-convict question to] totally . . . die away so that . . . it might be altogether forgotten that such a stain had ever rested on the colony.' Could this, some wondered, be the same man who once jibed, 'Once a convict, always a convict'? Macarthur hastened to save face, assuring them that though his arguments to end the division between exclusives and ex-convicts 'would be regarded as new to him, they were . . . opinions . . . he had always held'.[8]

Wentworth was absent from this meeting as well. But he would have read enough of the press criticism that Macarthur was trying to be all things to all people to realise that his opponent had done himself serious political damage. At the end of 1841, Macarthur compounded the damage when he acknowledged that reintroducing the very convict assignment system he had so long campaigned to end might be the only way to prevent the financial ruin of many settlers. The Tory *Sydney Morning Herald* (as it had been renamed by its new owner, John Fairfax) now attacked Macarthur for putting his 'love of Mammon' ahead of his 'love of character'. *The Australian*, so often Macarthur's opponent, now lauded him as the leader of what it christened the 'Transportation Recurrence Party'.

Sensing an opportunity to get bipartisan support for a renewal of convict assignment, *The Australian* looked for a leader from among those who had opposed Macarthur's earlier push to abolish transportation. The choice was between the now defunct Australian Patriotic Association's president, Sir John Jamison, who was old and infirm, its vice-president, Wentworth, who remained something of a political hermit, and its correspondence secretary, Dr William Bland. Although he was an ex-convict (a former naval surgeon, he had been transported for killing an opponent in a duel), Bland was a popular man. Despite his lack of political guile, *The Australian* endorsed him:

The Transportation recurrence party has a valuable ally in Dr Bland . . . [who has] the confidence of the public. Mr Wentworth, on the contrary, is one of those persons who was an influential man. His day is gone by. His opinion is worth nothing. He stands alone, and is altogether disregarded. Certainly he first taught the natives of this Colony what liberty was but he has betrayed them since and they have withdrawn their confidence from him.[9]

Not even that blast was enough to smoke Wentworth out of his self-imposed political exile. So he was absent, too, from the colony's Fifty-fourth Anniversary Dinner on 26 January, held at the Royal Hotel in George Street, the wealthier colonists' venue of choice. The 200 attendees listened as the dinner's chairman, Captain Maurice O'Connell, first said he would view with 'poignant regret' any return to transportation and assignment, and then contradicted himself by concluding that 'transportation should be continued . . . on public works'.

Wentworth also stayed away from a large public meeting a month later. Macarthur hoped the meeting would agree to a petition calling for an elected legislature. Instead it was a fiasco. One of the speakers claimed that the petition was 'founded on wealth and riches' and moved that any legislature be based on 'popular representation'. So Macarthur backtracked, blaming the defunct Australian Patriotic Association for the proposed narrow franchise. This slight prompted Dr Bland to object, amid great 'uproar and confusion'. Macarthur's motion later passed, but many at the meeting now judged him a poor leader. All the while, Wentworth stolidly continued to tend his peaches and pineapples.[10]

The Patriotic Association's agent, Charles Buller, might have double-crossed it over the abolition of transportation, but he had agreed with its members on the need for a legislature elected by ex-convicts and exclusives alike. With the issue of transportation out of the way, Buller moved to advance this part of the association's agenda, putting it to first one and then another Secretary of State.[11]

During the 1830s, Buller and Macarthur had agreed on the need to abolish transportation but disagreed on who should be entitled to vote for any legislature set up after that. While Macarthur had criticised Wentworth's draft Bills for allowing people with criminal records to vote, Buller had not only agreed that excluding ex-convicts 'would be illegal . . . and impolitic', but suggested that the Bills' proposed property franchise be widened to include mere tenants. This the association had readily accepted. And when it found out that Secretary of State Russell had introduced a Bill creating a blended legislature of thirty-six, of whom twenty-four would be elected by all voters occupying property worth £10 or more, the association wrote to Buller, 'This is so much in accordance with your views and ours.'

Although the Bill was later withdrawn, it established a precedent based broadly on Wentworth's Bill 'B' and set the scene for a more successful Bill soon afterwards. In its final letter to Buller the association armed him with evidence of Macarthur's conversion on the ex-convicts issue, enclosing an extract of the 1841 speech in which he admitted that 'the time had arrived when the long agitated emancipist question might be dropped, and that it would be unwise in the new bill to have any clause whatever upon the subject'.[12]

With proof that the colony's leading exclusive had changed his mind, Buller was now in an excellent position to lobby the new Secretary of State, Lord Edward Stanley. Three times Prime Minister during a long parliamentary career, Stanley had a reputation for 'masterly inactivity'. But in March 1842, Buller pushed him to reintroduce Russell's old Bill of 1840—the one based on Wentworth's Bill 'B'. Stanley then consulted many, including former Governor Bourke. And although the franchise was narrowed so that householders now had to occupy dwellings worth £20 instead of

Acquitted of no less than four different highway robberies in England, D'Arcy Wentworth made his fortune in New South Wales. (Artist unknown, British School, date unknown. Reverse portrait on glass. Vaucluse House Collection, Historic Houses Trust of NSW, presented by Members of the Historic Houses Trust)

The Old Bailey as D'Arcy Wentworth would have known it. The accused is on the right and the judge is on the left. At the top centre are the public galleries with the jury box below them. (By permission of the Guildhall Library, London)

No image of William
Charles Wentworth's
convict mother, Catherine
Crowley, is known to exist.
This image depicts how
she would have begun
her voyage to New South
Wales. (Convicts embarking
for Botany Bay, Thomas
Rowlandson 1756–1827,
nla.pic-an5601547, by
permission of the National
Library of Australia)

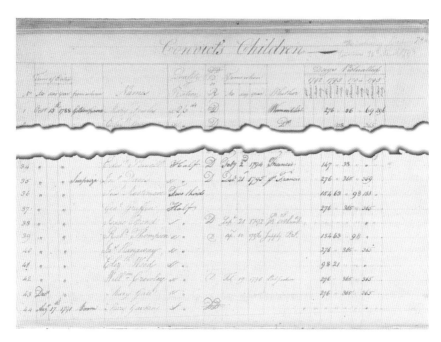

The Norfolk Island Victualling Book 1792–96 shows young William Crowley,
later known as William Charles Wentworth, listed as number 42 under the heading
'Convicts' Children'. (From the original held in the Mitchell Library, State Library of
New South Wales)

Lord Fitzwilliam was D'Arcy Wentworth's fabulously wealthy and well-connected kinsman and patron. (William Wentworth Fitzwilliam, 4th Earl Fitzwilliam 1748–1833, © National Portrait Gallery, London)

Queenborough on Norfolk Island was the hamlet where Wentworth spent his early childhood. (Attributed to John Eyre, from the original held in the Mitchell Library, State Library of New South Wales)

An engraving entitled *The Blue Mountains Pioneers* shows Wentworth waving his hat, a bareheaded Blaxland leaning forward and Lawson wearing a hat with his arm outstretched. (From the *Sydney Mail*, 25 December 1880, held in the Mitchell Library, State Library of New South Wales)

This is the title page to the first edition of the first book by an Australian-born author to be published. In it, Wentworth encouraged emigrants planning to settle in America to travel four times further to an autocratic penal colony. To make the colony more appealing, he demanded trial by jury and an elected legislature. (From the original held in the Mitchell Library, State Library of New South Wales)

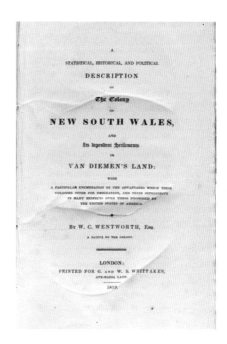

The 'Booby' Commissioner, John Thomas Bigge (1780– 1843). (By permission of the State Library of Queensland, Image no. 78178)

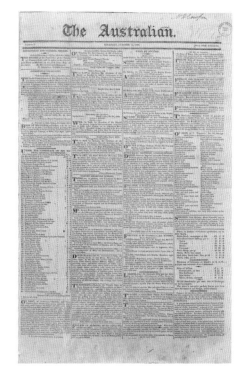

The front page of the first edition of the first independent newspaper published in Australia on Thursday 14 October 1824. In the editorial, Wentworth and Wardell championed the benefits of a free press. (From the original held in the Mitchell Library, State Library of New South Wales)

WENTWORTH, WM. CHAS.

A pencil sketch of the young William Charles Wentworth. (Copy of the original held in the Mitchell Library, State Library of New South Wales)

SARAH COX
See P 75

Wentworth and his client, Sarah Cox, misled the Court when they began an affair during her case against her fiancé for breach of promise. This affair blossomed into a partnership that was to last for 47 years. (William Nicholas, c 1852, watercolour and pencil, Vaucluse House Collection, Historic Houses Trust of NSW. Presented by Members of the Historic Houses Trust)

Ralph Darling, who Wentworth accused of murder. (Portrait of Ralph Darling, Governor of New South Wales, 1825–31, John Linnell, 1792–1882, nla. pic-an3291077, by permission of the National Library of Australia)

The Supreme Court and St James Church viewed from Elizabeth Street in 1842 looking much the same as they would have during the later years of Wentworth's career as a barrister. (The original watercolour by John Rae is held in the Mitchell Library, State Library of New South Wales)

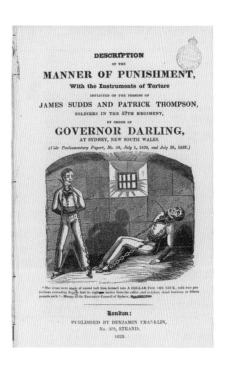

This drawing is based on a portion of Wentworth's letter seeking to impeach Governor Darling which was printed by order of the House of Commons in 1832. 'The set of irons were . . . so short', Wentworth charged, 'that he [Thompson] could not lie on either side without contracting his legs'. (The original is held in the Mitchell Library, State Library of New South Wales)

On 19 October 1831, Wentworth held a public barbeque to celebrate Governor Darling's departure. About 4000 people turned up, lining the shores in front of Vaucluse House to give Darling a drunken, jeering farewell as his ship made its way down the harbour. (Conrad Martens, c 1841, watercolour on card, Vaucluse House Collection, Historic Houses Trust of NSW, gift of Mrs Judith Willis and Mrs Edith Glennie, 1998)

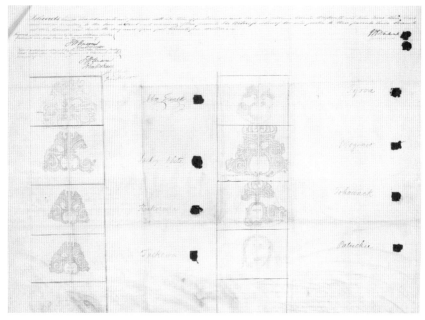

Pursuant to this agreement dated 15 February 1840, Wentworth and John Jones purchased the land between 'the degrees of forty and forty nine degrees south latitude'—the South Island of New Zealand—from its Maori owners.
(The original is held in the Mitchell Library, State Library of New South Wales)

A banner used by Wentworth and his running mate, William Bland, during the 1843 Legislative Council election for the District of Sydney. On polling day, 18 June, a number of these banners were destroyed in a riot during which one man was killed. (The original is held in the Mitchell Library, State Library of New South Wales)

The Reverend John Dunmore Lang (1799–1878), a sometime member of the New South Wales Legislative Council, was almost as scruffy, passionate and able as Wentworth himself. (By permission of the New South Wales Parliamentary Archivist)

Robert Lowe (1811–92), later Viscount Sherbrooke, was Wentworth's fierce opponent in the New South Wales Legislative Council. He later became Chancellor of the Exchequer in the British Government led by William Gladstone. (William Holt 1807–1871, nla.pic-an9633594, by permission of the National Library of Australia)

According to Robert Lowe, the New South Wales Legislative Council of 1843–1848 was 'as respectable, as enlightened, and as reasonable a body as ever met in any dependency of the Crown since the American Revolution'. The Chamber it met in is now used by the Legislative Assembly. (Dr Lang addressing the New South Wales Legislative Council in 1844, Jacob Janssen 1779–1856, nla.pic-an5600152, by permission of the National Library of Australia)

The young Henry Parkes (1815–96).
Later known as the 'Father of Federation',
Parkes acknowledged that Wentworth
had been his inspiration. (By permission
of the New South Wales Parliamentary
Archivist)

At this ceremony on 11 October 1852 in what is now 'Big School' at Sydney
Grammar, Fitzwilliam Wentworth's name was the first entered in Sydney University's
matriculation book. (Inauguration of the University of Sydney, nla.pic-an8416192, by
permission of the National Library of Australia)

James Macarthur (1798–1867) was, like Wentworth, Australian born. As young friends, middle-aged enemies and friends again in later life, their changing relationship was driven firstly by their disagreements over the role of ex-convicts and later by their common interest as large rural land holders. (By permission of John Macarthur-Stanham, Camden Park)

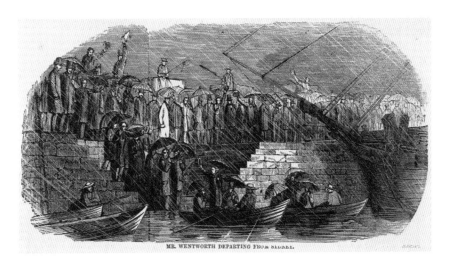

MR. WENTWORTH DEPARTING FROM SYDNEY.

Most cheered but some jeered as Wentworth left Circular Quay for London to lobby for the adoption of his Constitution Bill. (Mr Wentworth departing from Sydney in 1854, Walter G. Masson, nla.pic-an8017163, by permission of the National Library of Australia)

The length of Wentworth's lower legs, clearly visible in this photograph of him aged 72, hint at his great height. (Photographer unknown, c 1862, sepia toned photograph, Nielsen-Vaucluse Park Trust photograph album 5, Vaucluse House Collection, Historic Houses Trust of NSW)

Banned by her husband, Thomas Fisher, from seeing her parents for twenty years because he was embarrassed by their convict associations, the red-headed Thomasine was willful and wily enough to circumvent his edict. (Charles Adams, c 1844, plaster bust, Vaucluse House Collection, Historic Houses Trust of NSW)

Willie inherited his father's high intelligence but not his robust good health. (Artist unknown, British school 1855–59, pastel on paper, Vaucluse House Collection, Historic Houses Trust of NSW. Gift of W.C. Wentworth)

The Three Graces, Edith, Eliza and Laura, daughters of Sarah and William Charles Wentworth. (Hans Julius Gruder, 1868, oil on canvas, Vaucluse House Collection, Historic Houses Trust of NSW)

Left: At the age of 63, Sarah was still strikingly good looking. (Photographer unknown, c 1868, Vaucluse House Collection, Historic Houses Trust of NSW) Right: Aged 78 and in failing health, Wentworth nevertheless remained defiant, proudly posing in London in his squatter's corduroys. (A. Kens, c 1868, Vaucluse House Collection, Historic Houses Trust of NSW)

Seventy thousand people lined Sydney's streets to watch Wentworth's hearse make its way from St Andrew's Cathedral to Vaucluse following Australia's first state funeral. (From a copy of *The Illustrated Sydney News*, 10 June 1873, held in the Mitchell Library, State Library of New South Wales)

£10, ex-convicts as a class were not excluded from electing twenty-four of the blended council's thirty-six members. While this new Bill still placed many limitations on the council's powers to tax, spend and make laws independently of London, it was the beginning of representative government in Australia. Many claimed the credit, but it was Wentworth alone who had consistently struggled for almost a quarter of a century to bring this change about.[13]

Wentworth, being Wentworth, had already claimed the credit. Within a month of the public meeting during which Macarthur's petition for a representative legislature had been derided as 'founded on wealth and riches', Wentworth saw to it that a letter from Charles Buller to the Patriotic Association was prominently published in *The Sydney Morning Herald*. In his letter Buller noted the key role Wentworth's Bill 'B' was playing in the legislation being drafted for Lord Stanley, and hoped 'that at the close of the next session, I may congratulate you on having attained the object of your patriotic exertions'.[14]

Taking a risk that Stanley might not act as Buller predicted, Wentworth had the letter published anyway to enhance his own reputation as well as that of the association secretary, Dr Bland. After the New Zealand land-grab fiasco, Governor Gipps had struck Wentworth's name from the list of candidates recommended for appointment to the Legislative Council. And as Wentworth now planned how he would get there regardless by becoming one of the council's first twenty-four elected members, Bland became a crucial part of his strategy.[15]

An unofficial copy of Lord Stanley's new Act was published in the Sydney press on 10 December 1842, enough to get campaigning there underway. Just over a week later, Wentworth and Bland announced their intention to nominate for the District of Sydney. This district covered the same area as the Sydney City Council, established just a few months earlier. Other nominees for the district's two seats included a barrister named William Hustler; Sydney's first mayor, John Hosking; solicitor George Nichols; a wealthy merchant, Robert Cooper; and Captain Maurice O'Connell, a favourite of the conservatives and the grandson of Governor Bligh.

The first public meeting was called by O'Connell at the Royal Hotel on Boxing Day. O'Connell did well enough until he 'shirked' a question from George Nichols about whether his army obligations might conflict with his legislative duties. The very next day, Wentworth and Bland held their first public meeting at the same venue. Keen to answer the charge that he had 'betrayed' some of his poorer ex-convict friends by agreeing to the higher franchise of £20, Wentworth spoke of the need for compromise, even acknowledging that Macarthur had moderated his 'red-hot Tory views'. He could afford to be magnanimous, for his opponent George Nichols jumped up, withdrew his own nomination and argued that Wentworth and Bland should 'be returned . . . in that Assembly for which the people were principally indebted to them'. While *The Sydney Morning Herald* preferred O'Connell, *The Australian* praised Wentworth: 'Who was it who during the . . . Darling tyranny upheld . . . the liberty of the subject when menaced with the severest penalties?' it asked, before answering its own question: 'Let "Wentworth and Bland for Sydney" be your watchword.'[16]

On New Year's Day 1843, Lord Stanley's authenticated Act arrived in Sydney and campaigning began in earnest. In the District of Cumberland, which included the area around Parramatta, James Macarthur and William Lawson ran a joint campaign for the two seats on offer. They addressed seven meetings in six days, and *The Australian* declared that 'their election may now be considered certain'. *The Colonial Observer* was less enthused. It called Macarthur 'a tedious, longwinded . . . political trickster' and regretted that a 'plain man' like Lawson should be associated with him. In Camden many asked why Macarthur, the district's largest landowner, was not running there.[17]

In Sydney, Hustler and Cooper tried to stir up the local contest by calling a public meeting at the racecourse to protest the importation of 'Coolie' labourers from China and India. These low-paid workers were favoured by the Coolie Association—which included Wentworth, Lawson and O'Connell—as a means of making up the labour shortfall caused by the abolition of transportation. The issue attracted many extremists, and the meeting broke up in chaos after the secretary of the Coolie Association was chased around the racetrack by 300 'ragamuffins'. At the colony's anniversary dinner on 26 January, Wentworth spoke bluntly about the economic depression. 'They [the wealthy] ought to keep fewer carriages and fewer servants in the house,' he said, 'and more teams and more servants in the fields.' So confident of victory did Wentworth become that he went off campaigning for his brother D'Arcy, who had nominated for Northumberland Boroughs in the Hunter region. D'Arcy's opponent, Alexander Scott, was popular because he had set up an iron foundry that provided needed employment. So D'Arcy needed all the help he could get from his brother the local squire.[18]

Polling for each of the eighteen districts, some of which contained more than one seat, was to take place on different days, and it was possible for a candidate who had been unsuccessful in one seat to stand in another where an election was yet to be held. Sydney's nomination day came first, on 13 June. Apart from Wentworth and Bland, only O'Connell, Cooper and Hustler remained in the field to address the boisterous crowd of 8000 that gathered at Macquarie Place. On a show of hands, O'Connell and Cooper were declared elected. This declaration was then challenged, and a poll was scheduled for 18 June. On that day, Wentworth's and Bland's supporters paraded behind white banners that flew from blue-and-white poles. They contained a Union Jack in the top left-hand corner, an eight-pointed red star and the words 'Wentworth and Bland Australia's Hope and Sydney's Pride'. They were the earliest banners to bear any resemblance to the modern Australian flag. O'Connell's and Cooper's banners were green.

As the day wore on and rumours spread that Wentworth and Bland were well ahead in the count, an angry mob brandishing palings demolished one of Wentworth's campaign tents. But the booth captain they set upon owned a whaling ship and his crew, armed with harpoons, rushed to defend him. The mounted police arrived and the Riot Act was read, but the drunken mob swelled to over 400 and began to target Wentworth's supporters. Many were injured, and by the time order was restored one man lay dead. Despite their opponents' violent efforts, however, Wentworth and Bland, with 1275 and 1261 votes respectively, were declared elected. O' Connell came next with 733 votes, followed by Cooper's 365 and Hustler's 338.[19]

But there was no time for Wentworth to rest on his laurels. The following day was polling day for Northumberland Boroughs, and he hurried there by steamer to help his brother. At West Maitland he spoke briefly in support of D'Arcy, who went on to be elected. Fifty exultant supporters pulled the Wentworth brothers along in a carriage, shouting 'Wentworth for ever'. In Camden Macarthur's candidate defeated Charles Cowper, a prominent Anglican and sheep breeder who, unbowed, immediately nominated for Cumberland, where Macarthur and Lawson were the favourites. On nomination day, Wentworth seconded Lawson and delivered a blistering surprise attack on Macarthur's recent political reversals over trial by jury and ex-convicts' right to vote. Stunned by the ambush, Macarthur gave a speech that was likened to 'a barrel of Tom Underwood's ale—all froth and no substance'. There were two seats to be filled. Macarthur was beaten for the first by Cowper and for the second by Lawson—by just nine votes. Wentworth's verbal demolition of Macarthur had almost certainly helped Lawson across the line. In this way, Wentworth eclipsed Macarthur.[21]

Chapter 22

LEADER OF THE OPPOSITION

Top hats and frock coats were the uniform of choice for all but one of the twenty-four newly elected members of the Legislative Council as they filed into the first meeting with their twelve non-elected brethren on 1 August 1843. The venue—built for the purpose—was a simple chamber tacked on to the northern end of the Rum Hospital. Predictably the odd man out was Wentworth, who arrived wearing a squatter's corduroys, 'a contemptible affectation' *The Australian* said.

Wentworth expressed his regret that he would not be nominating for Speaker, 'the highest honour the Colony had to bestow'. *The Sydney Morning Herald* had earlier noted that 'the Speaker should be . . . cool and collected' and pointedly likened Wentworth's temper to gunpowder. For Wentworth, however, it was less an issue of temperament than that his 'public life had rendered him open to the imputation of partisanship'. But when Alexander McLeay was nominated, Wentworth did explode. Describing the former Colonial Secretary as a 'twice superannuated octogenarian', he reminded the members that McLeay had 'endeavoured to stifle' the creation of their newly constituted Council. But to Wentworth's fury, Darling's old cat's-paw was elected to the Speaker's Chair. The next day, Wentworth boycotted a visit to Government House during which his fellow councillors presented their new Speaker to Sir George Gipps. Still fuming, Wentworth then attempted to scuttle the Council's Vice Regal opening by moving that the Governor 'ought not to be received'. But he could not sway his colleagues, who had just enjoyed Gipps' hospitality.[1]

In an opening address to the Council on 3 August, Governor Gipps said he hoped there would be no rivalry between the official, nominated and elected members as they helped him to tackle the colony's 'monetary confusion'. This had been increased by the crash of the Bank of Australia and the Sydney Banking Company four months earlier, which was soon to plunge the colony into economic depression. Indeed, the spareness of the Council Chamber—with 'an entire absence of any attempt at grandeur . . . in its design'—arose from the colony's straitened finances. The Speaker even complained that he did not have enough candles to read by during evening sessions. One of the first items on the Council's agenda would be the Governor's 1844 Budget. But while the Council could pass laws, London and the Governor still had the power of veto. The Council had no control over Crown Lands; the Governor's Executive Council was still subject to direct instructions from London; and now local taxes worth £81,600 were each year to be automatically allocated to pay for Vice Regal, judicial and public service salaries, civil administration and public worship under Schedules to the Australian Constitutions Act. Wentworth, however, fully intended to use the Governor's Budget to make his point that if the colonists were to pay taxes, their government must answer to them for the way those taxes were spent.[2]

'The first Legislative Council,' said one of its members, Robert Lowe (who would later become Britain's Chancellor of the

Exchequer), 'was as respectable, as enlightened, and as reasonable a body as ever met in any dependency of the Crown since the American Revolution.' Apart from Lowe, its stars included Wentworth's sometime opponent the Rev. John Dunmore Lang; 'slippery Charlie' Cowper, who was to be five times Prime Minister of the colony; and the brilliant but acerbic barrister, journalist and farmer Richard Windeyer, whose district of Durham stretched north from the Hunter River. 'But towering over all in intellectual greatness, statesmanlike attributes and oratorical brilliancy,' Lowe's biographer wrote, 'was the un-wearying and determined champion of Australian liberties, William Charles Wentworth.'

Wentworth immediately became the Council's Leader of the Opposition, even if it later suited him to deny that there was one. From the beginning, the official and nominee members sat on two rows of high-backed leather benches to the Speaker's right (as the Premier and his party do today) while the elected members sat opposite, separated by a massive wooden table upon which was laid out the Bills for debate. With sittings usually beginning about 3 p.m., the elected members found themselves squinting into the afternoon sunlight which streamed in through the large Gothic windows on the chamber's northern wall. This light gave Wentworth a certain aura as he took the lead in tackling the Governor's lamented 'monetary confusion', introducing Bills to relieve solvent debtors, allow squatters to defer payment of bills by giving creditors security over future wool clips and permit them to use their livestock as collateral to borrow money without having to hand over their animals to their lenders. Everyone in New South Wales understood that Wentworth's lien on wool and livestock Bill was a revolutionary departure from English law, under which only fixed property like land could be given as security for a loan. Highlighting the problem squatters faced without such legislation, Wentworth said: 'Gentlemen with 10,000 sheep could not get credit for a bag of sugar or a chest of tea.' Nothing could have better symbolised the difference between the economic order of the new world and the old than hundreds of thousands of mortgaged sheep grazing on millions of acres of land that Australian squatters did not own. Although the Governor was diffident about Wentworth's Bill and the Secretary of State thought it would place lenders 'at the mercy of any dishonest borrower', the distinguished economic historian S.J. Butlin later said that Wentworth's Bill 'was . . . the most important measure taken' to combat the depression of the 1840s. The principle behind the Bill also helped to develop the grazing industry for the next hundred years.[3]

At a hearing of the Council's Select Committee on Monetary Confusion, Wentworth gave evidence as a director of the Bank of New South Wales. Asked to identify the causes of the colony's 'monetary embarrassment', he emphasised 'the cessation of transportation'. This meant, he said, that money now had to be 'sent out of the country to find a substitute for convict labour', particularly shepherds.

As a member of the Committee on Immigration, Wentworth cross-examined an employment agent. 'Are there a good many persons in Sydney . . . who go skulking about out of employment and will not take engagements?' 'Yes,' the agent replied, 'they comprise by far the greater portion of those who are out of employment in Sydney at the moment.' The Immigration Committee was charged with reviving free immigration, not the transportation Wentworth wanted. But its report did stress the demand for immigrant shepherds and the need to rescind the £1 an acre minimum price set for Crown land at auction. 'While some land around towns might be worth that,' Wentworth said, 'a vast quantity . . . [is] not worth tuppence.'[4]

The Committee on Distressed Mechanics and Labourers was chaired by John Dunmore Lang. It recommended immediate aid for families in 'actual destitution' and, more to Wentworth's liking, proposed that the unemployed should be drafted to rural areas where work at reasonable wages was available. However, Wentworth's narrow focus on squatters' interests could be sustained only for so long as the qualifications to vote in his Sydney electorate remained narrow. How long could the Member for Sydney continue to attend the Council in a squatter's corduroys? Wentworth understood that the answer depended on who had the vote. He also understood that he had only a limited time to achieve a constitutional settlement that protected squatters in a society increasingly dominated by immigrant tradesmen and labourers. Doing so remained his goal for the next decade. Brutal and self-serving as he often was, there was a tough consistency in his approach that set him apart from many of his more fickle colleagues.[5]

In his quest for a Constitution that would allow New South Wales to govern itself, Wentworth challenged London—and Governor Gipps—in large ways and small. He objected to local taxes being used to pay for the upkeep of the remaining convicts—who, after all, were British criminals. He demanded that local taxes collected for one purpose, for example judges' salaries under Schedule A of the Constitutions Act, but not fully spent should be used to make up shortfalls in other spending such as public worship under Schedule C before more local taxes were levied to cover any shortfall. And he tried to reduce the salaries of the government's lawyers. But Gipps remained unmoved.[6]

Wentworth's most effective ally against the Governor was Richard Windeyer, an enlightened, honest and uncompromising man who had become one of Sydney's leading barristers since Wentworth's retirement. The two men boycotted Speaker McLeay's presentation at Government House, tried to stop the Governor from attending the Council's ceremonial sitting and criticised the Governor's £5000 salary, demanding to know why Gipps was paid the same as the President of the United States. They also moved to strike out the judges' £1000 travelling allowance because, as Wentworth said, the Secretary of State knew they went on circuit when he set their pay. And they lashed the Governor for ignoring an arrangement agreed to by Governor Bourke whereby the colonists would pay for the police and jails in return for receiving all surplus land revenue. The colonists still paid for the police and jails, but all the land revenue now went to London. 'Is this not too much of a joke?' Wentworth bellowed. 'Is the colony to be bamboozled like this?' The public lined up to witness Wentworth and Windeyer in action, waiting impatiently on the front verandah of the old Rum Hospital before being signalled into a cylinder which supported a staircase. This took them to an upper gallery which seated fifty people, who could all watch the cut and thrust of debate on the floor of the chamber below. Demand was such that an extra attendant had to be hired between 3 and 10 p.m. to keep an eye on those queuing outside.[7]

Governor Gipps was in danger of being bamboozled too, by populist measures designed to ease the financial stress on local farmers and businessmen. Wentworth introduced a Bill that would have retrospectively limited interest on debts to 5 per cent, throwing nearly all lenders' calculations into confusion, and both men ignored London's free trade policy, demanding tariffs on imports like grain and flour to protect local farmers. Precisely because these measures were popular, Gipps, who no longer had a seat in the Council, had great difficulty mobilising effective Council allies. And Wentworth toyed with him. When an exasperated Governor complained about the Opposition's lack of restraint, Wentworth said he 'was not aware of any opposition'.

Wentworth soon found opposition of his own, however, in Robert Lowe, a champion Oxford debater, barrister and believer in free trade who also happened to be an albino. As a university student, Lowe had been forced to look so closely at his exam papers that 'his nose obliterated much that he wrote'. Still, the Governor took a shine to this young man with the snow-white hair, and appointed him to the Council in November 1843. Gipps hoped that Lowe would bolster the Colonial Secretary, Edward Deas Thompson, who was the

Government Leader in the Council now that the Governor himself was prohibited from taking part in debates. Although he was known for his 'calm good sense, strong reasoning powers and well informed mind', Thompson had been no match for Wentworth. And while Lowe did not win every round against Wentworth either, he checked his more grandiose pretensions, saying the decisions of a small colonial Council could not be compared 'to the laws of the Medes and the Persians'. One observer noted that 'Wentworth looked up like a fighting cock who had long been lord of the domain but who finds himself unexpectedly confronted by a rival'.[8]

Another unexpected rival was Thomas Fisher, the nephew of Wentworth's murdered partner Robert Wardell. Fisher had come from London to help Wentworth settle Wardell's estate. After being admitted to the Sydney Bar, he became besotted by the Wentworths' eldest daughter, Thomasine, whose orange-gold hair and high cheekbones turned many heads. An acquaintance of Fisher's noted that he 'pets and fondles her desperately'. A pedantic, fussy-looking little man, Fisher had, said the same associate, a 'selfish disposition . . . [and] a patronising air'. Childlike in some ways and strong-willed in others, Thomasine at first turned down Fisher's marriage proposal. But she soon relented and, although she was only just eighteen, Wentworth gave his blessing.

After the wedding, which took place in January 1844, Fisher broke off all contact with the Wentworths and refused to let Thomasine see her parents, a prohibition that lasted for twenty years. He was obsessed about being socially tainted by contact with his in-laws. 'We do not consider it worth our while to court the little gentleman's acquaintance,' Wentworth said loftily, hoping that Fisher would mellow. Sarah managed to evade Fisher's watchful eye and meet Thomasine from time to time. She also helped her daughter with washing and mending, especially after the birth of the Wentworths' first grandchild, Alice.[9]

As a member of the Crown Lands Committee, Wentworth had ended 1843 with a motion attacking the way the Government used Crown land to promote immigration. Revenues from such land should not be used to fund immigration, Wentworth argued. Rather, the promise of occupation of the land itself should be used to attract new settlers. At the time, the Governor was preparing regulations to control land beyond the nineteen counties squatters had been allowed to occupy. The squatters' £10 licence fee gave them no security of tenure or title, and they wanted both guaranteed. Instead, in April 1844, Gipps announced that a squatter's run would be limited to twenty square miles and that a separate annual licence fee, costing £10, would be needed for each run. For those like Wentworth who had many such runs, £10 now became hundreds. Predictably, they were outraged. At a furious public meeting in the Royal Hotel's lower grand saloon, which was 'sadly disproportionate in its width and height . . .', Wentworth loomed large, taking centre stage with a motion declaring that the new regulations rendered taxation by representation 'almost nugatory'. A Pastoral Association was formed. Even the Governor's pet Councillor, Robert Lowe, became a member, provoking the Governor to say his appointment was an act he had 'most reason to be sorry for'. (In fact, Lowe wanted to secure election to the Council in his own right, and was challenging the Governor to show potential voters he was not a government puppet.) With Wentworth and Lowe now united against him, Gipps had a major battle on his hands.[10]

Public interest in Council debates was intense, and in May 1844 a new gallery was opened above the Speaker's Chair to provide eight seats for 'gentlemen connected to the public press'. *The Sydney Morning Herald* and *The Australian*, being published daily, were allocated two seats each. By August, to the reporters' delight, Wentworth and Windeyer had the Governor's Budget estimates under siege. When Gipps asked the Council to consider a supplement of £8000 for the Judicial Department, Wentworth succeeded with a motion demanding that the Council consider the department's full budget of £28,000 or nothing at all. Nothing it was. But after applying the budget knife, the Governor found enough revenue from elsewhere, including the Schedules, to fund the department.[11]

By now Governor Gipps had modified his land regulations to recognise squatters' improvements and allow them to more easily purchase their runs. But the Council was not satisfied. Its Crown Land Grievance Committee demanded the abolition of licence fees, the introduction of fixed tenure and preemptive rights for squatters, which would give them the first option to buy the land they occupied. Above all, it demanded that the Council be given control of all revenue from Crown lands. According to Wentworth the government had no lawful authority to this income, which he estimated totalled at least £100,000 a year. 'The House must either put down this pretension,' he said, 'or this pretension must put down the House.' When the Council endorsed the committee's demands, Gipps wrote to London to criticise them.

Wentworth took advantage of the anger being directed at the Governor to establish a Committee on General Grievances, and used it to refine and consolidate his constitutional demands. Seconding Wentworth's motion, Reverend Lang likened the mover to 'one of the larger celestial bodies' that eclipse smaller planets in their shadow. The old barrister now had the whole colony as his client.

He started by cross-examining the Colonial Secretary Edward Deas Thomson on some fundamental constitutional questions:

—As a member of the Executive Council, do you conceive that you have any legal responsibility to any one; either to the legislature of the country, to the Governor, or to the home government?
—No, certainly not; I conceive that I am bound by my oath

to give advice to the best of my ability.

—Then you conceive that the discharge of your duties as an Executive Councillor, lies merely between yourself and your own conscience?

—Certainly.

—Do you conceive that there are any officers of this government, that stand in the relation to the legislature, that Cabinet Ministers in England stand to the Crown or to the Parliament?

—No, I do not consider that there are any.

—Then you not only consider that you yourself owe no responsibility to the legislature of the country but that none of the officers of the government owe any?

—Such is my opinion.

Wentworth thus established that the Governor's Executive Council, which had approved Gipps' disastrous land regulations, was unaccountable.[12]

Wentworth's report—because the General Grievance Committee's report was all Wentworth's work—was a masterpiece of advocacy. Objecting to the Civil List schedules that placed official salaries beyond the purview of the Council, Wentworth said they contravened the Act of 1778 that had prohibited Britain from taxing its American colonies without the consent of their local legislatures. On the issue of judges, Wentworth demanded that they be given tenure for the duration of their good behaviour rather than during the pleasure of the Crown. And on the all-important question of responsible government, he said:

The Legislative Council [must be given] the necessary privileges of a representative body which imply that control over the ministers and the administration of the colony which belongs to responsible Government . . . [and] which can only exist where the decision of the majority can occasion the choice—as well as the removal of the functionaries—who are entrusted with the chief executive departments. But to responsible Government there must belong responsible ministers . . . and the creation of some colonial tribunal for impeachments is an indispensable adjunct.[13]

The Legislative Council agreed. In December, it moved that the New South Wales Government be conducted 'on the same principle of responsibility as . . . the United Canadas'. In his report, Wentworth had not made clear what he meant by a 'representative body'. But the Committee on the Extension of the Elective Franchise, of which he was a member, had recommended that the vote be extended to 'every squatter possessed of no fewer than two hundred head of cattle or one thousand sheep'. This idea was endorsed in the report, which noted that 'A large portion of the class of squatters on the waste lands . . . consists of persons of reputable character and superior intellectual qualifications, and their flocks and herds constitute, in great measure, the wealth of the Colony.' But only a small number of the wealthiest squatters lived in Sydney. Extending the franchise, as the committee also recommended, to leaseholders paying as little as £10 a year would make Wentworth's seat less secure. Nevertheless, the committee's further recommendation to increase the number of seats for the Sydney District from two to six would help to counter this effect by giving Wentworth a better chance of being re-elected. However, no such increase could fully keep pace with a massive surge in immigration that would almost double Sydney's population by 1851, diluting Wentworth's electoral base and threatening his position as Leader of the Opposition.[14]

Chapter 23

COUNTED OUT

'On my advice, [Wentworth] has decided to place [his son] . . . with someone who is in the habit of taking charge of restive colts.' So wrote Robert Lowe to his friend the Reverend Richard Mitchell in 1846, asking him to find a 'Cambridge man' to take Willie under his wing while he prepared to study for the Bar. Wentworth's eldest son had arrived in England two years earlier to further his education. But Wentworth no longer had anyone there, as Lowe put it, to whom he could 'entrust a matter of so much difficulty'. Willie shared his father's high intelligence and auburn hair, but unlike his rough and robust father he was pale and pudgy.[1]

Lowe and his new ally Wentworth shared an interest in education. In October 1843, Wentworth had opposed John Dunmore Lang's move to give local authorities the power to build schools. '[This] would be beginning at the wrong end,' Wentworth said, '[without] some principle for . . . carrying out . . . education throughout the whole country.' Wentworth was referring to secular education. Charles Cowper, William Lawson and other Anglicans, by contrast, wanted to continue the church-supervised education system. In August 1844 Lowe's Select Committee on Education recommended that the colony adopt Lord Stanley's system, under which children of all faiths were taught together but given religious instruction by their own pastors and priests one day each week. Predictably, the Anglican bloc were against this.

Lowe soon resigned from the Council, a consequence of his falling out with the Governor for supporting the squatters. So it was left to another committee member, Joseph Robinson, to win over the Council's Anglican members. Solely as a compromise, Wentworth proposed that instead of having clergymen attend schools, students should be allowed one schoolday a week to obtain religious instruction elsewhere. Personally, he thought that 'this system rather taught too much religion, than too little'. His amendment prevailed by a single vote. But the Governor, fearing resistance from the clergy, declined to act. So in December, the amended motion was put to the vote again. Again it passed, with only Cowper, Lawson and three others holding out. And again the Governor declined to act. It was not until 1848 that a new Governor set up a General Educational Board to regulate schools according to Lord Stanley's system. But it was Lowe and Wentworth who had begun the push for what would eventually become one of the largest public education systems in the world.[2]

Aside from the married Thomasine and Willie in London, Wentworth and Sarah had eight children at home. The two youngest, Edith (born in 1845) and D'Arcy (1848) were younger than their niece, Thomasine's daughter Alice Fisher. Sarah had help from the older children to look after the younger ones, but for Wentworth the financial burden was relentless. 'Pressure of business,' Lowe said, had prevented Wentworth making the trip to London with Willie to help settle him there. Wentworth's entrepreneurial restlessness had seen him through the financial crisis of the 1840s in better shape than most, trading land and juggling mortgages. But hanging over his fragile financial arrangements was the constant threat of imminent bankruptcy. In September 1844, he wrote to warn Willie that 'the sudden and universal depreciation of property' had wiped out much of his fortune, and that the whole family might have to depend on Willie 'for the very means of subsistence'.

Wentworth grew so worried about money that in 1845 he set up a trust fund to provide an income for Sarah in case he went bankrupt. When the Bank of Australia failed in 1843 his £3250 stake in it became worthless, and now it threatened to ruin him. As Governor Gipps put it: 'The Bank . . . having been formed on the joint stock principle, every shareholder in it is liable for the debts of the bank to the full amount of his property.' The bank owed £230,000 and the interest burden was growing daily. Still, it had some assets, and Wentworth introduced a Bill to dispose of these. To raise £80,000 a sweepstakes was proposed, with every ticket allocated one portion of the bank's assets and two large estates as the biggest prizes. The Council passed the Bill. But although Gipps acknowledged that the Bank's land was presently 'unsaleable in any other way', he doubted the legality of a lottery and refused to assent to it.[3]

Wentworth's legislation to allow wool and livestock as collateral for loans had saved many deserving colonists from insolvency. But London disapproved, fearing that the pledging of 'things moveable', as Secretary of State Lord Stanley put it, would promote fraud. It infuriated Wentworth that London was still interfering in the local affairs of his country. How could a Whitehall bureaucrat stand in the boots of a squatter? Even though Gipps had shown flexibility by amending his squatting regulations, the Governor remained in 'an utter state of pupillage', Wentworth said, 'by that necessity for constant reference to Downing Street'. To Wentworth, this combination of delay and ignorance imperilled his own financial future as a squatter, a terrifying experience that he never forgot even after he again became a very wealthy man.[4]

★　　★　　★

Staunchly as he defended colonists' rights, Wentworth drew a stark line between them and Aboriginals. In 1838, at the Myall Creek sheep station near Inverell, some twenty-eight Aboriginals had been murdered by eleven Europeans. Some of the perpetrators of this massacre had escaped justice because a key Aboriginal witness, Davey, was not permitted—because he was Aboriginal—to take the oath at their trial. Citing this case, the Attorney-General put forward a Bill to allow Aboriginals to testify in court. The barrister Lowe opposed the Bill, saying that Aboriginals could not take an oath because they did not believe in God. Lowe called them 'untutored savages'. But Wentworth went much further. In a chamber which would see some appalling performances over the next 150 years, he delivered what is still probably its most shameful speech: 'It would be quite as defensible to receive as evidence in a Court of Justice the chatterings of the ourang-outang as of this savage race and [Wentworth] would as soon vote in favour of a Bill for that purpose as for the present measure.' The Bill was eventually defeated.[5]

The Council had been due to resume on 4 March 1845, but Governor Gipps delayed its opening until the end of July to await London's replies to its various demands and grievances. During the hiatus Wentworth's brother D'Arcy resigned his seat, and Robert Lowe, now described by *The Sydney Morning Herald* as a 'political dick swiveller' for abandoning the Governor to support the squatters, was elected in his own right as the member for St Vincent and Auckland, a district that stretched from Jervis Bay to Eden. On 29 July Gipps gave up waiting and opened the new session, declaring his 'support for popular representation'. Despite the confrontations of the previous year, Wentworth now claimed that the Governor's speech gave him 'unmitigated satisfaction'. A surprised *Herald* remarked:

He is at once the ablest and the weakest [member]—the most useful and mischievous . . . the ill effects of his ungovernable feelings and of the coarse and violent language in which his angry passions are poured forth are sometimes such as to defeat the good he would otherwise achieve . . . [but his] opening speech is happily exempt from all bad feeling.[6]

Less than a week later, a response finally arrived from London. Lord Stanley approved the Council's idea that surplus from one tax Schedule be used to top up any shortfall in another area before extra taxes were demanded. But he refused to give up London's taxing power. He also refused to lower the minimum price of Crown land or stop spending land revenue on immigrants, though he said that squatters should be allowed to occupy Crown Lands 'on fair terms' without having to purchase them. The *Herald* was satisfied, writing that 'the squatters will be able to go on pretty smoothly'. And for a while, it appeared that even Wentworth was content. Whereas during 1843 and 1844 there had been constant clashes over constitutional issues, Council debates during 1845 focused on lighthouses, the stealing of dead wood and a bridge over the Yarra River. And if Wentworth had been troubled by the time it had taken London to reply to the Council's grievances, he was not prepared to spend money to speed up their delivery. When a proposal was put up to slash the voyage to England from 120 days to sixty by introducing steamships via Singapore, Wentworth refused to agree unless the £40,000 cost was met by Whitehall.[7]

However, in late October 1845 the political temperature again began to rise when Wentworth moved that £1000 from Schedule C, where local taxes were automatically set aside for public religion, be paid to the Hebrew Congregation to help offset the cost of building a synagogue. 'Hebrews contributed just as much as Christians towards the revenue', Wentworth said, 'and Schedule C applied to public worship, not just Christian worship.' Backed by Lang's argument that it was the 'duty of the State to support truth wherever it was discovered', Wentworth won his motion. However, the Governor, at least initially, refused to pay even though there were over 1000 people who identified themselves as 'Hebrews' in the 1846 census. Whitehall backed the Governor and as late as 1853, when Wentworth tried to obtain a publicly funded stipend of £200 for the Hebrew minister, the Government refused to agree.[8]

A few days after the synagogue debate, Wentworth reignited the issue of taxation by representation with a Bill to prohibit local taxes being spent without the Legislative Council's permission. Ignoring a warning from the Colonial Secretary, Edward Deas Thomson, that he might oppose the Bill 'at every stage', Wentworth ploughed through a speech so dull that by the time he wound up the chamber was almost empty. No sooner had Windeyer commented on this—only eleven members being present at 6.45 p.m. when a minimum of twelve was required—than the Council adjourned for lack of a quorum. Perhaps the others had wandered off into the night in search of a meal, their members' room next door to the chamber having no kitchen of its own. With so-called 'party discipline' a thing of the future and only a couple of hand-bells of different frequencies to summon the Speaker and members, maintaining a quorum was difficult at any time, even for Wentworth when he was carrying on about legal technicalities.[9]

For whatever reason, Wentworth had been 'counted out'—a disaster, because it told London that the Legislative Council no longer cared about taxation by representation. Those members who did care now wrote to Francis Scott MP, the Council's parliamentary agent in London. They complained about Lord Stanley's assent to the Governor's squatting regulations, and his refusal to lower the minimum price of land as well as his refusal to let the Council determine how local taxes were spent. But in the Council itself these issues were left undebated. The Council rose for the year on 13 November, having sat for just sixty-one days compared to ninety-two the year before. All the letter to Scott did was to high-light the Legislative Council's abysmal record in 1845.[10]

It was not surprising, then, that Wentworth appeared subdued at a dinner given in his honour on 26 January. In the Sydney College hall that night, 250 people had gathered to hear 'the great man' honoured for his Lien on Wool Act and for his leading role in the fight for constitutional rights. But instead of giving the expected tub-thumping performance demanding the birth-rights of Englishmen, Wentworth spoke only of squatting. It was Lowe who, to loud cheers, threatened Britain with a repeat of 'the bloody and expensive [American] lesson' if it persevered with its present colonial policy. Had Wentworth lost his drive? Even his closest associates were starting to think so.[11]

About two weeks before the Legislative Council was due to reconvene, rumours began circulating that Speaker McLeay would be retiring. When sounded out to see if he would consider the Speaker's position Wentworth agreed, provided he could continue speaking out on controversial issues. That caveat—which would breach Parliamentary protocol—seemed to preclude his nomination. On 12 May 1846, the Governor opened the new Council session with what everyone knew would be his last speech in the chamber. A load of crushed bricks had been laid over the muddy front drive in anticipation of his arrival. Sitting on a special chair which had been covered in crimson morocco leather and stuffed with the best horsehair, Gipps congratulated himself on the improving local economy—to which Wentworth growled that it was only the Council, through measures such as the Lien on Wool Act, that had saved the colony from ruin.

Wentworth then gave notice of a motion to double the Speaker's salary to £1500, prompting a stunned *Sydney Morning Herald* to comment that it was 'impossible for [Wentworth's] bitterest enemy . . . to have suggested any thing . . . more damaging . . . [to] his character as a politician'. Two days later, Wentworth compounded this mistake by claiming that the Speaker should also be entitled to a dinner allowance, as was reported in the *Herald*:

> The Speaker's ability . . . to extend hospitality . . . would tend greatly to the dispatch of business by softening down those asperities which were apt to spring up in the warmth of debate. (Laughter).
>
> He was much surprised to hear members laugh for they could not be ignorant that . . . it was the practice of the Speaker of the Commons to give regular dinners to members during the session—it was not the mere dinners, for he would not suppose that the members wanted a dinner. (Great laughter) . . . They had become, as it were, an established part of the constitution. (Shouts of laughter).

Although Wentworth now refused the Chair for himself, the damage was done. 'Without these bi-weekly banquets,' Robert Lowe sneered, '[Wentworth says] the honour of the House cannot be preserved.' Like Lowe, Charles Cowper, Richard Windeyer and John Dunmore Lang were appalled by the hypocrisy of their leader, who had argued for salary cuts for all colonial officials. 'I could not sit down to bi-weekly feasts,' said one, '[because] fancy would ever be conjuring up some bloody Banquo's ghost—shades of displaced . . . clerks to push me from my seat.' With the Council laughing at him and with only Bland for support, Wentworth withdrew his motion. His leadership of the Opposition was now widely questioned.[12]

On 16 May 1846, Lord Stanley's final replies to the colonists' (really Wentworth's) grievances of December 1844 were published in the *Herald*. They were a slap in the face for Wentworth. His key demand, for the 'principle of legislative responsibility . . . conceded in Canada', was dismissed as 'so abstract and so vague'. The only grievance conceded was the demand for judges' tenure to be conditional on their good behaviour. On the same page of the newspaper the Governor gave notice of a Bill to restrain the extension of squatting and continue the budget of the border police, whose top priority was to collect taxes from squatters.[13]

It was not Wentworth but Windeyer who on 3 June was the first to voice his opposition to this Crown Lands Occupation Bill, which restrained squatters. It was Windeyer, rather than Wentworth, who moved that the Council object to continuing the tax on squatters by prerogative alone, without their consent. Lang and Lowe also spoke. Then, when all the other speakers had finished, Wentworth launched forth. It reminded some onlookers of his old tactics at public meetings where, having bided his time, he used to stride to the podium from the back of the hall. Now, he thundered, the Bill in question was all about taxation without representation. He viciously attacked Gipps and Stanley for taxing squatters through licence fees to pay for useless border police. In the Manaroo District, where squatters paid £2600 in assessment money, the police were seen only when collecting the money. This was all they did, Wentworth railed, apart from fetching their Commissioner's 'slippers or brushing his coat'. He recalled the story of a posse of border police who had made camp and were enjoying their tea. 'A carbine happened to fall,' Wentworth said, 'and astounded by the noise . . . they made off, and never stopped . . . till they had run a distance of forty miles.' Having thus tried to reassert his leadership, Wentworth sat down. Shortly afterwards, Windeyer's motion was carried. The Governor was contemptuous. 'It requires no reply,' he told the Speaker, 'and I do not intend to give it any.'[14]

Events now moved quickly.

On 10 June, Robert Lowe proposed a motion criticising the Government's unauthorised expenditure. Two days later, Wentworth reintroduced his Bill to prohibit local taxes being spent without the Council's permission. The day after that, Richard Windeyer moved 'a vote of thanks to Her Majesty for the change in the head of the Colonial Department'—Lord Stanley had been replaced by William Gladstone, later to be Prime Minister, on four occasions. Even though the Governor's new Budget estimates had yet to be considered, Wentworth next moved that the Council adjourn until 21 July. This was an audacious attempt to block the Governor's money supply by a leader struggling to reassert his authority. 'I should be ready to compel the Governor to consider [taxation by representation] by bringing the Executive to a deadlock,' Wentworth said, 'until some attention . . . [is] paid to the wishes of the House and the . . . community.' With Cowper, Lang and Lowe speaking in support of his motion Wentworth won overwhelmingly, and the House duly adjourned. Gipps declared later that Wentworth had proposed his motion 'with the avowed intention of [the Council] not meeting again . . . until after I . . . left the Colony'. In effect, the Legislative Council had deliberately shut itself down—counted itself out—as a protest against Gipps and as a message to his successor that the Council was not to be trifled with.[15]

But the Governor was not finished. He immediately issued a proclamation, proroguing the Council until 25 August. Writing to Colonial Secretary Gladstone two weeks later, Gipps noted, 'The adjournment of the Council . . . to 21 July, though doubtless intended to perplex me . . . gave me . . . a fair opportunity of proroguing them; and I shall, if necessary . . . extend the prorogation, so as to relieve Sir Charles Fitz Roy [the new Governor-in-waiting] from the necessity of meeting them immediately.'[16]

Chapter 24

ALLIES FALL OUT

As it turned out, Governor FitzRoy deemed it his duty to call the Legislative Council together at the earliest opportunity. He immediately promised the Council 'the most open . . . communication', saying he was relying on members' 'liberality' to approve the Budget estimates. Impressed, Wentworth promised that the Opposition would support the government 'where it deserved support'.[1]

Wentworth might not have understood it at the time but Fitz-Roy, who descended from an illegitimate son of King Charles II, posed a threat to the Leader of the Opposition. A Waterloo veteran, a former MP and a governor in the West Indies who had been popular for his conciliatory demeanour, the urbane and aristocratic FitzRoy was afraid of no one at the Colonial Office. Unlike the highly strung Gipps, who had defended London's prerogative, Fitz-Roy was his own man. When the Secretary of State threatened to recall him for being too generous in commuting quit rents, a form of land tax, FitzRoy coolly responded that he had acted in line with public opinion.[2]

Wentworth's Opposition leadership had survived so long as there was political capital in opposing the Governor. But this Governor was popular with the public; opposing him would be politically damaging. Back in September 1845, Wentworth's ally Richard Windeyer had become concerned that the watering down of new regulations for occupying Crown lands would give squatters possession in perpetuity. Calling the squatters 'cormorants', Windeyer accused them of conspiring with the government to lock out other settlers. Wentworth had replied that his squatter's right 'was the right of discovery and possession', while that of the Crown was only 'a legal fiction'. This confrontation had all the makings of a fatal political boil-over between close colleagues, but it simmered down when Gipps' obsessive defence of London's prerogative again gave the two men a common cause; Windeyer objecting on principle to squatters being taxed without their consent. Now, however, with the new Governor apparently on the colonists' side, bickering within the Opposition resumed. Before long, many of its members opposed Wentworth more than they opposed the Governor.[3]

In late September 1846 Robert Lowe, whose quest for popular support had by now led him to abandon the squatters, moved to reduce the minimum price of Crown land, making it easier for new settlers to buy and breaking the squatters' monopoly. Wentworth argued that the lands squatters occupied would be sold from under them, but his attempt to have the issue sidelined to a committee failed by one vote when Windeyer supported Lowe. Meanwhile, Wentworth had revisited funding for the synagogue, this time proposing that £1000 be provided from the Budget estimates to top up Schedule C. He also reintroduced his Bill to prohibit local taxes being spent without the Council's permission. But he immediately ran into trouble on both fronts. Cowper, Lowe and Windeyer refused to support him on the synagogue because they had always refused to supplement any Schedule in that way. And Cowper opposed Wentworth's Bill, to repeal all local laws which allowed taxes to be spent without the Council's permission, because it was 'legislating in the dark'. While Wentworth won these Council votes, his former allies were now circling.[4]

As they distanced themselves from Wentworth they drew closer to the new Governor, whose 1847 Budget estimates sailed through the Council. Wentworth continued to assert the Council's right to 'fix the detail of every amount'. But on this occasion, he said, he had 'no intention of asserting that right'. The Governor reciprocated, making good on his promise of open government by tabling a dispatch from Secretary of State Gladstone, marked 'private and confidential', which canvassed the idea of reintroducing transportation. While Gladstone denied any 'definite plan', he set out the 'general outlines of the course' he wanted FitzRoy to consider. These included the private assignment of convicts who had 'passed through their periods of probation' and the use of other convicts in gangs, to carry out road work that was too 'irksome' for immigrants. Rounding out the dispatch's subtle ambiguity, Gladstone asked for FitzRoy's 'reflections . . . upon [an] . . . interesting subject'.[5]

Keen to resurrect the private assignment of convict shepherds, Wentworth also played a subtle game, choosing to interpret Gladstone's ambiguity to suit his own ends. Since London had already settled on a renewal of transportation, Wentworth said, 'the only choice left was a choice of evils'. The greater evil, Wentworth argued, was the aggregation of convicts in road gangs; the lesser evil was their dispersal as shepherds. But Charles Cowper interpreted Gladstone's ambiguity differently. He claimed that the renewal of transportation itself was still an 'open question' and that the wider public 'had a full right to be heard'.

Cowper, however, was not a member of Wentworth's Select Committee into Transportation. So, despite Gladstone's oblique references to respecting 'the general sense of the colonists', Wentworth made no attempt to gauge public opinion. Instead, he cross-examined witnesses to establish that the assignment system was both beneficial to rehabilitation and a ready source of convict shepherds. This evidence, which assumed that the renewal of transportation was a *fait accompli*, disturbed the wider public. On 22 October 1846 a large public protest meeting chaired by Cowper expressed its 'alarm and regret', and Cowper agreed to present a petition to the Council.[6]

Wentworth and Cowper now vied for Council support. After briefly noting that the colonists, if asked, would veto any renewal of transportation, the Select Committee's report stressed that 'transportation is no longer an open question' and emphasised the desirability of an assignment system over the 'putrescent agency' of convict gangs. Wentworth begged off a full-scale Council debate, simply moving that the report be printed to allow, he said, more time to gauge public opinion. But his real aim was to make the report the Council's last word on the subject. To achieve this he stalled tabling it, 'for reasons it was unnecessary to explain', until the last sitting day. Cowper then moved that a dissenting report also be printed so the Council's views would be fully represented in London. But Wentworth deprived Cowper of a quorum and his motion lapsed. In this way, the report supporting convict assignment was sent off to London uncluttered by opposing views.[7]

By the time the Council next met, in May 1847, Gladstone had been replaced as Secretary of State by Henry Earl Grey, who was not believed to support transportation. Wentworth worried that the boom in British railway building would make it too expensive to attract any free men to replace convict shepherds. When Windeyer claimed that 'Wentworth seemed to look on coin as the only capital of the Colony', Wentworth shot back that 'it was easy for Windeyer with his little vineyard to talk about the inevitable tendency of wages to rise but . . . one shepherd had gone from 50 pounds last year to 70 pounds this year'. His only consolation was Grey's announcement that the Legislative Council would now have control of revenue from fines and land sales in the colony, a concession he had long struggled to obtain. Wentworth's pessimism was matched by the weather, which was so cold that the Council's four-month allocation of coal for its fireplaces had been ordered two weeks early, the Clerk hoping that when it ran out early the first weeks of spring would be unseasonally warm.[8]

Wentworth had recently welcomed a fellow squatter into the family when his eighteen-year-old daughter Fanny married John Reeve, a forty-two-year-old widower whose downward-turning moustache appeared to freeze his face in a permanent grimace. Reeve owned large numbers of livestock that he grazed over almost 70,000 acres in Gippsland. Wentworth approved the match and gave Fanny four allotments of land in Melbourne as a wedding present.

Despite her husband's wealth and prominence, Sarah Wentworth was still struggling against the disapproval of the colonial elite. When Sir Charles and Lady Mary FitzRoy, herself the daughter of a Duke, invited Sarah to Government House, the gossips reminded each other that Sarah had lived in sin with Wentworth and borne two of his children out of wedlock. In early June 1847 the Chief Justice, Sir Alfred Stephen, objected to Sarah's inclusion on the Governor's guest list. As a committee-man of the Temperance Society Sir Alfred was the complete opposite of his elder brother John, who had abetted Jane New's escape almost twenty years earlier. For him, Sarah's exemplary family life was of no account. It was a common view. As *The Sydney Morning Herald* put it, 'damaged female characters . . . should be uncompromisingly shut out . . . Whenever a woman falls, she falls forever . . . She becomes as it were socially dead.'[9]

But if Sarah was at all cast down by this brutal edict, Wentworth was buoyed by the arrival of a dispatch on the 'Squatting System'. Acknowledging the strength of a system that permitted land 'to be occupied for pasturage' and sold only 'at a high minimum price', The British government now granted squatters fourteen-year leases and set a minimum land price of £1 an acre. Where a high minimum price had once been a liability for the squatters who could not afford to buy and fretted about their tenuous occupation, now, with security of tenure, it became an asset. And with the rent for their leases set at £10 per 4000 sheep, it did not take the squatters long to leverage their more secure position into a demand for extra representation in the Legislative Council. Windeyer now compared the squatters to the English aristocracy. They, too, had first received their land under burdensome conditions which grew lighter as they grew stronger, until finally they forced the legislature to remove the conditions and surrender the land. 'And so it would be with the squatters,' he forecast. Supported by Cowper and Windeyer (who would be dead by year's end), Lowe moved to condemn the £1 per acre minimum because it prevented new settlers from buying, thereby further entrenching the squatter's advantage. But when he threatened to leave the colony if this motion was not passed, Wentworth threatened to leave the Council if it was not defeated. Lowe lost the motion—and remained in Sydney.

Comparing their debating styles, one observer noted that 'a growl from Wentworth has oftentimes more weight than an exquisitely polished sentence from Mr Lowe'. The fierce rivalry between these two talented opponents produced rhetorical combat of rare intensity. Positioned to the left of the Speaker (the government appointees were on his right), Wentworth and Lowe virtually sat on top of each other during their fierce exchanges. While the chamber is still used today by the Legislative Assembly, its gaudy green-and-gold Edwardian décor dates only to 1908. In the 1840s the austere boxlike chamber was mostly light brown, which contrasted with the dark-brown Speaker's chair and wooden gallery above it. So there was nothing to distract attention from debaters, whose skills would put today's politicians to shame.[10]

Relations between Lowe and Wentworth plumbed new depths during debate on a government Bill to raise a special tax to pay for an effective police force in the squatting districts. Lowe saw this as unfair to ordinary taxpayers. Wentworth accused Lowe of wishing to reduce the squatters to 'mere hewers of wood and drawers of water', and asked why Lowe did not become a squatter instead of trying to tear them down. Lowe answered that he did not think their company was good enough for him. 'A highwayman . . . having plenty of money might . . . ask him to join him,' Lowe said, 'but his reply would be: how did you come by this money?' Wentworth no doubt flinched at Lowe's blatant reference to his father's early career, but he had the satisfaction of seeing the government's Bill become law. Although workmen in the 'back passage', as the corridor behind the Speaker's Chair was known, had won a battle against the smell of lamp gas that was overwhelming the members, nothing, it seemed, could prevent Wentworth and Lowe from trying to overwhelm each other.[11]

Encouraged by the rift between Wentworth and Lowe, Cowper revisited Wentworth's Report on Transportation, urging the Council to consider it in light of public opinion and, he hoped, reject it. Wentworth protested feebly, but the report was roundly voted down. When finally given a chance, the Council sent a strong message to London that it repudiated Wentworth's report. Having thus rejected transportation, Cowper then proposed that the colony's urgent demand for labour be met by an annual intake of 20,000 free migrants. This was to be paid for by a loan using the land fund as security, an idea Wentworth now supported because 'under the circumstances . . . nothing better could be devised'. But Cowper tied himself in knots over the issue of Coolie labour from India and the South Pacific, saying 'they might well be good shepherds, but far better would it be . . . that those of their own colour . . . should be brought into this colony'. Still, Wentworth kept his own counsel. No doubt he had received private reports from his colleague Benjamin Boyd about the difficulties of employing Pacific Island labourers. Boyd had imported 200 Melanesians to work on his whaling and pastoral ventures, offering them the lowest possible wages. But most had found the climate too cold and the conditions unappealing, and drifted to Sydney. There workers protested the Melanesians' low pay and humanitarians claimed they were quasi-slaves; most were sent home within the year.[12]

As the 1848 election approached, Wentworth was handed a good old-fashioned constitutional issue. This was Earl Grey's proposal to establish directly elected municipal corporations, local government councils that would indirectly elect a Legislative Assembly. Although Wentworth had emphatically rejected such bodies in 1844, they had been introduced in New Zealand. Unaware that that experiment had failed and the corporations been suspended as unworkable, Wentworth and Lowe addressed a massive protest meeting in January 1848. They may have been on the same side of this question, but they still vied to outdo each other in condemnation of 'municipal juntas'. So Wentworth would have been chagrined to read press reports that he had received only 'loud cheers' compared to Lowe's 'deafening cheers'.[13]

When the Council resumed in March, however, Wentworth's anger over the municipal corporations plan was offset by news that 'exiles' were to be sent to the colony. Earl Grey had adopted the report of his Select Committee on Transportation. 'Convicts holding Tickets of Leave or Conditional Pardons may be sent to Australia,' Grey said, 'if they have been previously subjected to a reformatory punishment at home.' Grey agreed with Wentworth's report that the balance of the sexes should be equal, exiles should be accompanied by their spouses and, most importantly, there should be 'an equal importation of free migrants'. Wentworth had beaten Cowper by getting his report to London months before Cowper's Council motion rejecting it was passed. And he now tested the Council with a motion supporting 'Exileism'. After all the abuse heaped upon him so recently by Cowper and others over transportation, Wentworth was delighted that there was now broad support for this measure. Perhaps the colony was waking up to the fact that it did not have enough money to fund adequate migration. He 'cared not', the *Herald* reported, 'that people who refused indignantly . . . to take prisoners under the name of convicts should accept them . . . thankfully under the name of exiles . . . The rose by any other name would smell as sweet.' Cowper did not respond and so Wentworth's motion supporting exileism passed unopposed. Perhaps the precipitous fall in the number of convicts—from over 38,305 when transportation was abolished in 1840 to fewer than 5000 by 1848—combined with an acute shortage of any other labour contributed to the result.[14]

Wentworth next tackled Earl Grey's constitutional package which proposed a bicameral legislature. The lower house would be indirectly elected by municipal corporations, and an unspecified 'central authority' would deal with inter-colonial matters. Grey's other major proposal was the creation of the new Colony of Victoria to politically accommodate the 60,000 people now living in the Port Phillip District. With the mid-year election fast approaching, Wentworth seized the initiative with an attack on the new Constitution in a written petition of complaint known as a Remonstrance. The *Herald* immediately denounced its 'air of incivility—of half-uttered, half-suppressed braggadocio, bluster and bullying'. So Lowe and Cowper promptly offered a more respectfully worded alternative. But whereas Wentworth favoured a continuation of a hybrid Council, containing a mix of appointed and elected members—which would maximise the squatters' influence—Lowe and Cowper favoured separate lower and upper houses—the British model. When their view began to prevail in the Council Wentworth and the squatters joined with the government-appointed members, who were now aware of the suspension of New Zealand's municipal corporations, to adjourn the whole mess until after the looming election.

Sidelined in the furore was Wentworth's motion to establish 'a Congress from the various Colonial Legislatures . . . with power to enact laws on inter-colonial questions', the first Council reference to an Australian Federation. This visionary proposal, a response to Grey's suggestion of a 'central authority', was pushed to the sidelines in Wentworth's pre-election skirmishing with Cowper and Lowe. Wentworth was still a hero to the squatters, but for that very reason—as he well knew—he was now dangerously exposed in his own electorate.[15]

During the 1840s Europe suffered a severe economic downturn which, in 1848, exploded in violence. Revolutions convulsed Austria-Hungary, France, the German and Italian States and Poland, even spilling across the Atlantic into Brazil. When news of these revolutions reached Sydney Governor FitzRoy thought he might also be dangerously exposed, given that the New South Wales economy was similarly depressed, so he shortened the campaigning period to six weeks. In their Sydney electorate, Wentworth and William Bland were challenged by an appointed Council member, the merchant John Lamb, who was strongly backed by Lowe and Cowper. At a meeting of his supporters, Lamb claimed that Wentworth did not give Sydney's 'commercial interests . . . the weighty consideration . . . they deserved'. Then Lowe charged that because of Wentworth's self-interest on the land question, he was 'not a proper . . . representative'. Finally, Cowper noted Wentworth's tardiness in attending committee hearings. But it was Lowe's speech that received the loudest cheers.[16]

The day before, another public meeting had taken place. It drew many of Sydney's tradesmen, small businessmen and migrants, men who were tired of the squatters' interests being put ahead of their own yet unconvinced that John Lamb was their answer. Among the meeting's leaders was Henry Parkes, a thirty-four-year-old migrant who ran a struggling toy-and-trinket business. The crowd agreed to support Robert Lowe, because he was the only man capable of getting louder cheers than Wentworth.

After two weeks of dithering over whether to nominate for Sydney or for his South Coast seat, 'coquetting between his old love and his new' as the *Herald* put it, Lowe decided on Sydney. When he, Wentworth and the other candidates had been nominated, Lowe's friend Elias Weekes said that if they voted for Wentworth they must also vote for Mr Lowe 'to take care of him . . . being the only man . . . able to grapple with that intellectual giant'. In a defiant speech interrupted by cries of 'no Coolies, no cannibals', Wentworth defended the right of every individual 'to introduce any description of labour he liked so long as he paid for it out of his own pocket'. Referring to Lowe's betrayal of Governor Gipps and his abandonment of both the squatters and his South Coast seat, Wentworth asked 'what claim had a man like this to their confidence—a man who had betrayed every constituency which had yet trusted him'. In response, Lowe explained that he had sided with the squatters when they sought 'fixity of tenure' against the Crown but now opposed them because they sought it 'against the rights of the people'. Finishing with a sharp jab, Lowe claimed he 'had been consistent in fighting for liberty—the squatters had been consistent in fighting for money'.[17]

After a show of hands gave the result to Lowe and Lamb, Wentworth demanded a formal poll, winning the election by just 156 votes. Lowe came in a strong second. Wentworth had reminded his constituents that he was the man who had given them liberty of the press, trial by jury and the constitutional right of electing their representatives. But they were more likely to remember his hostility to migrant workers and his support for transportation. It was the votes of those migrant workers that had finally delivered a Sydney seat to someone who was not aligned with the squatters. 'The glory of a new era in . . . New South Wales is ours', Parkes wrote. 'To you virtuous working men . . . our congratulations on . . . victory are especially due.' Charles Cowper was returned along with William Lawson's son in Cumberland, and James Macarthur was elected unopposed in Camden. But the most astonishing result was in Melbourne, where separatists nominated Earl Grey in a protest vote to demonstrate the uselessness of sending any elected representatives to faraway Sydney. He could be no worse, they maintained, than John Dunmore Lang, whose Port Phillip seat had been declared vacant after he went lecturing overseas for two years. When Grey was proclaimed the winner, the legal advice was that there was nothing to prevent a British peer sitting in the Council. So Melbourne had the Secretary of State himself as an absentee member for the next two years. Back in London, however, he was already planning a double-cross on transportation. Later depicted in *Vanity Fair* as a cross between a frill-necked lizard and an urbane cricket, Grey had the lightning-quick survival instincts of a reptile when he was politically warmed up.[18]

Chapter 25

A SQUATTER'S CONSTITUTION

Published in August 1849 lines by Henry Parkes' ally Charles Harpur captured what many saw as Wentworth's war against his own electorate over the renewal of transportation and the form of a new Constitution.

> A Patriot?—He who has no sense nor heed
> Of public ends beyond his own mere need
> Whose country's ruin to his public fear
> Means only this—the loss of Windermere. [1]

After the failure of his first attempt at constitutional reform the new member for Melbourne, Earl Grey, tried again, this time giving the colonists a say. In what *The Sydney Morning Herald* lyrically called 'The Golden Dispatch', Grey proposed a blended Legislative Council similar to that of New South Wales for the three colonies of Port Phillip, Van Diemen's Land and South Australia. Noting the disagreement in New South Wales over whether the

Council should remain a mixture of elected and appointed members, as Wentworth and the squatters wanted, or be split into the two chambers favoured by Lowe and most city folk, the Secretary of State left it to the colonists 'to originate and discuss any changes for themselves'.

For many in Wentworth's Sydney's electorate, the interim continuation of a blended Council gave their local member and his squatting friends a head start. His less enthusiastic constituents worried that they would be 'driven into the polling-booths like sheep into a Wentworth squatting pen'.[2]

Meanwhile, Wentworth had real cause to fear being driven into bankruptcy. 'Commercial distress consequent upon the political convulsions . . . in Europe,' said Governor FitzRoy in late May 1849, 'has . . . [devalued] wool . . . and affected . . . property of every description'. One new insolvent was the Chief Commissioner of the Insolvent (Bankruptcy) Court himself. Wentworth's income from wool again plummeted. And the depressed value of his properties, some of which he needed to sell to pay his liabilities in the failed Bank of Australia, made things worse. In desperation, Wentworth attempted his own personal lottery to dispose of some of the properties, but he was blocked by the Attorney-General. And before the failed bank's affairs were finally wound up in 1851, he had to lease out Windermere and Belltrees and retreat with his family to Vaucluse. Supporting a motion to stop local revenue being deposited in British banks, Wentworth rounded on the Bank of Australasia, which had bought into the collapsed bank. Having 'extracted its pound of flesh from the colonial proprietors while the English ones got off scot-free', he said, it was 'not entitled to one farthing of Colonial revenue'.[3]

As a teenager in England Henry Parkes had attended the Birmingham Political Union's massive public meeting in 1832, where a crowd of some 250,000 gathered to support extending the franchise to owners or lessees of land worth £10 or more. But in late 1848, when Parkes proposed a similar pro-reform union for Sydney, his newfound champion Robert Lowe declined to be involved. Parkes pressed on regardless and formed the Constitutional Association. Its paper, *The People's Advocate*, asserted that since the European revolutions 'down-trodden labourers' could no longer be locked out of 'a fair share of political power'.[4]

This revolutionary fervour in Europe unsettled Lowe. He refused to attend a meeting called to advocate unemployment relief, saying the tradesmen of Sydney 'ought [not] to put themselves in the position of paupers . . . at the expense of their equally distressed fellow colonists'. But this Wentworth-like mood quickly passed as Lowe reversed himself yet again to accommodate his Sydney supporters. On 22 January 1849 he appeared at a public meeting of the Constitutional Association, which demanded a reduction of the £20 franchise to £10. James Macarthur and William Bland sent their apologies; Wentworth did not bother to do even that. Parkes spoke before Lowe—a sign that the balance of political influence was shifting. The ghostly white, blinking, darting albino had been overtaken by a physically imposing man whose direct gaze and strong jaw were framed by a full head of dark hair. Parkes had emerged from his Hunter Street toy and trinket shop to lead where Lowe was reluctant to go. The meeting resolved to support the £10 franchise—a move that would have far-reaching effects. But for the moment it was overshadowed by what everyone saw as Earl Grey's double-cross on transportation.[5]

On 22 January 1849, the *Herald* carried a story from a source in London that an official order, issued by Earl Grey, had again listed New South Wales as a convict destination. Under pressure, Governor FitzRoy then released a dispatch from the Secretary of State that confirmed the abolitionists' worst fears. After noting that the colony had agreed to accept 'exiles' only if they were accompanied by an equal number of free migrants, Grey said he would be sending out exiles alone because it was too late in the year to finance any accompanying migrants. At a public protest meeting on 9 March, and undaunted by the small size of the crowd, Charles Cowper and Lowe furiously denounced Grey's breach of faith and jumped back on the anti-transportation bandwagon. Wentworth did not attend, though he too was angered by the Secretary of State's double-cross because it destroyed public support for his own scheme for assigned convict shepherds. One speaker slyly expressed regret that Wentworth, who had denounced many other 'flagrant breaches' by the Colonial Office, was not present to denounce this 'outrage'. When a further dispatch from Grey was released indicating that 236 convicts were on their way in the transport ship *Hashemy*, Wentworth managed to water down Cowper's proposal, which would have banned exiles completely, to one that left room for the reception of some exiles, known as parolees.[6]

It took the arrival of the *Hashemy* itself to fire the protesters, who ignored June cold and rain to swarm to Circular Quay. Thanks to the organising ability of Henry Parkes and his fellow shopkeepers, many of whom closed for the day, 8000 showed up. Arriving an hour late, Robert Lowe had to stand on top of an omnibus to be heard. After thoroughly denouncing the renewal of transportation, he could not resist a dig at the absent Wentworth. By accusing him of abandoning his principles to secure a compromise with Cowper, Lowe revealed how vulnerable he felt over his own see-sawing on transportation. Parkes only added to his discomfiture when he told the crowd that not one word had been said about his class—the working class.[7]

Wentworth delayed his response until a Council debate on 12 June. It was Charles Cowper who had backed down, he said, by not ruling out exiles entirely. But he made it clear that he 'was as unwilling to receive convicts on the terms proposed by Earl Grey as anyone'. This time it was the usually urbane and unflappable Governor who proved uncompromising. When a delegation from the protest meeting arrived at Government House to present their petition, they found that the gates were locked, that the Governor would see only six of them and that it would have to be on another day. And when the delegation finally managed to ask FitzRoy to send back the *Hashemy*'s convicts, he replied testily that it was 'obviously impossible'.

This prompted a second mass meeting on 18 June, which petitioned for Grey's removal and for responsible government in the colony. While Lowe jeered that the Waterloo veteran FitzRoy was now afraid of just 'a few people', Henry Parkes attacked the absent Wentworth, calling him 'the gentleman who misrepresents the City of Sydney'. Parkes later wrote that 'agitation against the renewal of transportation brought together a band of influential men . . . and produced . . . consternation in the minds of the old colonial magnates [Wentworth included] who . . . had ruled with a particular order of absolutism . . . which characterised old Virginian society'.[8]

One sign of the pressure now being felt by these 'magnates' was the thaw in relations between Wentworth and James Macarthur. In 1843, Wentworth had destroyed Macarthur's election campaign for Cumberland. Now he asked the new member for Camden to nominate for the Speakership. Macarthur declined, chiefly because he feared official entertaining would cost him too much.[9]

During 1849, the Attorney-General tried to reintroduce his Aboriginal Evidence Bill. At first, Wentworth pointed out in lawyerly fashion that the Bill allowed Aborigines to give only 'collateral testimony'. This meant, he said, that the evidence of 1000 Aborigines might be defeated by that of one white man. Then, as he had done so often in the past, he let his racism off the leash: 'Any idea of serving subpoenas on . . . a wild man called Chicky Chicky or Chocky Chocky,' he said, '[is] perfectly absurd.' And the Bill was defeated by one vote. Wentworth remained more enlightened on the synagogue, this time proposing funding through an amendment to the Church Act. But Charles Cowper, that leading Anglican, blocked him, arguing that Wentworth's latest proposal amounted to an Appropriation Bill which could only be introduced by the government.[10]

A few days later, Wentworth laid himself open to another Cowper attack when he presented a petition from the proprietors of Sydney College to convert it into a university. After claiming a university with 'no religion at all' would give the colony's youth a 'more perfect education', Wentworth offered to make the college's valuable three-acre block and its £3000 building available for use as a university provided the proprietors were each able to present a student for university-level tuition. And he moved for a Select Committee to investigate the idea. In a vicious response, Charles Cowper claimed that 'the motion was founded on the Petition of a number of proprietors who were anxious to get rid of an ill managed institution which had never . . . been able to keep its head above water'. Wentworth should not be on the committee, Cowper continued, because his shareholding in the college presented a conflict of interest. But then came Cowper's main point. 'Wentworth . . . would have no religion at all taught there,' he said, and without that 'there could be no education worth anything at all'. Even so, Wentworth was made chairman of the committee. It noted that while Harvard had been established just twenty years after the arrival of the Pilgrim Fathers, Sydney was still waiting for a university after nearly sixty-two years. The committee recommended that capital funding of £30,000 and a further £5000 a year be set aside to establish a liberal university whose professors would all be laymen. When Wentworth introduced his Sydney University Bill, he said:

Clergy . . . ought to be excluded altogether from . . . [its] management . . . Its gates must be open to all whether they were disciples of Moses, of Jesus, of Brahmin, of Mohammed, of Vishnu or of Buddha. From . . . [it] would arise a long line of illustrious names—of statesmen, of patriots, of philanthropists, of philosophers, of poets and of heroes.[11]

Debate on the Bill dragged on for a year. The key sticking point was the composition of the university senate. Wentworth ultimately compromised, conceding that only twelve of the sixteen senators needed to be laymen. But the prohibition against a religious test was enshrined in the Bill, which became law on 1 October 1850. The University of Sydney itself was inaugurated at a ceremony in the old Sydney College premises two years later. One of its first students, William Charles Windeyer, son of Wentworth's late friend Richard, noted that the Chancellor, dressed in a robe of black and gold, read an address 'complimenting Mr Wentworth'. The inauguration was combined with a ceremony to mark the enrolment of the first twenty-four students, including Fitzwilliam Wentworth. In the classical tradition, the roll was in Latin and young Wentworth's name was at the top. The next column across was headed *Filius*, below which were the words *Guliilmi Caroli*. This translated as 'son of William Charles'. There was however no attempt to translate Fitzwilliam.[12]

In his University Bill, Wentworth had initially named himself, Robert Lowe and William Bland, among others, as lay senators. Lowe then asked whether 'it was a good principle to exclude the clergy as a body and to admit convicts into the government of an institution like this'. Grasping that he was the target of this question, Bland called Lowe 'a coward and a scoundrel', whereupon Lowe sued Bland for inciting him to breach the peace. He implied that Bland, who had originally been transported for killing a fellow officer in a duel, was trying to goad him into demanding satisfaction. Giving evidence on Bland's behalf, Wentworth claimed Lowe was such a coward that no insult could force him to fight, and the case was dismissed. Angry and humiliated, Lowe then resigned from the Legislative Council and, abandoning Henry Parkes and his Sydney supporters, sailed for London.[13]

Parkes nominated James Wilshire, a close colleague in the Constitutional Association and former Mayor of Sydney, to fill the vacant Sydney seat. Wentworth's old political ally William Bland also nominated—and received strong criticism from Parkes for supporting transportation. Wilshire, like Parkes, supported Chartism, a British political movement that sought universal suffrage, the principle of one vote one value and a secret ballot. Though taken for granted today, these demands were widely viewed with horror in 1849. In a by-election in which only a quarter of those eligible bothered to vote, Bland trounced Wilshire 601 votes to 219. It was a rough blow for Parkes. Wilshire's zeal and voters' apathy had delivered Sydney back into the hands of Wentworth's pro-transportation party. When a debt-laden Cowper resigned his Council seat a few months later Wentworth, now almost sixty, stood supreme, having also outlasted the other stars of 1843 including Lang, Lowe and Windeyer.[14]

Wentworth's political opponents were in awe of him. Describing the 'first champion of Australian liberty', *The People's Advocate* said:

With [a] . . . heavy, loose, drab coat and . . . mass of grizzled hair . . . there is something of the commanding ruin in . . . Wentworth. In his public speaking there is an inexcusable slovenliness and disrespectful bearing which would never be tolerated . . . if he did not possess superior intellect . . . There are times which witness him rise to the stature of a giant over his compeers. Few have equal power . . . to demolish an opponent's arguments; and none can command more forcible and original language . . . The tones of his voice are discordant and grating, sometimes running into a loud, harsh, impatient and decided drawl . . . His action is inelegant and random . . . His personal appearance is tall and athletic [but] slightly stooped . . . His countenance is florid and marked by courage and determination.[15]

But Wentworth's ascendancy was to be short-lived. Bland's financial troubles forced him to resign in June 1850, not long after the Reverend John Dunmore Lang arrived back in Sydney in search of another Council seat. During their first term on the Council Lang and Wentworth had had much in common, even on the squatting question. But since standing down in 1846 and travelling widely overseas, Lang had become more radical. In a series of public lectures during April 1850, he had advocated all things American—a federation, a republic and universal male suffrage. He also attacked the squatters. Wentworth's concern about Lang's reemergence was exacerbated by the fact that Lang shared many of his own best assets: commanding height, vigorous speech, wide knowledge, sharp wit and, at times, a shambolic personal appearance. For the same reasons, Parkes successfully courted Lang to stand in the Sydney by-election.[16]

Disconcerted by Lang's reemergence, Wentworth behaved erratically when the Council resumed. Having successfully slashed the Mounted Police budget from £3300 to £1100 a year earlier, because 'no one sees a mounted policeman', Wentworth moved at the end of June 1850 that £100 be allocated for a 'Queen's Cup' to breed horses for a local 'yeoman force'. Wentworth won his motion, lending weight to Lang's campaign argument that the 'Macquarie Street Squatting Club' needed to be cleaned out by equalising the electoral districts so a vote in Sydney would have the same weight as a vote in Bathurst. Lang's opponent for the vacant Sydney seat, John Holden, was a well-known racehorse owner, a fact that helped to make Lang's case. Rather than actively campaigning for Holden, Wentworth tried to block Lang's candidacy with a Bill, based on Commons practice, that would have prohibited ministers of religion from sitting in the Council. This was scotched when Attorney-General J.H. Plunkett pointed out that bishops sat in the House of Lords. And Lang had previously sat in the Council alongside Wentworth without exciting complaint.[17]

Wentworth also banked on the success of a colonial government campaign to discredit Lang via *The Sydney Morning Herald*. It involved allegations that Lang had fraudulently promoted a scheme which promised migrants passage to Moreton Bay and a grant of land in return for a fee paid to Lang. The British government had not agreed to this plan. And Lang made things worse by misleading Governor FitzRoy into thinking that it had. In doing so, his opponents claimed, Lang had attempted to defraud the colonial government of £3500. Lang was unbowed by the allegations and continued to emphasise his promise to extend the vote. Newspaper advertisements placed by Henry Parkes argued that 'those who contend for an enlargement of our elective privileges . . . will vote for . . . Lang who in 1843, resisted . . . Wentworth's mutilation of the franchise'. And they did vote for him: Lang beat Holden by just fifty-six votes.[18]

A rumour quickly spread that the fraud allegations might be used to prevent Lang from taking his seat. And when placards appeared all over the city calling on people 'to assemble at the Legislative Council Chamber to enforce [his] admission . . . should any objection . . . be made', the Speaker called on the Superintendent of Police to ensure a strong police presence. Although the Council's front fence that faced Macquarie Street comprised metal poles with spear tips, they were set in a low wall of soft Sydney sandstone, which Wentworth and many others feared could easily be breached. It would then be just a short run up a flight of steps to the Council's front door which, if broken down, would allow Lang's supporters to swarm through a thin cedar partition onto the floor of the chamber itself. As it turned out, no objection was taken to Lang's admission. Whether anyone was deterred from doing so by the threat of violence is unknown. Whatever the case Wentworth, who did not lack physical courage, was now obsessed by what he saw as the threat posed to the established order by mob violence.[19]

Now back in the Council, Lang immediately took the offensive, moving for a select committee to investigate the Moreton Bay affair. Responding to Wentworth's allegation that 'filthy lucre was at the bottom of [it] all', Lang reminded the House of a certain attempt to defraud the Maori people of New Zealand's largest island. Even so, Lang's bid for a committee was trumped by Wentworth, who succeeded with a motion that found Lang guilty of fraud. Outside the House, however, Lang remained a force. Ignoring the evidence, Parkes stirred up a crowd of 3000, claiming that Wentworth had persecuted Lang on behalf of 'convicts, Coolies and Chinamen'. Lang did not go to jail for the fraud, but he did later end up behind bars for defaming one of his Council colleagues who had supported Wentworth's fraud motion.[20]

Meanwhile, Wentworth had returned to his old populist standbys with a series of motions demanding responsible government and complete local control over colonial land, patronage and revenue. But when the debate was called on, it was clear that Wentworth had been rattled by Parkes' protest meeting in support of Lang. Having moved his responsible government motion Wentworth almost immediately withdrew it, saying it was not safe to proceed because, 'If the feelings that existed now were carried out, Sydney would be like Paris under the government of the people altogether.' The result was a fiasco, and on his final motion for the day he was counted out. Just how badly he had been shaken became clear in mid-September, when he opposed a move to reduce funding for local troops. 'He was afraid,' reported the [Herald], 'of those socialist and chartist principles which Lang . . . advocated to the mob at his beck and call.' Claiming that this mob 'had become ripe for . . . any outrage', Wentworth demanded that British troops stay in the colony until there was a 'national guard' to replace them.[21]

Back in London, Earl Grey refused to revoke his order listing New South Wales as a convict destination. His stubbornness soon triggered another Council motion to abolish transportation and a counter-motion to resume it, thereby setting the scene for one final showdown. Moderates, including the former Council member Charles Cowper, now combined with the likes of Parkes to re-energise public opinion. At a huge open-air meeting, a noisy crowd of 10,000 agreed to form an anti-transportation association. At the same time, James Macarthur flitted back and forth between the Council's factions trying to find a compromise. Wentworth, however, remained a defiant supporter of the exile-transportation idea. 'He was elected without any pledge,' reported the *Herald*, 'and had a right to exercise his own judgment even if his constituents differed from him.' In the end, Wentworth's heavily outnumbered pro-transportation faction simply walked out of the chamber, leaving the vote to their opponents. Despite Wentworth's posturing, transportation to New South Wales finally ended with a whimper—not a bang.[22]

Almost two years after Grey first foreshadowed it in his 'Golden Dispatch', the British government finally introduced a Bill for the 'better Government of the Australian Colonies'. Part of the government's plan was to promote FitzRoy to be Governor-General of all the colonies, whose vice-regal representatives were to accept his decisions in matters affecting more than one colony. Complementing this was the government's proposal that the colonies each have a single-chamber legislature and a £20 franchise, as New South Wales did. Many members of the Commons objected, arguing that if a single chamber dominated by squatters was given responsibility for remodelling itself, it would produce a squatters' constitution. However, the proposal for a single chamber was approved by a large majority.[23]

But the Lords were restless. Earl Fitzwilliam (the son of Wentworth's mentor, who had died in 1833) sniffily conceded that 'there were not the materials for a hereditary peerage' in New South Wales. Even so, he looked upon the single-chamber idea 'with great jealousy and alarm'. Other Lords noted that Robert Lowe, now back in England, had claimed there was strong colonial support for bicameral legislatures. In this climate, a petition to halve the franchise to £10, generated by Parkes' protest meeting of January 1849, demanded attention. And when a Lords amendment to create a bicameral legislature in each colony was lost by only two votes, the Secretary of State realised that he would have to give ground. So when a further amendment to halve the franchise was proposed, Grey accepted it.[24]

While this was a great victory for Parkes, Lang was in no doubt that the squatters had won overall. Their 'mock Legislature' would now fix the rules governing the next election, he said, and might yet agree to resume transportation. The next Constitution, too, was likely to be written by and for the squatters.[25]

P216

BICAMERAL

is

WITH TWO CHAMBERS

P219

OLIGARCH = GOVERNMENT

Chapter 26

WENTWORTH DEMANDS
SELF-GOVERNMENT

When the Legislative Council next met, in late March 1851, the item at the top of its agenda was consideration of the Australian Colonies Government Act, which set out how far Britain was prepared to let the colonies govern themselves. The struggle for self-government had always brought out the best in Wentworth, giving him a real chance of uniting the colony's factions. But his opportunity to lead the way now was overshadowed by the related proposal to create the new colony of Victoria out of southern New South Wales. This required a redrawing of electoral boundaries to take into account the older colony's reduced population, which was expected to fall from 265,000 to 187,000. The number of members in the Council as a whole would also change, though one-third still had to be government appointees. This was bound to be divisive. When Colonial Secretary Edward Deas Thomson introduced his Bill for an enlarged Council of forty-eight, including fourteen members from the counties, ten from the towns and eight from the squatting districts along with sixteen Crown nominees, the extent of the squatters' victory became clear. Sydney, with a population of 45,000, would return three members, while the county of Stanley, with 1500 people, was entitled to one, as were each of the squatting districts, which had even fewer people.[1]

The make-up of this enlarged Council, Wentworth said, would be a 'great improvement'. To the charge that he was an oligarch he replied that 'of the two extremes, oligarchy was better than socialism', a term brought into currency by the Revolutions of 1848. Wentworth was preoccupied by the ease with which Sydney's 'socialists' managed to convene 'hooting and yelling' meetings of 5000 whose deputations then demanded that the Governor give instantaneous replies to complex questions. And he freely admitted that over the preceding twelve months, these Sydney meetings had turned him against widening the franchise. Such a city was 'hardly worthy of representation at all', he said. 'The constant system of intimidation . . . render[s] the removal of the scat of government from these popular influences absolutely necessary.'[2]

John Dunmore Lang's response to Wentworth's blustering was popular with their mutual Sydney constituents. 'The Electoral Act avoid[s] the simple and plain test of population,' Lang said. Its main object was 'to bolster . . . the squatting interest'. But in a Council dominated by the squatters, Lang was ahead of his time. His amendment to increase Sydney's representation from three members to six was crushed. Ironically, because the British Parliament had already reduced the colony's voting qualification to £10, Wentworth's best chance of being re-elected in Sydney was actually to support Lang's amendment. Instead, he put the squatters first.[3]

If the colony's factions were at each other's throats over the Electoral Act, the Australian Colonies Government Act allowed them to collectively redirect their anger at Britain. Self-government in local matters seemed as far off as ever. London would still control territorial revenue. It would still dispense colonial patronage. It would still have a right of veto over colonial legislation. And worst of all, it had increased the sums that would be automatically diverted from colonial taxes to pay senior public servants. This time, Wentworth did unite the factions in protest. So great was his anger that he toyed with the idea of obstructing every measure in the Act. But as this might have triggered a revision of the new electoral package—to the squatters' disadvantage—he settled for a formal protest instead. Lang, for one, was suspicious of his motives. Noting that Wentworth and Earl Grey had disagreed on everything else, Lang said they both agreed 'in disliking the clause which reduced the existing franchise to ten pounds'. They were both oligarchs, 'and both prepared to cant'.[4]

However mixed Wentworth's motives might have been, on 8 April he established a committee to formalise his objections in a Declaration and Remonstrance against the Australian Colonies Government Act. What emerged above Wentworth's signature exactly three weeks later was a document as close as Australia ever got to a Declaration of Independence, the Report from the Select Committee on the New Constitution. It was produced as a basis for negotiation with Britain rather than to unilaterally sever ties with her. But it did set in train a process leading to Australia's political separation from Britain in local matters. It was a high point of Wentworth's public life, and for once he expressed himself with elegant simplicity:

We feel it to be a duty which we owe to ourselves, to our constituents and to posterity . . . to record our deep disappointment and dissatisfaction at the [new] Constitution . . . [in which] our reasonable expectations have been utterly frustrated . . . We hereby solemnly protest, insist and declare:

That the Imperial Parliament has not, nor of right ought to have any power to tax the people of this Colony . . .

That the revenue arising from public lands derived . . . by the labour and capital of the people of this Colony is . . . their property . . .

That . . . all Departments should be subject to the direct control . . . of the Colonial Legislature which should [appropriate] . . . the revenues of the colony . . .

That the whole patronage of the Colony should be vested in the Governor and the Executive Council unfettered by instructions from the Minister for the Colonies.

That plenary powers of legislation should be conferred upon and exercised by the Colonial Legislature . . . [and] no Bills should be reserved for [London] unless they affect . . . the Empire.

Solemnly protesting against these wrongs and declaring and insisting upon these our undoubted rights, we leave the redress of the one and the assertion of the other to the people whom we represent and the Legislature which shall follow us.[5]

Many years later, after one of the greatest careers in Australian public life, Henry Parkes put Wentworth's achievement in proper context:

Wentworth [denounced] the new party of reformers as . . . Communists [and] up-rooters of law and order . . . I was myself . . . denounced . . . as the 'arch-anarchist' . . . But to . . . Wentworth belongs the great merit of forcing public attention to the 'wrongs' of the colony, and with unwearied labours urging their 'redress' . . . His Declaration and Remonstrance is so important as one of the foundation-stones of the fabric of our constitutional liberties.[6]

The Council adopted Wentworth's Declaration and Remonstrance on 1 May, its last full sitting day before the 1851 election due in mid-September. Two weeks later, news broke that Edward Hargreaves had discovered a 'vast goldfield' near Bathurst. Having complained back in 1849 that assisted British migrants used Sydney merely as a staging post to California's goldfields, Wentworth immediately grasped the political significance of Hargreaves' find. Expecting a flood of gold diggers to return from California, Wentworth executed a rare about-face. 'A new and unexpected era . . . has . . . dawned . . . which must in a very few years precipitate us from a colony into a nation', he wrote. 'I shall in future . . . oppose the revival of transportation . . . and shall insist upon its immediate abolition in the whole of the [Australian] colonies.' Lang, fearing Wentworth might gain local campaign momentum from this reversal, accused him of conspiring with the Colonial Secretary to draft an Electoral Act that 'robbed men of their political rights'. Lang's accusation appeared in the press on 15 September, Sydney's nomination day, ensuring that Wentworth's opposition to giving the city more elected Council members was uppermost in the minds of those who swarmed into Macquarie Place to hear the candidates.[7]

Wentworth was the first to speak. After outlining the charges made against him—that he was a selfish squatter who had opposed the reduction in the franchise, voted against proper representation for Sydney and had until recently been in favour of transportation—Wentworth confronted Lang's supporters. 'If there [is] anything to add to this catalogue,' he bellowed, '[I] should be thankful to be reminded of it by any of [my] noisy and factious friends in front.' But for the squatters, Wentworth said, Sydney 'would have shrunk to a small fishing town'. And while he might have executed an about-face on transportation, Wentworth would not back down from his support for limiting the right to vote. 'Wherever the principle of universal suffrage has prevailed,' he argued, referring particularly to France, 'it has been the signal for rapine, massacre and bloodshed.' As for England's £10 franchise, there was a 'vast difference' between a £10 household there and a £10 household in Sydney. Lang took precisely the opposite view. For him, universal suffrage was 'first on the list of those great principles of progress'. He referred to Wentworth's claim that, under France's universal suffrage, 'property is theft' had become the national motto. 'It [is] a very old trick,' Lang said, 'to set the cry of "stop thief" by the thief himself.'[8]

The other candidates for Sydney were Charles Cowper, John Lamb and a little-known Catholic, Alexander Longmore. At 10 a.m., 11 a.m. and noon on polling day, Wentworth led the count. Lang was trailing, and some said his voters must be away digging for gold. But as the afternoon wore on, with his supporters badgering people to vote, Lang moved steadily up the list. When the final count was made he had won, with 1197 votes. Lamb was next, followed by Wentworth, with 998, Longmore and Cowper. Wentworth had just scraped into Sydney's third seat. Cowper was later returned as the member for Durham in the Hunter region. The number of immigrants to the colonies, which had fallen below 1000 in 1845, had surged to over 30,000 in 1848 and remained high thereafter. No doubt Sydney's share of this increase had contributed to Lang's majority.[9]

Speaking at the declaration of the poll, Wentworth regretted that 'there [is] a spirit of democracy abroad, which . . . [will] result in much mischief'. Even so, his election campaign had been an astonishing performance. The historian H.M. Green later noted how Wentworth 'could control men who hated him; how he could compel them to listen while he told them what he thought of them and in the end bend many of them to his purpose'.[10]

By the time the new Council met on 14 October 1851, Lang had resigned his hard-won seat owing to financial difficulties. And with a chastened Cowper now preoccupied with his investments in railways, Parkes noted that 'Wentworth is Master of the House'—a House that was now empowered to prepare a Constitution, subject to London's limitations on self-government. But though Wentworth was again the unchallenged leader of a chamber still dominated by squatters, he remained unnerved by the 'vociferous mob outside'. The sound of their rowdy demonstrations carried through the chamber's walls, prompting a motion demanding police action, which Wentworth supported. Such mobs only hardened Wentworth against democracy. But he swiftly re-established the committee that had produced his Remonstrance, demanding local control of patronage, revenues and taxation. When a colony supported itself, he said, 'it ought to be self-governing'. In an aggressive new move, he also demanded that Earl Grey be impeached for failing to act on earlier demands for self-government.

Despite the appointed members' opposition, his demand for complete self-government in local matters was endorsed by a large majority on 5 December. In many ways, it was a restatement of the Declaration and Remonstrance. But it also contained two seemingly contradictory demands for the Canadian system, one referring to government 'on the same terms as Canada'; the other to 'the establishment of a Constitution among us similar in its outline to that of Canada'. In return, the colony's taxpayers would assume the cost of their own government. The precise form of the Canadian pledge, another version of which had been unsuccessfully floated five years earlier, was to cause immense controversy when Wentworth's Constitution Bill was debated two years later.[11]

Having adjourned on 23 December, the House did not sit again until June 1852. By then the 'malignant star', as Wentworth called Earl Grey, had been replaced by Sir John Pakington, whose big ears and bushy sideburns made him resemble a monkey. Wentworth hoped the new Secretary of State would avoid Grey's 'systematic opposition' to the colony's wishes. But in case he should fail in this regard, Wentworth gave notice that the Governor's Budget estimates might not be considered until the Council's motion on complete self-government was answered. Supply might be blocked to force self-government. Wentworth continued this pressure by moving for a select committee to prepare a Constitution for the colony. So frenetic did Wentworth's activity become that the Clerk had to remind him to give adequate warning of the Committee's sitting days 'to avoid the considerable inconvenience of more than two Committees sitting at the same time'. The committee was to comprise 'the representatives of the people', as Wentworth called his squatting friends—although when a vote was forced, others including Charles Cowper and the Colonial Secretary were added. Fearing that members elected by the ever-growing number of city dwellers would dominate any Lower House, Wentworth stressed the need for an Upper House to act as a check and balance. In this, 'They [have] nothing to guide them,' he said, 'because they neither [have] the aristocracy of Great Britain nor the federative principle of America.' The committee's report, issued three months later, annexed Bills that proposed a solution. A Legislative Assembly was to be elected by men with leasehold estates worth as little as £10, which in the colony's booming gold economy meant that most men would be eligible to vote. But to balance this there was to be a Legislative Council of appointees, two-thirds of them chosen for life from men who had been elected to any previous Council—a leg-up for the squatters.[12]

When Wentworth's Constitution Bills came up for debate in December, he freely acknowledged his committee's internal disagreements. Some favoured a nominated Council, others an elected one. Some wanted one House; others, two. Still others wanted to keep a mixed House. Given these divisions, he feared that pursuing the Bills now would allow the Colonial Secretary to push through his proposal for a Council 'nominated by the Executive'. This, he said, would satisfy no one. It would be 'unjust' to those supporting a directly elected Upper House and equally unjust to those who, like himself, favoured one that was elected indirectly. So the Bills were adjourned to 1853.[13]

Wentworth's Constitution committee might have been disunited over the make-up of a new Parliament. But it had remained rock solid in its demands for self-government. And throughout 1852, Wentworth had continued his relentless push for complete legislative independence in local matters. Though there was a new man at the Colonial Office, his predecessor's dispatches continued arriving for some time, delayed by the long sea voyage. In one of these, Earl Grey rejected the Council's Declaration and Remonstrance because he doubted that it 'proceeded from a body accurately expressing the feelings of the community'. This was a severe blow to Wentworth. He counter-punched by moving to place a time limit on a Customs Bill to disrupt the government's income flow. 'If they [are] not prepared to do what . . . America [has] done, if they [are] not prepared even to levy war against the Queen,' Wentworth said, 'they had better retreat at once and . . . submit to be the laughing stock of Europe.' But this was too much, even for some of his squatting friends. Despite James Macarthur's support, Wentworth's proposal was roundly defeated. In a watered-down protest on 10 August Wentworth made pointed reference to British meddling which, he said, had led to the United States' Declaration of Independence and America's 'dismemberment from the British Empire'.[14]

Still under pressure to do something tangible Wentworth now moved that, rather than blocking supply completely, members should delay consideration of the 1853 Budget estimates by asking the Governor to prorogue the Council until 1 December. By then, he hoped, the attitude of the new Secretary of State would be clear. Failing that proposal, Wentworth warned, '50 times a night the House [will] be divided on every paltry sum'. *The Sydney Morning Herald* called this an attempted *coup d'état*. Although Wentworth had Charles Cowper's support this time, James Macarthur worried about 'the serious . . . consequences involved' and the motion was defeated.

Sensitive to Macarthur's criticism, Wentworth said he had thought hard before moving to block supply. But if it was necessary 'to upheave society to its centre to obtain those liberties without which they [cannot] live as Englishmen', he said, the goal was worth the risk. What particularly irritated him was the news that New Zealand, a colony of only 37,000 people, was obtaining constitutional concessions that were still being withheld from a colony containing 200,000. So he moved that before dealing with the 1853 estimates, the Council should decline to consider any future estimates until it received a favourable reply to its demand for self-government. This time the motion was carried, by twenty-four votes to twenty-three. Governor FitzRoy wrote to London that Wentworth had convinced the Council 'to pledge itself to refuse to vote the Supplies for . . . 1854' until London assented to self-government, and stressed 'the great . . . desire of . . . all classes . . . that this concession . . . be granted'.[15]

As Wentworth waited for Pakington's reply and mulled over options for a new Constitution, the gold rush was turning the colony upside-down. On 13 May 1851 a prospector had found a thirteen-ounce lump of gold near one of Wentworth's properties, later known as Lucknow, west of Bathurst. It was the colony's second major gold discovery, and within two weeks there were 1000 people digging 'upon a surface not more than a mile in extent', discovering nuggets weighing up to four pounds. On 3 June 1851, Bathurst's police inspector reported that 'a thousand pounds worth of gold was brought in here yesterday'. At first, Wentworth demanded royalties from the prospectors who were digging up his property but, finding them difficult to collect, he sold his land in April 1852 to Australia's first gold-mining company, the Wentworth Gold Field Company. It was a joint stock company with a paid-up capital of

£5000 and 3000 issued shares at £10 each; Wentworth was one of the directors. London's papers were soon carrying stories about the company's 'golden lode, found to contain 9.37 per cent of fine gold equivalent to 12,000 pounds per ton'. This find augmented Wentworth's already improved finances. In January 1851 he had £76,380 worth of assets, £33,440 worth of liabilities and an annual rental income of £4614 from properties all over the colony.[16]

The government, too, struggled to collect anything from the gold miners. Wentworth explored this shared problem when he examined the Chief Commissioner of the Gold Fields in evidence before a select committee. This hearing took place in the old chamber, which now doubled as a library and committee room. Located right next door to the new chamber, it looked out over Macquarie Street. And after its blinds had been removed 'to give some light', the spectacle of Wentworth's questioning must have amused those passing by on the verandah outside.

—Have you ever heard of men giving signals to each other by a whistle when the Commissioner has been going up the creeks?
—I have very often heard it myself, and have also very often seen people run away.
—Is the object of the whistle to bring the people to the Commissioner to pay their Licence?
—No, to run away, I have often caught them myself.
—As a matter of fact I suppose these people do not all willingly pay the Licence, they avoid it if they can?
—I do not suppose anybody would willingly pay anything to anybody.[17]

Wentworth also examined his police inspector brother D'Arcy, who advocated a passport system with checkpoints at Penrith and Hartley to stop servants running off to the diggings. For

Wentworth, revenues and runaways were linked issues. With more and more servants deserting for the goldfields, his Select Committee on Immigration recommended that new migrants indenture themselves for at least two years to repay some of the cost of their voyage out. He also recommended that the public funding for such voyages be increased by £50,000 pounds, no doubt hoping this would be offset by gold revenue, which he insisted should be controlled by the Council. But this demand crossed with a dispatch in which the Secretary of State made this very concession. By year's end, the Committee on Gold Fields Management could state that no one could mine gold, 'being the undoubted property of the Colony . . . without securing to the public revenue its legitimate share'.[18]

Just what this legitimate share was had been explored by Colonial Secretary Deas Thomson, who asked a committee witness whether in addition to a licence fee a duty might be charged on the export of gold. When the witness replied that 'this would give the mob orators an opportunity of holding forth about it', Wentworth interrupted:

—Are there many of these democratic haranguers at the diggings?
—No.
—Are not the diggers better employed than in going to hear what these ragamuffins say?
—The bulk of them go more for the fun than for anything else . . .
—Do you think men getting an ounce of gold a week would go from their holes to listen to these orators?
—They might for a rest . . .[19]

Wentworth's search for revenue extended to foreigners who, he said, should be charged a double licence fee if they set foot in New

South Wales. 'The use of the bowie knife and revolver [is] greater,' he said, 'because . . . [of the] influx of Californians . . . who neither improve our breed or our morals.' His proposal, accepted by the Council, was that all persons suspected to be aliens should be treated as such until they proved otherwise. But he was happy to import Indian Coolies, an idea also supported by the Council, because 'unlike the Chinese, these people [are] not anxious to escape from low wages'.[20]

Sir John Pakington's concession on the gold revenue had been a sign of things to come. And Wentworth's motion to block supply unless self-government was granted was the high-water mark of his and the colony's formal constitutional defiance. Thereafter, as London granted one concession after another, Wentworth shifted his focus to a rearguard action for a Constitution that would keep gold prospectors, immigrant mechanics, city dwellers, aliens, ragamuffins, democratic haranguers and just about anyone else but squatters at bay. As part of his squatters' defence strategy, Wentworth soon came to advocate a colonial aristocracy. These Botany Bay barons, his opponents joked, would be chosen from those who possessed the large noses and receding foreheads of their British counterparts. But Wentworth could not have looked more different. His colleagues spoke of:

A massive form . . . a slouching gait . . . a rough plebian appearance, of old clothes dragged on anyhow and of his . . . fumbling with his spectacles when he was called upon to speak. And then when he had struggled to his feet, his voice . . . harsh, his eloquence . . . rocky . . . he would rise suddenly into a broken sublimity of language and then growl and stutter again and defy the powers that were and clench his fist and appeal to the names of the great dead and close a lengthened effort of oratory with much ordinary claptrap.[21]

Wentworth more resembled the rough and roguish founders of the English and Irish aristocracies—William the Conquerer and Oliver Cromwell. And he had the same motive as they did: ensuring that he and his supporters had a controlling share of political power.

Chapter 27

THE DUKE OF VAUCLUSE

'Everything you have asked for has been granted.' With these words, the Governor announced to the reconvened Council on 10 May 1853 that the Secretary of State, Sir John Pakington, had at last agreed to the colony's demands for self-government.[1]

If Wentworth celebrated this culmination of his life's work he did so without his dependent family, who had sailed for London aboard the *Carnatic* on 28 February. Sarah, Fitzwilliam and the six younger Wentworth children had left indefinitely. With Willie already in England only Wentworth's married daughters, Thomasine Fisher and Fanny Reeve, remained behind. Wentworth appears to have been the driving force behind this momentous move, whose main purpose was furthering his children's education. Although Fitzwilliam had matriculated to Sydney University and paid £6 and 6s. for lecture fees, he did not end up going there, its founder preferring that his second son be sent to Cambridge, which offered a wider range of courses.

However, Wentworth remained interested in Sydney University.

Between 1851 and the end of 1853, he attended forty of the Senate's fifty-five meetings compared to James Macarthur's fifteen. His average fell in the last year only because of pressing Council business. Still, he was determined that Fitzwilliam go to Cambridge. Because he was seen as sickly Sarah wanted to go too, a move that would also allow her to keep an eye on Willie, who had been almost a decade in England and suffered from eye and ear trouble. For the couple's younger daughters, the move would afford a chance to learn foreign languages while moving away from the occasional, but still unpleasant, sting of social prejudice in Sydney. James Macarthur, who had finally dined at Vaucluse House in September 1852, found that 'the family are very quiet and nice looking . . . [Sarah being] . . . much more the Lady in manner and appearance than many who give themselves great airs of exclusiveness'. It was the Wentworth girls' own brother-in-law, Thomas Fisher, who remained the most prejudiced against them.[2]

When his family left Wentworth moved out of Vaucluse House, which was stripped of its furniture and advertised for lease. At first he rented a town house on Church Hill, and for a time continued with politics as usual.

At the end of 1852 Henry Parkes, the workers' champion, had been defeated in a by-election for a Sydney seat. Campaigning as an 'uncompromising radical', Parkes was trounced by a former mayor of Sydney, William Thurlow, and by voter apathy. He was devastated, but Wentworth had no doubt that his most formidable opponent's setback was only temporary.[3]

At about the same time, Sir John Pakington was succeeded as Secretary of State by the Duke of Newcastle, who was even more positively disposed towards the colony's demand for self-government than his predecessor, noting that 'the Legislative Council . . . favoured a constitution similar in its outlines to that of Canada . . . with an Elective Assembly and a Legislative Council to be nominated by the Crown'. On 20 May the following year, Wentworth re-established his select committee to draft a Constitution. The committee, he said, would perform a duty similar to its predecessor, which had disagreed only on the Upper House. The make-up of that chamber should therefore remain 'an open question'. But there was one more thing: the construction of a new Electoral Act, which he would 'do all in his power' to make conservative. Those elected to the committee included Colonial Secretary Deas Thomson, James Macarthur, Charles Cowper and James Martin (destined to be the only person ever to be Prime Minister and Chief Justice of New South Wales).[4]

Still smarting from his election failure, Henry Parkes wrote of the lack of public interest in the Constitution. 'It would be difficult to find a people on the face of the earth more intently occupied with . . . their private affairs.' Their elected representatives were no better, he noted: Wentworth and the Colonial Secretary were the only regular attendees at the select committee's meetings. Indeed, one member went so far as to say that despite all the talk of the Canadian Constitution, 'he doubted whether the House knew at the time what the constitution of Canada was'.[5] Although the Parliamentary library was by now located in the very next room to the Council chamber and, since 1846, the librarian had made a special point of collecting legislation affecting other colonies, 'particularly the Canadas', it seems that few members were interested in it.[5]

The public still had gold fever, and Wentworth somehow found time to chair a select committee on the Gold Fields Management Bill as well. One issue that arose there was whether Edward Hargreaves had been the first man to find gold 'in remunerating quantities', a discovery for which the Colonial Secretary had offered a £5000 reward. John Lister and James Tom both claimed the money was theirs. They conceded that Hargreaves had shown them 'the Californian method of obtaining gold by cradles' and that while in their company he had found some 'minute particles of gold'. But it was only later, they said, when they returned to the same spot without Hargreaves that they uncovered the sought-after 'remunerating quantities'. Lister was examined. Hargreaves was examined. And then the Colonial Secretary was examined—by Wentworth:

—What conclusions were drawn . . . when Mr Hargreaves . . . reported his discovery to the Government?

—He . . . produced . . . a few very minute specks . . . which were . . . not . . . indicative of a productive gold field . . . Then Mr Hargreaves proceeded to Bathurst . . . [and] transmitted to me . . . certain further specimens . . . that had been found since his last visit . . . [including] a small nugget.

—Did Mr Hargreaves apprise you that Messrs Tom and Lister had discovered the specimens?

—On the contrary, I understood that he claimed to be the discoverer himself, but he said he was working in conjunction with them.

In the end, the committee recommended that Hargreaves be given his £5000 but that Tom and Lister also be paid £1000 each. The committee further recommended that the miners' licensing system be continued to maintain supervision over 'bad characters', advice that reflected Wentworth's fears for public order.[6]

The day after Wentworth examined the Colonial Secretary, 28 July 1853, the Constitution committee's report was tabled, signed by Wentworth, with draft legislation annexed. Its main proposal was to manufacture a colonial aristocracy by bestowing hereditary titles on a small number of local worthies. This elite would elect Council members from among themselves. Wentworth adroitly distinguished this arrangement from the one already in existence in Canada. There, hereditary titles carried with them a hereditary right to sit in the Upper House, similar to the House of Lords in London. By adopting his proposal, Wentworth argued, the Council would redeem its pledge for a Constitution 'similar in its outline to that of Canada' but one that also contained an elective element.

What Wentworth did not say was that under the Canadian system Upper House members needed only to be 'discreet and proper' British subjects in order to be appointed for life, and the hereditary peerage provisions had never been acted on. The Scottish and Irish peers, who elected from among their number representatives who sat in the House of Lords, might have provided Wentworth with a better precedent. But knowing any peerage proposal would be met with scepticism by the Council, he thought his best chance to win over its members was to persuade them that in vowing to base the new Constitution on Canada's, they had implicitly promised a hereditary peerage as well. Another precedent, the election of Earl Grey to the Council in 1848, had been an act of protest, not an act of endorsement for either the peer or the peerage. The only prominent supporter of a local peerage was Supreme Court Justice John Dickinson, who had publicly proposed an Upper House of elected hereditary peers the previous year. But although Wentworth's plan was remarkably similar to the Judge's, he did not acknowledge Dickinson in his report. By contrast, in *Freedom and Independence for the Golden Lands of Australia*, published in London in 1852, John Dunmore Lang was happy to associate the plan with Dickinson. Any Cabinet minister who adopted it, he argued, 'would richly deserve impeachment'.[7]

Wentworth's report also proposed, 'as one of the more prominent legislative measures required', a General Assembly of the Australian Colonies to legislate on questions that transcended colonial borders, such as tariffs, railways, lighthouses, penal settlements, gold and postage. The Assembly would be overseen by a 'general Court of Appeal from the Courts of such Colonies'. Crude as it was, this was the first outline of the future Commonwealth of Australia to appear in an official report of a colonial legislature. FitzRoy had raised the issue of intercolonial relations seven years earlier, in a dispatch to

Gladstone pointing out that tariff barriers between colonies could destroy the Empire's free-trade policy. In response to Earl Grey's hint a year later that a 'central authority' ought to deal with such things, Wentworth had been the first to suggest 'a Congress from the various Colonial Legislatures . . . with power to enact laws on inter-colonial questions'. This visionary idea, as we have seen, fell victim to Wentworth's pre-election skirmishing with Cowper and Lowe in 1848. But Grey had it examined by the Privy Council's trade committee, which proposed a federal legislature—comprising a Governor-General and a single House of Delegates and elected by the colonial legislatures—to standardise intercolonial tariffs. The House of Lords rejected the idea and it went no further. Instead, Grey appointed FitzRoy as Governor-General of the Australian Colonies. The Lieutenant-Governors of individual colonies reported to him, in theory at any rate, to promote the common welfare.[8]

The most radical idea on federation had come from John Dunmore Lang, who in his 1852 book had proposed a Senate and House of Representatives for an independent Australia. Having met US President Martin Van Buren at the White House in 1840, Lang argued for an Australian President and Vice-President with much the same powers as their American counterparts. Wentworth described Lang's attempts to 'cut the painter' with Britain as 'absurd', but he saw some form of federation as essential. Pushing his plan for a General Assembly, he said, 'The establishment of such a body has become indispensable and ought no longer [to] be delayed.'

Wentworth's time on the Gold Fields Management committee had shown him what disharmony among colonial laws could cost: the committee, he fumed in his report, had been forced to recommend lowering the gold diggers' licence fee by the 'sudden and unexpected' reduction in the Victorian fee. Arguing that no single colony should be entitled to legislate on 'a great inter-colonial question like this', Wentworth wrote that 'such legislation should be entrusted only to a General Assembly' of all the colonies. But while he expressed hope that the Secretary of State would soon introduce a Bill 'for this express object', Wentworth declined to have his Constitution committee draft such a Bill for fear of igniting intercolonial rivalry and thus potentially delaying self-government for New South Wales. Victoria's Constitution committee, he knew, was diffident about the idea.[9]

Having denied any 'wish to sow the seeds of a future democracy', the Constitution committee's report appeared to do just that. The right to vote would be extended to all men who earned a salary of £100 a year or more or paid £40 a year for board and lodging or £10 for lodging only. As so often with Wentworth, the devil was in the detail. Additional elected members of Council, who would largely replace the government's nominee members, would be distributed among existing electoral districts. Any changes to these districts would require a majority of votes in the Council and a two-thirds majority in the Assembly; any changes to the Constitution Act itself would require a two-thirds majority in both chambers. These rules would carry over the squatters' domination of the Council into the new Assembly; the creation of colonial aristocrats would entrench that power in the new Upper House.[10]

Wentworth's opponents responded immediately, with a reinvigorated Henry Parkes at their helm. His newspaper *The Empire* burst into action, canvassing tests for choosing Wentworth's noblemen. Suggested criteria included being 'drunk as a lord' and 'rich as a lord'. With support from Charles Cowper and John Darvall, both Council members, as well as from the radical lawyer Daniel Deniehy, Parkes organised a protest meeting on 15 August 1853 at the Victoria Theatre in Pitt Street. Addressing almost 2000 people, who packed the massive theatre's boxes pit and gallery, Parkes, using Wentworth's own phrase from long ago, denounced the Council as a 'mongrel body'. Deniehy, who stood 5 ft. 2 in. tall and had the energy of a man twice his size, ridiculed what he branded

Wentworth's 'bunyip aristocracy'. Turning the theatre itself into a giant political prop, Deniehy conjured up a parade of its members:

> Let them walk across the stage in all the pomp and circumstance of hereditary titles. First then in the procession stalks the hoary Wentworth. But [I cannot] imagine that to such a head . . . [a garland of] strawberry leaves would add any honour. Next came the native aristocrat Mr James Macarthur . . . [I] would call him the Earl of Camden, and . . . [suggest] for his coat of arms . . . a rum keg.

With his audience convulsed by laughter, Deniehy declared that the British and Irish aristocracy was founded on the swords of William the Conqueror and Oliver Cromwell. 'But . . . how [have] Wentworth and his clique . . . conquered the inhabitants of New South Wales,' he asked, 'except in the artful dodgery of doctoring up a Franchise Bill?' A likeness of Oliver Cromwell hangs above the breakfast-room door at Vaucluse House, but there is no evidence that Wentworth ever saw himself as a Lord Protector.[11]

Maintaining the pressure, the very next day John Darvall tabled in the Council a petition protesting Wentworth's Constitution Bill, signed by 2630 people. Wentworth exploded in fury, hotly denying that his ideas for the Constitution had anything to do with his private ambition. Identifying the requirement for two-thirds majorities, the electoral districts and the colonial aristocracy as the disputed issues, he defended each in turn. As quick with American precedents as Lang when it suited him, Wentworth argued that Article Five of the US Constitution provided for amendments to be ratified by conventions of three-quarters of the states. In comparison, Wentworth said, his proposals for two-thirds majorities were moderate. On the question of electoral districts, he argued that representation should be based not on 'mere population, but [on] the great interests of the country'. The squatters' eight million sheep and half a million cattle provided an annual income of £2 million. By contrast, Sydney's merchants were 'simply engaged in exchanging one commodity for another . . . productive of absolutely nothing'. As for Sydney, it had 'really nothing to represent . . . except a large mass of people' who happened to be 'the most vacillating, ignorant and misled body of people in the Colony'.

Wedded to his idea for a local aristocracy, Wentworth reminded the Council of its agreement to establish a Constitution 'similar in its outline to that of Canada' and claimed that it was now 'bound by that compact'. Never mind that some British statesmen, especially William Gladstone, were now saying Canada needed an elected Upper House: two chambers elected on the same principle would be 'mere duplicates of each other'. Besides, Canada, split between its French and British citizens, was now no longer a 'precedent' for the 'one united race of this Colony'. Clearly sinking among the contra-dictions of his own argument, Wentworth pointed out that the 1791 Canadian Constitutional Act, which the Council had agreed (so he claimed) to use as a precedent, had been approved by those legen-dary parliamentarians Edmund Burke, William Pitt the Younger and William Wilberforce. Besides, he was bettering even them by proposing that a new local Upper House's members be elected by fellow aristocrats rather than sit solely by hereditary right.

To the charge that he wanted to be one of these aristocrats Went-worth replied that, as the *Herald* reported:

Whether he did or did not entertain that desire was . . . of little moment but admitting that he did, was it an improper object of ambition or was he to be denounced for cherishing the hope that some son of his could succeed him in the Coun-cils of his country?

Referring to American precedent, Wentworth noted that 'the great Washington . . . anxiously contemplated the introduction of hereditary titles'. But with the US having turned away from them, its 'democratic constitution . . . [is] working its own destruction and instead of being in the hands of the most talented men . . . it [is] in the hands of the . . . most incompetent'.[12] LIKE PRESIDENT TRUMP

When Wentworth finished, the debate was adjourned for a week. The next morning Parkes counter-attacked in *The Empire*:

> As Wentworth . . . stood there last night, the wreck of strong passions and of an able mind, he expressed . . . [opinions on] the power and monopoly of classes . . . which belong to the reign of Charles the First or . . . Louis the Fourteenth.[13]

The Sydney Morning Herald had initially supported Wentworth's aristocracy. But it now hoped he would disarm the opponents of a nominated Upper House by dropping his peerage proposal. As soon as Council sittings resumed, his growing band of critics there also went on the attack. James Martin said the Canadian Constitutional Act of 1791 was 'a dead letter', while Charles Cowper observed that the British government proposed 'to make Canada's Upper House elective'. Cowper also analysed how Wentworth's plan would distribute the fifty-four members of the Assembly among the colony's 206,000 inhabitants. The pastoral districts, with 31,000 people, would elect twelve members. The counties, with three times the population, would elect just twenty-six. Sydney, with 50,000, would elect four. Sydney hamlets would have two representatives for 10,000 people while the boroughs, with 25,000 people, would have ten. Cowper objected to the squatters' 'undue influence', arguing that 'every . . . 4000 people should have one representative'. People preaching politics on the goldfields would be no problem, he said, because 'so small an amount of crime [has] arisen' there.[14]

Of all the major Council figures, only James Macarthur fully shared Wentworth's fears about the mob. When Europe 'was rocked by the conflicting passions of democracy,' he warned, 'nothing but the bayonet could subdue the furious multitudes'. He endorsed Wentworth's plan for a local aristocracy as 'a very happy adaptation of the hereditary principle'—and ended with an encomium. The *Herald* reported it as follows:

> Our children's children should be enabled to lisp out the worthy name of their progenitors and the proudest name of all . . . would be . . . Wentworth . . . He had often been opposed to him . . . but . . . they had waged an honourable war . . . [Wentworth's] sole object was the good of his country . . . to protect it from those miserable intriguers whom he had withered with the lightening of his genius and shattered by his manly eloquence and . . . courage.

Thus the thirty-year feud between the Wentworth and Macarthur families ended in a last-ditch defence of their squatting and pastoral interests. But Macarthur's words of support were little comfort to Wentworth. Nowadays he regularly 'found himself denounced as a traitor'; one ruffian even demanded that he 'swing for his political crimes'. Overhearing someone pass on the common gossip that 'Wentworth is to be Duke of Vaucluse', he denied he wanted a peerage. 'When what little he had . . . was divided among ten [children],' he was reported as saying, 'there would not be sufficient for any one of them to maintain a hereditary title with honour.' Now that he could, by his own account, 'scarcely be called a squatter', he was able without any conflict of interest to identify others who might maintain a title with honour. 'Was there not a class in this colony peculiarly fitted to receive hereditary distinction—he meant that great and powerful class engaged in the sustenation of sheep and cattle and whom he might call the Shepherd Kings?'[15]

The Sydney Morning Herald reported that 'the proposal to create a class with hereditary honours . . . has been virtually given up', but it was still in the Bill as Wentworth wound up his reply on 2 September. 'It [is] probably the last important occasion when [my] voice [will] be heard within these walls,' Wentworth said as he pleaded for unanimous support for the new Constitution. When he sat down, the Speaker could not restrain 'a loud burst of applause from all sides . . . which . . . was taken up by the crowded gallery'. Perhaps his audience had warmed to Wentworth's confession that there was within him 'a flood of lava which ever and anon boils over'. 'It is rather the infirmity of my nature,' he said, 'than the passion of my heart.' Still, when the question was put amid loud cheers and clapping there were eight dissenters, including Cowper and Darvall. Further debate on the Committee stage of the Bill which examined its contents line by line was set down for 6 December. Wentworth said this would give the public time to digest his proposals.[16]

The public got indigestion. On 5 September, a further protest meeting brought over 3000 people to Circular Quay. Charles Cowper told the crowd that 'the helm was being wrested from the hands of the old pilot', immediately prompting the interjection that 'he [Wentworth] would have steered . . . on to Pinchgut', today's Fort Denison. Joining in the laughter, Cowper reminded his listeners that the people had been 'forced' to the helm once before over Wentworth's support for transportation. When Henry Parkes' turn came, he thundered that 'he wanted no Yankee Constitution but . . . by the God of his fathers he would never accept a Norfolk Island Constitution'. And then the pint-sized Daniel Deniehy spoke up. Dismissing the poem *Australasia* as a 'piece of trash', he compared Wentworth to the poem's metaphor for Britannia: 'tam'd Lion . . . bow'd by luxury', and noted that at Vaucluse the old poet was 'wallowing in soup, and pig, and claret'.

The Sydney Morning Herald reported that the meeting not only objected to Wentworth's Constitution but challenged the competency of the partially elected Legislative Council to draft one.[17]

To keep opposition to the Constitution Bill alive, a public dinner was organised to thank the 'minority of eight' who had voted against it on 2 September. John Darvall told the diners that Wentworth's attempt to fabricate a Constitution on the British model 'put him in mind of the Chinese tailor who, being told to make a pair of new breeches on the pattern of an old pair, copied his pattern so faithfully that he put a patch in the stern'.

Some of his critics' arguments hit home: by December, when debate resumed in the Council, Wentworth had replaced aristocrats with government nominees in his proposed Upper House. Some of his opponents wondered if that had not been his plan all along, especially when their amendment to popularly elect the Upper House was defeated. But their further amendment to increase the number of members for Sydney by one-third was lost more narrowly. And a week later a motion to reconsider this amendment resulted in a dead heat, broken only by the Speaker casting his vote with the 'ayes'. So the amendment to increase Sydney's representation by one-third was then voted on again. And this time, it was defeated by just one vote. Wentworth's proposal of four members for Sydney, rather than six, had squeaked home. 'The Session is over,' *The Sydney Morning Herald* said. 'The Bill is safe.'[18]

And Wentworth was about to leave for England.

Chapter 28

INDEPENDENCE AND FEDERATION

Having let Vaucluse House for three years in January 1854, Wentworth sailed for England on 20 March. James Macarthur now described him as the 'foremost' public man in Australia. But Macarthur's attempts to organise a fitting farewell were defeated by a combination of bad weather and a Council resolution to appoint Wentworth to lobby for the Constitution Bill in London. Although he stressed that he was 'going home', as the trip was then called, on family business, the Bill's critics insisted that his trip was a political lobbying exercise. Emerging from the Australian Club at about 3 p.m., Wentworth made his way to Circular Quay in driving rain. Accompanying him were just sixty people, including six ruffians hired by his political opponents. Stopping at Macquarie Place, the sodden little gathering attempted to ignore the troublemakers' interjections as Macarthur announced that funds were being collected for a statue of Wentworth. Such a gesture was 'more usually reserved for the dead than the living', Wentworth replied, assuring his supporters that he hoped soon to return.[1]

Wentworth, with his daughter Fanny Reeve and her husband John, got in a small boat and were rowed out to the *Chusan* in a slanting downpour. Being rowed from ship to shore was a bundle of three-month-old London papers. One paper headlined 'War' with Russia. Another, *The Times* of 15 December, reported Wentworth's speech attacking Sydney's merchants and its ordinary residents, that 'ignorant and misled' mass. 'One might imagine he was some courtier of Charles I,' *The Times* said. 'The practical English mind has little sympathy with such . . . invective.' (This piece was most likely written by Wentworth's old sparring partner, Robert Lowe, who since his return to London had become an editorial writer— work he continued after his election to the House of Commons in 1852.) So Wentworth was travelling towards another political storm. And in his wake he left a vacant seat, which Parkes won by a resounding majority.[2]

On 3 April, as the *Chusan* sheltered from a gale that prevented it from rounding Cape Leeuwin, Wentworth wrote to Macarthur to thank him for his public support in the face of 'rabid abuse':

> I trust I may arrive in London in time to hasten the ratification of our last great measure [because] if it is returned . . . [to the Colony] for amendment . . . it will no longer be possible to frame . . . a [conservative] constitution . . . My first interview with the Duke of Newcastle will show how the cat jumps.[3]

Sarah and their younger children were at the dock to meet him when the *Chusan* arrived on 2 June. They were full of news of their fifteen months in London. Among the highlights was seeing Queen Victoria, or at least her 'head and neck', as she rode by to open Parliament. The Parliament buildings Wentworth remembered from his time as a law student had burned down in 1834 and much work on the new buildings remained to be done, including completion of a giant tower to hold the clock Big Ben. Parliament itself was pre-occupied by a war, now two months old, which Britain and France had declared on Russia.

Eight days after Wentworth reached London, the Duke of New-castle left the Colonial Office. A man who one colleague said 'did not remember his rank unless you forgot it', Newcastle was none-theless happy to keep his appointment with Wentworth. Since he could no longer talk authoritatively about the Constitution Bills, their discussion turned to the 'defenceless state' of Sydney in the event of raids by Russian warships. Soon afterwards, Wentworth wrote to the Speaker in Sydney that since Britain was preoccupied with 'armaments in Europe', the colony must fortify the Heads at the entrance to Sydney Harbour and raise a militia itself. 'Perfect self-reliance,' Wentworth said, 'is the only safe principle the Aus-tralian Colonies can now adopt.'

A few days later Wentworth met Sir George Grey, the new Secretary of State. Grey told Wentworth that the Constitution Bills—which he had not had time to read closely—would not be dealt with during the present Parliamentary session. Wentworth wrote to Macarthur that the government was 'entirely absorbed' with the Crimean War. Nevertheless the senior Crown Law Officer Sir Frederic Rogers did find time to give his opinion on the Bills, and he was in no doubt that they raised the most important ques-tions he had ever dealt with. 'They are little less than a legislative declaration of independence,' he advised. 'What remains to com-plete colonial independence except command of the land and sea forces, I don't quite see.'[4]

In November, while Cabinet considered this proposal to take independence within the Empire close to its limit, the Wentworths moved to Brussels. There, their younger daughters would be able to learn French and German where they were spoken. And by making the ferry trip to London, Wentworth would still be able to attend political meetings. On 30 March 1855 he and a band of like-minded conservatives met at the New Hummums Hotel, Covent Garden, to establish the General Association of the Australian Colonies. The next day he wrote to Thomasine, in Sydney, about the possibility of staying in England 'if I get into Parliament and public life here'. In the meantime, he settled for chairmanship of the General Association, which set about lobbying Grey's successor as Secretary of State, Lord John Russell, to introduce the Constitution Bills with an amendment to provide 'for a federal assembly . . . to legislate on all inter-colonial questions', as suggested by Wentworth's Constitution committee.

On 17 May 1855 Russell introduced a Bill 'to confer a constitution on New South Wales', setting off a Parliamentary debate that would rage on for five weeks. But it was immediately clear to Wentworth that the Colonial Office had amended his Bills, paring back his claim for legislative independence while declining to provide for a federal Assembly. As he explained in a letter to the Speaker in Sydney, 'the clauses drawing a distinction between Imperial and Local subjects have been omitted; the old powers of [Crown] veto . . . have been restored and legislation by bare majorities . . . in all cases has been introduced'. He was furious about those 'bare majorities', which he described as 'dangerous and subversive' because they trumped his carefully crafted conservative safeguard of two-thirds majorities. But he could not risk the Bills being returned to Sydney for further consideration: if that happened, pressure to convert the proposed Upper House from one composed of nominees into an elected chamber might become overwhelming. So, after lobbying ministers behind the scenes, Wentworth supported Russell's Bills.[5]

His nemesis, the two-faced new MP Robert Lowe, was first on his feet to oppose them. Describing the proposed electoral districts as 'the iniquitous device . . . of a small . . . clique', Lowe claimed that those who had proposed a hereditary peerage were unfit to draft a Constitution. Wentworth's committee had not been concerned about what would be best for the colony, he said, but about what would be best for the few who made enormous fortunes. Of a non-elected Upper House, Lowe said:

> No materials for such a body existed in Australia because persons of the requisite education who were fitted to become members returned to England after acquiring wealth . . . If [the British government] established a Chamber of Peers out of the only materials they were able to obtain, they would have a large proportion of them passing through the Insolvent Court in a few years.

It must have been agony for Wentworth to have to sit silently in the public gallery while Lowe, the man he had branded a coward and whom he 'despised for lack of principle', weaved his way up and down the Commons Chamber attacking him at will. As he watched, Wentworth's keen political eye would have noticed how the House he remembered from his days as a law student had changed. Under the 1832 Reform Act many of the 'rotten boroughs' (including Old Sarum, which had only six voters) had been abolished, while new industrial cities like Manchester now had their own separate representatives. Wentworth surely worried about how those MPs would vote, being themselves the beneficiaries of drastic electoral reform. But fewer than one-third bothered to do so and Wentworth had the satisfaction of seeing Lowe's attempts to meddle with the new Constitution come to naught.[6]

On 20 July, Lord John Russell sent instructions to the new Governor of New South Wales, Sir William Denison, to implement the Constitution Act and assemble a legislature without delay. There was only one issue still unresolved, Russell said—the creation of a Federal Union of the Australian Colonies. The Secretary of State told Denison that the government had carefully considered Wentworth's federation model but decided that it would be inappropriate to include it in the new Act. However, Russell was prepared to consider any proposals emanating 'in concurrence from the respective Colonial Legislatures'. In other words, the colonies would all have to agree on, and initiate, a joint approach to London. But under responsible government, the colonies were moving apart rather than closer together. Now that their Lieutenant-Governors, for example, had been upgraded to Governors, the Governor-General's practical role had dwindled to nothing. If anyone in London was then capable of taking the federation of the Australian colonies further, the lifelong politician Russell was. But he had just been caught out trying to negotiate an end to the Crimean War, and the British press was accusing him of being 'willing to truckle to the Russians'. On the verge of a breakdown, he soon resigned.[7]

After Parliament's debates on the Constitution Bills were over, the Wentworths went on tour. Following two months at Aix-la-Chapelle in France, where Sarah noted that the cathedral held the bones of the Emperor Charlemagne, the greatest of Europe's medieval kings, they travelled through Switzerland before arriving in Paris. Having given up their house in Brussels, they rented a house on the Champs-Elysées with a view of the Eiffel Tower. 'We see the Empress pass,' Sarah said, 'whenever she comes to town.' Eliza and Isabella went to boarding school while the younger girls, Laura and Edith, attended a day school opposite the house. A frequent dinner guest was James Macarthur's brother William, who was attending the city's huge International Exhibition to showcase his collection of Australian woods.

The following year, after resettling in England, the Wentworths rented country estates, including one of the Duke of Marlborough's properties, where Wentworth entertained his political guests as they blasted away at pheasants. Between March and May 1856 he led three separate delegations to lobby the Secretary of State, the Chancellor of the Exchequer and the Prime Minister for 'first-class steam ships' to link Britain and Australia. With cost the sticking point, more progress was achieved through negotiations with private mail companies.[8]

Following the implementation of the new Constitution Act, the first Prime Minister of New South Wales, Stuart Donaldson, had lasted less than three months. His successor, Charles Cowper, lasted less than two. During his short time in office, Cowper had tried to offset his weak political and financial position by fiddling with tariffs. This angered *The Sydney Morning Herald*, which on 23 October 1856 strongly advocated a federal union to take control of such intercolonial issues. Cowper had by then been replaced as Prime Minister by Henry Watson Parker, whose most senior minister, Edward Deas Thomson, now strongly argued that tariffs 'ought to be submitted to some Federal Assembly representing all the Australian colonies'. When Wentworth became aware of this, he reactivated the General Association of the Australian Colonies. After an encouraging meeting with the Secretary of State, Henry Labouchère, Wentworth produced a draft Bill and an explanatory memorandum that were approved by an association meeting in London on 31 March 1857. 'A complete equality of representation, as between all the Australian Colonies, should be insisted upon,' the memorandum said 'without reference to the extent of their population in any Federal Assembly that may be formed.' The memorandum noted that such an Assembly could only be established by an Act of the British Parliament.[9]

To address British policy which required the colonies to agree on union and then initiate a joint request for it to London, Wentworth proposed that Parliament pass a 'permissive Act' enabling the colonies to federate themselves once they had agreed on the details. He also drafted a Bill which provided that two or more colonies might initially agree to join a federal union to be followed later by other colonies on equal terms. Western Australia was not to be included so long as it remained a penal colony and there was no mention of New Zealand, which was not part of the so-called 'Australian Group' of colonies. However, Queensland, which was then still part of New South Wales, and any other colony of the Australian Group 'not now in existence' could join later, provided none was a penal settlement. A Federal Assembly of the member colonies would have power to legislate on the growing list of intercolonial issues, including tariffs, railway gauges and a Court of Appeal. Although the Assembly was to appoint a President 'at the commencement of each session', no provision was made for a federal executive. All colonies, regardless of size, were to have equal membership, and they would collectively decide how to apportion costs. The Assembly's meetings, Wentworth claimed, would be short and would deal with little legislation, so they could be made 'perambulatory' and rotated through each member colony. Wentworth was calibrating his plan to appeal to the colonies' lowest common denominator and thus gain the widest possible support. The result would be a loose, ad-hoc arrangement rather than a close bond with a strong central government—a confederation rather than a federation. On 23 April 1857 he presented the plan to Henry Labouchère, taking with him a deputation of nineteen, including former members of the Legislative Councils of New South Wales, Victoria, South Australia and Tasmania. The Secretary of State's reaction to this phalanx of ex-politicians from the colonies was to seek advice from none other than Robert Lowe, now vice-president of the Board of Trade.[10]

No doubt relishing another opportunity to take his old foe apart, Lowe immediately homed in on the plan's weakest point: Wentworth's lowest-common-denominator approach. 'History teaches nothing with more uniformity,' Lowe said, 'than the failure of federations and their failure precisely in the point in which this federation is weakest, the powers of enforcing federal decisions against individual states.' To overcome this flaw, Lowe argued, the British government would have to establish a federal executive and judiciary as well as a federal legislature. Only then would Wentworth's idea be turned into a workable federation. But having just enhanced the individual colonies' powers in their respective Constitution Acts, Lowe claimed that it would be 'very rash to interfere prematurely' by transferring some of these powers to a federal body, until 'we have something [a proposal] more authentic from each colony'. Then Lowe twisted the knife, saying there was no provision for popular representation in the Association's proposed federal assembly, while the plan for equal representation for all colonies would disadvantage larger ones like New South Wales. This was enough to put off Labouchère, a stolid man who had a reputation for efficiency and calm. But it is easy to imagine Lowe, with his darting, vengeful intelligence, running rings around him. A month after Wentworth's delegation presented their plan, the Secretary of State replied that he would not introduce the Bill they wanted because it was unlikely the colonies 'would consent to entrust such large powers to an Assembly'. Even if they did initially agree, Labouchère said, 'the result would . . . probably be dissention and discontent'. Nevertheless, the Secretary of State did circulate the Association's proposal to the colonies to seek their views. While the colonial press generally supported Wentworth's efforts to promote the case for federal union, *The Melbourne Herald* called him and his Association 'a body of . . . holiday-making colonists'. Henry Parkes scolded them as a 'knot of gentlemen in England who took upon themselves . . . without the slightest authority to recommend legislative action'. On 26 January 1858, these gentlemen organised a dinner at the Albion hotel in Aldgate Street, London, to celebrate the colony's seventieth anniversary. Federation still seemed years away.[11]

Responding to Labouchère's circular, the leader of the government in the Legislative Council, Edward Deas Thomson, had established a select committee in August 1857 that proposed a federal model based on Wentworth's General Association draft. But when a similar committee in Victoria shied away from specifics and simply recommended general discussions at a federal conference, the New South Wales committee fell into line with it. The following month, Charles Cowper became New South Wales Prime Minister for the second time. He agreed with Henry Parkes that the Legislative Assembly should concentrate on liberalising Wentworth's squatter-favouring Constitution. When the select committee's proposal was listed for the Assembly's consideration Cowper opposed a debate, saying 'much valuable time' would be wasted. Within days an election was called, and Cowper won it convincingly. So no one was surprised when, at the opening of the new Parliament in March 1858, the Governor said 'the question of a Federal Legislature . . . may without inconvenience be deferred'. And it was—for over forty years.[12]

In November 1855, Sarah had written of her intention to return to Sydney. 'I like it best,' she said, '[while] the elder children like it better here.' But a series of disasters put off any thought of moving. In early 1856 Fanny had a baby son, but five months later he died. Soon afterwards, Isabella was struck down by gastric fever and died within weeks. Then Wentworth himself fell dangerously ill with influenza. 'His age and hard living,' noted William Macarthur, 'are beginning to tell heavily.' Sarah Eleanor, D'Arcy and Fitzwilliam also became ill. So in the summer of 1857, Wentworth, Sarah Eleanor and D'Arcy were packed off to take the waters near Munich. Sarah later joined them for a tour of Europe, which ended abruptly in Corfu when Sarah Eleanor became too sick to go on. Wentworth returned to London on business, but the others remained on the island with her. Just before Christmas, she died of lung disease. Wentworth wrote rather clinically to his wife:

> If she be put in lead . . . her remains may . . . be consigned to Australia. In the meantime you had better arrange . . . a plain tablet . . . 'Sacred to the Memory of Sarah Eleanor, third

daughter of W.C. Wentworth & Sarah his wife of Vaucluse, Australia. She was born on the   day of   1834 and died the   day of December 1857'. Fill up these blanks and leave money in the bank for the tablet before you leave Corfu.[13]

Although D'Arcy recovered his health, Fitzwilliam's lungs suffered in the English climate. So he gave up his studies and went off to New Zealand, where he purchased one of the largest sheep runs in Otago. For Willie, however, things turned out tragically. Extremely bright although not quite right in the head, he struggled along with his legal studies although his passion was chemistry. He became convinced that he had discovered something that had 'baffled the most scientific men for fifty years'. Even the great electrochemist Michael Faraday took an interest. But Willie's constant testing of batteries and gases took a toll on his health, and he complained to Sarah that his 'brain was getting affected'. Coincidentally, Faraday had also suffered mental health problems. After finally being admitted to the Bar in July 1858, Willie had a breakdown so severe that one doctor recommended he be committed to an asylum. Instead, Wentworth moved his family out of London to St John's Wood, where Willie died on 31 March 1859. 'Willie's stomach after death turned quite a dark olive colour,' Sarah wrote to Thomasine. 'I have been enquiring about a copy of dear Willie's likeness. When it is ready I will send you one.'[14]

As the plaster busts of Sarah Wentworth and Thomasine Fisher at Vaucluse House attest, the Wentworths were partial to likenesses of all types. Wentworth had a full life-sized figure of himself sculpted by the renowned Pietro Tenerani in Rome, and travelled there twice for sittings. Back in Sydney, there was a heated debate about another likeness of Wentworth by 'an Italian master'. In October 1859, Henry Parkes moved that this likeness, a painting that had been 'lying at the Chamber of Commerce', be permanently hung in the Legislative Assembly chamber. Although he did not support

Wentworth's politics, Parkes said the Assembly 'should . . . hon-our . . . a man most conspicuous for breadth of character, power of intellect, untiring energy and masculine eloquence'. This drew immediate fire from John Dunmore Lang. 'One of Wentworth's most prominent services,' Lang shot back, 'was the infamous Con-stitution Act.' The Assembly voted by a margin of one, the casting vote of the Speaker, to hang Wentworth's portrait. The image, which shows him grimly holding a rolled paper in both hands like a schoolmaster about to administer punishment, gazes down on the chamber to this day.[15]

One argument put against so prominently displaying his likeness was that Wentworth might return to Sydney and be re-elected, in which case hanging his portrait 'would be giving him undue influ-ence'. Indeed, despite the family upsets and tragedies, Sarah and her husband continued to dream of returning to Vaucluse; early in 1859, Wentworth even contemplated making the voyage alone. But persistent illness in the family—the latest mishap was Eliza's fall from a horse—kept them both in England. They were also detained there by Wentworth's legal proceedings. Sarah wrote to Thoma-sine that 'we are not going to Sydney now till Papa gives evidence in Lloyd's case'. Wentworth had sued J.C. Lloyd in 1859, alleg-ing a conspiracy to defraud him of a station on the Namoi River. When the Wentworths finally left England with Eliza, Laura, Edith and D'Arcy aboard the *Benares* in February 1861, Sarah wrote with some misgiving that they would soon be back. 'The law suit will oblige us to return to England,' she said.[16]

A month before they set sail, Wentworth chaired a dinner at the Clarendon Hotel for Sir John Young, who was about to replace Sir William Denison as Governor of New South Wales. By this time, the colony had been further shrunk by the enlargement of South Australia and the 1859 creation of Queensland as a separate colony. Owing to intercolonial rivalry, Young was not appointed

Governor-General as Denison and FitzRoy had been. Even so, the dinner's forty guests included William Gladstone, now Chancellor of the Exchequer; Sir Frederic Rogers, now permanent head of the Colonial Office; and James Macarthur, who had arrived in London the previous June.

Proposing a toast to Young, Wentworth lamented that:

The influx . . . of men of . . . turbulent character and ultra-democratic notions from America . . . together with the adoption of manhood suffrage and the destruction of . . . safe-guards . . . [in] the Constitution . . . [places] the other colonists in a powerless minority [and causes] incessant changes in the Ministry . . . [with] no . . . hope for improvement.

Thanking Wentworth for his 'frank and sincere warning', Young said he hoped that he would find things in a better state than Wentworth feared. Gladstone, who had been responsible for Young's appointment, reassured him that Wentworth exaggerated. The gathering, by this stage embarrassed and uncomfortable, finally relaxed when Sir Stuart Donaldson, whose term as the first Prime Minister of New South Wales had been short and stormy, forecast that after a period of struggle 'the sound sense . . . of the community . . . [will] assert itself'. And they all agreed with Gladstone that 'Australia [is] fortunate in being exempt from the fatal element of slavery which was creating such unhappy dissensions in America.'[17]

Chapter 29

MR PRESIDENT

On 18 April 1861, while the *Benares* was still at sea, Wentworth's brother-in-law Richard Hill sailed out from Coogee Bay to meet the ship and present Wentworth with an advance copy of a welcoming address. The committee which drew up the address had hired the steamer *London* to accompany its hero up the harbour, once the *Benares* had cleared South Head. Despite Prime Minister Cowper's opposition, the Legislative Assembly had resolved by a one-vote margin to adjourn for the day. The *London*, adorned with the words 'Wentworth Welcome Home', was packed with about 1000 people, including several Cabinet ministers and Parliament's Presiding Officers. As the two vessels steamed side by side, the *Benares* stopped briefly near Vaucluse Bay, where Sarah and the children disembarked amid loud cheers. All the while, Wentworth remained secluded below decks as he composed his reply to the address—miffing some of his admirers on board the *London* who had hoped to catch a glimpse of him. After the ships reached Circular Quay and the passengers were assembled onshore, James Martin publicly welcomed Wentworth as 'the first of all our public men'. Cowper, meanwhile, was seen quietly paying his personal respects.[1]

As he rode in a carriage to Vaucluse House, Wentworth passed through a city transformed. Now housing 100,000 people, Sydney was spreading out in all directions with a network of roads already laid to support future subdivisions in today's eastern suburbs. Reaching the family estate, he came upon a shambles. The Wentworths already knew that in 1858 their departed tenant had left the garden 'in a most disgraceful state'. But Sarah's sister, Maria Hunt, who had lived at Vaucluse since, had let the house itself become dreadfully run down.[2]

In politics Wentworth found a similar mess. In just five years there had been seven Prime Ministers: Stuart Donaldson, Charles Cowper, Henry Watson Parker, Cowper again, William Forster, John Robertson, and now Cowper for a third time. Six years earlier, the British Parliament had adopted Lord John Russell's proposal that simple majorities of the New South Wales legislature would be sufficient to amend its Constitution—discarding Wentworth's carefully crafted safeguard requiring two-thirds majorities. And by the end of 1858, Cowper had legislated to give every adult male the vote and equalise the sizes of electoral districts. There was now a clash between the popularly elected Legislative Assembly and the appointed Legislative Council, still dominated by squatters. These appointees' five-year terms were shortly to expire, and the Constitution dictated that their successors were to be appointed for life.

Central to this clash between the Assembly and the Council was former Prime Minister Robertson's proposal to sell off Crown land in small blocks, allowing buyers to pay by instalments. Robertson, a radical pastoralist whose description of himself as a 'mere denizen of the bush' camouflaged a shrewd political brain, was determined to democratise the distribution of land, but the squatters would have none of it—and they still had the power to block him. However, their blocking power could be overcome by appointing extra members who would vote for the reforms. The only question was whether the Governor would appoint the Prime Minister's preferred nominees.[3]

In December 1860, Prime Minister Robertson had fought a general election over the land reform issue, and thirty-five of the fifty-three candidates who supported his policy were elected to the Assembly. So passionate was Robertson about the issue that he then stepped down as Prime Minister to concentrate on getting his land reform Bills through the Assembly. That done, he resigned his Lower House seat and was appointed to the Council, where he intended to shepherd his Bills through the final stages of enactment. When the Council's squatter members gutted his Bills with amendments Robertson and Cowper, his successor as Prime Minister, lobbied Governor Sir John Young to stack the Council by appointing twenty-one new members who would support the Bills. After some hesitation Young agreed. As he explained to his superiors in London:

> The choice, if choice it can be called . . . was either to accept the advice of the ministers or break with them, backed as they are by six-sevenths of the Assembly and by the people in a cry which was all powerful . . . at the general elections.

When the Council president learned of the new appointees, he refused to take the chair. Standing on the upper step in front of it, he explained that he had resigned in protest at this attempt to stack the chamber. He then withdrew, leaving the Clerk no option but to adjourn 'until the next sitting day', which happened to be 14 May—the day after the terms of all the existing Council members expired. 'I never contemplated when I lent my hand to framing . . . the Constitution,' Wentworth said, 'that any Ministers . . . would have the audacity to sweep the streets of Sydney . . . to swamp the House by the introduction of twenty-one members.'[4]

With the Parliament adjourned for six months, Cowper had time to consider whom he would recommend to the Governor for lifetime appointment to the Council. Helpfully, *The Sydney Morning Herald* suggested some criteria: 'Can the proposed Councillor write? Can he spell? Can he speak grammatically?' Wentworth, meanwhile, was receiving the accolades of those who could in the form of a congratulatory address from Sydney University for his gift of £200 to fund the Wentworth Medal for the best English essay. As speculation mounted about who the new Councillors might be, it was even reported that Wentworth might be made President of the Council and that 'the Ministers themselves are divided'.

The rumour proved accurate. On 25 June Wentworth was named as president of a Council that still had jurisdiction over today's Northern Territory as well as New South Wales. Having only recently denounced the Prime Minister 'in terms of unmeasured contempt' over the way in which his changes to the Constitution had caused chronic political instability, Wentworth executed a stunning about-face. This was all the more remarkable because he had agreed upon taking the job that 'the Land Bill should pass [and] the Legislative Council should be elective'. The Macarthurs, James and William, were in no doubt that he had been 'got at' by Slippery Charlie Cowper. They were right. Cowper had 'gradually . . . dispelled' Wentworth's 'strong prejudices' against taking Council office. No doubt the status of the job, and its £1200 salary, appealed to the man who had wanted to be a Presiding Officer since 1843. Appointment to the Council for life was the equivalent today of being made a Life Peer in Britain; the role of President was seen at the time as 'somewhat analogous to that of Lord High Chancellor of England'. But Wentworth was also driven by his desire for political stability. And he stipulated a condition, based partly on his morbid fear of mob violence and the concern he shared with the Governor, that 'the agitation of the land question . . . [had] driven the people wild':

The Council is not to be swamped on any future occasion, until after the rejection by it of some vital question upon which the opinion of the country had previously been taken, after a dissolution of the Assembly for that express purpose.[5]

On 3 September 1861, Wentworth formally took the chair as President in a corrugated-iron building that had been prefabricated in England for use as a church on the Victorian goldfields; it is still used by the Council today. As he surveyed the members on their red leather benches from his opulent presidential Chair Wentworth would have admired the rich cedar panelling and fine wallpaper, set off by exquisite gilding. But he knew that, out of sight, all this was being held together by a steel frame and waste wood salvaged from the structure's packing containers. Not everything about the chamber was as it appeared to those sitting in the public gallery—a metaphor for the President himself over the coming months.

Opening the session that immediately followed Wentworth's formal claim of the presidential Chair, the Governor asked for 'a speedy . . . settlement of the land question . . . [and] the constitution of the . . . Council on an Elective basis'. Before the month was out, John Robertson reintroduced his land Bills. From the government's point of view, Wentworth generally behaved well. But at one point he was unable to contain himself over a clause that sought to bring unsettled lands within settled districts. As the *Herald* reported:

Why was it sought to disturb the 43,000,000 acres of leased land when there were 122,000,000 acres to pick from without disturbing existing interests . . . The Minister was robbing the squatters . . . without whom the Colony would have been one of the most miserable holes in the universe, not half as good as the sands of Arabia where luckily for the Arabs, there was no Minister for Lands to interfere.

Robertson joined in the general laughter, but he still won this vote convincingly. Shortly thereafter, the land bills that had recently been so controversial became law.[6]

Until now, Bills to make the Legislative Council elective had been just as controversial. One way or another, no fewer than four such Bills had been stalled since 1859. In December 1861, when the government introduced a bill giving all adult males the right to vote in Council elections, the proposal was promptly referred to a select committee chaired by Wentworth. Although he acknowledged that the Council should be subject to the 'elective principle', Wentworth quoted the 'extreme liberal' political philosopher John Stuart Mill to stress the importance of balance, which could not be achieved if the two Houses were elected in the same way. So the committee proposed a high property qualification for Council electors and recommended a quota system of proportional voting rather than the winner-take-all system used in those Assembly electorates which returned a single member. In addition to the thirty Council members to be elected by this system (under which the colony would be treated as one electorate), Wentworth proposed that ten members drawn from former presiding officers and the like be appointed for life. After meeting on twenty-one separate days, the committee produced a Bill which the Council finally passed on 8 October 1862. Wentworth immediately stood down as President. His task of drafting a Bill 'to prevent . . . any future attacks on the Council's independence', he explained, was now complete. Still, he said, he feared that the property qualification was too low for electors and nonexistent for members.

The Bill had clearly been a difficult compromise for Wentworth, and the Attorney-General congratulated him on his 'able and courteous manner' in the Chair. 'Mr Wentworth has behaved admirably as President and so indeed have all members,' Cowper told Parkes. 'The construction of that House has been a great success.' So successful was it that when the Bill came before the Assembly Cowper quietly let it lapse, preferring reasonable appointees to popularly elected members. In an astonishing finale to his public life, Wentworth, that champion of the so-called 'bunyip aristocracy', had devised an Upper House that was too liberal for Charles Cowper, the leading liberal of the day.[7]

On 23 June 1862, in the Great Hall of Sydney University, a statue of Wentworth by Pietro Tenerani paid for by public subscription and shipped from Rome was unveiled. Seven feet tall and carved from white marble, it portrayed Wentworth in the act of making an address, his right arm raised and two fingers extended. To an audience that included the Governor, the Speaker, the Chancellor and the Mayor of Sydney, James Martin, soon to be Prime Minister, made a wonderful speech complimenting Wentworth on his 'bold and masterly advocacy of freedom without licence'. Referring to Wentworth's role in establishing the university, Martin said 'its doors are open with a wise and comprehensive liberality to the members of every creed, class and condition'. Wentworth himself was absent. 'I was not present,' he said, 'it having been decided by the Senate that I ought not to be there or take any part in the proceedings.' Perhaps the Senators thought that the Great Hall was not big enough for both Wentworth and his statue. Or perhaps they decided that, this not being a political event, Wentworth could not be trusted to control himself. All the same, it was a strange decision from a body that claimed to champion 'liberality'.[8]

Sarah, too, was being feted, her days as a social outcast well and truly over. Sir John and Lady Young had come to know her on Corfu, where Sir John had been British High Commissioner, and she was now regularly invited to Government House. Word of her status spread, and Sarah wrote that 'all the nice families . . . call on us'. Her son-in-law, Thomas Fisher, was 'the only one', she said, who still thought the Wentworth family 'a disgrace'. The ultimate social accolade came in September 1862 when the Vice-Regal couple, along with ministers and parliamentarians, attended the Wentworths' ball at Roslyn Hall, in today's Kings Cross. Larger than Vaucluse House, Roslyn Hall was also much closer to the city. This suited most of the guests, who feasted on a sumptuous dinner prepared by a former Government House chef. It was the first and only time the Wentworths entertained in Sydney on such a large scale, and the evening was a great success.

Five weeks later the Wentworths boarded the *Bombay*, bound for Britain.[9]

Sarah hated to leave Vaucluse, where her recent improvements included a shark-proof bathing enclosure. But Wentworth's ongoing litigation in Lloyd's case left her no choice. On Wentworth's behalf, his agent Thomas Mort had sold a Namoi River station to grazier J.C. Lloyd and others in 1853. Six years later, Wentworth claimed he had been unaware that Mort was one of the buyers. He therefore argued he had been defrauded of the now much more valuable property. Mort insisted that he had disclosed his interest as a purchaser. The case turned on whether Wentworth had known of Mort's interest and, if so, when he first learned of it. As the proceedings had been commenced in London, one of the key questions put to witnesses on commission in Sydney was whether Mort's purchase had been discussed during the sale by Wentworth and his solicitor, Gilbert Wright. Mort's lawyer asked Wright, 'Did Mr Wentworth ever say anything to you on . . . his dealings with Mort?' Wentworth objected that any answer was privileged and the question was not pressed. But he was uneasy, fearing that his objection would be seen in London as an attempt to block damaging evidence. He was also worried about the 'very considerable' costs of the case to date. Now the Wentworths were setting off to attend a hearing in London scheduled for 11 March 1863.[10]

The day before the *Bombay* departed, Sir John Young wrote to the Secretary of State:

The Ministers have earnestly urged . . . that if a . . . Baronetcy is to be conferred . . . it should be . . . on Mr Wentworth . . . Men of . . . all shades of opinion . . . [pronounce] him the colonist most distinguished by genius and service . . . [He] lent a powerful and willing aid toward remedying the evils [of] general instability . . . produced by four general elections in four . . . years. His appearance and influence have been eminently serviceable to . . . order and good government at this critical period.

As Wentworth set sail, *The Sydney Morning Herald* bade farewell to 'the legislator of Australia' with the hope that 'mild and genial suns—if he can find them in old England—may light his passage over the brief space which must separate three score years and ten from the . . . [place from which] no traveller returns'.[11]

Chapter 30

HIS BONES AND HIS MEMORY

While the Wentworths' passage to England with their Aboriginal servant Bobby was incident-free, another ship carrying their papers was wrecked. This added to Wentworth's difficulties as he prepared for Lloyd's case. After seven days of hearings in April 1863, his claim was dismissed. Among other things, the judge concluded that Wentworth had hidden his knowledge of Mort's interest by refusing to let his own solicitor, Gilbert Wright, answer the key question in the case. So Wentworth appealed to the House of Lords, which heard his case the following year. The Lord Chancellor said the judge had ignored the principle of solicitor/client privilege in his finding against Wentworth, but dismissed his appeal on other grounds. Ordered to pay costs, Wentworth formally objected to the 'enormous' amount involved, but again he was rebuffed. Some speculated that he was forced to pay out more in legal bills than the £29,860 (now $3 million) he had received for the original station sale.[1]

According to one report, the adverse judgment in Lloyd's case made Wentworth look ten years older. For the first time he looked his age, although a photograph of him dressed in his squatter's corduroys still had about it an air of proud and upright defiance. Wentworth's exact age at the time was a cause of confusion. On 25 October 1864 Sarah, who at fifty-nine was still strikingly attractive, wrote to Thomasine, 'Tomorrow is Papa's birthday [and] he will be 74 years old', but the 4 was later overwritten by a 3 and then by a 2. The date of these alterations is unknown.

Wentworth took a keen interest in his origins, perhaps to reassure himself that D'Arcy Wentworth had been his father. In September, he had travelled to Ireland to seek out his surviving relatives. One Irish cousin in Portadown thought he looked exactly like the elder Wentworth who, he said, even shared the same tone of voice. 'At Armagh we saw an aunt of Papa's, ninety-six years old', Wentworth's daughter Laura wrote. 'She was very pleased to see Papa and thinks him very like her own father.' Apart from his father's identity, Wentworth had long been concerned about his illegitimacy. In 1827 he had had his mother Catherine Crowley's remains reinterred with those of D'Arcy Wentworth under the headstone 'Here lie the mortal remains of D'Arcy Wentworth . . . Also of Catherine his wife'. In fact D'Arcy never married. But this did not stop the Privy Council in the lawsuit brought by Wentworth's half-brothers and sisters, who challenged their father's will, from referring to Wentworth as D'Arcy's legitimate child. No doubt it relied on Wentworth's claim that this was the case.[2]

Of all his ten children, Laura was perhaps closest to him. She tried to persuade him to accept Christ, even resorting to taking him breakfast in bed and then reading him the 103rd Psalm. Laura noted with mixed feelings that when the family went to church Wentworth remained at home, quietly reading his Bible in the dining room. But she was never quite sure about her father's beliefs. Most likely Wentworth believed in God, because the motto on his coat of arms was 'In God is Everything'. But he did not change his view that organised religion had too much politics in it. Whether he believed in Jesus Christ remains an open question. In the summer of 1867, however, after hearing of James Macarthur's death, he wrote, 'I little thought when I last saw him that we were to meet no more in this world', suggesting that he believed in the next.[3]

Despite losing a fortune on Lloyd's case Wentworth still had enough money to travel widely outside England during the 1860s, visiting Ireland, Corfu, Paris, and Schwalbach and Kreuznach in Germany. On more than one occasion, he talked seriously of returning to New South Wales. As late as 1871, Sarah thought that Wentworth would 'be able to go to Sydney in a good steamer with a good doctor', though a year earlier he had more realistically said of Vaucluse, 'I never expect to see it again myself.' But he did assume that Sarah would return to live at her 'endeared' Sydney home after his death.

Now occupied by Wentworth's in-laws Robert and Maria Hunt, Vaucluse continued to cause problems. Despite Thomas Fisher's contempt for the Wentworth family, when he and Thomasine returned to Sydney in late 1866, following a long time in England, the Wentworths allowed them to stay at Vaucluse. But this arrangement came to an end after just six months when, following a dispute with the Hunts, Fisher complained to Wentworth. Accepting Fisher's side of the story, including an allegation that Mrs Hunt had stripped the fruit trees and cut down the green bananas 'in an act of paltry malice', a disgusted Wentworth cancelled Robert Hunt's power of attorney and transferred it to Fisher. And he encouraged Fisher to remain at Vaucluse, pointing him to 'some very fair sherry . . . in the cellar'. All he asked in return was that Vaucluse be maintained. The Hunts meanwhile threatened Fisher with an action for slander. Over the next year or so Wentworth sided with Fisher, providing helpful tips about Vaucluse's problems, including an invasion of snakes. On 21 April 1869 Wentworth wrote from his favourite London haunt, the Conservative Club, 'it might not . . . be a bad plan to pay 3d per head for all snakes killed within the fences of Vaucluse . . . but take proper precautions that the same snakes are not presented twice for payment'.[4]

Helped by the fact that Fisher was 12,000 miles away, Wentworth now developed a tolerable working relationship with him. But the Fishers' return had also been tinged by tragedy. The Wentworths' eldest grandson, William Wentworth Fisher, twenty-two, was working at a property Wentworth part-owned, Haddon Riggs (now Haddon Rig), located between Dubbo and Brewarrina, where he formed a relationship with a half-Aboriginal woman who was then cohabiting with an Aboriginal horse-breaker. More than once the woman had gone to be with young Fisher, and more than once the horse-breaker had reclaimed her. Finally, after the intervention of the Haddon Riggs superintendent, the Aboriginal couple left. The devastated Fisher armed himself with a rifle and tried to follow them on horseback, but the station hands stopped him. So Fisher walked away into the bush. Some time later, his body was found at the base of a sapling that had a broken strap attached to it. 'Death had been caused by suffocation,' the Coroner's report said, 'produced by strangulation.'

Bitter recriminations followed. Wentworth, fearing for Thomasine's sanity, made plans to 'go out to the Colony' to sell his share in Haddon Riggs. Meanwhile, his partner there, John Christie, drowned in the Macquarie River after an alcoholic fit brought on, some said, by the Wentworths' anger at William Fisher's death. So Wentworth was dismayed in 1870 when his son Fitzwilliam decided to buy Haddon Riggs outright. It did not sit well with Sarah's plan for Vaucluse 'to remain the home of all the family, from Fitzwilliam to the rest, for 99 years'. Overcoming his disappointment with Fitzwilliam's decision, Wentworth remained intensely interested in Haddon Riggs, advising his son at one point that 'a good plan before the next shearing [is] to get . . . battens cut to make yards for the washed sheep to lie on until they are shorn'.[5]

Throughout the 1860s, the Wentworths rented various properties both in London and in the country. 'Papa is dull', Sarah said, 'if he remains in one place too long.' Wherever they were, the English winters proved too much for their Aboriginal servant Bobby, who went home after shivering through three. Sarah regretted bringing him over, saying, 'He is naturally so clever and sensible that I hope he will be content to go back to Vaucluse.' The closest Wentworth now got to anything Australian was an occasional appearance, health permitting, at London gatherings of Australian expatriates. His deteriorating health, a combination of lung and heart problems worsened by old age, restricted his mobility, although as late as July 1870 Sarah managed to take him to Germany. 'The change,' she said, 'has always benefited Papa.'

A few months beforehand the Wentworths had moved to Merly House, near Wimborne in Dorset, an enormous pile of eighteen bedrooms built for a West Indian planter. Though this mansion was pretentious, the Wentworths remained less so than others. 'Some people are so absurd,' Sarah said, 'to say that Papa's father was a son of Lord Fitzwilliam.' According to rumour only, Wentworth had declined a baronetcy (a hereditary knighthood) when it was offered to him. But he was delighted to be elected as a Fellow of the Royal Geographic Society. Above all, however, he remained a squatter at heart. In November 1871, when he could no longer write, he dictated a letter to Sarah for one of his station managers in Australia. 'I am glad to find', he said, 'that the sheep washing machine answers so well and I trust that the wool will in consequence be got up in an unusually clean manner.'[6]

On 20 March 1872, at the age of eighty-one, Wentworth died, 'peacefully passing from this world' as Sarah said. *The Illustrated London News* of 27 April, which had been provided by the family with a later birth date, reported that Wentworth, who had been 'conspicuous in the foremost rank of Australian . . . statesmen, died in the seventy-ninth year of his age'. The span of Wentworth's life had been as large as the man himself. At the time of his birth, messages had taken six months to get from London to Sydney by sailing ship. Now they took only six hours when tapped out on the newly opened transcontinental telegraph. And the penal settlement of just over 2000 people into which Wentworth was born had been transformed into six colonies with a combined population approaching 2 million, where trial by jury and freedom of the press were accepted without question.

As Sarah grieved the loss of 'the light of our dwelling', the thoughts of others turned to grandiose plans for remembrance. Eliza Wentworth wanted to know whether the Sydney authorities would allow 'a recumbent figure of dear Papa in marble' to be built on top of a large tomb in the cathedral. Sarah, however, worked on carrying out Wentworth's wish to be buried inside 'the large single rock . . . on the slope from Parsley Hill' as seen from the 'long drawing room side' of Vaucluse House. Eliza abandoned her plan, but the public reaction to the news of Wentworth's death was such that even in egalitarian Sydney, a grandiose cathedral monument might not have been out of the question. On 6 August 1872 the Legislative Assembly, on the motion of the Prime Minister, Sir James Martin, resolved to offer the Wentworth family a state funeral, Australia's first. In seconding the motion, Henry Parkes admitted that he had never spoken to Wentworth 'in his life' before conceding that his opponent's early struggles 'were of a priceless character in repelling arbitrary power'. In death Wentworth had finally united his former Council colleagues, who all stood silently in their places to signify their assent when the Speaker put the motion. And by March 1873 Henry Parkes, now Prime Minister himself, was writing anxiously to Sarah to inquire about the name and arrival date of the vessel carrying Wentworth's remains.[7]

The year 1872 had not been all bad for the Wentworth family, which celebrated three marriages in the northern autumn. As he got older Wentworth's forceful and abrupt way of speaking, no doubt exacerbated by his deafness and the crankiness of old age, had embarrassed and unsettled his children's friends. So it may just have been a coincidence. It may, in the girls' case, have been the £25,000 they each inherited, or their striking auburn hair and penetrating brown eyes. But Edith, then D'Arcy and then Laura all got married within months of their father's death. What Wentworth would have thought of Edith's husband, who was Robert Lowe's nephew, it is difficult to say. Lady Sarah Macarthur described him as 'a silly little High Church curate'.

Other family news proved more predictable. Thomas Fisher wrote to Sarah within four months of Wentworth's death, declining to act as executor of his estate and at the same time complaining about having to pay from his own pocket the cost of employing a gardener at Vaucluse.[8]

Wentworth's body was returned to Sydney aboard the *British King*, and his funeral was fixed for 6 May 1873, a Tuesday, which was declared a public holiday. From early morning, barriers across George Street, at Haymarket in the south and Market Street in the north kept a large area in front of St Andrew's Cathedral free of traffic for the arrival of the family, the Governor, the Prime Minister, the Chief Justice, the Mayor and a long list of other worthies, carefully organised according to the protocol of the day. At the start of the service the polished cedar coffin, covered in wreaths made from native plants at Vaucluse, was borne down the aisle to Beethoven's Funeral March, after which the bishop conducted a Church of England service. While the pillars of church and state were paying homage to a man who detested organised religion, 70,000 spectators lined the route to Vaucluse in big crowds from the cathedral to the Woolloomooloo omnibus stand and smaller clusters along the rest of the way. Near Hyde Park, a dense throng elbowed each other for room until the funeral procession of over 130 coaches approached, whereupon 'the noisy hum of conversation was immediately stilled'. The only exception was in front of the coffin, where a group of 'Native Australians'—about 400 Australian-born Europeans—marched. To their annoyance they were soon joined by half a dozen 'barefoot and bedraggled' Aboriginals, whose very presence, *The Sydney Morning Herald* said, 'publicly disputed' the Europeans' claim to be 'Native Australians'.

Once the procession reached Vaucluse, Sir James Martin continued the European tribute:

> William Charles Wentworth was one of the first born of the first generation of native Australians . . . [After] the advantage of an English education . . . he came back . . . to his native country . . . [which was] then little better than a large prison . . . What he claimed for himself he claimed also for others and so while contending for a free press, for trial by jury, and for a share in the making of the laws by which he was to be governed, he fought the battle of the humblest as well as of the highest . . . For half a century he took a leading part in . . . public affairs.[9]

Summing up the funeral from the other side of the continent, *The Perth Gazette* of 6 June 1873 noted that 'the people of New South Wales have proved themselves capable of a deep . . . reverence towards the first of their Australian-born countrymen who has attained eminence in the world'.[10]

In all the grandiloquence, it was perhaps *The Freeman's Journal* of 3 May 1873 that came closest to capturing Wentworth the man:

> That passionate and untameable spirit is quenched now . . . His bones and his memory are all that are left . . . This was a man really great . . . [whose] undying patriotism . . . will carry down the memory of the squinting eyes, the repellant manner, the harsh voice, and, in speaking, the disagreeable delivery, the violent emphasis, and the foaming mouth. Our

descendants will read his orations and will admire . . . the breadth of character shining through. They will recognise that he who spoke these words must have been emphatically a *man* . . . When we wish to raise our young men above the petty manoeuvrings and sharp practice of later politics . . . [and] show them in short the noble figure of a true patriot, we shall take them to the grave and repeat to them the history of William Charles Wentworth.[11]

Whatever may have been the practice for young politicians in the years immediately following Wentworth's death, there is hardly a politician today who would know, let alone visit, where Wentworth is buried. Indeed, in the legislative chamber where some of Wentworth's greatest speeches were made, few members now pause to reflect about why his portrait hangs there. And the public think of Wentworth, if they think of him at all, as that explorer who crossed the Blue Mountains near Wentworth Falls. In America, Wentworth would still be revered as that republic's founding fathers are. But Wentworth understood, as one of the first European Australians, that this was not going to be the Australian way. And with his dislike of many things American, he would not have minded.

In modern lists of the greatest Australians Wentworth's name is usually towards the bottom, an understandable placing given the contemporary obsession with celebrity. But Wentworth would have understood that too; a celebrity of his time and place, he knew only too well how quickly Australian public opinion could change. Without a revolution like the United States had, or even an insurrection like Canada's, there is no history of conflict to highlight for today's Australians just what a struggle Wentworth had against 'arbitrary power' to win his 'legislative declaration of independence', freedom of the press and trial by jury—achievements that flowed from New South Wales to every other Australian colony and ultimately to the Commonwealth itself. While these constitutional milestones were passed as a matter of course in many British colonies, none of them was inevitable in New South Wales, which began as a glorified jail.

Many others, including Bland, Cowper, Hall, Hayes, Jamison, Lang, Lowe, Macarthur, Parkes, Wardell and Windeyer, also deserve great credit. But as each of them acknowledged at one time or another, Wentworth's contributions stood head and shoulders above their own. In 1872, Parkes said: 'I have lived long enough to know that in his Constitution . . . [Wentworth] was careful with the pains-taking care of a man having a fatherly regard for his country to make the broad foundation for it.'

Like so many other historical figures, the driven personality that impelled Wentworth to great things was matched by utterly obnoxious behaviour. So often his intelligence, energy and courage were offset by his intolerant, loud and self-serving ways. His contempt for Aboriginals was as unacceptable then as it is now. And his self-serving opposition to democracy rightly casts a shadow over his reputation. But it is a longer shadow than it should be due largely to his still-born 'bunyip aristocracy', which has made it easy for his critics to lampoon him. The fact is that Wentworth ended up advocating and voting for an elected Upper House based on a system of proportional representation—a model opposed by that great liberal Charles Cowper and not bettered in terms of implementation until the Legislative Council was reconstituted in 1978.[12]

Wentworth at heart remained a Whig who believed in a narrowly elected, aristocratic Parliament to balance the power of the Crown. It was only political necessity that pushed him to support a wider franchise, and only then on terms designed to preserve the squatters' power for as long as possible. Yet this did not mean that he had a narrow vision for Australia. On his departure for England in 1854, Wentworth said:

Whatever may be my destiny, believe me that my latest prayer shall be for the happiness and prosperity of the people of Australia, for its rapid expansion into a nation which shall rule supreme in the southern world.

In London, as in Sydney, Wentworth had led the first serious push to unite the colonies to end the petty rivalries over tariffs that he saw as holding back their combined prosperity and expansion. Wentworth's greatest opponent, Henry Parkes, who was acknowledged as the 'Father of Federation' by Australia's first Prime Minister, Edmund Barton, in turn acknowledged Wentworth's role in showing him the way:

> So far back as July 28 1853 . . . Wentworth . . . [said] 'One of the most prominent legislative measures required by . . . *the colonies of the Australian group generally,* is the establishment *at once* of a Legislative Assembly, to make laws in relation to intercolonial questions . . .' Wentworth did not say that a federal legislature would be required towards the close of the century but 'at once' thirty-nine years ago . . . If Wentworth were still living he would be a decided advocate for federation, for he was its decided advocate at a time when the reasons in support of it were not one hundredth part so strong as they have since become.[13]

Nine years after Parkes wrote these words, the Australian federation came into being.

Wentworth, a convict's illegitimate child who rose from the bottom of the putrescent pile of transportation to help shape a new nation, attracted sycophantic praise, rabid abuse and every sentiment in between. But the last word should go to Sarah, his partner for forty-seven of his eighty-one years. 'I who knew him best,' she said, 'can appreciate the grand and noble nature and yet so simple in all the worldly matters.'[14]

COLONIAL BOUNDARIES

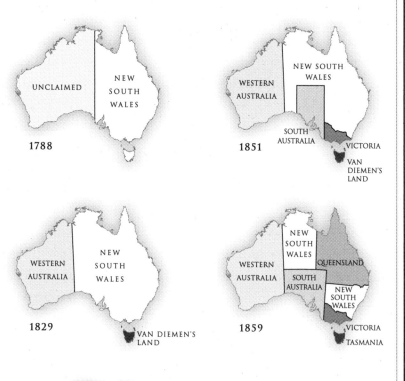

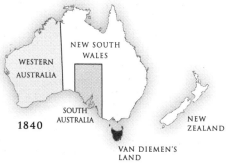

1788

1829

1840

1851

1859

Note 1: These maps show the colonial boundaries in the year indicated
Note 2: In 1840 New Zealand was a dependency of New South Wales
Note 3: Between 1851 and 1861 the Governor of New South Wales was also the Governor–General of all the colonies

NOTES

Each numbered note covers all the material in the main text back to the previous numbered note. Some notes cover one paragraph. Others cover more than one.

NOTES ON THE WENTWORTH PORTRAIT

1 *Votes and Proceedings of the New South Wales Legislative Assembly*, 11 October 1859; *Herald*, 12 October 1859.

2 M. Stapleton, *Australia's First Parliament*, Parliament of New South Wales, Sydney, 1995, p. 125.

3 W.C. Wentworth to Lord Fitzwilliam, 15 January 1817, Mitchell Library, A756.

INTRODUCTION

1 J. Ritchie, *The Wentworths Father and Son*, Melbourne University Press, 1999, p. 239; C.M.H. Clark, *A History of Australia*, Volume IV, Melbourne Univerrsity Press, Melbourne, 1978, p. 35.

2 *The People's Advocate*, 25 August 1849; S. Butler, *The Dinkum Dictionary*, 3rd Edition, Text Publishing, Melbourne, 2009, p. viii.

3 A.C.V. Melbourne, *Early Constitutional Development in Australia*, University of Queensland Press, Brisbane, 1963 pp. 419–20; W.C. Wentworth to the Speaker, 8 July 1854, *Votes and Proceedings of the Legislative Council of NSW*, 12 September 1854.

4 'The Late William Charles Wentorth', *Legislative Assembly Proceedings*, 6 August 1872, reported in The Sydney Morning Herald, 7 August 1872.

5 C.M.H. Clark, *A History of Australia*, Volume III, Melbourne UniversityPress, 1979, pp. 320–21 & Volume IV, 1999, pp. 261–62; www.law.mq.edu.au/scnsw; www.parliament.nsw.gov.au/prod/web/common.nsf/key/pre1991Hansard

6 C.M.H. Clark, *A History of Australia*, Melbourne University Press, Melbourne, Volumes I, II, III & IV first published in 1962, 1968, 1973, & 1978 respectively; A.C.V. Melbourne, *William Charles Wentworth*, Queensland University Press, Brisbane, first published in 1934; J. Ritchie, *The Wentworths Father & Son*, Melbourne University Press, Melbourne, first published 1997; C. Liston, *Sarah Wentworth Mistress of Vaucluse*,

Historic Houses Trust, Sydney, 1988; P. Cochrane, *Colonial Ambition*, Melbourne University Press, Melbourne, 2006; M. Persse, 'Wentworth, William Charles (1790–1872)', *Australian Dictionary of Biography* [ADB], Volume2, Melbourne University Press, Melbourne,1967, pp. 582–89.

CHAPTER 1   PLUCKED FROM THE PUTRESCENT PILE

1 Report of the Select Committee of the NSW Legislative Council on the Renewal of Transportation, 31 October 1846.

2 J.J. Auchmuty, 'Wentworth, D'Arcy (1762–1827)', *Australian Dictionary of Biography*, Volume 2, Melbourne University Press, 1967, pp. 579–82; J. Eddy, 'Wentworth, D'Arcy (1762–1827)', *Oxford Dictionary of National Biography* [ODNB], Oxford University Press, London, 2004, Volume 58, pp. 125–26; S. M. Farrell, 'Watson-Wentworth, Charles (1730-1782)', *ODNB*, Volume 58, pp. 118–25.

3 Earl of Albemarle, *Memoirs of the Marquis of Rockingham*, Richard Bentley, London, 1852, Volume I, p. 250; A.G. Olson, *The Radical Duke*, Oxford University Press, London, 1961, pp. 151–52; J. Fortescue, ed., *Correspondence of King George III 1760-83*, Frank Cass, London, 1967, Volume V, p. 392.

4 D. Wilkinson, 'Fitzwilliam, William Wentworth, second Earl Fitzwilliam in the peerage of Great Britain and fourth Earl Fitzwilliam in the peerage of Ireland (1748–1833)', *ODNB*, Volume 19, pp. 969–73; Ritchie, *The Wentworths*, pp. 2, 9; Auchmuty, D' Arcy Wentworth, *ADB*, Volume 2, pp. 579–82; <www.nationalarchives.gov.uk/currency> [18 January 2008].

5 *The Times*, 17 and 18 January 1787; Ritchie, *The Wentworths*, pp. 13, 15; Evidence of John Harris to Commissioner Bigge, 16 August 1820, Mitchell Library [ML] Bonwick Transcripts, Box 1, p. 269; *The Times*, 13, 18 July 1787; Thomas Alger, Violent Theft, 11 July 1787, the Proceedings at the Old Bailey ref: t17870711-9.

6 D'Arcy Wentworth, Mary Wilkinson, otherwise Looking, Theft with Violence: Highway Robbery, Theft: receiving Stolen Goods, Theft with Violence: Highway Robbery, Theft with Violence; Highway Robbery, 12 December 1787, The Proceedings of the Old Bailey, ref: t17871212–7.

7 *The Times*, 13 November 1789, Ritchie, *The Wentworths*, pp. 18–20; J.M. Beattie, 'Garrow, Sir William (1760-1840)', *ODNB*, Volume 21, pp. 546–48; D'Arcy Wentworth, Theft with Violence: Highway Robbery, 9 December 1789, The Proceedings of the Old Bailey, ref: t17891209–1; *The Times*, 10 December 1789; 'Barrington, George (1755?–1804)', *ADB*, Volume 1, pp. 62–63; W. Tench, *A Narrative of the Expedition to Botany Bay*, J. Debrett, London, 1789, p. 46; Ritchie, *The Wentworths*, p. 27.

8 M. Flynn, *The Second Fleet*, Library of Australian History, Sydney, 2001, pp. 30–32, 37–40, 229; Ritchie, *The Wentworths*, pp. 31–33; *The Times*, 30 December 1789; S. Macarthur Onslow, *Some Early Records of the Macarthurs of Camden*, Angus & Robertson, Sydney, 1914, pp. 4–13; M. Steven, 'Macarthur, John (1767–1834)', *ADB*, Volume 2, pp. 153–59; A. Needham, *The Women of the* Neptune, A-1 Instant Printing P/L, Dural, 1992, p. 61.

9 Evidence of John Harris to Commissioner Bigge, 16 August 1820, ML BT Box 1, p. 269; *The Times*, 30 December 1789; Flynn, *The Second Fleet*, pp. 42–49, 61; Ritchie,

The Wentworths, pp. 22, 33–36, 39–40; Macarthur Onslow, *The Macarthurs*, pp. 9, 17; Report of the Commissioners of His Majesty's Navy, 15 February 1792, in *Accounts and Papers Relating to Convicts on Board the Hulks and those Transported to New South Wales*, House of Commons Papers, 10, 26 March 1792, p. 63.

10 G. Mackaness, *Admiral Arthur Phillip*, Angus & Robertson, 1937, p. 256.

11 Flynn, *The Second Fleet*, p. 414; B.H. Fletcher, ed., *An Account of the English Colony in New South Wales by David Collins*, Volume I, A.H. & A.W. Reid, Sydney, 1975 (originally published in 1798), p. 106; S. De Vries, *Historic Sydney*, Pandanus Press, Sydney, 1999, p. 11; Ritchie, *The Wentworths*, p. 46.

12 William Charles Wentworth [Wentworth] to D'Arcy Wentworth, 15 January 1824 and Martha Johnston to D'Arcy Wentworth, 3 February 1826, both in D'Arcy Wentworth's Papers, ML A754–2; Ritchie, *The Wentworths*, p. 22.

13 Norfolk Island Victualling Book, 1792–96, ML A1958; *The Illustrated London News*, 27 April 1872; Sarah Wentworth to Thomasine Fisher, 25 October 1864, ML A868; Flynn, *The Second Fleet*, p. 229; Persse, 'William Charles Wentworth', *ADB*, Volume 2, pp. 582–89; Ritchie, *The Wentworths*, pp. 22, 47.

14 C.M.H. Clark, *A History of Australia*, Volume I, Melbourne University Press, 1962, p. 329.

CHAPTER 2   CURRENCY LAD

1 J. Hunter, *An Historical Journal of the Transactions at Port Jackson and Norfolk Island*, John Stockdale, London, 1793, p. 188; F. Clune, *The Norfolk Island Story*, Angus & Robertson, Sydney, 1967, pp. 28–29; M. Hazzard, *Punishment Short of Death*, Hyland House, Melbourne, 1984, p. 38.

2 Hunter, *Journal*, pp. 197, 579; R. Nobbs, *Norfolk Island 1788–1814*, Library of Australian History, Sydney, 1988, p. 114; P. Fidlon, ed., *The Journal and Letters of Lieutenant Ralph Clark 1787–1792*, Australian Documents Library, Sydney, 1981, pp. 180, 184, 186, 191, 202; L.A. Gilbert, 'Considen, Dennis (–1815)', *ADB*, Volume 1, pp. 242–43; Charles Cookney to D'Arcy Wentworth, 17 August 1797, ML A751.

3 Nobbs, *Norfolk Island*, p. 119; Ritchie, *The Wentworths*, pp. 67–68; Charles Cookney in Account with Mr D. Wentworth, 25 March 1794, ML A754–2; Hazzard, *Punishment Short of Death*, p. 40.

4 Fitzwilliam to D'Arcy Wentworth, 24 June 1793, ML A754–2; Wilkinson, Fitzwilliam, William Wentworth, *ODNB*, Volume 19, pp. 969–73; Cookney to D'Arcy Wentworth, May 1794, ML A754–2.

5 *Advertiser*, 20 January 1792, as quoted in Ritchie, *The Wentworths*, p. 64.

6 Norfolk Island Victualling Book; A.G.L. Shaw, 'King, Phillip Gidley (1758–1808)', *ADB*, Volume 2, pp. 55–61; Nobbs, *Norfolk Island*, p. 61; Clune, *Norfolk Island Story*, p. 51.

7 Dundas to Grose, 15 November 1793; Hunter to Portland, 30 April 1796; D'Arcy Wentworth's Commission, 1 April 1796, all in F. Watson, ed., *Historical Records of Australia [HRA]*, Series I, Volume I, The Library Committee of the Commonwealth Parliament, Canberra, 1914, at pp. 458, 561–62, 691–92 respectively; Nobbs, *Norfolk Island*, p. 214; Cookney to D'Arcy Wentworth, 30 August 1797, ML A754–2; M.H.

Ellis, *John Macarthur*, Angus & Robertson, Sydney, 1955, p. 165; De Vries, *Historic Sydney*, p. 8.

8 Clark, *A History of Australia*, Volume I, p. 135; Patterson to King, 18 September 1800, *HRA*, Volume II, p. 544. Hunter to Portland, 1 May 1799, *HRA*, Volume II, p. 367; Return of Land Grants, 6 February 1800, *HRA*, Volume II, pp. 462–63; Ritchie, *The Wentworths*, p. 81; Hunter to D'Arcy Wentworth, 21 December 1799, ML A751.

9 Ritchie, *The Wentworths*, p. 83; P.J. Fulton, ed., *The Minerva Journal of John Washington Price*, Miegunyah Press, Melbourne, 2000, pp. 150–51; W.C. Wentworth, *Australasia*, G. & W.B. Whittaker, London, 1823, p. 3.

10 King to Patterson, 8, 18 September 1800, *HRA*, Volume II, pp. 542–45; Grose to Foveaux, 25 June 1799, ML A753; B.H. Fletcher, 'Foveaux, Joseph (1767–1846)', *ADB*, Volume 1, pp. 407–09; Fulton, *The Minerva Journal*, p. 150; 'Barrington, George (1755?-1804)', *ADB*, Volume 1, pp. 62–63; *The Times*, 10 December 1789.

11 Ritchie, *The Wentworths*, pp. 88, 93; Fitzwilliam to D'Arcy Wentworth, 30 July 1802, ML A754–2; S. Mourot, *This Was Sydney*, Ure Smith, Sydney, 1969, p. 18; P. Fidlon, *The Journal of Arthur Bowes Smyth*, Australian Documents Library, Sydney, 1979, p. 128.

12 Cookney's Account with D'Arcy Wentworth, 1803–09, ML A754–2; Cookney to D'Arcy Wentworth, 31 October 1803, ML A754–2; William and D'Arcy Wentworth to their father, 24 July 1804, ML A756; D'Arcy Wentworth Jr to his father, 4 July 1805, ML A755; Cookney to D'Arcy Wentworth, n.d., ML A754–2; Cookney to D'Arcy Wentworth, 13 April 1805, ML A754–2; Cookney to D'Arcy Wentworth, 19 June 1805, ML A754–2.

13 Mrs Cookney's postscript to a letter from William to his father, 11 August 1805, ML A756; Cookney to D'Arcy Wentworth, 8 October 1805, 31 December 1805, 10 June 1807, 14 November 1807, 29 April 1808, all in ML A754–2; Cookney's Account with D'Arcy Wentworth, 1803–09; *Gentleman's Magazine*, October 1842, pp. 433–34.

14 Castlereagh to Bligh, 30 December 1807, *HRA*, Volume VI, p. 200; Wilkinson, Fitzwilliam, William Wentworth, *ODNB*, Volume 19, pp. 969–73; Cookney to D'Arcy Wentworth, 25 November 1809, ML A754–2; Cookney's Account with D'Arcy Wentworth, 1803–09; John Macarthur to Elizabeth Macarthur, 3 May 1810, in S. Macarthur Onslow, *The Macarthurs*, pp. 194, 198; Ellis, *Macarthur*, p. 348.

CHAPTER 3   A VERY VALUABLE INVESTMENT

1 *The Sydney Gazette [Gazette]*, 24 March 1810.

2 Bligh to Windham, 31 October 1807, *HRA*, Volume VI, p. 188; Bartrum, *Proceedings of a General Court Martial of Lieut.-Col. Geo. Johnston on a Charge of Mutiny for Deposing on 26 January 1808, William Bligh*, Sherwood, Neely and Jones, London, 1811, pp. 102, 105, 205, 209–211, 236; Bligh to Castlereagh, 30 April 1808, *HRA*, Volume VI, pp. 426–29; N.D. McLachlan, 'Macquarie, Lachlan (1762–1824)', *ADB*, Volume 2, pp. 187–95.

3 Introduction, *HRA*, Volume VI, p. xxxiv; *Gazette*, 7, 14 January, 24 February 1810; Bartrum, *Johnston's Court Martial*, p. 230.

4 Ritchie, *The Wentworths*, pp. 104, 141; Macquarie to Castlereagh, 8 March 1810, *HRA*, Volume VII, p. 224; M.H. Ellis, *Lachlan Macquarie*, Angus & Robertson, Sydney, 1952, p. 114.

5 Auchmuty, 'D'Arcy Wentworth', *ADB*, Volume 2, pp. 579–82; Ritchie, *The Wentworths*, p. 135; C.M.H. Clark, *A History of Australia*, Volume II, Melbourne University Press, 1979, p. 41; Ellis, *Macquarie*, p. 231; *Gazette*, 19 October 1810; C.M.H. Clark, *Select Documents in Australian History*, Volume I, Angus & Robertson, 1970, p. 434, quoting Commissioner Bigge.

6 Ritchie, *The Wentworths*, p. 133; *Gazette*, 31 March, 19 May, 29 December 1810; Macquarie to Castlereagh, 8 March, 30 April 1810, 18 October 1811, *HRA*, Volume VII, pp. 223, 253–54, 384; Ellis, *Macquarie*, p. 192. Liverpool to Macquarie, 19 May, 17 November 1812, *HRA*, Volume VII, pp. 486–87, 597; Mourot, *This Was Sydney*, pp. 22–23.

7 Ritchie, *The Wentworths*, p. 135; Clark, *A History of Australia*, Volume I, p. 278; State Records Authority of NSW, Agency No. 1047: Provost Marshal <www.investigator. records.nsw.gov.au/Details/Agency-Detail.asp?Id=1047> [22 April 2007]; *Gazette*, 26 October 1811, 11, 18 January, 1 February, 19 December 1812, 2 January 1813.

8 Wentworth, Blaxcell and Riley to Macquarie, 4, 23 March, 18 December 1812, 11 January 1813, 5 October 1814, ML A761; Macquarie to Wentworth, Blaxcell and Riley, 17 September, 30 December 1812, 10 February 1813, ML A761.

9 Ritchie, *The Wentworths*, p. 148; Wentworth to William Moore, 4 June 1815, ML A756; *Gazette*, 11 December 1813, 22 January; Agreement between D'Arcy Wentworth, William Campbell, William Wentworth, Alexander Riley and Garnham Blaxcell, January 1814, ML A752.

10 *Gazette*, 22 October 1814.

11 A.T. Yarwood, *Samuel Marsden*, Melbourne University Press, 1977, p. 150. Wentworth to William Moore, 4 June 1815, ML A756.

CHAPTER 4   BLAXLAND, LAWSON AND WENTWORTH

1 Clark, *A History of Australia*, Volume I, p. 277; Clark, *Select Documents*, Volume I, p. 405; *Gazette*, 22 May 1813.

2 J. Conway, 'Blaxland, Gregory (1778–1853)', *ADB*, Volume 1, pp. 115–17; E.W. Dunlop, 'Lawson, William (1774–1850)', *ADB*, Volume 2, pp. 96–97; Ritchie, *The Wentworths*, pp. 66, 134; Account of Stock Issued, 17 November 1812, *HRA*, Volume VII, p. 628.

3 G. Blaxland's letter and 'Narrative' sent to Commissioner Bigge, 28 November 1819 in J.A. Richards, ed., *Blaxland-Lawson-Wentworth 1813*, Blubber Head Press, Hobart, 1979, pp. 173–76; G. Blaxland to J.O. Parker, 10 February 1823, in F. Walker, ed., *A Journal of a Tour of Discovery Across the Blue Mountains NSW in 1813 by Gregory Blaxland*, Sydney, 1913, pp. 10-12; T.M. Perry, *Australia's First Frontier,* Melbourne University Press, Melbourne, 1965, pp. 27–28.

4 F. Walker, *Blaxland's Journal*, p. 13; G. Blaxland to Sir Joseph Banks, 10 November 1816, in J.A. Richards, *Blaxland-Lawson-Wentworth*, pp. 99–105, 150; W.C. Wentworth, *Journal of an Expedition Across the Blue Mountains*, 11 May to 6 June 1813, ML Safe 1/22a.

5 F. Walker, *Blaxland's Journal*, pp. 15–23; J.A. Richards, *Blaxland-Lawson-Wentworth*, pp. 85, 86.

6 F. Walker, *Blaxland's Journal*, pp. 23, 24, 27; J.A. Richards, *Blaxland-Lawson-Wentworth*, pp. 13, 15–17, 87, 88; C. Cunningham, *Blue Mountains Rediscovered*, Kangaroo Press, East Roseville, 1999, pp. 53, 65–66, 70; R. Brownscombe, *On Suspect Terrain*, Forever Wild Press, 2004, pp. 163, 183.

7 F. Walker, *Blaxland's Journal*, pp. 27–32; J.A. Richards, *Blaxland-Lawson-Wentworth*, pp. 88–90; R. Brownscombe, *On Suspect Terrain*, pp. 183, 225.

8 F. Walker, *Blaxland's Journal*, pp. 34–41; G. Blaxland to L. Macquarie, 15 June 1815, in J.A. Richards, *Blaxland-Lawson-Wentworth*, pp. 145–46 and generally at pp. 88–90; R. Brownscombe, *On Suspect Terrain*, p. 225.

9 F. Walker, *Blaxland's Journal*, p. 41; Wentworth to Lord Bathurst, 18 January 1817, in J.A. Richards, *Blaxland-Lawson-Wentworth*, p. 181; *Gazette*, 12 June 1813.

10 W.C. Wentworth, *Journal*, ML Safe 1/22a; *The Journal of William Lawson*, in J.A. Richards, *Blaxland-Lawson-Wentworth*, p. 104.

11 G. Blaxland to Sir Joseph Banks, 10 November 1816, in J.A. Richards, *Blaxland-Lawson-Wentworth*, p. 150; Government and General Orders, 10 June 1815, *HRA*, Volume VIII, p. 569; Cunningham, *Mountains Rediscovered*, pp. 143–44.

12 *Gazette*, 12 February 1814; Cunningham, *Mountains Rediscovered*, p. 145.

13 *Gazette*, 10 June 1815; G. Blaxland to L. Macquarie, 15 June 1815, in J.A. Richards, *Blaxland-Lawson-Wentworth*, pp. 145–6.

14 J.E.B. Currey, ed., *Reflections on the Colony of New South Wales by George Caley*, Lansdowne Press, Melbourne, 1966, pp. 6–22, 116, 195; Cunningham, *Mountains Rediscovered*, pp. 55, 83, 86, 111; G. Blaxland to Sir Joseph Banks, 10 November 1816 and G. Blaxland to Commissioner Bigge, 28 November 1819, both in J.A. Richards, *Blaxland-Lawson-Wentworth*, pp. 149–51, 173–76 and see also p. 34.

15 Dunlop, 'Lawson, William', *ADB*, Volume 2, pp. 96–97; Wentworth, *Australasia*, p. 13.

16 J.A. Richards, *Blaxland-Lawson-Wentworth*, p. 32.

CHAPTER 5   A SHOWDOWN LOOMS

1 Ritchie, *The Wentworths*, p. 169; *Gazette*, 9 March 1816.

2 Fitzwilliam to Wentworth, 25 December 1816, ML A757; Agreement between Wentworth and J. Griffiths, 25 February 1816, ML MSS.8/1; D'Arcy Wentworth to Wentworth, 16 April 1816, ML A752; Wentworth to Alexander Riley, 25 August 1818, ML A756.

3 *Gazette*, 30 March 1816; Ritchie, *The Wentworths*, p. 169; D'Arcy Wentworth to Wentworth, 16 April 1816, ML A752.

4 Wentworth to D'Arcy Wentworth, 16 August 1816, ML A756.

5 Ritchie, *The Wentworths*, p. 161; John Macarthur to Elizabeth Macarthur, 9 December 1816, in Macarthur Onslow, *The Macarthurs*, p. 285.

6 Wentworth to D'Arcy Wentworth, 7 February 1817, ML A756; Ritchie, *The Wentworths*, p. 165; Wentworth to Fitzwilliam, 18 December 1816, 15 January 1817, ML

A756; Fitzwilliam to Wentworth, 16 January 1817, ML A757; Wentworth to Earl Bathurst, 18 January, 22 April 1817, in J.A. Richards, *Blaxland-Lawson-Wentworth*, pp. 181–86.

7 Wentworth to D'Arcy Wentworth, 10 April 1817, ML A756.

8 Wentworth to D'Arcy Wentworth, 10 April 1817, ML A756; H. King, *Elizabeth Macarthur and Her World*, Sydney University Press, Sydney, 1980, pp. 65, 90.

9 Fitzwilliam to Cookney, 9 August 1818, ML A757; Cookney to Wentworth, 21 July, 11 August 1818, ML A757.

10 Macquarie to the Duke of York, 25 July 1817, *HRA*, Volume IX, pp. 447–48; Sanderson, Forster and Grant to Molle, *HRA*, Volume IX, p. 453; Molle to Macquarie, 24 June 1817, *HRA*, Volume IX, p. 456; D'Arcy Wentworth to Macquarie, 8 September 1817, ML A753; Macquarie's Charges against the Officers of the 46th Regiment, *HRA*, Volume IX, p. 460; Macquarie to Bathurst, *HRA*, Volume IX, p. 554.

11 D'Arcy Wentworth to Fitzwilliam, 16 December 1817, ML A753; Wentworth to A. Riley, 19 November 1819, ML A756; Ritchie, *The Wentworths*, p. 176, Wentworth to D'Arcy Wentworth, 24 April 1817, ML A756; Cookney to D'Arcy Wentworth, 15 April 1817, ML A754–2; *The Times*, 8 March 1817; Wentworth to H.G. Bennet, 16 March 1817, ML A756; Wentworth to D'Arcy Wentworth, 22 March 1817, ML A756; J. Ritchie, *Punishment and Profit*, Heinemann, Melbourne, 1970, pp. 29–30; N. Thompson, 'Bathurst, Henry, third Earl Bathurst (1762–1834)', *ODNB*, Volume 4, pp. 354–55; Petition of the Settlers of NSW respecting the Conduct of Governor Macquarie, *Journals of the House of Commons*, 28 January to 16 December 1817, p. 148.

12 C.H. Currey, 'Bent, Jeffrey Hart (1781–1852)', *ADB*, Volume I, pp. 87–92; Proceedings before the Superintendent of Police, 6 September 1815, *HRA*, Volume IX, pp. 16–17; C. H. Currey, *The Brothers Bent*, Sydney University Press, Sydney, 1968, pp. 121, 146, 152; Mourot, *This Was Sydney*, p. 28.

13 Currey, *The Brothers Bent*, p. 153; House of Commons, *Report of the Select Committee on Transportation*, 10 July 1812, Minutes of Evidence, p. 45; Fitzwilliam to Cookney, 9 August 1818, ML A757; Cookney to Wentworth, 21 July, 11 August 1818, ML A757; Ritchie, *Punishment and Profit*, pp. 30, 51, 61.

CHAPTER 6   HUMILIATION

1 Wentworth to J. Macarthur Jr, 24 August 1818, ML A756; Wentworth to Alexander Riley, 25 August 1818, ML A756; John Macarthur Jr to his mother, 5 March 1818, ML A2911; Ellis, Macarthur, pp. 480–81.

2 Wentworth to D'Arcy Wentworth, 25 May 1818, ML A756.

3 Wentworth to D'Arcy Wentworth, 25 May 1818, ML A756; Wentworth to John Macarthur Jr, 29 July 1818, ML A756; Wentworth to D'Arcy Wentworth, 10 November 1818, ML A756; Ritchie, *The Wentworths*, p. 175; H. King, *Elizabeth Macarthur*, pp. 86–91; M. Steven, 'Macarthur, John (1767–1834)', *ADB*, Volume 2, pp. 153–59; J.M. Ward, *James Macarthur Colonial Conservative, 1798–1867*, Sydney University Press, Sydney, 1981, p. 24.

4 Wentworth to D'Arcy Wentworth, 10 November 1818, ML A756; Wentworth to A. Riley, 19 November 1818, ML A756.

5 T.C. Hansard, *The Parliamentary Debates*, London, 1819, Volume 39, cc. 468–69; H.G Bennet, *Letter to Viscount Sidmouth, Secretary of State for the Home Department, on the Transportation Laws, the State of the Hulks, and of the Colonies in New South* Wales, J. Ridgway, London, 1819; Ritchie, *The Wentworths*, p. 177.

6 Wentworth to D'Arcy Wentworth, 14 February 1819, ML A756; Wentworth to H.G. Bennet, 12 February 1819; ML A756; Wentworth to D'Arcy Wentworth, 13 April 1819, ML A756; J.M. Beattie, Sir William Garrow, *ODNB*, Volume 21, pp. 546–48.

7 Wentworth to D'Arcy Wentworth, 14 February 1819, ML A756.

8 Hansard, *Debates*, 1819, Volume 39, c. 471; Wentworth to D'Arcy Wentworth, 13 April 1819, ML A756.

9 D'Arcy Wentworth, Theft with Violence: Highway Robbery, 9 December 1789, The Proceedings of the Old Bailey, ref: t17891209–1; Fitzwilliam to Wentworth, 9 February 1821, ML A757.

10 Clark, *Select Documents*, Volume I, p. 18; Wentworth to D'Arcy Wentworth, 13 April 1819, ML A756.

CHAPTER 7   THE FIRST BOOK

1 Wentworth to D'Arcy Wentworth, 4 May 1819, ML A756.

2 W.C. Wentworth, *A Statistical, Historical, and Political Description of The Colony of New South Wales and its Dependent Settlements in Van Diemen's Land with a Particular Enumeration of the Advantages which these Colonies offer for Emigration, and their Superiority in many Respects over those Possessed by the United States of America*, G. and W.B. Whittaker, London, 1819. J. Wantrup, *Australian Rare Books 1788–1900*, Hordern House, Sydney, 1987.

3 Wentworth to D'Arcy Wentworth, 25 May 1818, ML A756.

4 Wentworth, *A Statistical etc Description*, 1819, pp. viii, 4, 60, 64, 65, 86, 87.

5 Wentworth, *A Statistical etc Description*, 1819, pp. 2, 159, 160, 166–69, 172, 175.

6 Wentworth, *A Statistical etc Description*, 1819, pp. 212, 251, 253, 255, 266, 270–78, 327, 410; Commons, *Committee on Transportation*, 1812, Report, pp. 6, 14; Steven, 'Macarthur, John, *ADB*, Volume 2, pp. 153–59.

7 Wentworth, *A Statistical etc Description*, 1819, pp. 337, 345–48; Commons, *Committee on Transportation*, Report, p. 13.

8 Wentworth, *A Statistical etc Description*, 1819, pp. 355–57; Melbourne, *Early Constitutional Development of Australia*, p. 69.

9 Wentworth, *A Statistical etc Description*, 1819, pp. 357–62; Commons, *Committee on Transportation*, Report, p. 8; Hansard, *Debates*, 1819, Volume 39, cc. 468–69.

10 Wentworth, *A Statistical etc Description*, 1819, pp. 365, 375; Commons, *Committee on Transportation*, Report, p. 7.

11 Wentworth, *A Statistical etc Description*, 1819, pp. 383, 422, 425.

12 Wentworth to D'Arcy Wentworth, 24 August 1819, ML A756; *Edinburgh Review*, Volume xxxii, July 1819; D'Arcy's 'affectionate sister' to D'Arcy Wentworth, 6 May

1822, ML A754–2; J. Macarthur Sr to J. Macarthur Jr, 20 February 1820, in S. Macarthur Onslow, *The Macarthurs*, p. 337.

13 Wentworth to D'Arcy Wentworth, 24 August 1819, ML A756; Ritchie, *The Wentworths*, p. 182; *The Times*, 28 August 1819; Wantrup, *Australian Rare Books*, pp. 117–18; W.C. Wentworth, *A Statistical etc. and a Word of Advice to Emigrants*, 2nd edition, London, 1820, pp. xiv–xvii, 441, 477, 479; Clark, *Select Documents*, pp. 405–06.

CHAPTER 8   A BOOBY COMMISSIONER

1 Wentworth to D'Arcy Wentworth, 6 July 1819, ML A756.

2 J. Macarthur Sr to J. Macarthur Jr, 20 February 1820, in S. Macarthur Onslow, *The Macarthurs*, p. 329.

3 Wentworth to D'Arcy Wentworth, 13 April 1819, ML A756; Ritchie, *The Wentworths*, p. 176; Wentworth to D'Arcy Wentworth, 9 August 1819, ML A756.

4 Wentworth to D'Arcy Wentworth, 24 August 1819, ML A756; L. Colley, *Britons*, Pimlico, London, 2003, p. 264; C.W. Colby, ed., *Selections from the Sources of English History*, Longmans Green, London, 1920, pp. 298–300; Wilkinson, second Earl Fitzwilliam, *ODNB*, Volume 19, pp. 969–73.

5 Wentworth to D'Arcy Wentworth, 24 August 1819, ML A756; Ritchie, *The Wentworths*, p. 182; J.M. Bennett, 'Bigge, John Thomas (1780–1843)', *ODNB*, Volume 5, pp. 693–94; Ritchie, *Punishment and Profit*, p. 54; Macquarie to Bathurst, 10 October 1823, Commons Papers relating to New South Wales, 25 June 1828; Copy of a further letter from Bathurst to Bigge, 6 January 1819, in Australiana Facsimile Editions No. 69, Libraries Board of South Australia, Adelaide, 1966.

6 Ritchie, *Punishment and Profit*, pp. 54, 55, 119, 139, 158, 323; Ritchie, *The Wentworths*, pp. 187–90; Bigge to D'Arcy Wentworth, 25 January 1812, ML A754–1; J. Macarthur Sr to J. Macarthur Jr, 20 February 1820, in S. Macarthur Onslow, *The Macarthurs*, pp. 324–25, 329.

7 Ritchie, *Punishment and Profit*, p. 237; The Bigge Reports, Biographical Note, in Australiana Facsimile Editions No. 70, Libraries Board of South Australia, Adelaide, 1966; Bigge Report on Agriculture and Trade, pp. 86, 109; Bigge Report on The Colony, p. 86.

8 Macquarie to Bathurst, 10 October 1823 and Macquarie to Bathurst, 27 July 1822, both in House of Commons Papers Relating to New South Wales, 25 June 1828; Bigge Report on The Colony, pp. 148–49, 174–75; Clark, *Select Documents*, p. 310.

9 Ritchie, *Punishment and Profit*, p. 224; Macquarie to Duke of York, 25 July 1817, *HRA*, Volume IX, p. 448; Bigge Report on Judicial Establishments, p. 90.

10 Wentworth to Alexander Riley, 25 August 1818, ML A756; Bigge Report on Judicial Establishments, p. 40; Bigge Report on The Colony, p. 175.

11 W.C. Wentworth, *A Statistical etc Description*, 3rd edition, London, 1824, Volume I, pp. 348–50.

12 Wentworth, *A Statistical etc Description*, 1824, Volume I, pp. 387–89; Ritchie, *Punishment and Profit*, p. 240.

CHAPTER 9 TRANSITION

1 Cookney to D'Arcy Wentworth, 30 August 1822, ML A754–1; Wentworth's Middle Temple Degree of the utter Bar, 8 February 1822, ML A758; Cookney to D'Arcy Wentworth, 9 August 1821, ML A754–2; Cookney to D'Arcy Wentworth, 28 May 1820, ML A754–2; Cookney to D'Arcy Wentworth, 26 December 1821, ML A754–2; Ritchie, *The Wentworths*, pp. 169, 190; Eddy, D'Arcy Wentworth, *ODNB*, Volume 58, pp. 125–26; Fitzwilliam to Wentworth, 31 December 1823, ML A757.

2 Wentworth to D'Arcy Wentworth, 18 March 1823 ML A756; Ritchie, *The Wentworths*, pp. 200, 202.

3 J. Macarthur Jr to his mother, 5 March 1818, ML A2911; J. Macarthur Jr to J. Macarthur Sr, 1 June 1821, ML A2911; J. Macarthur Sr to J. Macarthur Jr, 20 February 1820, in S. Macarthur Onslow, *The Macarthurs*, p. 338; J. Macarthur Jr to James Macarthur, 24 March 1822, ML A752; D'Arcy Wentworth, Reports of Trials, 1787, 1789, ML D185; C.H. Currey, *Sir Francis Forbes*, Angus & Robertson, Sydney, 1969, p. 75.

4 Wentworth to D'Arcy Wentworth, 18 March 1823, ML A756; *Gazette*, 18 March 1824; Wentworth, *Australasia*, pp. viii, ix, 12, 22; Currey, Forbes, p. 251.

5 Wentworth, To Miss Taylor on her Birthday, 17 May 1823, ML A756; Ritchie, *The Wentworths*, p. 175; Wentworth to A. Riley, 27 October 1820, ML A756; A. Riley to Wentworth, 31 October 1820, ML A756;

6 W.C. Wentworth to D'Arcy Wentworth, 11 May 1820 ML A756; Cookney to D'Arcy Wentworth, 30 August 1822, ML A754–2; Wentworth to D'Arcy Wentworth, 18 March 1823, ML A756.

7 Wentworth, *A Statistical etc Description*, 1824, Volume I, pp. 223 and Volume II, pp. 59, 98.

8 Currey, *Sir Francis Forbes*, pp. 21–46; 4 G. IV, c. 96; Hansard, *Debates*, 1823, Volume 9, cc. 1447–52; Ritchie, *The Wentworths*, p. 202; W.J.V. Windeyer, *Lectures on Legal History*, 2nd edition, Law Book Company, Sydney, 1957, p. 310.

9 Wentworth, *A Statistical etc Description*, 1824, Volume I, pp. 326, 338–39, 387; Melbourne, *Early Constitutional Developments*, p. 86.

10 Wentworth, *A Statistical etc Description*, 1824, Volume I, p. 383; Wentworth, *Australasia*, p. ix; Ellis, *Macquarie*, pp. 520–21; *Gazette*, 22 July 1824.

11 R. Else-Mitchell and J. Bennett, The Charter of Justice of NSW, Standard Publishing House, Sydney, 1974; Fitzwilliam to Wentworth, 31 December 1823, ML A757; C.H. Currey, 'Wardell, Robert (1793–1834)', *ADB*, Volume 2, pp. 570–72; Wentworth, *A Statistical etc Description*, 1824, Volume I, pp. 20–29; Wardell v Howe, *Australian,* 29 March 1827; R.B. Walker, *The Newspaper Press in New South Wales*, Sydney University Press, Sydney, 1976, p. 6.

12 Wentworth v Jones, *Australian*, 24 November 1825; *Gazette*, 22 July 1824.

CHAPTER 10 PLEADERS AND PAPERS

1 Wentworth v Jones, *Australian*, 24 November 1825 and *Gazette*, 24 November 1825.

2 *Gazette*, 18 March, 1 April 1824.

3 *Gazette*, 22 July 1824; Clark, *A History of Australia*, Volume II, p. 52; J.D. Heydon,

'Brisbane, Sir Thomas Makdougall (1773–1860)', *ADB*, Volume I, pp. 151–55; Ritchie, *The Wentworths*, pp. 137, 208; J. Broadbent and J. Hughes, eds, *The Age of Macquarie*, Melbourne University Press, Melbourne, 1992, pp. 22, 66.

4 Division of the Profession, *Gazette*, 16 September 1824; J.M. Bennett, *A History of the New South Wales Bar*, Law Book Company, Sydney, 1969, p. 34; R. Annable, *A Setting for Justice*, University of New South Wales Press, Sydney, 2007, pp. 19, 52, 69, 74; Currey, *Forbes*, pp. 5, 47, 71–3.

5 C. Chambers for Wentworth to J. Norris, 18 January 1825, ML A1440; Wentworth to The Attorney General, 15 April 1825, ML A1440; R. Wardell and Wentworth to The Attorney General, 4 March 1825, ML A1440; Bennett, *History of the Bar*, p. 36; *Australian*, 25 November 1824; Mourot, *This Was Sydney*, p. 28; Currey, *Forbes*, p. 70.

6 *Australian*, 14 October 1824.

7 Brisbane to Bathurst, 12 January 1825, *HRA*, Volume XI, pp. 470–71; *Australian* and *Gazette*, 14 October 1824; *Australian*, 29 September 1825.

8 R v Gillman; *Australian*, 14, 21, 28 October 1824; *Gazette*, 21, 28 October 1824.

9 *Australian*, 21 October 1824; *Gazette*, 21 October, 4 November 1824; J.M. Bennett, 'The Establishment of Jury Trial in New South Wales', *The Sydney Law Review*, Volume 3, 1959–61, pp. 469–70.

10 *Australian*, 28 October 1824; D. Bairstow, *A Million Pounds A Million Acres*, Self-published, Sydney, 2003, pp. 4–5; Ritchie, *The Wentworths*, p. 218; *Gazette*, 2 December 1824.

11 R v Sheriff of New South Wales, *Australian*, 13, 27 January 1825; *Gazette*, 3 February 1825.

12 Wentworth to Brisbane, 26 February 1825, ML A1440; Wentworth to Major Ovens, 19 March 1825, ML A1440; *Australian*, 7 April 1825; Jeans, *An Historical Geography*, p. 93.

13 Ritchie, *The Wentworths*, p. 212; Liston, *Sarah Wentworth*, pp. 17, 24–25; Cox v Payne, *Australian*, 19 May 1825; *Gazette*, 19 May 1825.

14 Liston, *Sarah Wentworth*, p. 17; J.V. Byrnes, 'Howe, Robert (1795–1829)', *ADB*, Volume 1, pp. 557–59; *Australian*, 7, 28 April, 23 June 1825; *Gazette*, 7 April 1825.

CHAPTER 11   SHOOT THE ATTORNEY-GENERAL

1 *Australian*, 24 February 1825; *Gazette*, 24 February 1825; Brisbane to Bathurst, 4 March 1825, *HRA*, Volume XI, p. 529.

2 *Gazette*, 3 March, 21 April 1825; *Australian*, 3 March 1825; Brisbane to Bathurst, 4 March 1825, *HRA*, Volume XI, p. 529.

3 R v Howe, 18 April 1825 and R v Mitchell (No. 1), 19 April 1825, *Australian*, 21 April 1825; R v Mitchell (No. 2), 1 August 1825, *Australian*, 4 August 1825; Mitchell v Howe, 8 October 1825, *Australian* and *Gazette*, 13 October 1825; Currey, *Forbes*, pp. 128–32.

4 R v Cooper, 12 February 1825, *Australian*, 17 February 1825; R v Wentworth, Campbell and Dunn, 17 June 1825, *Australian*, 23 June 1825; *Gazette*, 20 September 1825.

5 *Australian*, 10 October 1825; *Gazette*, 31 March, 21 July, 10, 17 October 1825.

6 Rowe v Wilson, 28 November 1825, *Gazette*, 5 December 1825; D.S. Macmillan, ed., *Two Years in New South Wales* (written by Peter Cunningham in 1827), Angus & Robertson, Sydney, 1966, p. 34.

7 Minutes of Proceedings of the Legislative Council from 25 August 1824 to 22 November 1825, Sydney, 1847, pp. 2, 29; *Australian*, 26 May 1825.

8 *Australian*, 28 April 1825; John Macarthur Jr to his father, 27 December 1824, ML A2911; S. Macarthur Onslow, *Elizabeth Macarthur*, p. 128.

9 *Australian*, 27 October 1825; Liston, *Sarah Wentworth*, p. 17; Ritchie, *The Wentworths*, p. 215; M.J.B. Kenny, 'Hall, Edward Smith (1786–1860)', *ADB*, Volume 1, pp. 500–02.

CHAPTER 12   THE CALM BEFORE THE STORM

1 'Darling, Sir Ralph (1772–1858)', *ADB*, Volume I, pp. 282–86, *Gazette*, 16, 28 January 1826; Darling to Hay, 1 May 1826, *HRA*, Volume XII, pp. viii-ix, 254; Currey, *Forbes*, p. 176; R. Border, 'Scott, Thomas Hobbes (1783–1860)', *ADB*, Volume 2, pp. 431–33.

2 Walker v Scott (No. 1), 21 December 1825, *Gazette*, 26 December 1825; Walker v Scott (No. 2), 19 January 1826, *Gazette*, 26 January 1826; Bannister to Darling, 14 April 1826, *HRA,* Volume XII, p. 277; Forbes to Wilmot Horton, 6 February 1826, Catton Papers, Australian Joint Copying Project, Reel M791.

3 R v Broadbear and Broadbear, 5 June 1826, *Gazette*, 7 June 1826.

4 Broadbear and Wife v McArthur [sic] et al., 14, 27 March 1827, *Gazette,* 17, 29 March 1827; Protest by T.H. Scott against judicial conduct of J. Stephen, 24 May 1837, *HRA*, Volume XIII, pp. 322–23.

5 Dr - The Office of W.C. Wentworth - Cr 1825, ML A758; Deposition of J. Cogill, 9 May 1826, *HRA*, Volume XII, pp. 331–32; Ritchie, *The Wentworths*, p. 208; Bennett, *History of the NSW Bar*, p. 36; *Abstract of Accounts at the Female Orphan School, HRNSW*, Volume XIII, p. 353; Currey, *Forbes*, p. 251; Macmillan, ed., *Two Years in New South Wales*, p. 252.

6 *Gazette*, 29 March 1826, 27 June 1828; Ritchie, *The Wentworths*, p. 209; Spencer v Jeffrey, 3 May 1826, *Australian*, 6 May 1826.

7 *Gazette*, 29 March 1826; Halloran v Hall, 22 May 1826, *Gazette,* 27 May 1826; *Australian*, 24 May 1826; *The Monitor*, 26 May 1826.

8 R v Howe, 20 October 1826, *Australian*, 21 October 1826; *Gazette*, 25 October 1826; *Monitor*, 27 October 1826; Forbes to Horton, 15 December 1826, *HRA*, Series IV, Volume I, pp. 669–79; Currey, *Forbes*, p. 189.

9 Currey, *Forbes*, p. 167; *Gazette*, 29 July 1826; *Australian*, 9 February, 30 August 1826.

10 J.D. Heydon, 'Sir Thomas Brisbane', *ADB*, Volume 1, pp. 151–55; V. Parsons, 'Goulburn, Frederick (1788–1837)', *ADB*, Volume 1, pp. 463–64; *Australian*, 1, 11 November 1826; *Gazette*, 9 September, 6 December 1826.

11 Ritchie, *The Wentworths*, p. 213; Liston, *Sarah Wentworth*, p. 17; *Gazette*, 17 June, 27 September 1826; *Australian*, 17 June 1826.

12 R.F. Holder, *Bank of New South Wales*, Volume 1, Angus & Robertson, Sydney, 1970, pp. 11, 12, 66; *Gazette*, 2 December 1824, 5 December 1825; Ritchie, *The Wentworths*, p. 209.

13 *Australian*, 26 January, 9 February, 23 March, 29 April, 13, 17 May 1826; *Gazette*, 26 January 1826; Holder, *Bank of New South Wales*, p. 67; S.J. Butlin, *Foundations of the Australian Monetary System 1788–1851*, Sydney University Press, Sydney, 1968, pp. 164, 192.

14 Holder, *Bank of New South Wales*, pp. 56, 67; *Gazette*, 22 March 1826.

15 Holder, *Bank of New South Wales*, p. 74; Ritchie, *The Wentworths*, p. 244; Darling to Bathurst, 4 December 1826, *HRA*, Volume XII, pp. 716–17.16 *Australian*, 25 November 1826.

CHAPTER 13   THE STORM BREAKS

1 *Australian*, 29 November 1826.

2 *Australian*, 2, 6, 9, 13, 20, 27 December 1826; Forbes and Stephen to Darling, 13 December 1826, *HRA*, Volume XII, pp. 755–56; Wentworth to Murray, 1 March 1829, *HRA*, Volume XIV, pp. 825–26.

3 *Australian*, 11 November 1826.

4 Darling to Hay, 15, 16 December 1826, *HRA*, Volume XII, pp. 761–65.

5 *Gazette*, 15, 20, 27 January 1827; *Australian*, 18 January 1828.

6 Darling to Hay, 9 February 1827, *HRA*, Volume XIII, pp. 96–101.

7 *Gazette*, 1 January, 3 April 1827; Wardell v Howe, 29 March 1827, *Australian*, 3, 7 April 1827.

8 Darling to Horton, 26 March 1827, *HRA*, Volume XIII, pp. 192–93; *HRA*, Volume XIII, pp. vi, vii, ix, xii–xiv; Bannister v Wardell, 29 March 1827, *Gazette*, 31 March, 30 April 1827; 8 Geo IV, No. 2.

9 *HRA*, Volume XIII, pp. xii–xiv; *Australian*, 16 May 1827; *Gazette*, 23 May 1827.

10 R v Lowe, 18 May 1827, *Australian*, 23 May 1827; *Gazette*, 2 January 1828; Wentworth, *Australasia*, p. 5.

11 Liston, *Sarah Wentworth*, p. 18; Wentworth, *A Statistical etc Description*, 1819, p. 13.

12 Ritchie, *The Wentworths*, pp. 228–30, 235–38; *Gazette*, 9, 11 July 1827.

13 R v Hall, 13 September 1827, *Gazette*, 19 September 1827; R v Edward Smith Hall (No. 1), in T.D. Castle and B. Kercher, *Dowling's Select Cases 1828 to 1844*, Francis Forbes Society, Sydney, 2005, p. 771; Annable, *A Setting for Justice*, pp. 61–62, 69, 71–72, 77; Currey, *Forbes*, p. 74.

14 R v Wardell (No. 1), 26 June 1827, *Australian*, 29 June 1827; R v Wardell (No. 2), 12, 14 September 1827, *Gazette*, 17 September 1827; *Australian*, 30 October 1827; R v Wardell (No. 3), 22 December 1827, *Australian*, 26 December 1827.

15 John Macarthur Sr to John Macarthur Jr, 16 May 1827, Mitchell Library Reel CY 752B; Darling to Horton, 26 March 1827, *HRA*, Volume XIII, p. 193; Darling to Goderich, 10 October 1827, *HRA*, Volume XIII, p. 548.

16 Darling to Goderich, 14 December 1827, *HRA*, Volume XIII, p. 642; *Australian*, 2 November 1827.

17 *Gazette*, 14 December 1827; *Australian*, 21 December 1827; Currey, *Forbes*, p. 255.

18 Darling to Goderich, 14 December 1827, *HRA*, Volume XIII, p. 638; A. McLeay, Government Order No. 43, 13 December 1827, *HRA*, Volume XIII, p. 646; Darling to Goderich, 15 December 1827, *HRA*, Volume XIII, p. 647.

19 Ex parte Wardell and Wentworth, 28 December 1827, *Monitor*, 31 December 1827; Ex parte Wardell and Wentworth, 31 December 1827, *Australian*, 2 January 1828; Darling to Hay, 10 January 1828, *HRA*, Volume XIII, pp. 692–94; Forbes to Horton, 7 March 1828, Catton Papers, Australian Joint Copying Project, Reel M791; Currey, *Forbes*, pp. 306–07; Annable, *A Setting for Justice*, p. 71.

20 *Gazette*, 24 November 1827; Melbourne, *Early Constitutional Development*, pp. 137, 145.

CHAPTER 14   A LITTLE CRACKED IN THE UPPER STOREY

1 Ovens to Lindesay, 17 December 1827, *HRA*, Volume XIII, pp. 730–33.

2 *Gazette*, 17 October, 9 November, 3 , 21 December 1827; Darling to Hay, 15 February 1828, *HRA*, Volume XIII, pp. 784–85.

3 *Australian*, 9, 18, 30 January 1828; Darling to Hay, 15 February 1828, *HRA*, Volume XIII, pp. 784–85.

4 *Australian,* 9 January 1828; *HRA*, Volume XIV, p. v; Liston, *Sarah Wentworth*, pp. 18, 20.

5 R. Griffin, 'Early History of the Estate', in R. Griffin and J. Hughes, eds, *Vaucluse House*, Historic Houses Trust, Sydney, 2006, pp. 9–12.

6 Memorial of George Cookney, 27 November 1826, *HRA*, Volume XIII, pp. 526–27; Report on the Office of Colonial Architect, 25 March 1826, *HRA*, Volume XIII, pp. 528–29; Darling to Goderich, 27 September 1827, *HRA*, Volume XIII, pp. 525–26.

7 Ritchie, *The Wentworths*, p. 239; Griffin and Hughes, *Vaucluse House*, pp. 110–11.

8 A.C. Howe, 'Huskisson, William (1770-1830)', *ODNB*, Volume 28, pp. 974–80; C.J. Finlay, 'Mackintosh, Sir James (1765–1832)', *ODNB*, Volume 35, pp. 674–79; Hansard, *Debates*, 1828, Volume 18, cc. 1427, 1559, 1564–65.

9 S.G.P. Ward, 'Murray, Sir George (1772–1846)', *ODNB*, Volume 39, pp. 905–06; *Gazette*, 30 June 1828; Hansard, *Debates*, 1828, Volume 18, cc. 1456–63; Currey, *Forbes*, pp. 294–95.

10 Melbourne, *Early Constitutional Development*, pp. 152–62; B.H. Fletcher, *Ralph Darling A Governor Maligned*, Oxford University Press, Melbourne, 1984, pp. 230, 233–34.

CHAPTER 15   DARLING EMBARRASSED AND EMBARRASSING

1 Wentworth to Murray, 1 March 1829, *HRA*, Volume XIV, pp. 835, 854–55; Fletcher, *Darling*, p. 272; Currey, *Forbes*, p. 354 .

2 Wentworth to Murray, 1 March 1829, *HRA*, Volume XIV, pp. 810, 818, 820, 824, 830; Examination of P. Thompson, 23 April 1827, *HRA*, Volume XIV, p. 862.

3 Darling to Murray, 24 March 1829, *HRA*, Volume XIV, p. 690; Wentworth to Darling, 14 April 1829, *HRA*, Volume XIV, p. 714; Darling to Murray, 28 May 1829, *HRA*, Volume XIV, pp. 793, 800; Executive Council Minute No. 20, 21 May 1829, *HRA*, Volume XIV, p. 872; Wentworth to Darling, 14 May 1829, *HRA*, Volume XIV, p. 897.

4 Currey, *Forbes*, pp. 355–60; Ex parte Wentworth, in re Mansfield, 30 September 1829, *Australian*, 2 October 1829.

5 R v Mansfield (No. 1), 3, 26 June 1830, *Gazette*, 8, 29 June 1830; Currey, *Forbes*, pp. 355–60.

6 Hansard, *Debates*, 1830, Volume 22, cc. 1314–15; Hansard, *Debates*, 1830, Volume 25, cc. 436–50, 1110-14; Annable, *A Setting for Justice*, p. 78.

7 R v Hayes, 14 April, 8 June 1829, *Australian*, 17 April, 9 June 1829; Hansard, *Debates*, 1830, Volume 25, c. 856; Currey, *Forbes*, pp. 362–63.

8 Darling to Twiss, 7 July 1829, *HRA*, Volume XV, p. 70; Hansard, *Debates*, 1830, Volume 25, cc. 856, 1126.

9 In re Tyler R. v Rossi and Others, 25 April, 13, 27, 30 June, 1 July 1829, *Gazette*, 28 April, 16 June, 4 July 1829; Darling to Murray, 6 July 1829, *HRA*, Volume XV, p. 53; Kenny, Edward Smith 'Hall', *ADB*, Volume I, pp. 500–02.

10 In re Jane New, 16, 18, 21 March 1829, *Gazette* 17, 19 March 1829, *Australian*, 20 March 1829, *HRA*, Volume XIV, pp. 765–71; Currey, *Forbes*, pp. 341–43; C. Baxter, *An Irresistible Temptation*, Allen & Unwin, Sydney, 2006, pp. 121–26.

11 Hayes v Hely, 16 March 1830, *Australian*, 17 March 1830; In re Jane New, 21 March 1829, in *HRA*, Volume XIV, pp. 765–71; Currey, *Forbes*, pp. 343–45.

12 Currey, *Forbes*, p. 348; Murray to Darling, 30 January 1846, *HRA*, Volume XV, p. 346.

CHAPTER 16   VAUCLUSE INTRIGUE AND CELEBRATION

1 Baxter, *An Irresistible Temptation*, p. 158; Liston, *Sarah Wentworth*, pp. 20–21; Darling to Murray, 29 June 1829, *HRA*, Volume XV, pp. 28–29; Darling to Goderich, 27 April 1831, *HRA*, Volume XVI, pp. 252–53.

2 Currey, *Forbes*, p. 330; *Australian*, 17 July 1829.

3 Baxter, *An Irresistible Temptation*, p. 322.

4 Liston, *Sarah Wentworth*, pp. 20–22; N.D. McLachlan, 'Eagar, Edward (1787–1866)', *ADB*, Volume 1, pp. 343–44; N.D. McLachlan, 'Edward Eagar (1787–1866): A Colonial Statesman in Sydney and London', *Historical Studies Australia and New Zealand*, Volume 10, No. 40, May 1963; Marriage and Burial Register, 5–4188, New South Wales Registrar General, Volume 25, p. 14; Joseph Fowles, *Sydney in 1848*, Ure Smith, Sydney, 1973, pp. 10–12.

5 *Australian*, 3, 10 February 1830.

6 *Australian*, 10 February 1830; *Monitor*, 10 February 1830; Melbourne, *Early Constitutional Development*, p. 152; *Gazette*, 11 February 1830; Fletcher, *Darling*, pp. 284–85; *Monitor*, 20 February 1830; Introduction, *HRA*, Volume XIV, p. xii.

7 Hayes v Hely, 16 March 1830, *Australian,* 17 March 1830; Hall v Hely, 17 March 1830, *Australian*, 19 March 1830; Introduction, *HRA*, Volume XIV, p. xv.

8 Hall v Mansfield (No. 1), 1 April 1830, *Gazette*, 6 April 1830; Hall v Mansfield (No. 2), 2 April 1830, *Australian*, 7 April 1830; Hall v Mansfield (No. 3), 3 April 1830, *Australian*, 7 April 1830; Statement re P. Clynch by A. Macleay, July 1830, *HRA*, Volume XV, p. 597; Annable, *A Setting for Justice*, pp. 20, 64, 69, 71, 77; R v Hall (No. 1), 25 September 1828, *Australian*, 26 September 1828; Hall v Scott, 6 April 1830, *Gazette*, 10 April 1830; Introduction, *HRA*, Volume XIV, p. xvi; Darling to Murray, 1 December 1830, *HRA*, Volume XV, p. 822.

9 R v Farrell, Dingle and Woodward, 27, 28 June, 23 July 1831, *The Sydney Herald* [became *The Sydney Morning Herald* on 1 August 1841, hereafter in both cases referred to as *Herald*], 11 July 1831, *Gazette* 26, 30 July, August 1831; Annable, *A Setting for Justice*, pp. 67, 73.

10 D.W.A. Baker, 'Mitchell, Sir Thomas Livingstone (1792–1855)', *ADB*, Volume 2, pp. 238–42; R v West, 12 October 1831, *Gazette*, 22 October 1831; *Australian*, 14 October 1831; R v West, 17, 18 October 1832, *Herald*, 18, 22 October 1832.

11 Currey, *Forbes*, pp. 371–74; Fletcher, *Darling*, pp. 286–88; Replies by R. Darling to Criticism in Parliament, 22 December 1830, *HRA*, Volume XV, pp. 851–63; Darling to Goderich, 3 October 1831, *HRA*, Volume XVI, pp. 400–02.

12 *Monitor*, 19 October 1831; *Gazette*, 20 October 1831; *Australian*, 21 October 1831.

CHAPTER 17   ECHOES FROM THE PAST

1 Fletcher, *Darling*, pp. 1–4; H. King, *Richard Bourke*, Oxford University Press, Melbourne, 1971, pp. 4, 90, 104, 108; L. Bredvold and R. Ross, *The Philosophy of Edmund Burke*, University of Michigan Press, Ann Arbor, 1970, pp. 1–11; G.B. Smith, 'Fitzwilliam, Charles William Wentworth, third Earl Fitzwilliam in the peerage of Great Britain and fifth Earl Fitzwilliam in the peerage of Ireland (1786–1857)', *ODNB*, Volume 19, pp. 973–74; Charles William, Earl Fitzwilliam and Sir Richard Bourke, *Correspondence of Edmund Burke*, Francis and John Rivington, London, 1844; M. Waugh, *Forgotten Hero Richard Bourke, Irish Governor of New South Wales 1831–1837*, Australian Scholarly Publishing, Melbourne, 2005, pp. 2–3.

2 F.K. Crowley, 'Stirling, Sir James (1791–1865)', *ADB*, Volume 2, pp. 484–88; *Australian*, 23 December 1831; *Gazette*, 24 December 1831.

3 King, *Bourke*, p. 135; Ward, *James Macarthur*, pp. 24, 46, 48–49; Ellis, *Macarthur*, pp. 522–29, 584–85.

4 *Gazette*, 1, 3 December 1831, 21 January 1832; *Monitor*, 3 December 1831, 21 January 1832; *Australian*, 20 January 1832; Introduction, *HRA*, Volume XVIII, p. xii.

5 Ward, *Macarthur*, p. 53; King, *Bourke*, pp. 150, 152, 154, 157; Hansard, *Debates*, 1832, Volume 13, cc. 1089, 1104, 1106, 1114–15; *Gazette*, 29 January 1833; *Monitor*, 30 January 1833; *Herald*, 31 January 1833; *Australian*, 1 February 1833; Introduction, *HRA*, Volume XVIII, p. xii.

6 Earle v Nowlan, 4 April 1832, *Gazette*, 7 April 1832; A. Dowling, ed., *Reminiscences of a Colonial Judge*, Federation Press, Sydney, 1996, p. 17; Currey, *Forbes*, p. 258.

7 R v Lewis and Others, 18 May 1832, *Gazette*, 19 May, 5 June 1832, *Herald*, 21 May, 4 June 1832, *Australian*, 25 May 1832.

8 Fletcher, *Darling*, p. 202; Liston, *Sarah Wentworth*, p. 42.

9   New South Wales Legislative Council, Minute No. 4, 3 September 1829; Liston, *Sarah Wentworth*, pp. 23, 25, 26, 32, 33; Griffin and Hughes, *Vaucluse House*, pp. 23, 34–37.

CHAPTER 18   EXIT WARDELL

1   *Australian*, 17 March 1827; N. Gray, 'Dumaresq, Henry (1792–1838)', *ADB*, Volume 1, pp. 333–35; A. Halloran, 'Some Early Legal Celebrities', *Journal and Proceedings of the Royal Australian Historical Society [JRAHS]*, Volume X, 1924, Part VI, pp. 344–45; Currey, *Forbes*, p. 195.

2   Legislative Council Minutes No. 17, 21 April 1830, No. 2, 8 April 1834; Legislative Council, Magistrates' Returns: G. Blaxland, 25 March 1834, W. Lawson, 22 March 1834, J. Macarthur, 31 March 1834; Currey, *Forbes*, pp. 416–20.

3   Farringdon v Elder, 18 June 1834, *Herald*, 26 June 1834.

4   R v Cullen, Doyle and Walsh, 4 August 1834, *Herald*, 11 August 1834; R v Bridgens, 14 August 1834, *Gazette*, 19 August 1834, *Herald*, 28 August 1834; Forbes, Dowling and Burton to the Governor, 27 August 1833, Chief Justice's Letter Book 1824–35, pp. 352–57, State Records of NSW, 4/6551.

5   R v Jenkins and Tattersdale, 20 September 1834, *Gazette*, 25 September 1834; J. Connell, ed., *Sydney*, Oxford University Press, Melbourne, 2000, p. 63.

6   *Gazette*, 13 September 1834; *Australian*, 11 November 1834.

7   *Gazette*, 25 September 1834; *Australian*, 2 June 1829; *Gazette*, 8 September, 1 October 1829; *Australian*, 18 November 1834; *Herald*, 6 November 1834; Adjourned Meeting of the Bar, *Australian*, 18 November 1834.

8   Forbes, Darling and Burton to the Govenor, 27 August 1833, Chief Justice's Letter Book 1824–35, pp. 352–57; State Records of NSW, 4/6551; *Gazette*, 12 February 1835.

9   Ex parte O'Shaughnessy, in re Lang, 2 June 1835, *Gazette*, 4 June 1835; D.W.A. Baker, 'Lang, John Dunmore (1799–1878)', *ADB*, Volume 2, pp. 76–83; D.W.A. Baker, ed., *Reminiscences of my Life and Times by John Dunmore Lang*, Heinemann, Melbourne, 1972, pp. 107–08.

10 R v Kay and others, 16 November 1835, *Gazette*, 19 November 1835; Liston, *Sarah Wentworth*, p. 34; Annable, *A Setting for Justice*, pp. 26, 75.

CHAPTER 19   THE AUSTRALIAN PATRIOTIC ASSOCIATION

1   *Australian*, 12 July 1833; *Monitor*, 13 July 1833; *Gazette*, 6 June, 13, 16 July 1833; B.H. Fletcher, 'Sir John Jamison in New South Wales 1814–1844', *JRAHS*, Volume 65, June 1979, Part 1, pp. 5, 10, 19.

2   *Australian*, 29 August 1834; *Monitor*, 30 August 1834; *Gazette*, 30 August 1834; *Herald*, 1 September 1834.

3   *Gazette*, 30 May 1835; *Herald*, 1 June 1835; *Australian*, 2 June 1835; *Monitor*, 3 June 1835; Bourke to Glenelg, 26 December 1835, *HRA*, Volume XVIII, pp. xiv, 251–52; M.E. Chamberlain, 'Bulwer, (William) Henry Lytton Earle, Baron Dalling and Bulwer (1801–1872)', *ODNB*, Volume 8, pp. 666–69.

4 D. Shineberg, 'Jones, Richard (1786–1852)', *ADB*, Volume 2, pp. 24–25; Ward, *James Macarthur*, pp. 59–60; *Gazette*, 24 November 1835; *Australian*, 4 December 1835; King, *Bourke*, pp. 158–60; W. Bland, *Letters to Charles Buller M.P. from the Australian Patriotic Association*, D.L. Welch, Sydney, 1849, pp. 191–212; Melbourne, *Early Constitutional Development*, p. 207; Currey, *Forbes*, p. 497.

5 Ward, *James Macarthur*, pp. 60-61.

6 Fletcher, *Darling*, pp. 328–31; *Monitor*, 13 April 1836; *Herald*, 14, 18 April 1836; *Australian*, 15 April 1836; Fowles, *Sydney in 1848*, p. 50.

7 *Australian*, 3 June 1836; A. Atkinson, 'Macarthur, James (1798–1867)', *ODNB*, Volume 35, pp. 12–13; J.D. Heydon, 'Macarthur, James (1798–1867)', *ADB*, Volume 2, pp. 149–53; Glenelg to Bourke, 5 January 1836, *HRA*, Volume XVIII, p. 258; Ward, *James Macarthur*, pp. 16, 22, 27, 44; Likeness of James Macarthur in *The Illustrated Sydney News*, 16 March 1865, p. 5.

8 Ward, *James Macarthur*, pp. 67–74; Liston, *Sarah Wentworth*, pp. 24, 25, 42.

9 Currey, *Forbes*, pp. 504–05, 511, 514; Ward, *James Macarthur*, pp. 69–74; J. Macarthur, *New South Wales, Its Present State and Future Prospects*, D. Walther, London, 1837, pp. 266–70, 279–80.

10 J.D. Lang, *A Historical and Statistical Account of New South Wales, both as a Penal Settlement and as a British Colony*, Cochrane and M'Crone, London, 1834; Ward, *James Macarthur*, pp. 75–80; Melbourne, *Early Constitutional Development*, pp. 225–27.

11 Melbourne, *Early Constitutional Development*, p. 224; Select Committee on Transportation Report, Ordered to be Printed on 14 July 1837, pp. ii, 89, 134, 241; Ward, *James Macarthur*, p. 80; Liston, *Sarah Wentworth*, p. 34; Chamberlain, Henry Lytton Bulwer, *ODNB*, Volume 8, pp. 666–69; H.J. Spencer, 'Buller, Charles (1806–1848)', *ODNB*, Volume 8, pp. 613–17.

12 *Australian*, 3, 15 January, 12 February 1839; *Gazette*, 9, 14 February 1839; *Monitor*, 11 February 1839; A.W. Martin, 'Parkes, Sir Henry (1815–1896)', *ADB*, Volume 5, pp. 399–406; A.W. Martin, *Henry Parkes A Biography*, Melbourne University Press, Melbourne, 1980, p. 29.

13 Hansard, *Debates*, 1838, Volume 42, c. 479; Hansard, *Debates*, 1839, Volume 49, cc. 1239–43; Bland, *Letters to Buller*, pp. 140–41; Ward, *James Macarthur*, pp. 82–83; Melbourne, *Early Constitutional Development*, pp. 240–44; Currey, *Forbes*, p. 512; Clark, *Select Documents*, Volume I, p. 406.

14 Ward, *James Macarthur*, pp. 79, 103.

CHAPTER 20   WENTWORTH BUYS UP NEW ZEALAND

1 H. King, 'Bourke, Sir Richard (1777–1855)', *ADB*, Volume 1, pp. 128–33; *Herald*, 4, 7 December 1837; *Australian*, 5 December 1837; *Gazette*, 5, 7 December 1837; Introduction, *HRA*, Volume XIX, pp. viii, ix; 'Hindmarsh, Sir John (1785–1860)', *ADB*, Volume 1, pp. 538–41.

2 Melbourne, *Early Constitutional Development*, pp. 199, 249; Liston, *Sarah Wentworth*, pp. 29, 34–35; Cavenagh v Wentworth, 1, 3 July 1837, *Herald*, 6 July 1837.

3 Gipps to Glenelg, 3 April 1839, *HRA*, Volume XX, pp. 81–82.

4 Melbourne, *Early Constitutional Development,* pp. 172–73; H.C. Evison, *Te Wai Pounamu The Greenstone Island,* Aoraki Press, Wellington, 1993, pp. 53–58; J.W. Davidson, 'Busby, James (1801–1871)', *ADB,* Volume 1, pp. 186–88.

5 E. Sweetman, *The Unsigned New Zealand Treaty,* Arrow Printery, Melbourne, 1939, pp. 1, 182, 186; P. Moon, *Hobson Governor of New Zealand 1840–1842,* David Ling Publishing, Auckland, 1998, pp. 51–52.

6 R.L. Jellicoe, *The New Zealand Company's Native Reserves,* Government Printer, Wellington, 1930, pp. 4–7; Sweetman, *Unsigned New Zealand Treaty,* p. 40.

7 Moon, *Hobson,* pp. 40–41, 43–44; Sweetman, *Unsigned New Zealand Treaty,* pp. 55–58; J. Prest, 'Russell, John [formerly Lord John Russell], first Earl Russell, (1792–1878)', *ODNB,* Volume 48, pp. 295–307.

8 Evison, *Te Wai Pounamu,* pp. 114–15, 133; Moon, *Hobson,* p. 59; H.C. Evison, 'The Wentworth-Jones Deeds of 15 February 1840', *The Turnbull Library Record,* Volume 28, 1995, p. 44; *Sydney Herald,* 31 January 1840.

9 Gipps to Russell, 16 August 1840, *HRA,* Volume XX, pp. 761–62; Evison, *The Wentworth-Jones Deeds,* pp. 44–45; Sweetman, *The Unsigned New Zealand Treaty,* pp. 61–62.

10 Agreement between W.C. Wentworth and John Jones of Sydney with Maori chiefs for purchase of land in New Zealand, 15 February 1840, ML MSS 7574.

11 Moon, *Hobson,* pp. 95, 107, 110, 116; *Australian,* 4 April 1840; Evison, *The Wentworth-Jones Deeds,* pp. 55–56.

12 Evison, *The Wentworth-Jones Deeds,* p. 56; *Herald,* 6 July 1840; Sweetman, *Unsigned New Zealand Treaty,* pp. 77, 78, 81, 103, 108, 110, 130, 142.

13 Evison, *Te Wai Pounamu,* p. 131; Archives New Zealand, William Charles Wentworth, OLC 1, Box 23, pp. 497–99; Jellicoe, *The New Zealand Company's Native Reserves,* p. 24.

CHAPTER 21   WENTWORTH ECLIPSES MACARTHUR

1 *Australian,* 18 January 1842, *Herald,* 11 July 1840; Melbourne, *Early Constitutional Development,* p. 246; Ward, *James Macarthur,* p. 92.

2 Liston, *Sarah Wentworth,* pp. 25, 27, 28, 34, 35; Griffin and Hughes, *Vaucluse House,* p. 39; *Gazette,* 24 October 1837; *Australian,* 21 June, 11 November, 14, 16 December 1842; J.S. Sheldon, *The Big School Room at Sydney Grammar,* Sydney Grammar School Press, Darlinghurst, 1997, p. 116; J. Cobley, 'Bland, William (1789–1868)', *ADB,* Volume 1, pp. 112–15; C. Turney, *Grammar,* Allen & Unwin, Sydney, 1989, pp. 10–14; A. Barcan, *A Short History of Education in New South Wales,* Martindale Press, Sydney, 1965, p. 57; S.H. Smith & G. T. Spaull, *History of Education in New South Wales,* George Philip & Son, Sydney, 1925, p. 62; *Herald,* 19 December 1842.

3 Liston, *Sarah Wentworth,* pp. 28, 29, 38; Laura Wentworth to Thomasine Wentworth, n.d., ML A868.

4 Griffin and Hughes, *Vaucluse House,* p. 36; Wentworth, *A Statistical etc Description,* 1819, pp. 459–60; *Australian,* 13 January 1830, 13 February, 22 September 1841, 16 September 1842.

5 Butlin, *Foundations of the Australian Monetary System,* pp. 315–23; Griffin and Hughes, *Vaucluse House,* pp. 36–38, 56.

6 Liston, *Sarah Wentworth*, pp. 35–37; Ward, *James Macarthur*, pp. 94–98; Clark, *Select Documents*, Volume I, pp. 293–94.

7 Ward, *James Macarthur*, pp. 100–01; Clark, *Select Documents*, Volume I, pp. 405, 409.

8 *Australian*, 9, 30 January, 6 February 1841; *Gazette*, 9 January 1841; *Herald*, 6 February 1841.

9 *Australasian Chronicle* [*Chronicle*], 9 January, 11 February 1841, 6 January 1842; *Monitor*, 3, 8 February 1841; *Herald*, 22, 25, 29 December 1841; Ward, *James Macarthur*, pp. 111–12; Fletcher, *Jamison*, p. 21; *Australian*, 18 January 1842; Walker, *The Newspaper Press in NSW*, p. 32.

10 *Australian*, 27 January, 17 February 1842; *Herald*, 28 January 1842; Ward, *James Macarthur*, pp. 114–16; Fowles, *Sydney in 1848*, pp. 50–53.

11 Spencer, 'Charles Buller,', *ODNB*, Volume 8, pp. 613–17.

12 Jamison, Wentworth and Bland to Buller, 20 June 1840 in Bland, *Letters to Buller*, p. 26; Jamison and Bland to Buller, 29 February 1840 in Bland, *Letters to Buller*, pp. 82–83; Hansard, *Debates*, 1840, Volume 52, cc. 360–61; Jamison and Bland to Buller in Bland, *Letters to Buller*, pp. 154–55; Ward, *James Macarthur*, pp. 101–02; Jamison, Wentworth and Bland to Buller, 15 February 1840 in Bland, *Letters to Buller*, p. 160; J. Macarthur, *New South Wales*, p. 266.

13 Melbourne, *Early Constitutional Development*, pp. 269–76; Ward, *James Macarthur*, pp. 116–19; Hansard, *Debates*, 1842, Volume 61, c. 814; A. Hawkins, 'Stanley, Edward George Godfrey Smith, fourteenth earl of Derby (1799–1869)', *ODNB*, Volume 52, pp. 178–87.

14 *Herald*, 21 March 1842.

15 Ward, *James Macarthur*, pp. 101–02; Bland, *Letters to Buller*, p. xxxi; Cobley, Bland, *ADB*, pp. 112–15.

16 M.M.H. Thompson, *The Seeds of Democracy*, Federation Press, Sydney, 2006, pp. 23–25; *Colonial Observer* [*Observer*], 28 December 1842; Ward, *James Macarthur*, p. 120; *Herald*, 19, 28, 29 December 1842, *Australian*, 30 December 1842.

17 *Australian*, 2, 16 January 1843; Thompson, *Seeds of Democracy*, pp. 39, 44, 57, 59; *Observer*, 18 January 1843; J.M. Ward, 'Cowper, Sir Charles (1807–1875)', *ADB*, Volume 3, pp. 475–79; C.H. Currey, 'Therry, Sir Roger (1800–1874)', *ADB*, Volume 2, pp. 512–13.

18 *Herald*, 18, 28 January 1843; *Chronicle*, 21 February 1843; Thompson, *Seeds of Democracy*, p. 81.

19 Griffin and Hughes, *Vaucluse House*, p. 19; Thompson, *Seeds of Democracy*, pp. 111–17; *Herald*, 20 June 1843.

20 Thompson, *Seeds of Democracy*, pp. 122, 132–35; *Maitland Mercury*, 24 June 1843; Ward, *James Macarthur*, pp. 132–34; *Herald*, 28 June 1843; *Observer*, 28 June 1843.

CHAPTER 22   LEADER OF THE OPPOSITION

1 *Herald*, 4 July, 2, 3, 4 August 1843; *Australian*, 2 August 1843; Thompson, *Seeds of Democracy*, pp. 139–43; M. Stapleton, ed., *Australia's First Parliament House*, Sydney, 1995, p. 38.

2 *Votes and Proceedings of the NSW Legislative Council*, 3 August 1843; Melbourne, *Early Constitutional Development*, pp. 270–79; Fowles, *Sydney in 1848*, p. 79; The Clerk to Lewis, 16 September 1843, NSW Parliamentary Archive, No. 43/60.

3 J.F. Hogan, *Robert Lowe Viscount Sherbrooke*, Ward and Downey, London, 1893, pp. 19, 21, 25 ; D. Clune and K. Turner, eds, *The Premiers of New South Wales*, Volume 1, Federation Press, Sydney, 2006, p. 35; Butlin, *Foundations of the Australian Monetary System*, pp. 340–1; *Votes and Proceedings*, 8 August, 15 September 1843, 30 December 1844; Melbourne, *Wentworth*, p. 66; S.H. Roberts, *The Squatting Age in Australia 1835–1847*, Melbourne University Press, Melbourne, 1964, pp. 206–07; Introduction, *HRA*, Volume XXIII, p. xii; Gipps to Stanley, 7 October 1843, *HRA*, Volume XXIII, p. 180; The terms Prime Minister and Premier were used interchangeably in the nineteenth century—see Clune and Turner, *The Premiers of New South Wales*, p. 7; Liston, *Sarah Wentworth*, p. 53; The Clerk to Lewis, 16 August 1843, NSW Parliamentary Archive, No. 43/60; The Clerk to Colonial Secretary, 18 September 1843, NSW Parliamentary Archive, No. 43/84.

4 Evidence of W.C. Wentworth before the Select Committee on Monetary Confusion, 25 October 1843; Evidence of J. Johnson before the Select Committee on Immigration, 11 September 1843; *Votes and Proceedings*, 18 October 1843.

5 Report of the Select Committee on the Petition from Distressed Mechanics and Labourers, 24 November 1843; Legislative Council debates, *Herald*, 21 December 1843.

6 *Votes and Proceedings*, 12, 19, 27 October, 2 November, 20 December 1843.

7 J.B. Windeyer, 'Windeyer, Richard (1806–1847)', *ADB*, Volume 2, pp. 615–17; Thompson, *Seeds of Democracy*, p. 143; Council debates, *Herald*, 4, 20 August, 7 September, 17 October 1843; Fowles, *Sydney in 1848*, pp. 76–77; The Clerk to Colonial Secretary, 18 September 1843, NSW Parliamentary Archive, No. 43/84.

8 A. Halloran, 'Some Early Legal Celebrities', *JRAHS*, Volume 12, Part 1, 1927, p. 52; R. Knight, *Illiberal Liberal*, Melbourne University Press, Melbourne, 1966, pp. 50–63; R.L. Knight, 'Lowe, Robert, Viscount Sherbrooke (1811–1892)', *ADB*, Volume 2, pp. 134–37; A.P. Martin, *Life and Letters of Rt. Hon. Robert Lowe Viscount Sherbrooke*, Volume I, Longmans, Green & Co., London, 1893, p. 192; Council debates, *Herald*, 9, 28 October 1843; Melbourne, *Early Constitutional Development*, p. 292; R. Therry, *Reminiscences of Thirty Years' Residence in NSW & Victoria*, Sampson Low & Co., London, 1863, pp. 232, 234.

9 Thomas Callaghan's Diary, 16 May 1842, 6 January 1843, 23 July 1844, ML A2122/1; Liston, *Sarah Wentworth*, pp. 43–46.

10 *Votes and Proceedings*, 15 August, 20 December 1843; Melbourne, *Early Constitutional Development*, pp. 283, 296–98; *NSW Government Gazette*, 2 April 1844; *The Australian Daily Journal*, 10 April 1844; Protest of the Pastoral Association, 16 May 1844, in *Votes and Proceedings*, 30 May 1844; Knight, *Illiberal Liberal*, pp. 63, 74; Hogan, *Lowe*, p. 55; A. Powell, *Patrician Democrat The Political Life of Charles Cowper 1843–1870*, Melbourne University Press, Melbourne, 1977, p. 22; Melbourne, *Wentworth*, p. 109; Fowles, *Sydney in 1848*, pp. 50–53.

11 Council debates, *Herald*, 2, 9, 29, 30 August, 13 September 1844; The Clerk to the Speaker, 25 May 1844, NSW Parliamentary Archive, No. 44/84.

12 Melbourne, *Early Constitutional Development*, pp. 298–300; Council debates, *Herald*, 6, 22 June 1844; *Votes and Proceedings*, 13 June 1844; Evidence of E.D. Thomson before the Select Committee on General Grievances, 31 August 1844.

13 Report of the Select Committee on General Grievances, 6 December 1844.

14 Council debates, *Herald*, 7 June 1844; Votes *and Proceedings*, 13 June, 27 November, 23 December 1844; Report of the Select Committee on Extension of the Elective Franchise, 27 September 1844; Melbourne, *Early Constitutional Development*, pp. 304–06; Connell, *Sydney*, p. 58.

CHAPTER 23   COUNTED OUT

1 Lowe to Mitchell, 30 November 1846, in Martin, *Life and Letters of Robert Lowe*, pp. 287–88; Liston, *Sarah Wentworth*, pp. 37–38.

2 Council debates, *Herald*, 11, 17 October 1843; Powell, *Patrician Democrat*, pp. 23–24; Report of the Select Committee on Education, 28 August 1844; Knight, *Illiberal Liberal*, p. 90; *Votes and Proceedings*, 10 October, 17 December 1844; Gipps Education Message to the Legislative Council, 27 November 1844; Smith & Spaull, *History of Education in NSW*, pp. 78–86.

3 Martin, *Life and Letters of Robert Lowe*, p. 288; Gipps to Stanley, 1 January 1845, *HRA*, Volume XXIV, pp. 164–70; *Votes and Proceedings*, 11 October 1844; Butlin, *Foundations of the Australian Monetary System*, pp. 349–50; Stanley to Gipps, 17 May 1845, tabled in the Legislative Council on 8 October 1845; Wentworth to W.C. Wentworth Jr, 7 September 1844, ML A756; Liston, *Sarah Wentworth*, pp. 24, 25, 37.

4 Report of the Select Committee on the Lien on Wool Act, 14 October 1845; Melbourne, *Early Constitutional Development*, p. 301; Report of the Select Committee on General Grievances, 6 December 1844.

5 Council debates, *Herald*, 21 June 1844; R v Kilmeister (No. 1), 15 November 1838, *Gazette*, 20 November 1838; R v Kilmeister (No. 2), 26 November 1838, *Australian*, 27 November 1838; D. Kirkby, D. Kirby and C. Bourne, *Law, History and Colonialism*, Manchester University Press, Manchester, 2001, p. 143.

6 Council debates, *Herald*, 31 December 1844, 30, 31 July, 19 August 1845; *Herald*, 20 March 1845.

7 Council debates, *Herald*, 6 August, 3 September 1845; *Votes and Proceedings*, 1844, 1845.

8 Council debates, *Herald*, 25 October 1845, 21 September 1853; Fowles, *Sydney in 1848*, p. 66.

9 Council debates, *Herald*, 19 December 1844, 18, 29 October 1845; P.L. Reynolds, *Legislative Architecture in NSW*, Legislative Council, Sydney, 1976, p. 13; The Clerk to Lewis, 16 August 1843, NSW Parliamentary Archive, No. 43/60.

10 Council debates, *Herald*, 3, 11, 29 October, 8, 14 November 1845; McLeay to Scott, 8 November 1845; *Votes and Proceedings*, 13 November 1845.

11 Knight, *Illiberal Liberal*, pp. 115–16.

12 *Herald*, 1 May 1846; Council debates, *Herald*, 13 May 1846; Dr Stuart to J. Stuart, 2 June 1846, NSW Parliamentary Archive, PRS 25 LC1; Reynolds, *Legislative Architecture*, p. 13; The Clerk to Gordon, 7 May 1846, NSW Parliamentary Archive, No. 46/24.

13 *Herald*, 16 May 1846.

14 Council debates, *Herald*, 4, 5, 6, 10 June 1846; Melbourne, *Early Constitutional Development*, p. 284.

15 Council debates, *Herald*, 11, 13, 14 June 1846.

16 *Herald*, 16 June 1846; Gipps to Gladstone, 25 June 1846, *HRA*, Volume XXV, pp. 109, 116.

CHAPTER 24   ALLIES FALL OUT

1 Council debates, *Herald*, 9 September 1846.

2 Introduction, *HRA*, Volume XXV, p. x; Knight, *Illiberal Liberal*, pp. 146–47.

3 Council debates, *Herald*, 23 October 1845.

4 *Votes and Proceedings*, 25 September 1846; Council debates, *Herald*, 11, 16, 17, 26 September, 15, 17 October 1846; *Votes and Proceedings*, 15, 24, 25 September 1846.

5 Council debates, *Herald*, 8 October 1846; Gladstone to FitzRoy, 30 April 1846, tabled in the Legislative Council on 7 October 1846.

6 Council debates, *Herald*, 9, 10, 14 October 1846; *Votes and Proceedings*, 13 October 1846; Evidence of John Dobie, Thomas Barker and Charles Logan to the Select Committee on Transportation, 15, 16 October 1846; *Herald*, 23 October 1846.

7 Report of the Select Committee on Transportation, 31 October 1846; Council debates, *Herald*, 28, 31 October, 2 November 1846; Knight, *Illiberal Liberal*, p. 163.

8 Council debates, *Herald*, 5 May 1847; Powell, *Patrician Democrat*, p. 33; Melbourne, *Early Constitutional Development*, pp. 119, 348; Council debates, *Herald*, 15 May 1847; The Clerk to Buchanan, 15 May 1847, NSW Parliamentary Archive, No. 47/56.

9 Liston, *Sarah Wentworth*, pp. 47–51; *Herald*, 27 May 1847; M. Rutledge, 'Stephen, Sir Alfred (1802–1894)', *ADB*, Volume 6, pp. 180–87; C. Baxter, *An Irresistible Temptation*, Allen & Unwin, Sydney, 2006, p. 369.

10 Grey to FitzRoy, 29 November 1846, tabled 1 June 1847; Melbourne, *Early Constitutional Development*, pp. 302, 307; Council debates, *Sydney Herald*, 29 May, 10, 19, 23, 24 June 1847; Knight, *Illiberal Liberal*, p. 179; H.M. Green, *Wentworth as Orator*, D.S. Ford, Sydney, 1935, p. 18; Liston, *Sarah Wentworth*, p. 53; Stapleton, *Australia's First Parliament*, p. 90.

11 Council debates, *Herald*, 12, 14 August 1847; The Clerk to Colonial Secretary, 4 June 1847 and Dr Nicholson to Australian Gas Light Company, 2 October 1847, both in NSW Parliamentary Archive, PRS 25 LC1; Dr Nicholson to Brown, 31 March 1847, NSW Parliamentary Archive, PRS 25 LC1; Fowles, *Sydney in 1848*, p. 81.

12 Council debates, *Herald*, 16 September 1847; Council debates, *Herald*, 22 September, 2 October 1847; Knight, *Illiberal Liberal*, pp. 169–75.

13 Grey to FitzRoy, 31 July 1847, tabled in the Legislative Council on 21 March 1848; Powell, *Patrician Democrat*, p. 37; Hansard, *Debates*, 1847, Volume 95, cc. 1004–06; Knight, *Illiberal Liberal*, p. 181; *Herald*, 19, 21 January 1848.

14 Grey to FitzRoy, 3 September 1847, tabled in the Legislative Council on 21 March 1848; Council debates, *Herald*, 10 April 1848; Clark, *Select Documents*, Volume I, pp. 405–06.

15 *Sydney Herald*, 26, 28 April; Council debates, *Herald*, 1, 3, 4, 10 May 1848; Melbourne, *Early Constitutional Development*, pp. 349–51; Knight, *Illiberal Liberal*, pp. 182–85; Powell, *Patrician Democrat*, pp. 37–39; see generally: Papers relative to the Proposed Alterations in the Constitution of the Australian Colonies, tabled in the Legislative Council on 25 May 1849; *Votes and Proceedings*, 28 April 1848.

16 Powell, *Patrician Democrat*, p. 42; *Herald*, 5 July 1848; Thompson, *Seeds of Democracy*, p. 206.

17 Martin, *Parkes*, pp. 47–49; *Herald*, 12, 20 July 1848.

18 Thompson, *Seeds of Democracy*, pp. 192–93, 197; Martin, *Parkes*, p. 50; Powell, *Patrician Democrat*, p. 43; *Herald*, 20 July 1848; Ward, *James Macarthur*, p. 139; J.D. Lang, *Freedom and Independence for the Golden Lands of Australia*, Longmans, London, 1852, p. 218; *Vanity Fair*, 8 May 1869.

CHAPTER 25 A SQUATTER'S CONSTITUTION

1 *The People's Advocate* [*Advocate*], 18 August 1849; H. Parkes, *Fifty Years in the Making of Australian History*, Longmans, London, 1892, p. 9.

2 Grey to FitzRoy, 31 July 1848, tabled in the Legislative Council on 22 May 1849; *Herald*, 17 November 1848; Lang, *Freedom and Independence*, p. 218.

3 Council debates, *Herald*, 18 May 1849, 13 June 1850; Butlin, *Foundations of the Australian Monetary System*, pp. 196, 258, 350–54; Knight, *Illiberal Liberal*, p. 209; Liston, *Sarah Wentworth*, pp. 54–55.

4 Knight, *Illiberal Liberal*, pp. 206–09; Parkes, *Fifty Years*, p. 10.

5 Knight, *Illiberal Liberal*, p. 210; *Herald*, 24, 26 January 1849.

6 *Herald*, 22, 26, 27 January, 9, 10 March 1849; Grey to FitzRoy, 8 September 1848, tabled in the Legislative Council on 22 May 1849; Council debates, *Herald*, 23, 24, 30 May, 1, 2, 6 June 1849; Ward, *James Macarthur*, pp. 158–59.

7 *Herald*, 12 June 1849; Knight, *Illiberal Liberal*, pp. 219–20; Martin, *Parkes*, pp. 56–57.

8 Council debates, *Herald*, 13 June 1849; *Herald*, 15, 19 June 1849; Martin, *Parkes*, p. 59; Parkes, *Fifty Years*, pp. 16–17.

9 Ward, *James Macarthur*, p. 153.

10 Council debates, *Herald*, 29 June, 29 August 1849.

11 Council debates, *Herald*, 1, 7 September 1849; Report from the Select Committee on the Sydney University, 21 September 1849.

12 Council debates, *Herald*, 5 October 1849; *Votes and Proceedings*, 10 October 1849; Turney, *Grammar*, pp. 23–27; Sheldon, *The Big School Room*, p. 145; G.L. Fischer, *The University of Sydney 1850–1975*, Edwards and Shaw, 1975, pp. 14–15.

13 Knight, *Illiberal Liberal*, pp. 246–50; Ward, *James Macarthur*, p. 165.

14 Martin, *Parkes*, pp. 47, 56, 60; *Herald*, 19, 20, 22 December 1849; Powell, *Patrician Democrat*, p. 45.

15 *Advocate*, 25 August 1849.

16 D.W.A. Baker, *Days of Wrath*, Melbourne University Press, Melbourne, 1985, pp. 203–04, 290–92, 297, 301.

17 Council debates, *Herald*, 30 August 1849, 21, 29 June, 6, 10 July 1850; Baker, *Days of Wrath*, pp. 301–02.

18 Baker, *Days of Wrath*, pp. 257–67; *Herald*, 9, 11, 12, 13, 14, 20, 24, 25 July 1850.

19 The Clerk to Day, 30 July 1850, NSW Parliamentary Archive, No. 50/81; Fowles, *Sydney in 1848*, pp. 76–77; Tender for varnishing and French polishing work issued by the Legislative Council Office, 25 March 1847, NSW Parliamentary Archive, PRS 25 LC1.

20 Council debates, *Herald*, 7, 15, 17, 21, 22 August 1850; *Votes and Proceedings*, 21 August 1850; Baker, *Days of Wrath*, pp. 314–15, 321–23, 327, 329.

21 *Votes and Proceedings*, 27 August 1850; Council debates, *Herald*, 28 August, 13 September 1850.

22 Council debates, *Herald*, 12 June, 29, 31 August, 4, 28, 30 September, 1 October 1850; Parkes, *Fifty Years*, p. 18; Martin, *Parkes*, p. 66; Ward, *James Macarthur*, pp. 160–63.

23 Hansard, *Debates*, 1850, Volume 108, cc. 554, 609, 976, 979–80; Hansard, *Debates*, Volume 109, cc. 1288, 1303–04, 1315; Hansard, *Debates*, 1850, Volume 110, cc. 606, 622, 1397, 1423–26; Introduction, *HRA*, Volume XXV, p. xi; Melbourne, *Early Constitutional Development*, pp. 374–75.

24 Hansard, *Debates*, Volume 111, cc. 511–14, 943–44, 948–49, 1041–42, 1047–48; Thompson, *Seeds of Democracy*, p. 213.

25 Lang, *Freedom and Independence*, p. 185.

CHAPTER 26   WENTWORTH DEMANDS SELF-GOVERNMENT

1 *Votes and Proceedings*, 28 March 1851; Council debates, *Herald*, 5 April 1851; Thompson, *Seeds of Democracy*, p. 219; Clark, *Select Documents*, Volume I, p. 405.

2 Council debates, *Herald*, 9, 12 April 1851.

3 Council debates, *Herald*, 17, 18 April 1851.

4 Council debates, *Herald*, 9 April 1851.

5 Report of the Select Committee on the New Constitution, 29 April 1851; Council debates, *Herald*, 2 May 1851.

6 Parkes, *Fifty Years*, pp. 25, 28–29.

7 Council debates, *Herald*, 3, 6, October 1849, 2 May 1851; *Sydney Herald*, 15 May, 29 July, 15, 16 September 1851; Thompson, *Seeds of Democracy*, pp. 221–26.

8 *Herald*, 16 September 1851.

9 *Herald*, 17 September 1851; Thompson, *Seeds of Democracy*, pp. 225–26; Clark, *Select Documents*, Volume I, p. 214.

10 *Empire*, 18 September 1851; Green, *Wentworth as Orator*, p. 19.

11 Baker, *Days of Wrath*, p. 342; Powell, *Patrician Democrat*, p. 52; Melbourne, *Wentworth*, p. 79; Melbourne, *Early Constitutional Development*, p. 382; Council debates, *Herald*, 15, 17 October, 1 November, 8 December 1851; *Votes and Proceedings*, 5 December 1851; 13 and 14 Victoria, Chapter 59.

12 Council debates, *Herald*, 9, 10, 11, 17 June 1852; Report of the Select Committee on the Proposed New Constitution, 17 September 1852; The Clerk to Wentworth, 11 July 1852, NSW Parliamentary Archive, No. 52/5.

13 Council debates, *Herald*, 13 December 1852.

14 Council debates, *Herald*, 23 July 1852; *Votes and Proceedings*, 10 August 1852.

15 Council debates, *Herald*, 19, 20, 26 August 1852.

16 D'Arcy Wentworth to Inspector General of Police, 3 June 1851, in *Votes and Proceedings*, 1852, Volume 2, p. 559; G. Butler Earp, *The Gold Colonies of Australia*, Routledge and Co., London, 1852, pp. 140–41; 'Lucknow', *The Age*, 8 February 2004; Report from the Select Committee on the Wentworth Gold Field Company's Bill, 12 August 1853; *The Times*, 30 September 1852; Melbourne, *Wentworth*, p. 95.

17 Evidence of J.R. Hardy and D'Arcy Wentworth before the Select Committee on the Management of the Gold Fields, 22 September, 26 November 1852 respectively: The Clerk to Lewis, 24 April 1849, NSW Parliamentary Archive, No. 41/23; Stapleton, *Australia's First Parliament*, p. 39.

18 Reports of the Select Committee on Immigration, 6 July, 1 October, 28 December 1852; Report of the Select Committee on the Management of the Gold Fields, 22 December 1852; Council debates, *Herald*, 9, 16 September 1852.

19 Evidence of G.S. Lang before the Select Committee on the Management of the Gold Fields, 8 December 1852.

20 Council debates, *Herald*, 15, 23 December 1852.

21 Green, *Wentworth as Orator*, pp. 15–16.

CHAPTER 27 THE DUKE OF VAUCLUSE

1 Council debates, *Herald*, 11 May 1853.

2 J. Hughes, *Report on Select List of Manuscripts Relating to Vaucluse House and the Wentworth Family*, compiled for the Historic Houses Trust, 20 September 1982, p. 140; Liston, *Sarah Wentworth*, pp. 38, 56, 58, 64; Report from the Senate of the University of Sydney for the year 1852, 3 January 1853; Fischer, *Sydney University*, p. 16; H. Kennedy, *Attendance of Fellows at Meetings of the Senate from 3 February 1851 to 28 November 1853*, Report of the Senate for the year 1853, Legislative Council Vote, and Proceedings, 1854.

3 Liston, *Sarah Wentworth*, p. 59; Martin, *Parkes*, pp. 108–11.

4 Council debates, *Herald*, 11, 21 May 1853; Melbourne, *Early Constitutional Development*, pp. 399–400; Pakington to FitzRoy, 18 December 1852, ordered to be printed by the Council on 11 May 1853.

5 Thompson, *Seeds of Democracy*, pp. 232–33; Council debates, *Herald*, 28 May 1853; The Clerk to Richardson, 26 December 1846, NSW Parliamentary Archive, No. 46/217; Stapleton, *Australia's First Parliament*, p. 39.

6 Evidence of E.D. Thomson before the Select Committee on the Gold Fields' Management Bill, 27 July 1853; Report of the Select Committee on the Gold Fields' Management Bill, 20 September 1853; Council debates, *Herald*, 9 June 1853.

7 Report from the Select Committee on the New Constitution, 28 July 1853; The

Constitutional Act, 1791, 31 George III, Chapter 31, Sections III-VI; J. McLaughlin, 'Dickinson, Sir John Nodes (1806–1882)', *ADB*, Volume 4, pp. 71–72; Lang, *Freedom and Independence*, pp. 136–37.

8 J. Ward, *Earl Grey and the Australian Colonies 1846–1857*, Melbourne University Press, Melbourne, 1958, pp. 30, 92–99, 109–16, 191–93, 230–33; Introduction, *HRA*, Volume XXVI, pp. xii–xvii; Report from the Select Committee on the New Constitution, 28 July 1853; Council debates, *Herald*, 17 August 1853; see generally: Papers relative to the Proposed Alterations in the Constitution of the Australian Colonies, tabled in the Legislative Council on 25 May 1849.

9 Lang, *Freedom and Independence*, pp. 32–34; Council debates, *Herald*, 17 August 1853; Report of the Select Committee on the Gold Fields' Management Bill, 20 September 1853; Ward, *Grey and the Australian Colonies*, pp. 339–40.

10 Report from the Select Committee on the New Constitution, 28 July 1853.

11 Report from the Select Committee on the New Constitution, 28 July 1853; *Votes and Proceedings*, 2 August 1853; Martin, *Parkes*, pp. 111–13; *Herald*, 16 August 1853; Fowles, *Sydney in 1848*, p. 34.

12 Council debates, *Herald*, 17 August 1853; Council debates, *Herald*, 17 August 1853.

13 Martin, *Parkes*, p. 114.

14 Council debates, *Herald*, 17, 19, 24, 25, 31 August 1853.

15 Council debates, *Herald*, 1 September 1853.

16 Council debates, *Herald*, 23 August, 3 September 1853.

17 *Herald*, 6, 7 September 1853.

18 Council debates, *Herald*, 8, 9, 10, 21, 22, 23 December 1853.

CHAPTER 28   INDEPENDENCE AND FEDERATION

1 Council debates, *Herald*, 22 December 1853; *Herald*, 21 March 1854; Martin, *Parkes*, p. 119; Baker, *Days of Wrath*, pp. 364–65; Thompson, *Seeds of Democracy*, pp. 244–45.

2 *Herald*, 23 March 1854; Knight, 'Lowe, Robert', *ADB*, Volume 2, pp. 134–37; Martin, *Parkes*, pp. 120–23; *The Times*, 15 December 1853.

3 Wentworth to James Macarthur, 3 April 1854, Macarthur Papers, Volume 27, ML A2923, CY Reel 955.

4 Sarah Wentworth to Thomasine Fisher, 11 March 1854, ML A868; Wentworth to the Speaker of the Legislative Council, 8 July 1854, *Votes and Proceedings*, 12 September 1854; Wentworth to James Macarthur, 15 July 1854, Macarthur Papers, Volume 27, ML A2923, CY Reel 955; D. Munsell, 'Clinton, Henry Pelham Fiennes Pelham, Fifth Duke of Newcastle-under-Lyme (1811–1864)', *ODNB*, Volume 22, pp. 148–51. Melbourne, *Early Constitutional Development*, pp. 417–20.

5 Liston, *Sarah Wentworth*, pp. 62–63; Wentworth to Thomasine Fisher, 31 March 1854, ML A1441; Hansard, *Debates*, Volume 138, c. 719; Wentworth to the Speaker of the Legislative Council, 3 July 1855, *Votes and Proceedings*, 2 October 1855; Ward, *Grey and the Australian Colonies*, pp. 343–46.

6 Hansard, *Debates*, Volume 138, cc. 719, 723, 725, 1989, 1997, 2005, 2012, Volume 139, cc. 102, 108, 109; Sarah Wentworth to Thomasine Fisher, 27 June 1854, ML A868.

7 Russell to Denison, 20 July 1855, tabled in the Legislative Council on 31 October 1855; Melbourne, *Wentworth*, p. 99; Ward, *Grey and the Australian Colonies*, p. 285; Prest, Earl Russell, *ODNB*, Volume 44.

8 Sarah Wentworth to Amelia Hunt, 2 August 1855, ML A868; Sarah Wentworth to Thomasine Fisher, 7 October, 5 November, 2 December 1855, ML A868; Liston, *Sarah Wentworth*, pp. 64–65; *The Times*, 11 March, 29 April, 4 May 1856, 4 January 1858.

9 Clune and Turner, *The Premiers of NSW*, Volume I, pp. 15, 35, 55; *Sydney Morning Herald*, 23, 30 October 1856; Ward, *Grey and the Australian Colonies*, pp. 356, 361–62; Federation Correspondence tabled in the Tasmanian Parliament on 22 October 1861.

10 Ward, *Grey and the Australian Colonies*, pp. 363–67; *The Times,* 24 April 1857; R. Hughes, *The Fatal Shore*, Pan Books, London, 1988, pp. 572, 580.

11 Melbourne, *Wentworth*, p. 100; Ward, *Grey and the Australian Colonies*, pp. 367–70; *The Times*, 9, 23 January 1858; Federation Correspondence, 1861.

12 *Herald*, 21 October, 2 December 1857; Ward, *Grey and the Australian Colonies*, pp. 455–64.

13 Sarah Wentworth to Thomasine Fisher, 5 November 1855, 8 October 1856, 20 August 1857, ML A868; Liston, *Sarah Wentworth*, pp. 66, 68; Wentworth to Sarah Wentworth, 3 January 1858, ML Wentworth Family Legal Documents, Box 4.

14 Sarah Wentworth to Thomasine Fisher, no date, ML A868, p. 165; same correspondents, 21 July 1857, ML A868; same correspondents, 23 April 1859, ML A868; Wentworth Jr to Thomasine Fisher, no date, ML A868; Liston, *Sarah Wentworth*, pp. 70–73; M. Bragg, *12 Books that Changed the World*, Hodder & Stoughton, London, 2006, p. 221.

15 Griffin and Hughes, *Vaucluse House*, p. 56; John Alexander Letter Book, 10 June 1858, ML MSS 3843; Liston, *Sarah Wentworth*, pp. 70, 72; *Votes and Proceedings of the Legislative Assembly,* 11 October 1859; *Herald*, 12 October 1859.

16 *Herald*, 12 October 1859; Liston, *Sarah Wentworth*, p. 76; Sarah Wentworth to Thomasine Fisher, 20 February 1858, ML A868; Sarah Wentworth to Thomasine Fisher (1859/1860) ML A868; Sarah Wentworth to Thomasine Fisher, 25 January 1861, ML A868.

17 *Herald*, 13 May 1861; Ward, *James Macarthur*, pp. 257, 259; J.M. Ward, 'Young, Sir John [Baron Lisgar] (1807–1876)', *ADB*, Volume 6, pp. 455–57.

CHAPTER 29   MR PRESIDENT

1 *Herald*, 17, 19 April 1861; Council debates, *Herald*, 18 April 1861; Clune and Turner, *The Premiers of NSW*, Volume I, p. 48.

2 *Herald,* 19 April 1861; John Alexander Letter Book, 9 January 1858, ML MSS 3843; Liston, *Sarah Wentworth*, pp. 77–78; Clark, *Select Documents*, Volume II, p. 666; Mourot, *This Was Sydney*, pp. 54–55.

3 Clune and Turner, *The Premiers of NSW,* Volume I, pp. 15, 35, 48, 55, 69, 81; D. Clune and G. Griffith, *Decision and Deliberation,* The Federation Press, Sydney, 2006, pp. 19, 67, 68; B. Nairn, 'Robertson, Sir John (1816–1891)', *ADB,* Volume 6, pp. 38–46.

4 Nairn, 'Sir John Robertson', *ADB,* Volume 6, pp. 38–46; C.H. Currey, 'The First Proposed Swamping of the Legislative Council of New South Wales', *JRAHS,* Volume 15 (1929), pp. 282–91.

5 *Herald,* 10, 16 May, 1, 5, 7, 25 June, 20 July 1861; Fischer, *Sydney University,* p. 26; Young to Newcastle, 20 July 1861, CO 201/518. Emmeline Parker to William Macarthur, 7 May 1861, ML A2959; Clune and Turner, *The Premiers of NSW,* Volume I, p. 48; Clune and Griffith, *Decision and Deliberation,* pp. 83, 84, 88, 112; Currey, *The First Proposed Swamping,* p. 285.

6 *New South Wales Parliament,* NSW Government Printer, 1985; Council debates, *Herald,* 4, 27 September, 2, 11 October 1861; Clune and Griffith, *Decision and Deliberation,* p. 123; Stapleton, *Australia's First Parliament,* p. 39; Reynolds, *Legislative Architecture in NSW,* p. 23.

7 Clune and Griffith, *Decision and Deliberation,* pp. 145–148; Report from the Select Committee on the Legislative Council Bill, 21 August 1862; Council debates, *Herald,* 10 October 1862; Clune and Turner, *The Premiers of NSW,* Volume I, p. 48.

8 *Herald,* 24 June 1862; Wentworth to Thomasine Fisher, 22 September 1862, ML A868; Liston, *Sarah Wentworth,* pp. 80–81.

9 Sarah Wentworth to Thomasine Fisher, 21 July 1861, 21 May 1862, ML A868; Liston, *Sarah Wentworth,* pp. 80–82; Legislative Council, *Votes and Proceedings,* 17 September 1862.

10 Sarah Wentworth to Thomasine Fisher, 20 December 1861, ML A868; Wentworth v Lloyd, X HLC 589; Wentworth to Thomasine Fisher, 20 September 1862, ML A868.

11 Young to Newcastle, 21 October 1862, CO 201/523; *Herald,* 22 October 1862.

CHAPTER 30   HIS BONES AND HIS MEMORY

1 Liston, *Sarah Wentworth,* pp. 83, 85; Wentworth v Lloyd, 32 Beav. 467; Wentworth v Lloyd, X HLC 589; Wentworth v Lloyd (No. 2), 34 Beav. 454.

2 Liston, *Sarah Wentworth,* pp. 15, 83; Sarah Wentworth to Thomasine Fisher, 25 October 1864, ML A868; Laura Wentworth to Thomasine Fisher, 25 September, 7 October 1864, ML A868; Ritchie, *The Wentworths,* p. 230; Towns v Wentworth [1858], 14 ER 794 at 800.

3 Laura Wentworth to Thomasine Fisher, May 1865, Lancaster Gate, 1865, December 1869, ML A868; A.C.V. Melbourne, *William Charles Wentworth,* The Discovery Press, Penrith, 1972, p. 68b; Clark, *A History of Australia,* Volume IV, p. 262.

4 Wentworth Family Movements 1853–1880, compiled by Joy Hughes for the Historic Houses Trust, 20 September 1982; Wentworth to Thomasine Fisher, 23 February, 14 June 1869, ML A1441; Sarah Wentworth to Thomas Fisher, 17 May 1870, January 1871, ML A868; Wentworth to Thomas Fisher, 29 June, 24 July, 22 December 1867, 1, 24 January, 22 May, 1868, 25 February 1869, ML A1441.

5 Depositions concerning William Fisher's death, 1868, ML A868; Wentworth to Thomas Fisher, 29 July 1868, ML A1441; Liston, *Sarah Wentworth*, pp. 96–98; Sarah Wentworth to Thomas Fisher, 22 May 1868, ML A868; Wentworth to Thomas Fisher, 17 May 1870, ML A868.

6 Liston, *Sarah Wentworth*, p. 85; D.S. Macmillan, 'The Australians in London', *JRAHS*, Volume 44, pp. 163–64; Wentworth to Thomas Fisher, 1 December 1869, ML A1441; Sarah Wentworth to Thomas Fisher, November 1869, 14 July 1870, 9 August 1871, ML A868; K.S. Inglis, *The Australian Colonists*, Melbourne University Press, Melbourne, 1974, p. 249; *The Times*, 11 March 1868; Sarah Wentworth for Wentworth to unknown, 29 November 1871, ML A441.

7 Liston, *Sarah Wentworth*, p. 101; *The Illustrated London News*, 27 April 1872; Sarah Wentworth to Thomas Fisher, 11 May 1872, May-June 1872, ML A868; Eliza Wentworth to Thomasine Fisher, 16 May 1872, ML A868; Assembly Debates, *Herald*, 7 August 1872; Henry Parkes to Sarah Wentworth, 14 March 1873, ML A758; Clark, *Select Documents*, Volume II, p. 664.

8 Liston, *Sarah Wentworth*, pp. 88, 105; Sarah Wentworth to Thomas Fisher, September 1872, 4 October 1872, November 1872, ML A868; Lady Sarah Macarthur to Mrs Macarthur-Onslow, February 1873, ML A2969.

9 *Herald*, 7 May 1873; Liston, *Sarah Wentworth*, pp. 106–08.

10 *The Perth Gazette*, 6 June 1873.

11 *The Freeman's Journal*, 3 May 1873.

12 Assembly debates, *Herald*, 7 August 1872; Melbourne, *William Charles Wentworth*, p. 112; Clune and Griffith, *Decision and Deliberation*, pp. 503–15.

13 J. Quick and R.R. Garran, *The Annotated Constitution of the Australian Commonwealth*, Legal Books, Sydney, 1976, p. 93; Clune and Turner, *The Premiers of NSW*, Volume I, p. 137; Parkes, *Fifty Years*, p. 332; Melbourne, *Wentworth*, p. 109.

14 Sarah Wentworth to Thomas Fisher, May-June 1872, ML A868.

BIBLIOGRAPHY

PRIMARY SOURCES

The author's notes and research files are held by the Mitchell Library, State Library of New South Wales.

Mitchell Library

Wentworth Family Letters, 1867–1902, A868

D'Arcy Wentworth, Correspondence, 1783–1808, A751

D'Arcy Wentworth, Correspondence, 1809–1816, A752

D'Arcy Wentworth, Correspondence, 1817– 20, A753

D'Arcy Wentworth, Correspondence, 1821–1827, A754–1

D'Arcy Wentworth, Supplementary Papers, mainly letters, 1785–1826, A754–2

D' Arcy Wentworth (the younger), Papers, 1805–58, A755

William Charles Wentworth, Correspondence, 1804–63, A756

Letters to William Charles Wentworth, 1814–57?, A757

William Charles Wentworth, Miscellanea, 1816–45, A758

Wentworth family—Papers, 1783–1827, A761

W.C. Wentworth, Legal Letter Book, 1825–6, A1440

William Charles Wentworth, Business and Estate papers, 1853–1872, A1441

Agreement between W.C. Wentworth and John Jones of Sydney with Maori chiefs for purchase of land in New Zealand, 15 February 1840, MSS 7574

John Alexander Letter Book, 10 June 1858, MSS 3843

Thomas Callaghan's Diary, A2122/1

Catton Papers, Australian Joint Copying Project, Reel M791

John Harris, Evidence to Commissioner Bigge, 16 August 1820, Bonwick Transcripts, Box 1

John Macarthur Jr Correspondence, 1810–31, A2911

Macarthur Papers, Miscellaneous MSS, 1787–1888, D185

James Macarthur, In-letters, 1819–67, A2923

Macarthur family, 1838–1930, Wine—memoranda, accounts, A2969

Lady Parker—Papers, 1829–89, A2959

Norfolk Island Victualling Book, 1792–96, A1958

NSW Parliamentary Archives

Copies of Vouchers Relating to Minor Expenses, PRS 0025.LC1

Miscellaneous Letter Book 1842–1855, PRS 0020.LC1, Copies of Letters Sent

Archives New Zealand

William Charles Wentworth, OLC 1, Box 23

State Records of New South Wales

Chief Justice's Letter Book, 1824–1835, 4/6551

House of Commons Papers

Report of the Commissioners of His Majesty's Navy, 15 February 1792

The Parliamentary Debates, London, 1810–62

Petition of the Settlers of NSW Respecting the Conduct of Governor Macquarie, 1817

Report of the Select Committee on Transportation, 1812

Bigge Report on Judicial Establishments, 1823

Bigge Report on The Colony, 1822

Bigge Report on Agriculture and Trade, 1823

Papers Relating to New South Wales, 1828

Report of the Select Committee on Transportation, 1837

New South Wales Legislative Council Papers

Records of Legislative Council Proceedings from 1824

<www.parliament.nsw.gov.au/prod/web/common.nsf/key/pre1991Hansard> [2006–08]

Minutes of Proceedings of the Legislative Council from 25 August 1824 to 22 November 1825, 1847

Minute No. 4, 3 September 1829

Minutes No. 17, 21 April 1830 and *No. 2*, 8 April 1834

Magistrates' Returns: G. Blaxland, 25 March 1834, W. Lawson, 22 March 1834, J. Macarthur, 31 March 1834

Votes and Proceedings of the NSW Legislative Council, 1843–62

Minutes of Evidence before the Select Committee on Monetary Confusion, 1843

Report of the Select Committee on Immigration together with Minutes of Evidence, 1843

Report of the Select Committee on the Petition from Distressed Mechanics and Labourers together with Minutes of Evidence, 1843

Report of the Select Committee on General Grievances together with Minutes of Evidence, 1844

Report of the Select Committee on Education, 1844

Protest of the Pastoral Association, 1844

Report of the Select Committee on Extension of the Elective Franchise, 1844

Report of the Select Committee on the Lien on Wool Act, 1845

Report of the Select Committee on the Renewal of Transportation, 1846

Papers relative to the Proposed Alterations in the Constitution of the Australian Colonies, 1849

Report from the Select Committee on the Sydney University, 1849

Report of the Select Committee on the New Constitution, 1851

Report of the Select Committee on the Proposed New Constitution, 1852

Report of the Select Committee on the Management of the Gold Fields together with Minutes of Evidence, 1852

Reports of the Select Committee on Immigration, 1852

Report from the Select Committee on the Wentworth Gold Field Company's Bill, 1853

Report of the Select Committee on the Gold Fields' Management Bill together with Minutes of Evidence, 20 September 1853

Report from the Select Committee on the New Constitution, 1853

Report from the Senate of the University of Sydney for the year 1852, 1853

Report of Attendance of Fellows at Meetings of the Senate from 3 February 1851 to 28 November 1853, 1853

Report from the Select Committee on the Legislative Council Bill, 1862

Tasmanian Parliament

Federation Correspondence, 1861

Court Reports

D' Arcy Wentworth, Mary Wilkinson, otherwise Looking, Theft with Violence: Highway Robbery, Theft: receiving Stolen Goods, Theft with Violence: Highway Robbery, Theft with Violence; Highway Robbery, 12 December 1787, The Proceedings of the Old Bailey, ref: t17871212–7

Kercher, B., *Decisions of the Supreme Courts of New South Wales 1788–1899*, <www.law.mq.edu.au/scnsw> [2006–08]

D'Arcy Wentworth, Theft with Violence: Highway Robbery, 9 December 1789, The Proceedings of the Old Bailey, ref: t17891209–1

Bartrum, *Proceedings of a General Court Martial of Lieut.-Col. Geo. Johnston on a Charge of Mutiny for deposing on 26 January 1808, William Bligh*, Sherwood, Neely and Jones, London, 1811

Castle T.D. and Kercher, B., *Dowling's Select Cases 1828 to 1844*, Francis Forbes Society, Sydney, 2005

Thomas Algar, *Violent Theft*, 11 July 1787, the Proceedings of the Old Bailey, ref: t17870111-9

Towns v *Wentworth* [1858], 14 ER 794

Wentworth v *Lloyd*, 32 Beav. 467

Wentworth v *Lloyd*, X HLC 589

Wentworth v *Lloyd (No. 2)*, 34 Beav. 454

Newspapers

Advertiser, 1792

Australian, 1824–43

Australasian Chronicle, 1841–42

Australian Daily Journal, 1844

Colonial Observer, 1842–43

Edinburgh Review, 1819

Empire, 1851

Freeman's Journal, 1873

Gentleman's Magazine, 1842

Illustrated London News, 1872

Illustrated Sydney News, 1854–1873

Maitland Mercury, 1843

Monitor, 1826–41

People's Advocate, 1849

Perth Gazette, 1873

Sydney Gazette, 1810–39

Sydney Herald, 1831–41

Sydney Morning Herald, 1841–72

The Times, 1787–1858

Vanity Fair, 1869

Memoirs, Letters and other Documents

Albemarle, Earl of, *Memoirs of the Marquis of Rockingham*, Richard Bentley, London, 1852, Volume I

The Bigge Reports, Biographical Note, in Australiana Facsimilie Editions No. 70, Libraries Board of South Australia, Adelaide, 1966

Bland, W., *Letters to Charles Buller M.P. from the Australian Patriotic Association*, D.L. Welch, Sydney, 1849

Bredvold, L. and Ross, R., eds, *The Philosophy of Edmund Burke*, University of Michigan Press, Ann Arbor, 1970

Clark, C.M.H, *Select Documents in Australian History*, Angus & Robertson, Sydney, 1970

Colby, C.W., ed., *Selections from the Sources of English History*, Longmans Green, London, 1920

Copy of a further Letter from Bathurst to Bigge, 6 January 1819, in Australiana Facsimile Editions No. 69, Libraries Board of South Australia, Adelaide, 1966

Currey, J.B., ed., *Reflections on the Colony of New South Wales by George Caley*, Lansdowne Press, Melbourne, 1966

Fletcher, B.H., ed., *An Account of the English Colony in New South Wales by David Collins*, Volume I, A.H. & A.W. Reid, Sydney 1975 (originally published in 1798)

Fidlon, P., ed., *The Journal and Letters of Lieutenant Ralph Clark 1787–1792*, Australian Documents Library, Sydney, 1981

Fidlon, P., ed, *The Journal of Arthur Bowes Smyth*, Australian Documents Library, Sydney, 1979

Fortescue, J., ed., *Correspondence of King George III 1760–83*, Frank Cass, London, 1967, Volume V

Fulton, P.J., ed., *The Minerva Journal of John Washington Price*, Miegunyah Press, Melbourne, 2000

Hughes, J., *Report on Select List of Manuscripts Relating to Vaucluse House and the Wentworth Family*, compiled for the Historic Houses Trust, 20 September 1982

Hunter, J., *An Historical Journal of the Transactions at Port Jackson and Norfolk Island*, John Stockdale, London, 1793

Macarthur Onslow, S., *Some Early Records of the Macarthurs of Camden*, Angus & Robertson, Sydney, 1914

Martin, A.P., *Life and Letters of Rt. Hon. Robert Lowe Viscount Sherbrooke*, Volume I, Longmans, Green & Co., London, 1893

Richards, J.A., ed., *Blaxland-Lawson-Wentworth 1813*, Blubber Head Press, Hobart, 1979

Walker, F., ed., *A Journal of a Tour of Discovery Across the Blue Mountains NSW in 1813 by Gregory Blaxland*, Sydney, 1913

Watson, F., ed., *Historical Records of Australia*, Series I, Volumes I–XXVI, The Library Committee of the Commonwealth Parliament, Canberra, 1914–1925

Wentworth Family Movements 1853–1880, compiled by Joy Hughes for the Historic Houses Trust, 20 September 1982

Wentworth, W.C., *Journal of an Expedition Across the Blue Mountains*, 11 May to 6 June 1813, ML Safe 1/22a

SECONDARY SOURCES

Annable, R., *A Setting for Justice*, University of New South Wales Press, Sydney, 2007

Atkinson, A., 'Macarthur, James (1798–1867)', *Oxford Dictionary of National Biography*, Oxford University Press, 2004 [*ODNB*] London, Volume 35, pp. 12–13

Atkinson, A., *The Europeans in Australia*, Volume 1, Oxford University Press, Melbourne, 1998

Atkinson, A., *The Europeans in Australia*, Volume 2, Oxford University Press, Melbourne, 2004

Auchmuty, J.J., 'Wentworth, D'Arcy (1762–1827)', *Australian Dictionary of Biography*, [*ADB*], Volume 2, Melbourne University Press, Melbourne, 1967, pp. 579–82

BIBLIOGRAPHY

Bairstow, D., *A Million Pounds A Million Acres*, Self Published, Sydney, 2003

Baker, D.W.A., *Days of Wrath*, Melbourne University Press, Melbourne, 1985

Baker, D.W.A., 'Lang, John Dunmore (1799–1878)', *ADB*, Volume 2, pp. 76–83

Baker, D.W.A., 'Mitchell, Sir Thomas Livingstone 91792–1855)', *ADB*, Volume 2, pp. 238–42

Baker, D.W.A., ed., *Reminiscences of my Life and Times by John Dunmore Lang*, Heinemann, Melbourne, 1972

Barcan, A., *A Short History of Education in New South Wales*, Martindale Press, Sydney, 1965

'Barrington, George (1755?–1804)', *ADB*, Volume I, pp. 62–63

Baxter, C., *An Irresistible Temptation*, Allen & Unwin, Sydney, 2006

Beattie, J.M., 'Garrow, Sir William (1760–1840)', *ODNB*, Volume 21, pp. 546–48

Bennet, H.G., *Letter to Viscount Sidmouth, Secretary of State for the Home Department, on the Transportation Laws, the State of the Hulks, and of the Colonies in New South Wales*, J. Ridgway, London, 1819

Bennett, J.M., *A History of the New South Wales Bar*, Law Book Company, Sydney, 1969

Bennett, J.M., 'Bigge, John Thomas (1780–1843)', *ODNB*, Volume 5, pp. 693–94

Bennett, J.M., 'The Establishment of Jury Trial in New South Wales', *The Sydney Law Review*, vol. 3, 1959–61

Border, R., 'Scott, Thomas Hobbes (1783–1860)', *ADB*, Volume 2, pp. 431–33

Bragg, M., *12 Books that Changed the World*, Hodder & Stoughton, London, 2006

Broadbent, J. and Hughes, J., *The Age of Macquarie*, Melbourne University Press, Melbourne, 1992

Brownscombe, R., *On Suspect Terrain*, Forever Wild Press, 2004 <www.fwp.com.au>

Butler Earp, G., *The Gold Colonies of Australia*, Routledge and Co., London, 1852

Butler, S., *The Dinkum Dictionary*, 3rd edition, Text Publishing, Melbourne, 2009

Butlin, S.J., *Foundations of the Australian Monetary System 1788–1851*, Sydney University Press, Sydney, 1968

Byrnes, J.V., 'Howe, Robert (1795–1829)', *ADB*, Volume 1, pp. 557–59

Chamberlain, M.E., 'Bulwer, (William) Henry Lytton Earle, Baron Dalling and Bulwer (1801–1872)', *ODNB*, Volume 8, pp. 666–69

Clark, C.M.H., *A History of Australia*, Volume I, Melbourne University Press, Melbourne, 1962

Clark, C.M.H., *A History of Australia*, Volumes II and III, Melbourne University Press, Melbourne, 1979

Clark, C.M.H., *A History of Australia*, Volume IV, Melbourne University Press, Melbourne, 1999

Clune, D. and Griffith, G., *Decision and Deliberation*, The Federation Press, Sydney, 2006

Clune, D. and Turner, K., *The Premiers of New South Wales*, Volume I, Federation Press, Sydney, 2006

Clune, F., *The Norfolk Island Story,* Angus & Robertson, Sydney, 1967

Cobley, J., 'Bland, William (1789–1868)', *ADB*, Volume 1, pp. 112–15

Cochrane, P., *Colonial Ambition,* Melbourne University Press, Melbourne, 2006

Colley, L., *Britons,* Pimlico, London, 2003

Connell, J., ed., *Sydney,* Oxford University Press, Melbourne, 2000

Conway, J., 'Blaxland, Gregory (1778–1853)', *ADB*, Volume 1, pp. 115–17

Cramp, K.R., *William Charles Wentworth of Vaucluse House, RAHS,* 1934

Crowley, F.K., 'Stirling, Sir James (1791–1865)', *ADB*, Volume 2, pp. 484–88

Cunningham, C., *Blue Mountains Rediscovered,* Kangaroo Press, East Roseville, 1999

Currey, C.H., 'Bent, Jeffrey Hart (1781–1852)', *ADB*, Volume I, pp. 87–89

Currey, C.H., *Sir Francis Forbes,* Angus & Robertson, Sydney, 1969

Currey, C.H., *The Brothers Bent,* Sydney University Press, Sydney, 1968

Currey, C.H., 'The First Proposed Swamping of the Legislative Council of New South Wales', *JRAHS,* Volume 15 (1929)

Currey, C.H., 'Therry, Sir Roger (1800–1874)', *ADB*, Volume 2, pp. 512–13

Currey, C.H., 'Wardell, Robert (1793–1834)', *ADB*, Volume 2, pp. 570–72

'Darling, Sir Ralph (1772–1858)', *ADB*, Volume I, pp. 282–86

Davidson, J.W., 'Busby, James (1801–1871)', *ADB*, Volume 1, pp. 186–88

Dear, L. and Barr, J., *Australia's First Patriot,* Angus & Robertson, Sydney, 1911

De Vries, S., *Historic Sydney,* Pandanus Press, Sydney, 1999

Dowling A., ed., *Reminiscences of a Colonial Judge,* Federation Press, Sydney, 1996

Dunlop, E.W., 'Lawson, William (1774–1850)', *ADB*, Volume 2, pp. 96–97

Eddy, J., 'Wentworth, D'Arcy (1762–1827)', *ODNB*, Volume 58, pp. 125–26

Ellis, M.H., *John Macarthur,* Angus & Robertson, Sydney, 1955

Ellis, M.H., *Lachlan Macquarie,* Angus & Robertson, Sydney, 1952

Else-Mitchell R. and Bennett, J., *The Charter of Justice of NSW,* Stoddart Publishing House, Sydney, 1974

Evison, H.C., *Te Wai Pounamu The Greenstone Island,* Aoraki Press, Wellington, 1993

Evison, H.C., 'The Wentworth-Jones Deeds of 15 February 1840', *The Turnbull Library Record,* Volume 28, 1995

Farrell, S.M., 'Watson-Wentworth, Charles (1730-1782)', *ODNB,* Volume 58, pp. 118–25

Finlay, C.J., 'Mackintosh, Sir James (1765–1832)', *ODNB*, Volume 35, pp. 674–79

Fischer, G.L., *The University of Sydney 1850-1975,* Edwards and Shaw, Sydney, 1075

Fitzwilliam, Earl and Bourke, Sir Richard, *Correspondence of Edmund Burke,* Francis and John Rivington, London, 1844

Fletcher, B.H., 'Foveaux, Joseph (1767–1846)', *ADB*, Volume 1, pp. 407–09

Fletcher, B.H., *Ralph Darling A Governor Maligned,* Oxford University Press, Melbourne, 1984

BIBLIOGRAPHY

Fletcher, B.H., 'Sir John Jamison in New South Wales 1814–1844', *Journal and Proceedings of the Royal Australian Historical Society* [*JRAHS*], Volume 65, June 1979, Part 1

Flynn, M., *The Second Fleet*, Library of Australian History, Sydney, 2001

Fowles, J., *Sydney in 1948*, Ure Smith, Sydney, 1973

Gilbert, L.A., 'Considen, Dennis (–1815)', *ADB*, Volume 1, pp. 242–43

Gray, N., 'Dumaresq, Henry (1792–1838)', *ADB*, Volume 1, pp. 333–35

Green, H.M., *Wentworth as Orator*, D.S. Ford, Sydney, 1935

Griffin, R., 'Early History of the Estate', in *Vaucluse House*, eds R. Griffin and J. Hughes, Historic Houses Trust, Sydney, 2006

Halloran, A., 'Some Early Legal Celebrities', *JRAHS*, Volume 10, 1924, Part VI

Halloran, A., 'Some Early Legal Celebrities', *JRAHS*, Volume 12, Part 1, 1927

Hawkins, A., 'Stanley, Edward George Godfrey Smith, Fourteenth Earl of Derby (1799–1869)', *ODNB*, Volume 52, pp. 178–87

Hazzard, M., *Punishment Short of Death*, Hyland House, Melbourne, 1984

Heydon, J.D., 'Brisbane, Sir Thomas Makdougall (1773–1860)', *ADB*, Volume 1, pp. 151–55

Heydon, J.D., 'Macarthur, James (1798–1867)', *ADB*, Volume 2, pp. 149–53

'Hindmarsh, Sir John (1785–1860)', *ADB*, Volume 1, pp. 538–41

Hirst, J.B. *Freedom on the Fatal Shore*, Black Inc., Melbourne, 2008

Hogan, J.F., *Robert Lowe Viscount Sherbrooke*, Ward and Downey, London, 1893

Holder, R.F., *Bank of New South Wales*, Volume 1, Angus & Robertson, Sydney, 1970

Howe, A.C., 'Huskisson, William (1770–1830)', *ODNB*, Volume 28, pp. 974–80

Hughes, R., *The Fatal Shore*, Pan Books, London, 1988

Inglis, K.S., *The Australian Colonists*, Melbourne University Press, Melbourne, 1974

Jeans, D.N., *An Historical Geography of New South Wales to 1901*, A.H & A.W. Reed, Sydney, 1972

Jellicoe, R.L., *The New Zealand Company's Native Reserves*, Government Printer, Wellington, 1930

Kenny, M.J.B., 'Hall, Edward Smith (1786–1860)', *ADB*, Volume 1, pp. 500–02

King, H., 'Bourke, Sir Richard (1777–1855)', *ADB*, Volume 1, pp. 128–33

King, H., *Elizabeth Macarthur and Her World*, Sydney University Press, Sydney, 1980

King, H., *Richard Bourke*, Oxford University Press, Melbourne, 1971

Kirkby, D., Kirby, D. and Bourne, C., *Law, History and Colonialism*, Manchester University Press, Manchester, 2001

Knight, R.L., *Illiberal Liberal*, Melbourne University Press, Melbourne, 1966

Knight, R.L., 'Lowe, Robert, Viscount Sherbrooke (1811–1892)', *ADB*, Volume 2, pp. 134–37

Lang, J.D., *A Historical and Statistical Account of New South Wales, both as a Penal Settlement and as a British Colony*, Cochrane and M'Crone, London, 1834

Lang, J.D., *Freedom and Independence for the Golden Lands of Australia*, Longmans, London, 1852

Liston, C., *Sarah Wentworth Mistress of Vaucluse*, Historic Houses Trust, Sydney, 1988

'Lucknow', *The Age*, 8 February 2004

Macarthur, J., *New South Wales, Its Present State and Future Prospects*, D. Walther, London, 1837

Mackaness, G., *Admiral Arthur Phillip*, Angus & Robertson, Sydney, 1937

Macmillan, D.S., 'The Australians in London', *JRAHS*, Volume 44

Macmillan, D.S., ed., *Two Years in New South Wales* (written by Peter Cunningham in 1827), Angus & Robertson, Sydney, 1966

McLachlan, N.D., 'Eagar, Edward (1787–1866)', *ADB*, Volume 1, pp. 343–44

McLachlan, N.D., 'Edward Eagar (1787–1866), A Colonial Statesman in Sydney and London', *Historical Studies Australia and New Zealand*, Volume 10, No 40, May 1963

McLachlan, N.D., 'Macquarie, Lachlan (1762–1824)', *ADB*, Volume 2, pp. 187–95

McLaughlin, J., 'Dickinson, Sir John Nodes (1806–1882)', *ADB*, Volume 4, pp. 71–72

Martin, A.W., *Henry Parkes A Biography*, Melbourne University Press, Melbourne, 1980

Martin, A.W., 'Parkes, Sir Henry (1815–1896)', *ADB*, Volume 5, pp. 399–406

Matthew, H.C.G., 'Gladstone, William Ewart (1809–1898)', *ODNB*, Volume 22, pp. 383–409

Melbourne, A.C.V., *Early Constitutional Development of Australia*, University of Queensland Press, Brisbane, 1963

Melbourne, A.C.V., *William Charles Wentworth*, The Discovery Press, Penrith, 1972

Moon, P., *Hobson Governor of New Zealand 1840–1842*, David Ling Publishing, Auckland, 1998

Mourot, S., *This Was Sydney*, Ure Smith, Sydney, 1969

Munsell, D., 'Clinton, Henry Pelham Fiennes Pelham, Fifth Duke of Newcastle-under-Lyme (1811–1864)', *ODNB*, Volume 22, pp. 148–51

Nairn, B., 'Robertson, Sir John (1816–1891)', *ADB*, Volume 6, pp. 38–46

Needham, A., *The Women of the Neptune*, A-1 Instant Printing P/L, Dural, 1992

New South Wales Parliament, NSW Government Printer, 1985

Nobbs, R., *Norfolk Island 1788–1814*, Library of Australian History, Sydney, 1988

Olson, A.G., *The Radical Duke*. Oxford University Press, London, 1961

Parkes, H., *Fifty Years in the Making of Australian History*, Longmans, London, 1892

Parsons, V., 'Goulburn, Frederick (1788–1837)', *ADB*, Volume I, pp. 463–64

Perry, T.M., *Australia's First Frontier*, Melbourne University Press, Melbourne, 1965

Persse, M., 'Wentworth, William Charles (1790–1872)', *ADB*, Volume 2, pp. 582–89

Powell, A., *Patrician Democrat The Political Life of Charles Cowper 1843–1870*, Melbourne University Press, Melbourne, 1977

Prest, J., 'Russell, John [formerly Lord John Russell] First Earl Russell (1792–1878)', *ODNB*, Volume 48, pp. 295–307

BIBLIOGRAPHY

Quick, J. and Garran, R.R., *The Annotated Constitution of the Australian Commonwealth*, Legal Books, Sydney, 1976

Reynolds, P.L., *Legislative Architecture in NSW*, Legislative Council, Sydney, 1976

Ritchie, J., *Punishment and Profit*, Heinemann, Melbourne, 1970

Ritchie, J., *The Wentworths Father and Son*, Melbourne University Press, Melbourne, 1999

Roberts, S.H., *The Squatting Age in Australia 1835–1847*, Melbourne University Press, Melbourne, 1964

Rutledge, M., 'Stephen, Sir Alfred (1802–1894)', *ADB*, Volume 6, pp. 180–87

Shaw, A.G.L., 'King, Phillip Gidley (1758–1808)', *ADB*, Volume 2, pp. 55–61

Sheldon, J.S., *The Big School Room at Sydney Grammar*, Sydney Grammar School Press, Darlinghurst, 1997

Shineberg, D., 'Jones Richard (1786–1852)', *ADB*, Volume 2, pp. 24–25

Smith, G.B., 'Fitzwilliam, Charles William Wentworth, Third Earl Fitzwilliam in the peerage of Great Britain and Fifth Earl Fitzwilliam in the peerage of Ireland (1786–1857)', *ODNB*, Volume 19, pp. 973–74

Smith, S.H. and Spaull, G.T., *History of Education in New South Wales*, George Philip & Son, Sydney, 1925

Spencer, H.J., 'Buller, Charles (1806–1848)', *ODNB*, Volume 8, pp. 613–17

Stapleton, M., ed., *Australia's First Parliament House,* Parliament of New South Wales, Sydney, 1995

State Records Authority of NSW, Agency No. 1047: Provost Marshal <www.investigator.records.nsw.gov.au/Details/Agency-Detail.asp?Id=1047> [22 April 2007]

Steven, M., 'Macarthur, John (1767–1834)', *ADB*, Volume 2, pp. 153–59

Sweetman, E., *The Unsigned New Zealand Treaty*, Arrow Printery, Melbourne, 1939

Tench, W., *A Narrative of the Expedition to Botany Bay*, J. Debrett, London, 1789

Therry, R., *Reminiscences of Thirty Years' Residence in NSW & Victoria*, Sampson Low & Co., London, 1863

Thompson, M.M.H., *The Seeds of Democracy*, Federation Press, Sydney, 2006

Thompson, N., 'Bathurst, Henry, Third Earl Bathurst (1762–1834)', *ODNB*, Volume 4, pp. 354–55

Turney, C., *Grammar*, Allen & Unwin, Sydney, 1989

Walker, R.B., *The Newspaper Press in NSW 1803–1920*, Sydney University Press, Sydney, 1976

Wantrup, J., *Australian Rare Books 1788–1900*, Hordern House, Sydney, 1987

Ward, J.M., 'Cowper, Sir Charles (1807–1875)', *ADB,* Volume 3, pp. 475–79

Ward, J.M., *Earl Grey and the Australian Colonies 1846–1857*, Melbourne University Press, Melbourne, 1958

Ward, J.M., *James Macarthur Colonial Conservative, 1798–1867*, Sydney University Press, Sydney, 1981

Ward, J.M., 'Young, Sir John [Baron Lisgar] (1807–1876)', *ADB,* Volume 6, pp. 455–57

Ward, S.G.P., 'Murray, Sir George (1772–1846)', *ODNB*, Volume 39, p. 905–06

Waugh, M., *Forgotten Hero Richard Bourke, Irish Governor of New South Wales 1831–1837*, Australian Scholarly Publishing, Melbourne, 2005

Weekes, J.W., *William Charles Wentworth*, Friends of Historic Houses Trust, Sydney, 1993

Wentworth, W.C., *A Statistical, Historical, and Political Description of The Colony of New South Wales and its Dependent Settlements in Van Diemen's Land with a Particular Enumeration of the Advantages which these Colonies offer for Emigration, and their Superiority in many Respects over those Possessed by the United States of America*, G. and W.B. Whittaker, London, 1819; 2nd Edition, London, 1820; 3rd Edition, London, 1824

Wentworth, W.C., *Australasia*, G. and W.B. Whittaker, London, 1823

Wilkinson, D., 'Fitzwilliam, William Wentworth, second Earl Fitzwilliam in the peerage of Great Britain and Fourth Earl Fitzwilliam in the peerage of Ireland (1748–1833)', *ODNB*, Volume 19, pp. 969–73

Windeyer, J.B., 'Windeyer, Richard (1806–1847)', *ADB*, Volume 2, pp. 615–17

Windeyer, W.J.V., *Lectures on Legal History*, 2nd edn, Law Book Company, Sydney, 1957

Yarwood, A.T., *Samuel Marsden*, Melbourne University Press, Melbourne, 1977

INDEX

The abbreviation 'WCW' refers to William Charles Wentworth; the abbreviation 'D'AW' refers to his father, D'Arcy Wentworth.